Surf's Up

Brian Wilson & The Beach Boys

Peter Do

new modern

First published in the UK in hardback in 2025
This paperback edition published in 2026 by New Modern
An imprint of Putman Publishing
Mermaid House, Puddle Dock, Blackfriars, London, EC4V 3DB

@newmodernbooks
@newmodern_books

Paperback ISBN: 978-1-917923-37-8
eBook ISBN: 978-1-917923-36-1
Audio ISBN: 978-1-917923-35-4

A CIP catalogue record for this book is available in the British Library.

Publishing and editorial: Pete Selby, James Lilford and Eleanor Porter
Typesetting: Marie Doherty

1 3 5 7 9 10 8 6 4 2

New Modern is an imprint of Putman Publishing
www.newmodernbooks.co.uk
www.putmanpublishing.co.uk

MIX
Paper | Supporting responsible forestry
FSC® C018072

Printed and bound in Great Britain by Clays Ltd, Elcograf S.p.A.

Praise for *Surf's Up*:

'A smorgasbord of magical wonder'
★★★★★★★★★ *Classic Rock*

'[A] beguiling montage of essays about one of America's most bewitching and bewildering bands. Some of the finest ever writing about this brilliant yet complicated collective'
★★★★ *Mojo*

'A sophisticated, immensely detailed study of a pop phenomenon as absorbed and absorbing as the best literary biographies'
Roger Lewis, *Mail on Sunday*

'A brilliant book'
Stuart Maconie

'Doggett steers a sure course between deep Brian worship and the beckoning shallows, between trivia and telling detail'
Ian Penman, *London Review of Books*

'A thoughtful recalibration of the Beach Boys story … Doggett is scrupulously fair in his analysis. A sad tale well told'
★★★★★★★★ *Uncut*

'Captures all [their] messy brilliance. It is to the author's credit that even those who know plenty about the band's highs any many lows will find much to enthrall them here'
Irish Independent

'An enthralling book. We thoroughly recommend it'
Word in Your Ear

'Particularly poignant … tasteful and compassionate'
★★★★★ *Shindig*

'Razor-sharp profiles [and] anecdotes galore … Peter Doggett mixes precise literary and in-depth research with an impartial critical assurance. The book might well be the last word on the subject'
Chris Charlesworth, *Just Backdated*

Dedicated to Mike Grant;
and, of course, to Rachel

PETER DOGGETT has been writing professionally about popular music and 20th-century culture since 1980. His many books include *You Never Give Me Your Money*, about the breakup of the Beatles and its aftermath; *There's a Riot Going On*, chronicling the links between rock music and revolutionary politics in the late 1960s and early 1970s; and a biography of David Bowie's 1970s recorded output, *The Man Who Sold the World*. He lives in London.

Contents

Introduction

'Til I Die

In the crazy world of corporate entertainment, there is always an anniversary.

To mark forty years since the release of the Beach Boys' *Pet Sounds* album, its creator, Brian Wilson, was persuaded to revive his joyously melancholy song cycle at theatres in five American cities. Squeezed between these events was the briefest of transatlantic visits, for a single show at London's Adelphi Theatre on 12 November 2006. This, the promoter promised, would be a landmark occasion: it would reunite Wilson with fellow Beach Boy Al Jardine for the first time on a British stage since 1980; and it would also be the final performance of the entire *Pet Sounds* cycle in Europe. Neither claim turned out to be true.

Jardine was mysteriously absent, leaving Wilson as the solitary Beach Boy among the spectacularly versatile musicians who had supported him for almost a decade. For the first time as a live performer, Brian was now surrounded by a crew numerous and expert enough to reproduce the most delicate textures of his music. They had acted as his orchestra when he first revisited *Pet Sounds* in 2000; then his psychological and musical crutch as the agonising *SMiLE* project from 1966/67 was finally brought to some kind of fruition.

If his musicians were a guarantee of musical safety, they did nothing to calm their frontman's inescapable paranoia. Every audience was a desert of accusing eyes, deadening Wilson with their expectation, a damning array of judges whose adulation was as unsettling as the rejections that shadowed his past.

His insecurities stretched back across decades of clumsy therapeutic intervention, reckless medication, drug-induced hallucinations and the numbing stress of artistic responsibility – all the way, in fact, to his childhood. It was then that, through birth, accident or malice, he lost most of his hearing in his right ear. This disability left him violently sensitive to loud noise, a crippling weakness in a musician required to perform in front of over-cranked speakers and shrieking teenage fans. More pervasive still was the sense of inferiority and failure that had been bullied into him, from the nursery onwards, by his cruelly abusive but equally wounded father.

His multipartite role as the creative engine of the Beach Boys – composer, producer, arranger, musician, vocalist, sergeant-major, standard-bearer – heightened the pressure upon this emotionally fragile young man. Time after time, he broke under the strain, without ever loosening himself from the shackles imposed upon him by commercial expectations and his fellow Beach Boys.

None of the other songs he composed during the 1960s depicted the frailty of his psyche with the coruscating honesty of 'I Just Wasn't Made for These Times', which provided a cathartic near-climax to the psychological odyssey of *Pet Sounds* in 1966. Back then, Brian Wilson worked at home while the touring line-up of the Beach Boys – his brothers Dennis and Carl, his first cousin Mike Love, his school friend Al Jardine and his replacement, Bruce Johnston – touted his wares around the world. They had neither the instrumental capability nor the inclination to offer such an intensely personal account of weakness to their adolescent admirers. By the time Wilson was able to premiere the song in public himself, in 2000, he had endured and survived a literally mind-boggling succession of psychological traumas. His team of minders had determined that he was finally ready to meet the challenge of facing his global audience in the flesh. The message of this song – 'I guess I just wasn't made for these times' – was no less appropriate then than in his creative prime.

The first time Wilson and his band toured with a repertoire built around *Pet Sounds*, his friend, disciple and sideman, Jeffrey Foskett, carefully doubled Brian's vocal parts to obscure any obvious flaws. By 2006, however, Wilson felt confident enough to assume the role he had originally designed for himself. That night at London's Adelphi, he embarked on the two-octave run to the summit of the first verse, only for his voice to crack and shatter at the peak. The knowledgeable audience winced in sympathy. Second time around, the climb required him to lament the 'cop out' of his 'fair-weather friends' – and out of defiance or pride, he conjured up the mental and vocal strength to hit the note, and its implications, head on.

A triumph, then, of resolution over despair? But wait. Brian Wilson could not always keep his demons at bay. In the same show, the run of Beach Boys classics led him to the ostensibly benign 'Break Away', a perennial favourite in Britain. And it was here that his emotional disarray darkened the stage.

Perhaps because a therapist had suggested it as a device to overcome his fear of performing, Brian had taken to acting out the words of his songs with extravagant hand gestures. The Beach Boys' onstage frontman, Mike Love, had added the same novelty to the group's stage repertoire back in 1962 and had never grown out of it. Now Brian Wilson extended that technique from the banal to the ridiculous, his arms paddling through imaginary waves as he sang the group's early surf hits.

The lyrics of 'Break Away' reflect the desire to propel oneself beyond the reach of romantic disappointment. The narrator declares that he can 'break away from that lonely life' until 'my world is new'. Anodyne enough, you might think. But for the composer, the song concealed a tripwire in front of a crevasse. After an apparently innocent reference to consoling voices in his head, the narrator finds the key to unlock his sadness by realising that it is entirely self-created. 'Found out it was in my head,' he explains, 'found out it was my head.'

At the Adelphi, Brian Wilson rushed guilelessly towards those lines and then suddenly realised what he was about to sing. His arms fell to his side as if a puppeteer had cut his strings, his face stricken with anguish. He looked panicked, bereft, exposed beyond human endurance; until, a few seconds later, the chorus offered melodic relief and he was swept back under control by the tireless beauty of his own music.

What had triggered his moments of despair? On the most obvious level, it seemed as if Wilson had been reminded all too publicly of one of the cruellest manifestations of his prolonged mental illness: his auditory hallucinations. It's common enough for people to 'hear' their own verbal commentary on their lives, but Wilson's voices were threatening in the extreme. Their message was simple: 'We're going to kill you'. Their frequency and strength were so alarming that Brian had always taken them at their devilish word.

If that was not unsettling enough, the very creation of 'Break Away' was surrounded by insecurity and fear. It was assembled across a seven-week period in the spring of 1969, at a moment when the Beach Boys were enduring the final rites of their increasingly disputatious relationship with their American record label, Capitol. The song was released as a single in late May, just as the group (minus Brian) arrived in Britain for a lengthy European tour. Their arrival was overshadowed by news from home.

Brian had chosen this moment to announce that the Beach Boys were facing a financial crisis. 'We're pretty low on money,' he declared. 'We owe everybody money and if we don't pick ourselves off our backsides and have a hit record, we'll be in worse trouble.' 'Break Away', he explained, was therefore a 'make or break' record for them, which was unfortunate, as Capitol had no intention of spending money on promoting it to the US market.

In Brian's reading of the situation, the blame lay everywhere but with him: office expenses, too many extravagant releases by artists handled by their production company (though the Beach Boys were effectively the only act on the roster), and the profligacy and selfishness of his bandmates: 'A lot of the guys started throwing money around, buying cars, houses and other things, and pretty soon the cash started dwindling.' Yet they were exactly the 'guys' who were now promoting 'Break Away' to their most loyal market, in Britain and continental Europe, where it duly became a sizeable hit. They were also about to venture behind the Iron Curtain for a rare excursion into the Soviet bloc by an American pop band. Their schedule involved rowdy, ecstatically received shows in Prague, where Mike Love dedicated 'Break Away' to the newly ousted liberal Czechoslovak leader, Alexander Dubček. When the trip was over, Brian Wilson's reliably calm younger brother, Carl, was required to reassure the American media that 'We are not bankrupt ... we are still worth a lot'. But the odour of failure remained.

If it wasn't the lyrics to 'Break Away' that triggered Brian's distress decades later, or the circumstances of its release, there was another, even more unsettling association to the song. His father, thwarted songwriter Murry Wilson, had channelled the frustration of his own musical journey into a rampant desire that his three sons should succeed – but only on his terms. He established a regime of rigid discipline, psychological bullying and severe physical punishments that fixed all three boys in their roles for life: Brian the hapless *Wunderkind*, unable to decipher his father's mercurial moods; Dennis the delinquent teenage rebel, compelled to defy Murry's will; and Carl the eternal peacemaker, determined to avert conflict at all costs.

By sheer force of character, Murry Wilson established himself as the Beach Boys' producer, manager, music publisher, goad, tormentor and, for good measure, moral guardian – until the group rebelled and banished him from any active role in their careers. But he was still Brian's father and, as each man battled loneliness and personal dislocation in the late 1960s, they were able to achieve brief interludes of placidity. In early 1969, Murry Wilson was struck by the way that TV host and comedian Joey Bishop would signal an advertising break: 'Let's break away for a minute'. He brought that phrase to Brian as the impetus for a song and sketched out the lyrical content without, apparently, being aware that he was also creating a verbal portrait of his son's mental torture. For reasons lost in the dynamics of this most complex of families, the father chose to be credited as co-songwriter on the single under the name 'Reggie Dunbar'. A matter of weeks later, Murry rewarded his son by selling off his musical copyrights, apparently behind Brian's back – although, as ever with the Beach Boys, the story was not quite that simple.

'Break Away' was not merely a song, then: it was a family psychodrama in miniature. But strip back the emotional debris and you are left with three minutes of exquisite beauty – enough in itself to justify the Beach Boys' reputation, even if it was their only record. It was the product of Hollywood's top session musicians and pop's finest-ever vocal arranger, guiding the tireless efforts of five superb vocalists. The genius was in their harmonies, especially across the 'tag' (as the Beach Boys dubbed their penchant for filling the closing seconds of their records with complex, circular vocal refrains). Layer upon layer of exquisitely recorded voices wrapped around each other, with each melodic line (delivered with rich, multi-dubbed harmonies) staking its claim to the ear's attention. It was a cavalcade of musical complexity, a seamless mesh of perhaps thirty or forty different vocal performances, arranged with such dexterity that it seemed at once impossible and natural. 'Break Away' was the epitome of pop perfection; and yet it represented barely a dot on the epic landscape of the Beach Boys' recording career.

One member of the 1969 Beach Boys was entirely absent from the creative process for that song: middle brother Dennis Wilson. He was distracted by a man, a commune, a cult and a way of thinking that resulted in one of the most savage ritual murders in American history. And that, too, is part of the group's history of madness; of idealism curdled in corruption and despair; of Californian sunshine shadowed by darkness; of harmony and dissonance balanced in perilous limbo.

The story of the Beach Boys isn't one narrative arc: it's a sometimes disturbing and often confusing tangle of achievements and failures, impulses and compulsions, success and excess. That's why this book isn't a simple chronological account of a band of popular musicians, but a collage of different perspectives, following individual strands of their career to their necessary conclusions. In these pages you will find plenty of evidence to brand the Beach Boys as the most dysfunctional group of musicians ever to succeed in the pop industry. But, I hope, you will also come away with a sense of awe at their creative ambition and unwavering love for their music. Those are the feelings that have captivated and moved me for the many decades that I have been immersing myself in their songs.

Presenting ... the Beach Boys

BRIAN WILSON (active in the group 1961–96, 2011–12)
Eldest of the three Wilson brothers. Musical prodigy with a stunning grasp of how to construct vocal harmonies, influenced by, but not restricted to, his love of records by the Four Freshmen. Competent pianist and bassist; excellent singer until his voice is damaged by poor lifestyle choices. In his twenties, undoubtedly the most brilliant arranger working in popular music, as well as being a composer with a peerless grasp of melody and counterpoint. Relentlessly bullied by his father as a kid, which triggers his addictive personality. Suffered from schizo-affective bipolar disorder (wrongly diagnosed as schizophrenia or paranoid schizophrenia).

MIKE LOVE (active 1961–present)
First cousin of the three Wilson brothers. Outwardly self-confident performer and public personality, whose bravado masks a sensitivity kept private from audiences. Forceful and often compelling vocalist in his younger years, albeit with a limited range. His admitted tendency towards an addictive personality is held in check by his decades-long devotion to the practice and belief system of Transcendental Meditation (TM). Married and divorced on many occasions. The only Beach Boy present in every line-up of the band, testifying to his relentless drive to succeed. Adept and clever lyricist, building on his childhood love of poetry and other literature.

DENNIS WILSON (active 1961–83)

The middle of the three Wilson brothers, and easily the most reckless. Natural rebel with evidence of attention deficit disorder, leaving him prone to clash with any form of authority, from his father upwards. Hedonist in every area of life, from sex to driving fast cars; skilled if untrained exponent of many sports and competitions, including surfing and drag racing. Effective though not expert drummer; charismatic live performer; haunting baritone voice, severely damaged by physical attack in the 1970s. Highly addictive personality with little self-control in any area of his life. Outwardly the least talented Beach Boy in the group's early years, but quickly develops after 1966 into composer of romantic, deeply emotional songs, for which he learns to become an imaginative arranger and producer. Falls into extreme addiction problems, the indirect cause of his fatal drowning accident.

CARL WILSON (active 1961–81, 1982–97)

Youngest of the three Wilson brothers. Grooms himself as the family peacemaker from an early age in a bid to avoid the severe punishments meted out to his older brothers. Carries this trait into the Beach Boys, where it shapes an obsessively serious attitude to the band's music and their responsibilities as live performers; seen as difficult by those who don't share his devotion to duty. Arguably possesses the most beautiful of all the band's voices, taking even his brothers by surprise. Talented lead guitarist from his early teens, who also masters keyboards and, as his eldest brother withdraws, all aspects of record-making and arranging. Sporadic composer of gorgeous melodies, who sacrifices his own creativity for the greater cause of keeping the Beach Boys in motion. Stress of his role demonstrated by the lifelong addiction to tobacco which results in his fatal lung cancer.

ALAN 'AL' JARDINE (active 1961–62, 1963–98, 2011–12)

School and college friend of Brian Wilson. Teenage fan of commercial folk music, which remains his deepest musical love. Initially opts to prioritise his medical studies, but returns to become a dependably talented vocalist on record and stage, a more-than-capable rhythm guitarist and a budding composer of folk-rooted songs. Sometimes indecisive about his creative impulses, which restricts his writing and solo recording activities. Reliable right-hand man to Love and the Wilson brothers until Carl Wilson's death shatters the group's unity, after which a bitter feud erupts between him and Mike Love. In his eighties, sounds almost unchanged as a vocalist from his youth.

DAVID MARKS (active 1962–63, 1997–99, 2008, 2011–12, 2014–15)

Pre-teen hellraising friend of Carl and Dennis Wilson, who becomes skilled guitarist ideally suited for rock 'n' roll and surfing songs. Replaces Al Jardine during early 1960s, but falls out with the Wilsons' father and is encouraged to leave the band. Returns to cover for the ailing Carl Wilson, then sporadically tours with the band in subsequent years. The Beach Boy most likely to supply lurid details of immoral behaviour on the group's early tours and still offering occasional very humorous insights into the group's dynamics in his late seventies.

BRUCE JOHNSTON (active 1965–72, 1978–2026)

Chicago child adopted by successful Los Angeles businessman and raised amidst some wealth. Launches musical career in mid-teens and masters a wide range of skills, from piano to arranging, producing, songwriting and singing. Forms a creative partnership with producer/singer Terry Melcher and volunteers to cover for Brian Wilson at 1965 concerts – a short-term role that expands to dominate his life. Self-mockingly calls himself the group's all-round schlockmeister, but also expert composer of romantic ballads with a smaller catalogue than he might have achieved outside the group. Acts as the Beach Boys' in-house critic and adviser after returning as producer and then full-time performer from 1978. Famously clean-leaving and keen surfer into old age.

RICKY FATAAR (active 1971–74)

Youngest of the Fataar brothers who form the South African R&B/rock group the Flames, later known as Flame. Excellent drummer who also masters keyboards and other instruments. Subsequently enjoys successful career as drummer with acts such as Bonnie Raitt, and briefly as actor/musician with Eric Idle's fictional band, the Rutles. Co-writer of several effective songs for the Beach Boys with Blondie Chaplin.

BLONDIE CHAPLIN (active 1972–73)

Fellow member of the Flames/Flame with Ricky Fataar. Co-writer with him of several Beach Boys songs; also strikingly powerful and soulful vocalist on his own and other people's songs. Excellent lead guitarist who also plays bass and other instruments. Establishes sporadic solo career after leaving the Beach Boys, before working with former members of the Band and the Byrds. Later becomes regular touring member of the Rolling Stones' line-up, before joining Brian Wilson's live band for several tours.

Our Team: The Auxiliary Beach Boys

RON ALTBACH

Expert keyboardist known as the Professor, introduced to Mike Love in 1970s through their mutual interest in TM. Former member of hit pop-rock band King Harvest; later co-writer/producer of late '70s Beach Boys songs and member of their touring band for several years; creator of *Beach Boys Suite*, a surprisingly tasteful orchestral tribute album.

ADRIAN BAKER

British vocalist/multi-instrumentalist first known for his one-man pastiches of US acts such as the Beach Boys and the Four Seasons. Teams up with Mike Love in 1980s for various recording projects and subsequently tours with the Beach Boys as a substitute for Brian Wilson.

GLEN CAMPBELL

Top-of-the-range LA session guitarist in the 1960s while also beginning career as country/pop singer which enables him to become one of the world's most successful entertainers in the 1970s and 1980s. Performs as session-man on many early Beach Boys records; tours with the group as replacement for Brian Wilson during a six-month run in 1964–65. Performs the Wilson-produced/written single, 'Guess I'm Dumb'.

ED CARTER

Regular member of the Beach Boys' live ensemble and sometime contributor to their studio recordings between 1968 and 1995. Affable, reliable stage presence; highly skilled musician on guitar and bass as required.

DARYL DRAGON

Keyboardist and songwriter who becomes part of the touring Beach Boys line-up from 1967 to the early 1970s. Also co-writes and produces several early 1970s recordings with Dennis Wilson. Subsequently pop star as the male half of Captain & Tennille, alongside the Beach Boys' only female touring member, Toni Tennille.

BOBBY FIGUEROA

Rock-solid live and studio drummer with the Beach Boys for several decades, from the late 1960s onwards. Utterly dependable whether as second drummer alongside Dennis Wilson or with Mike Kowalski. Soulful vocalist given little opportunity to sing with the Beach Boys.

JEFF FOSKETT

Teenage Beach Boys aficionado who cheekily turns up at Brian Wilson's house to express his love for the band's music. Subsequently establishes his multiple musical talents – multi-instrumentalist, harmony singer, producer, composer, ideal substitute for Brian Wilson's voice – through a lengthy involvement with Brian and the band, not least as the 'secret' member featured on their 2012 reunion album.

BILLY HINSCHE

Teenage member of the 'celebrity' pop group, Dino, Desi & Billy, who turns down the chance to become a fully-fledged Beach Boy, opting to go to college. Subsequently becomes an enduringly loyal member of the group's touring band, treated by all with the respect due to a 'real' Beach Boy. Performs as keyboardist and guitarist, and regular backing singer. Becomes Carl's brother-in-law when Wilson marries Annie Hinsche.

MATT JARDINE

Al Jardine's son, first joining the Beach Boys on stage as a child percussionist. Recruited as tour manager in the mid-1980s and subsequently a regular part of the live band as a singer and musician until shortly after his father falls out with the band in the late 1990s.

MIKE KOWALSKI

Like Bobby Figueroa, a dependable powerhouse drummer for the Beach Boys on stage and often on record, from the late 1960s through the next forty years.

CHARLES LLOYD

Jazz flautist and saxophonist of much renown, who meets the Beach Boys through TM connections. Appears occasionally on their records from the early 1970s onwards, and tours regularly with them for several years, especially in the late 1970s, when he is also a member of Mike Love's spin-off band, Celebration.

CARLI MUÑOZ

Highly talented keyboards player, singer and songwriter, who establishes close personal and professional relationships with Carl and especially Dennis Wilson. Tours with the Beach Boys for several years, but most enduring addition to their catalogue is his work with Dennis Wilson as composer and producer of several remarkable pieces in the late 1970s.

JOHN STAMOS

Keen drummer and amateur guitarist with a more than passable voice, who indulges his passion for the Beach Boys' music as occasional guest artist in concert from the 1980s onwards. Very popular actor in teen dramas and soaps; mastermind of the group's TV movies, *The Beach Boys: An American Family*.

DEAN TORRENCE

With Jan Berry, forms the rock 'n' roll/pop/surfing duo Jan & Dean and records a long series of hit singles in early 1960s, many of them co-written by Brian Wilson. Famously sings the uncredited lead vocals on the Beach Boys hit 'Barbara Ann'. Subsequently designs several of their album covers, before teaming up with Mike Love on various musical ventures from the 1980s onwards.

MARILYN WILSON

Marries Brian Wilson at the age of sixteen in 1964, but already by then a recording veteran alongside her sister Diane and cousin Ginger in the vocal trio, the Honeys. The two sisters become Spring/American Spring for early 1970s album co-produced by Brian. Regular contributor of harmony vocals to Beach Boys records; mother of Brian's eldest children, Carnie and Wendy, who both enjoy musical success with the trio Wilson Phillips. Introduces Brian to therapist Eugene Landy during the darkest period of their marriage.

Friends: Producers & Playmates

TONY ASHER

Advertising copywriter who collaborates as lyricist with Brian Wilson on *Pet Sounds*, and a handful of Wilson's solo songs.

ROGER CHRISTIAN

Disc jockey and lyricist skilled at capturing the sounds and thrills of hot rod racing and other teen obsessions with early 1960s rock 'n' roll hits. Collaborates with Brian Wilson on many songs 1962–63.

JAMES GUERCIO

Member and producer of rock band Chicago; founder of Colorado recording complex, Caribou. Encourages several Beach Boys to join Chicago for mid-1970s sessions, inspiring the two bands to tour together on several occasions, to great acclaim. Later plays with, produces and even briefly manages the Beach Boys.

GREGG JAKOBSON

Lyricist and friend of Dennis Wilson from the late 1960s onwards, who helps him compose several of his best-loved songs and provides emotional support during the aftermath of his turbulent encounters with Charles Manson.

STEVE KALINICH

Poet and lyricist who works with all three Wilson brothers in the late 1960s and occasionally afterwards; his verses are featured on an album produced by Brian Wilson.

EUGENE LANDY

Possibly the most notorious 'celebrity' therapist of all time, thanks in most part to his controversial involvement with Brian Wilson – first in 1975–76, then subsequently for a decade after 1982. Embeds himself so deeply in Brian's life that he is credited as his co-producer and co-songwriter on Brian's early solo efforts. Subsequently blamed for misdiagnosing and mistreating Brian's mental afflictions, with dire effects.

STEVE LEVINE

Hit 1980s producer with Culture Club, persuaded by Bruce Johnston to produce the group's self-titled 1985 album – an experience he finds taxing and upsetting.

TERRY MELCHER

Regular creative partner of Bruce Johnston in the early 1960s; highly successful producer of the Byrds, in 1965 and 1970, and his mother, Doris

Day; works on many hits and albums by Paul Revere & the Raiders in the 1960s. Talented singer and songwriter; musical legacy overshadowed by his links to Charles Manson. Recovers to co-write and produce the last big Beach Boys hit, 'Kokomo'.

ANDY PALEY

Phil Spector discovery in the 1970s who becomes in-demand producer, songwriter, instrumentalist and singer. Works on many solo projects with Brian Wilson, siding with Brian during his time with Eugene Landy.

VAN DYKE PARKS

Child film star, uniquely talented composer, lyricist, arranger and producer, who collaborates with Brian Wilson on the *SMiLE* project in both the twentieth and twenty-first centuries. Also composes the songs on the *Orange Crate Art* album for Wilson to sing. Highly articulate and intelligent conversationalist and observer of culture, young and old.

JACK RIELEY

Disc jockey who talks his way into becoming the Beach Boys' career adviser between 1970 and 1973. Appoints himself as lyricist for three albums' worth of collaborations with Brian and Carl Wilson. Subsequently records one mid-1970s concept album in the tradition of the Beach Boys' *Holland*.

DIANE ROVELL

Elder sister of Marilyn Wilson and therefore Brian Wilson's sister-in-law during the 1960s and 1970s. Fellow member with Marilyn of the Honeys and Spring. Production supervisor for the Beach Boys for many years, and assistant of sorts to Brian in the 1970s, a role that occasionally entails taking over Marilyn's marital responsibilities in unusual ways.

DARIAN SAHANAJA

Founder member of the Wondermints and crucial player in the final twenty-five years of Brian Wilson's solo career as keyboardist and arranger of his touring band. Brian's helpmate in resurrecting and completing the *SMiLE* project.

JOE THOMAS

Record company executive, songwriter and producer, who enters the Beach Boys' story as producer of their *Stars and Stripes* country album. Subsequently masterminds portions of Brian Wilson's solo career, easing him towards less experimental, smoother music. Collaborates with the Beach Boys on their 2012 reunion album and live record.

GARY USHER

Prolific producer/writer from the early 1960s Los Angeles pop scene, responsible for many surfing, hot rod and other rock 'n' roll masters. Collaborates on several key songs with Brian Wilson early in the Beach Boys' career. Their partnership is resumed less happily on an abortive mid-1980s solo project.

DON WAS

Co-founder of funk/rock band Was (Not Was), who becomes in-demand producer with penchant for enabling veteran acts to rediscover their original creativity. Produces Brian Wilson's TV special and album *I Just Wasn't Made for These Times*. Also attempts to produce a 1995 Beach Boys album which is abandoned after inter-group disputes.

MURRY WILSON

Frustrated songwriter and father of three of the original Beach Boys. Uses his force of will and abrasive personality to fight his sons' cause in their early career, but proves too domineering in the recording studio. Sacked by the group as their manager in 1964, though the bullying he has inflicted since their childhoods haunts all three sons for the rest of their lives.

We're Together Again

Greenford, west London: 24 September 1988

By the late 1980s, disappointment was lodged deep in the psyche of every committed Beach Boys fan. The group's decision-making, individual and collective, had been steering resolutely towards disaster for at least fifteen years. After a peerless decade of musical dexterity and artistic daring, stretching from their earliest surfing anthems to the sophisticated maturity of their *Holland* album, the Beach Boys had drifted into self-parody and putrefaction. Once a hallmark of excellence, they existed in the 1980s solely as the soundtrack for mindless regurgitations of nostalgia and hedonism, all subtlety lost in the party atmosphere of the arenas they struggled to fill.

If the true spirit of the Beach Boys survived, it was only in the souls and hearts of those who relished something more profound than a backdrop to frat-boy boorishness and cheerleaders in bikinis. Nowhere in the world was there a more concentrated, more loyal, more betrayed core of admirers than in Britain, the nation that had held the group's reputation aloft as it sank beneath the waves in their American heartland.

In September 1988, 250 or 300 of these diehards had trooped, as loyal subscribers, to the tenth annual convention run by the British fanzine *Beach Boys Stomp* and paid their £5 admission fee. Previous events had delivered attractions tailored for this uniquely fervent crowd: renditions of Beach Boys songs by fellow fans; grainy video footage of vintage Beach Boys TV cameos beamed onto a large screen; record stalls filled with rare and often illicit Beach Boys gems; and even the first public airing of legendary lost recordings by the group, smuggled out of their Brother Records archive and unveiled to one of the few audiences in the world who might recognise their significance.

After several hours, though, the tenth convention seemed to be dissolving into chaos and anticlimax – a state that, as seasoned followers of the group, Beach Boys aficionados knew only too well. Harassed organisers emerged from behind the stage curtains at regular intervals to apologise for unspecified 'technical problems'. Meanwhile, the increasingly disgruntled fans milled about, having already exhausted the novelty value of the meagre distractions on offer.

Eventually, the curtains parted and veteran British session singer Tony Rivers took the stage with a handful of friends. His pedigree stretched back to 1960s covers of Beach Boys surf tunes with his own band, the Castaways, and his outfit's flawless vocal harmonies briefly calmed any disquiet. But no sooner had their performance got into its stride than they were signalled to leave the stage, to a collective groan of disappointment. Once more the curtains closed and the mood in the hall congealed into a cynical sense of bad faith.

The surroundings offered no relief. The Parish Centre of Our Lady of the Visitation Catholic Church in the unprepossessing west London suburb of Greenford resembled (from the outside) a miniature industrial warehouse and (from within) a primary school hall. The rumble of disapproval slowly grew and, if the assembled fans had been there to celebrate a punk band instead of the Beach Boys, a riot might have broken out. There was little sense of anticipation when an organiser emerged to announce that, at last, the show was ready to resume. The curtains edged apart, slowly revealing a Yamaha DX7 keyboard, a pair of microphones and a seated figure clad in pristine white trousers and a red-and-white Hawaiian shirt.

There was a profound, baffled silence that seemed to stretch for hours, and then hysteria caught flame among the 250 or so fans standing in the hall. People gasped aloud, or cried out in disbelief, and then their amazement erupted into a crescendo – a prolonged howl that reached beyond mere pleasure into some primaeval tsunami of ecstasy. It was true. The man on the stage really was their hero: Brian Wilson. Men in their thirties or forties wept openly; others tried to prove to themselves that they had not lost their minds. And all of them, all of us, applauded as if only our hands could express the love we felt for the man before us – who sat at the keyboard looking bewildered, visibly shaking, yet somehow still in command.

I might have been the only member of that crowd who knew in advance that something startling might happen. The previous night, I'd rung my friend Mike Grant, the editor of *Beach Boys Stomp*, to apologise for the fact that I wouldn't make it to the convention because I was unwell. Mike's response had been uncharacteristically blunt: 'No, you will be coming'. I rephrased my regrets, only for Mike to interrupt me. 'Believe me,' he said, 'if you don't come tomorrow, you will regret it for the rest of your life.' He barely budged under my follow-up questions, but didn't deny it when I finally insisted: 'You mean Brian Wilson is going to be there?'

The incongruity was obvious – a rock legend would travel 6,000 miles to appear before a smattering of fans in a church hall? And this was not any rock legend. This was a man famous for combining musical genius with psychological collapse. He was one of rock's unhappy band of great lost talents, occupying this dark pantheon with other casualties of fame such as Syd Barrett, Skip Spence and Sly Stone. At his peak in the 1960s, startling creativity flowed from his soul until comparisons with Mozart, Bach or Beethoven began to seem unremarkable. Then, afflicted by extreme paranoia and psychic damage exacerbated by hallucinogenic drugs, he had disintegrated in public. Soon, the effortless genius had become an obese recluse, a tortured bear of a man whose rare appearances before an audience evoked a tragicomedy of discomfort and confusion. Every few years, his family and his bandmates would encourage the myth that 'Brian is back', only for Wilson's erratic behaviour to prove precisely the opposite.

Then, under the strictest of regimes imposed by controversial psychiatrist Dr Eugene Landy, Brian had embarked on a hesitant, precarious recovery. By 1988, at the age of forty-six, he was slimmer than he'd been since his late teens and ready, at last – twenty years after friends first encouraged him to leave the Beach Boys – to begin a solo career. That summer, he issued a remarkably coherent debut album and submitted to interviews on major US TV shows. But he had still rarely dared to attempt a performance without the ambiguous support of his family band. When *Beach Boys Stomp* dared to ask whether Brian might make some kind of contribution to their convention – a short message, perhaps, even a video link-up – Dr Landy sensed an opportunity. 'I thought it would be good for Brian,' Landy told me with the patronising air of a schoolmaster as he watched his client perform from the side of the hall. 'He needs to be able to do this.' Then he resumed his stocky, superior pose, alpha male to his client's problem child.

Wilson appeared unconvincing at first, stumbling through 'Surfer Girl' – which he'd sung at hundreds of Beach Boys performances since 1962 – as if he was making it up from scratch. But as he moved into two songs from his new album, his nervousness seemed to dissolve. He even felt emboldened to add an unfamiliar verse to 'Love and Mercy', about a despair too stark for even God to heal. He completed his set with the effervescent 'Night Time' and basked in another preternaturally raucous ovation.

'I couldn't believe it,' he recalled a few days later. 'I thought, those people are going nuts for *me*.' He lapped up the adulation like a proud toddler who'd just taken his first steps before a room of adoring aunts. But his ordeal had only just begun. For the second stage of his rehabilitation, Dr Landy had arranged for Brian to sit behind a table at the front of the stage and sign autographs for everyone in the hall – all 250 of them.

'When they came up, one by one, I thought, oh my, how cute is *this*.' That's how Brian chose to remember it. But his body language betrayed another story. His fans wanted nothing more menacing than the chance to thank their hero for what he had brought to their lives. But as each person moved in for a handshake, Brian reeled back in his chair, his torso at a 45-degree angle, his face creased with panic. It was as if he had been asked to greet a procession of spitting cobras. He listened uncomfortably to each paean of praise, muttered a word of thanks and then scribbled his signature before the next agent of agony arrived in front of him. His involuntary contortions continued for more than an hour, as the line slowly edged towards him. He kept glancing over at Dr Landy, who was standing nonchalantly perhaps twenty yards away.' Landy's complacent smile never wavered: he merely nodded an instruction to his client to stay in his chair and soak up the pain.

I waited my turn towards the end of the line, part professional observer, part awestruck admirer. I was clutching an album by Brian's recently deceased brother Dennis, until Mike Grant rightly scolded me: 'Don't show him that! You'll freak him out.' Instead, I pulled out a copy of *Bay Area Music*, a magazine I'd found at a memorabilia stand during the long hours of inactivity that afternoon. 'Brian Wilson: Trouble in Mind' the cover announced, alongside a matinee-idol style shot of the forty-six-year-old icon, brooding and uneasy. Within, journalist Jerry McCulley sensitively drew out reminiscences and revelations from the recalcitrant 'genius'. 'Every day I go through a few minutes of word dilemmas,' Wilson admitted, 'of feeling like I'm rejected or I don't have enough love from my girlfriends or my phone friends.' Dr Landy was 'a total life expert' and 'the only person in the world that has total superiority over me', although 'it's not a control thing at all'.

And so it continued, each declaration of faith in his muse ('Creativity cuts a hole right in glass') punctured by a shard of reality: 'I've run out of melodies. I'm on a dry cycle right now … and it just pisses me off.' Most unsettling was his reflection on the group he had once imagined and masterminded: 'I don't want to get entangled with those darn Beach Boys, because I know what happens when I do. I always regret it. It's a fight inside my head to keep my sanity within the Beach Boys. I'm very much alienated to the group personally.' Then, a few paragraphs later: 'I love being with them, you know what I mean? I want to retract that statement that I didn't want to be with the Beach Boys.'

These ambiguities were no more suitable fare for a fleeting encounter than reminding the agonisingly nervous performer of his late brother. Faced by Wilson's uneasy presence, I acted not as journalist but as fan.

I could not muster anything more original to say to him than the truth: 'Thank for your music, it's meant so much to me'. Brian didn't recognise any warmth in my words, or anyone else's; they were just a ritual to be endured. He reeled back as he grasped my hand for a few seconds, then scrawled 'To Peter – Brian Wilson' across his photograph. I felt blessed to be in his company, and guilty at having conspired in the mortification of a creature too vulnerable for this world, for this audience, for this stage or any other.

What I didn't know, and neither did Brian, was that Dr Landy would prove to be right: this torment was merely the precursor to decades of touring as a solo artist, in which Brian would soak up the applause of crowds across the globe, without apparently gaining a moment of solace or self-congratulation as his reward.

This, then, was Brian Wilson – the founder, leader and prime mover of the Beach Boys; a self-contained musical genius unmatched among his peers; a consummate explorer in sound. In the studio, players and vocalists alike obeyed his commands in the confidence that he could create music beyond the grasp of their merely human imaginations. Brian was repaid with worship and acclaim by generations of his fellow artists; with loyalty and betrayal from those closest to him; and with sixty years of mental anguish which he demonstrated in miniature on that west London stage.

The Beach Boys would sometimes achieve remarkable things without him, but at heart, as his equally tormented brother Dennis once admitted, they were only 'his messengers'. His story, and theirs, began in childish innocence, haunted by parental strife, and maintained the same unstable course throughout their creative lives. All of us who watched it unfold, in Greenford and beyond, relished and applauded the epic scope of his music, as well as having to claim their share of responsibility for the toll it exacted on Brian Wilson's psyche. Sometimes love and mercy turn out to be bittersweet.

The Boys on the Beach

The other Beach Boys, from Hawaii to Cornwall

Once upon a time, there were the Five Beach Boys, who crooned sweet harmonies on bandleader Johnny Long's 1948 rendition of 'Home'. A decade later, there were Beach Boy lifeguards on the beach in Waikiki, some of whom recorded easy-listening versions of Hawaiian songs to the accompaniment of guitars, ukuleles and other supposedly ethnic instruments. And don't forget a brief interlude when steel guitar ace Jerry Byrd assembled his own team of Beach Boys for a pair of 1953 singles.

In Stamford, Texas, they were a local dance band, cunningly located more than 300 miles from the nearest beach. In Cornwall, England, they were at least within easy reach of the sand and they dubbed themselves the Fabulous Beach Boys at the height of the surf guitar boom of 1962. In Malaya, the Japanese band the Spacemen were billed as the Beach Boys when they cut a selection of local dance tunes. In Atlantic City, the same era produced an instrumental trio concentrating on those familiar Hawaiian melodies; they were just the Beach Boys, with no claim to being Fabulous. In Tampa, the Beach Boys were a barbershop quartet, tunefully serenading the crowd of dignitaries at a museum opening. And over in California, a twisting combo who liked to be known as the Latin Beach Boys turned up on a concert bill at the Hollywood Bowl in November. Alongside them were such familiar purveyors of the surfing sound as Dick Dale and the Del-Tones, and Jan & Dean, as well as the

Seven Surfs – but not, on this occasion, a more familiar set of claimants to the Beach Boys brand.

The most serious set of alternative Beach Boys could conceivably have launched a legal claim to the name, had they still been together. In 1959, Kapp Records of New York issued a bouncy, danceable tune entitled 'Bathing Beauty', backed by the gentler 'On the Beach at Sunset'. The artists? The Beach Boys. Some disc jockeys picked up on one side or other of the single; an occasional journalist gave them a mention in the American press. They were even tipped as possible chart contenders by *Billboard* magazine, alongside other novelties such as Carole King's 'Short Mort'. But whereas she went on to become one of the most successful songwriters of the 1960s, the original Beach Boys and their 'Bathing Beauty' were swiftly forgotten.

So too were various visual projects scheduled for filming in 1962. That year, *The Beach Boys* was supposed to be an adventure movie starring George Maharis; or, alternatively, a Gallant Productions television series featuring teenage starlet Tuesday Weld alongside newcomer Dick Lewis. Neither of them was made, and even if they had been, their titles would not have survived – because by the end of 1962, the Beach Boys meant only one thing in American entertainment: the five-man surfing combo led by three Wilson brothers, a cousin and a friend.

There was still room for other types of beach boys to take their place in American society, however. In Hawaii, 'beach boy' was a generic term for local young men who taught tourists how to surf or paddled them along the shore in canoes. In Miami, 'beach boys' were a much larger community, still associated with the tourism industry, but with a more dubious reputation. They worked on the sand, or even more often around hotel swimming pools, supplying services that varied from the useful to the altogether seedy.

'A lot are pseudo gigolos,' said a Miami Beach police chief in 1964. 'They prey on women – in many cases much older women – who are on vacation and are looking for a good time. On the other hand, a lot are family men who have steady jobs where they've worked for years.' Jack Murphy, known to his friends as 'Murf the Surf', was keen to defend his breed. 'Being a beach boy is a profession, just like being a waiter or cook or pilot,' he insisted. 'It's annoying to us to have the word beach-bum brought up – just because we don't have a suit and tie on and work in swimsuits.'

His defence would have sounded more convincing if Murf the Surf wasn't one of a trio of young Miami men who had been arrested for stealing artefacts from a New York museum, among them the legendarily valuable Star of India sapphire. They were swiftly caught and, a few months later, the treasure was recovered undamaged. But their unabashed arrogance and rebellious demeanour turned them into folk heroes whose exploits ensured that 'beach boys' would continue to signify thieves and rogues to every section of the American public that wasn't enchanted by the (sometimes) less controversial achievements of the singing quintet from California.

Ride the Wild Surf

The Beach Boys and surfing culture

As the Beach Boys sang, 'Surfin' is the only life, the only life for me' – and that made sense, because they came from California, the home of what *Billboard* magazine called 'the kookiest, wildest and most refreshing fad within memory'. So potent was its impact as a sport and a lifestyle that, as a reporter noted in 1963, 'it has already engulfed Hawaii and Australia, and is reaching into Japan'. Even those parts of the United States that were not within hundreds of miles of a beach or a white-topped wave were falling for the surfing style, it seemed.

Billboard went on to explain why its appeal had spread across the landlocked states: 'It's a fad that belongs to the teen and 20 set, an age group most inclined to ardently follow the unorthodox. Surfing is a sport that connotes courage and, as such, has become a status symbol among youngsters who strive to be linked or "in" with anything that is related to surfing. Those who can't afford the gear can be part of the crowd through the music and dance.' In California, it seemed, there were at least 100,000 surfers active along the shoreline. They were serviced by at least 100 manufacturers of surfboards, dozens of surfer stores and two magazines published in Hollywood, which chronicled the craze and carried its magic far beyond the sand of Venice Beach, Doheny State Beach or Malibu.

The surfing scene didn't end there, of course. It was carried around the world by surf guitar bands and, after the arrival of the Beach Boys, countless other groups of young people joined together to preach the joys of catching waves in song. To exploit and extend this passionate sound, in 1962 and 1963 record companies crammed the market with titles aimed exclusively at the surfing market. Capitol Records, who released the Beach Boys' music, even prepared a *Surfing Dictionary* that was sent to record stores across North America to be given away free to any kid anxious to know more.

The year 1962 had ended with a World's Fair of Surfing at Santa Monica, at which the Beach Boys inevitably performed. Attendees could also enjoy a display of surfing art (artist Robert Irwin was winning a national reputation for his decorated surfboards), a vintage collection of boards and a parade of woodies – restored and revamped station wagons, in other words, with wood-panelled sides, perfect for transporting surfer boys and girls to the beach. There was also a craze for revived disused hearses. They had once been unsaleable on the used-car market but suddenly became a status symbol for the serious surfer.

There was only one flaw in this celebration of California's native culture: it didn't come from California. In fact, it was a symbol of American colonialism rather than an unalloyed badge of national pride. As *Billboard* magazine had noted, surfing had indeed 'engulfed' Hawaii, for the simple reason that the sport was invented there. Then – short version of complicated history – the Americans arrived and tried to wipe surfing out.

The influx of English-speaking folk into the natural paradise of Hawaii began when Captain Cook's expedition on the British naval vessel, HMS *Resolution*, touched shore in 1778. He named the archipelago the Sandwich Islands and then set sail towards North America. The following year, he led the *Resolution* back to Hawaii. Legend has it that the natives regarded him as a god, but this appears to have been an invention motivated by the widespread belief that no non-white population could possibly fail to worship their colonisers' superior spirit and strength. When some of the local population resisted theft and pillage by the Cook party, the captain dubbed them 'insolent' and vowed to kidnap their king. In the ensuing struggle, Cook was beaten over the head with a club and then stabbed to death, meeting his end in the Hawaiian surf.

The indigenous population of the Hawaiian Islands was then believed to be around 800,000. Within fifty years, it had been reduced by five-sixths. By 1890, only 40,000 people lived there, the remainder having fallen prey to illnesses brought in by outsiders. The same period also saw a determined cultural invasion from the United States, beginning with an influx of Christian missionaries in the 1820s. Their mission was to wipe out 'savage' native traditions. And one of the most pervasive and pernicious, as far as the evangelists were concerned, was the Hawaiian sport of surfing. This, it was claimed, 'would only hinder the heathens' moral progress' if it was allowed to continue unchecked. One of the foremost reasons for banning the sport was that it encouraged unmarried and barely clad young men and women to mingle unchaperoned in the sea. Indeed, many Hawaiian relationships began in the surf, as teenage girls and boys found love among the waves.

Even the most puritanical American visitors, however, found it hard to argue against the spectacle and skilful practice of surfing. As it was too deep-rooted to eradicate, the US chose to exploit it. First, they had to quell the local opposition which had rumbled against the visitors for more than a century. In 1893, American troops overthrew the Hawaiian queen in an act that even President Grover Cleveland had to admit was 'illegal'. Five years later, the US claimed total ownership of the Territory of Hawaii (though it took another sixty years for Hawaii to become a fully-fledged American state).

This unchallenged rule from Washington allowed American businessmen to translate Hawaiian tradition into an annex of US tourism. Alexander Hume Ford was the man credited with transforming surfing from a pariah sport into a prize attraction for visitors. The novelist Jack London lent his talents to Ford's crusade, the two men ensuring that they sold surfing as a white sport, on the basis that the natives must be too lazy to take part in anything so virile. From there, capitalism had its inevitable way, from the formation of canoe clubs and surfing societies on prime beaches to the staging of annual carnivals of the sea and surf. In return, the pick of the local surfers – men such as Duke Kahanamoku and George Freeth – were paid handsomely to sell surfing to the Californians. Beaches in the Los Angeles area were highlighted as ideal venues, although the sport only took hold after World War Two, during which most of the shore had been reserved for military use. Technology played its part, producing new surfboard designs that were lighter to carry and easier to control.

Three cultural events consolidated the West Coast surfing industry. The first was a novel, *The Ninth Wave*, by Eugene Burdick. Its political background was scarcely sunny, but its milieu captivated young readers – among them teenager Bruce Johnston. Three years later, in 1959, another surf-based novel, *Gidget* by Frederick Kohner, was translated into the first American beach movie – a Hollywood genre that focused exclusively on the joys and sorrows of teenage surfers and sun worshippers. And in 1961, the photographer and film-maker John Severson founded *Surfer* magazine, intended from the start to establish the serious credentials of the surfing scene beyond teen dramas and bikini-clad starlets.

For anyone who, like the young Beach Boys, grew up within easy reach of a California surfing beach, the pull of the sand and sea was almost visceral. Not that the group could claim to be masters of the waves. Carl Wilson was too plump as a teenager to ride a surfboard comfortably. His oldest brother, Brian, hated the entire experience: 'It's dangerous. You get hit on the head with a surfboard.' Al Jardine tried harder but with little more success: 'Dennis tried to get me out there a couple of times. But it proved to be a daunting experience. The front of the board kept making its way into the sand and I kept following it headlong.' Mike Love claimed that he 'knew how to ride a wave', though it wasn't his sport of choice (he preferred cross-country running).

This left one original Beach Boy who was a natural surfer, who had the physique and the charisma and the swagger and the style to epitomise everything that was attractive about the sport, even if he wasn't necessarily the most adept surfer on the scene. That was Dennis Wilson, of course, the man who went fishing with his cousin Mike Love one day and returned home with the idea that his brother Brian should form a group and sing about surfing. Soon enough, there was a second surfing Beach Boy in the band: Bruce Johnston, who took to the waves as soon as he'd read *The Ninth Wave* and kept up the sport way beyond the age when most men have opted for less energetic pursuits. It cemented his relationship with Dennis, the way that fishing united Dennis and Mike, and although there were occasional accidents along the way, like the 2006 tumble on the Santa Barbara shore that saw Bruce briefly hospitalised, he continued to preach the surfing gospel.

Meanwhile, Brian Wilson stayed home and waited for other people to bring him the language and the mystique of surfing. Dennis Wilson supplied the original inspiration; Mike Love translated the lifestyle into rock 'n' roll lyrics that scanned and rhymed and syncopated; and Jimmy Bowles, the brother of one of Brian's first girlfriends, supplied the list of prime surfing spots that filled the band's biggest early hit, 'Surfin' USA'. Five years later, Mike Love went out for a nostalgic trip into the waves near Camp Pendleton with his buddy Bill Jackson and returned to Brian's house high on the experience and eager to write a song entitled, suitably enough, 'Do It Again'. 'I don't like it,' said Bruce Johnston at the time, but he still sang on it, and it became the Beach Boys' second and last British number-one single. (The closest they came after that was with a novelty rap revival of a surfing instrumental tune, 'Wipe Out', with the Fat Boys.)

Ironically the Beach Boys' championing of surf culture brought them no respect from the people who lived that life every day. According to 1962–63 Beach Boys member David Marks, authentic surfers 'really resented us for exploiting their sacred cult. It wasn't really a sport back then. It was like a cult. It was a gang. The local people didn't really like the idea of us doing all this stuff about surfing when we weren't really doing it ourselves. Dennis and I were the only ones who really took it seriously.'

That opposition wasn't what brought the Beach Boys' run of surfing anthems to an end after 1963 (apart from 'Do It Again', of course, and 1964's 'Don't Back Down', which was inspired more by Brian Wilson's desire to stand up to his fears than by life on the beach). Surfing, Brian announced definitively in summer 1964, was 'strictly passé'. His brother Carl toed the same line: 'Surfing is out now as a social thing.' And Mike Love was nervous that surfing would 'probably be a tag' applied to the Beach Boys for the rest of their lives. In later years, he would recount his frustration about Capitol Records promoting them as the US's number-one surfing band when they were trying to sell *Pet Sounds* or 'Good Vibrations'. (Indeed, some reviews of *Pet Sounds* insisted that the album maintained that vintage sound: the *Honolulu Star-Advertiser* called it a 'summertime sizzler'.)

That wasn't quite the end of the crossover between rock 'n' roll and the surfing lifestyle. 'Surf City has gone punk,' claimed an Associated Press article in 1981. The piece focused on a new strand of 'violence and vandalism' that was marring California's beaches. There were pitched battles between local surfers and tourists involving swearing, fistfights and even jousting with surfboards. 'Robberies and drug deals are routine,' the article continued. 'Roving gangs terrorize bathers – picking pockets, snatching purses and ripping off jewellery.' Inevitably, there was surf punk music to accompany this menacing new wave, as instrumental bands channelled the visceral energy of punk into guitar riffs borrowed from twenty-year-old surf instrumentals.

If there was ever a time when Dennis Wilson could have emerged as a cultural pacesetter once again, this was it: he had the beach-bum look, the fearlessness and the genuine surfing experience to stand aloft this wave. Instead, he and the other Beach Boys kept their distance and left bands such as the Surf Punks (of course) and Agent Orange to dominate the scene. The Beach Boys never stopped singing about surfing, but somewhere between 1962 and 1982, their vintage hits passed from expressions of teenage hedonism into quaint slices of 1960s Americana, as far removed from the beach as Brian Wilson had always been.

California Calling

The Beach Boys in their home state

This was the California dream, laid out in *Life* magazine just after VJ Day, 1945: 'Californians live in a land where the sun shines 355 days of the year ... where towering mountains and endless beaches flank a countryside of incredible fertility ... Californians have evolved a unique way of life which is physically the most comfortable and attractive way of life enjoyed in any region of the US ... This Californian way of life flourishes chiefly in the southern half of the state. There the people live half indoors and half out. They dress for comfort rather than social elegance. They spend much of their time in automobiles' – visiting drive-in stores and, in time, cinemas.

Don't forget those California girls: thanks to *Life* magazine again, this time in 1962, we learned that the Golden State could boast 'the prettiest, biggest, lithest, tannest, most luscious girls this side of the international dateline'.

There was only one drawback to California circa 1945, according to *Life*: 'It has not yet made any artistic or intellectual advance comparable to that which it has made in the mode of physical living.' No worries: it had Hollywood – and, from 1955, the Disneyland complex in Anaheim, which the Wilson family from Hawthorne visited twice a year. Soon after 1945, it also grew a surfing culture that would be sold to the rest of the US by Hollywood and the TV industry in the form of lovable, kooky Gidget, played by Sandra Dee. And in 1961, of course, the burgeoning surf industry provided California with its soundtrack, courtesy of the Beach Boys.

For the group's chief composer, Brian Wilson, the responsibility of reflecting West Coast teenage life was very real. 'Our songs tell stories about teeners,' he explained in 1965, 'what they do and what their feelings are. We base them on activities of healthy California kids, who like to surf, hot rod and engage in other outdoor fun.' Looking back almost twenty years later, his brother Carl reflected that 'Brian created this whole world at home at his piano, and people were mad to get to California. There was an awe connected to California and the beach and the way we lived. But it wasn't the real California so much as the California in Brian's songs.'

The 'real California' wasn't entirely real, either. What lured millions of people from the inner US to the West Coast was a series of promises: endless summer, opportunities for wealth, healthy living for kids, an end to poverty and economic ruin. All the original Beach Boys came from families who had migrated west in the hope of meeting that dream, which was fulfilled by their descendants in the 1960s. 'I've always had the feeling that California was the Mecca of the West,' Al Jardine said in 1982, 'that all of the answers and all of life's pleasures were here.'

But there were other visions of California that painted a more troubled picture: racial discrimination in Los Angeles, most of all, which haunted the lives of African Americans until their anger exploded in the so-called Watts Rebellion of 1965. (The Watts district of Los Angeles is only a couple of miles from Hawthorne, where the Wilsons grew up. Not a hint of that unrest or its fiery revolt surfaced in the Beach Boys' music nor was ever mentioned in their interviews – proof that segregation worked to protect privileged whites from reality as well as oppress other races.)

California was where a movie star, Ronald Reagan, could become governor and then president. It was where the Mouseketeers led by Annette Funicello could provide a fantasy role model for young girls across the nation. It was where kids grew taller and fitter than any of their American cousins. But it also became the US capital of cults and quacks, gurus and shysters, who might be selling a universal panacea, a quick fix for global harmony, or a race war that would leave the dune-dwelling cult members as the inheritors of the world. Erik Davis wrote a profile of Brian Wilson in 1990, in which he focused on the strange spectrum of West Coast culture. 'Myths the size of California elect their own pantheons,' he pronounced. 'Ours has Ronald Reagan and Charles Manson at either end; and the Beach Boys may be the only bridge between those deranged poles.' In time, the group would certainly come to mirror every facet of Californian life, from the eternal sunshine to the full gamut of corporate and individual derangement.

Nobody could deny the physical beauty of what, in 1962, *Life* magazine had dubbed the 'Great Golden Land in the West'. The problem with paradise, though, is that it is easy to tarnish – to pave it over, as Joni Mitchell had it, 'and put up a parking lot'. Nature could bite back at the inhabitants in the form of earthquakes. 'Tell everybody to think real hard that there will not be an earthquake in California,' Al Jardine begged in 1969. 'I'm afraid everyone going around believing it will happen might cause it to happen.'

It transpired that earthquakes weren't the only natural phenomena endangering life in California. The difference was that the others were directly caused by humankind. The comedian Carl Reiner called the pollution-based cloud that hung over the city of Los Angeles 'the worst weather in the world'. Beach Boys lyricist Van Dyke Parks noted in the late 1960s that 'there is smog on the basin', the heart of Los Angeles surrounded by mountains and sea. Jardine called out the contradiction of trying to hold your breath when you drove into the city, while also breathing to stay alive. 'There is a psychological problem with smog,' he concluded. Parks extended his revulsion from the automobile fumes that triggered the smog to the strip malls and reckless urbanisation that represented the unchecked expansion of Los Angeles. 'Everyone feels the alienation, the dehumanisation,' he claimed in 1967. 'I see the horror of it all as I drive out to Palm Springs. I see the real horror, but people in their conditioned situations don't see the horror.'

Few people were more 'conditioned' from Californian realities than celebrities – pop stars among them. To their credit, the Beach Boys were early adopters of an environmentalist viewpoint. Their proselytising began with healthy food in the late 1960s and soon expanded to the wider effects of humanity on the land they loved. These concerns culminated in the 1971 album *Surf's Up*, with songs that warned of chemicals that poisoned rivers and oceans alike, and pollution that was choking the very trees helping to provide the oxygen we breathe. 'It was totally into ecological things,' Mike Love explained. 'We had a picture of the Salt Flats on the inner sleeve and the cover was an Indian … Like, this is the way the "red man" went and this is the way everybody is going to go if they don't tighten up.'

You can trace those environmental concerns through the rest of their career: Mike Love and Brian Wilson protesting against plans to drill for oil off Santa Monica; Love and Dennis Wilson composing 'Pacific Ocean Blues' about the slaughter of wildlife by pelt hunters; Love campaigning to defend the redwood trees that were among the state's greatest natural wonders; Bruce Johnston joining the advisory board of the Surfrider Foundation to save California beaches from developers; the entire group sending out ecological messages with the *Summer in Paradise* album, right down to the EcoPak cover design. Distress at what was happening to the California environment was also one of the prevailing themes of Van Dyke Parks' 1995 collaboration with Brian Wilson, *Orange Crate Art*.

Mike Love was adamant that part of the Beach Boys' role in California culture was 'bringing a new optimism into the way people think about the problems of pollution and violence'. That optimism was increasingly hard to maintain, it seemed. Al Jardine became so disillusioned about pollution and smog that he moved his family upstate to the almost deserted area of Big Sur, where mountain slides and forest fires were more pressing dangers.

Other Beach Boys were more concerned by the dramatic shift in urban culture exemplified by riots and other episodes of violence. 'The Los Angeles and Southern California we sang about doesn't exist anymore,' Bruce Johnston lamented in 1990. 'I got out of LA after a body was dumped in my street and left there for six hours. More than two miles inland from the beach isn't safe anymore.' Mike Love identified another fear: 'Now you get murdered there for having a good car. It used to be the promised land. Now there's nothing but earthquakes, fire and drive-by shootings.' So much for the hope expressed by commentators in the 1950s that California would produce 'an anxiety-free future', so rich were its natural assets. Paradise was easier to ruin than it was to keep, it seemed.

Not only were the individual Beach Boys fleeing Los Angeles for a more pleasant life elsewhere: the city was also destroying their heritage. Or so it seemed to the Wilson family when planners routed Century Freeway, alias I-105, through parts of Hawthorne. Among the buildings demolished was the old Wilson family home at 3701 W 119th Street, where the group worked up their first song, 'Surfin''. Twenty years later, the site of that house – well, not the actual site, which is now under the interstate, but a nearby wall – was designated as California Historical Landmark 1041: 'Site of the Childhood Home of the Beach Boys' (or three of them, at least). A monument, loosely based on the cover of the *Surfer Girl* album, was unveiled there in 2005 at a ceremony attended by Brian Wilson, Al Jardine and David Marks. (Mike Love and Bruce Johnston presumably weren't invited, because of the band's internal politics.) The Beach Boys were now a part of the official state history, even if California was no longer the California they once knew.

Home Alone in Hawthorne

The birth of the California Saga

All great traditions require a creation myth, and the Beach Boys are no exception.

The story goes that the three Wilson brothers were left alone by their parents with food money for the weekend. Dennis Wilson suggested they should form a band and sing about surfing. They hired instruments with the cash, didn't eat for three days and then surprised their mom and dad with a finished song – and a surefire hit: 'Surfin''.

That's the way it plays out in the TV movies. The dictatorial Murry Wilson looks furious as he stomps through the door, but his boys touch his heart with their youthful energy and rousing vocal harmonies. Murry takes their career in hand and, within a matter of days, they are stars.

Reality wasn't quite that simple. Forming the Pendletones (as they initially named themselves) wasn't an instant decision but the culmination of a months-long process of locating a sound, fine-tuning a line-up and then exploiting Murry Wilson's slightly outdated music business contacts as efficiently as they could. About fifty pages of James B. Murphy's forensic biographical study, *Becoming the Beach Boys 1961–1963*, were devoted to the journey from first considering a band to making a record.

Given a rare opportunity to explain the process in depth, individual Beach Boys were able to illuminate different facets of the myth.

Al Jardine concentrated on his musical rapport with Brian Wilson: 'It gelled so quickly and seemed so natural. It was instantaneous chemical reaction, spontaneous combustion. It seemed like we found each other. And it was all just there for the taking. You don't appreciate it at the time.' To this day, Jardine recalls the words with which Brian Wilson would scold the fledgling band towards musical perfection. 'Think sharp,' Brian would lecture them. 'If you don't do that, you'll always sing flat.' Missing from Al's reminiscences was a substantive difference between their musical visions: he wanted to found a modern folk group with Brian, who instead was looking to recreate the jazzy harmonies and vocal purity of the Four Freshmen.

Enter the younger two Wilson brothers, both devoted to contemporary rock 'n' roll. Carl's 'origin' moment centred on Dennis: 'Listening to a group on his transistor radio, [he] swore we could sing better than they could and tossed out the idea of forming our own group. He promptly forgot the suggestion. The rest of us thought he had a great idea, but we didn't follow through. Later, Mike and Dennis returned from a fishing trip where they'd talked themselves into a state of high excitement about the group plan. They were so jazzed up, they rushed home to tell us about it.'

At this point, there was zeal but no core. As Dennis recalled, the three Wilsons, cousin Mike Love and Brian's friend Jardine gathered regularly at the Wilsons' home, exploring how they might sound. 'The five of us, Al included, began practising vocal harmonies every chance we had. Mostly we sang Coasters songs and Four Freshmen arrangements, as Brian was high on their style of vocalising.'

It was Jardine who first secured an audition, working with a folk group called the Islanders. Brian Wilson was invited to fill out their sound as they performed for writer/producers Hite and Dorinda Morgan and their son Bruce. They were old acquaintances of Murry Wilson, who hoped that Brian, Al and their chums would record some of his songs. After the Morgans had politely turned the Islanders away, Brian and Al arranged to return with the family group. They probably showed off their harmonies on some R&B covers, before the Morgans told them that they needed fresh material. Up piped Dennis Wilson with (depending on whom you believe) either the suggestion that surfing would make a great subject for a song or, perhaps, the bold but blatantly untrue statement that he and his brothers had already written a surfer's anthem. The five young men began to assemble the rudiments of a doo-wop-style surfing novelty, fuelled by Dennis's command of the sporting idiom. And after several auditions, rewrites and taped rehearsals, the Pendletones were finally ready to record a single.

As Carl Wilson remembered it, 'It was my guitar, Alan had the upright bass and Brian played a single snare drum with a pencil. And that was it. Brian took his shirt off and put it over the drum because it was too loud. We did it all at once, with Michael on one microphone and the rest of us on another.' The backing vocals comprised riffs based on recent hits such as Jan & Dean's 'Heart and Soul' and Gene Chandler's 'Duke of Earl'. Mike Love's presence at the microphone was evident from the start: he sounded cool, cocky, even slightly tough – one of the kids from the street, not a professional flown in to masquerade as a teenage rebel.

Various tapes from the gestation process of 'Surfin'' have been unearthed down the years. During an early rehearsal at the Wilsons', the boys are constantly threatening each other that they will 'pop you in the mouth': they all sound about thirteen. Al Jardine isn't there that day, as Brian threatens Dennis he'll bring Al in as a replacement if Dennis doesn't shape up. Mike might be the lead singer and Dennis the one true surfer, but Brian is unmistakeably the leader. He arranges the group's harmonies by getting them to stand closer or further from the mic and gives them the kind of encouragement he would have learned from his dad: 'Now, just sing out naturally … don't hold back … Stand with your hands on your hips, you get a lot more breathing.'

Transferred to the Morgans' studio, the group barely touch their instruments, relying on the vocals to fill the soundscape. The addition of Al Jardine's voice fills any holes left by Carl and Dennis's youthful inexperience. And then at last they are recording for real. Even as amateurs with no drum kit, one electric guitar (Carl) and a stand-up bass (Al), they suddenly sound like a rock 'n' roll band. The speed of that transformation is remarkable, though it pales alongside how far they would progress over the year ahead.

For the flipside, they are encouraged to record a Morgan original tune, a skeletal novelty called 'Luau'. For this side, Brian's cultured croon is the featured voice, with Dennis also allowed a brief, unsophisticated spotlight. Nobody would ever have listened to this cut again if it didn't carry the name of the Beach Boys – for that was the group credited on the record, not the Pendletones or (a short-lived suggestion) the Surfers. The boys were mildly disgruntled by not being consulted about Hite Morgan's decision, but that was forgotten the first time they heard themselves singing on a local radio station. 'Dennis was thrilled,' Carl recalled, 'because he was living it. He went to school and his friends said, "We were on our way home from the beach, totally exhausted from riding the waves all day. We heard your record come on and it turned us on so much that we went back to the beach."'

The Beach Boys were no longer a front-room fantasy but a functioning reality, with a live schedule before them and local fans following them around. Hyping a record across the US in the days before international media organisations seized control of the music industry was a haphazard task. Unless an act was already established, they would break out in one regional market and then (maybe) get picked up in other areas. As a record about surfing made in California, it made sense that the Beach Boys' debut would sell there and become a minor local sensation. What nobody involved in the release can have expected was that it would eventually show up on the national charts – a long way down, with number 75 its *Billboard* peak, but something to boast about, nonetheless.

It was as 'Surfin'' undertook that laborious climb into the Top 100 that one of the five Beach Boys decided to leave. 'I threw it all away,' recalled Al Jardine. 'I quit the band and went back to college, like an idiot. By some strange quirk, Brian was really mad at me. He wouldn't accept it. Thank goodness.'

While Jardine choose dentistry as a more solid future than rock 'n' roll, the Beach Boys required a replacement. David Lee Marks (born

22 August 1948) hailed from New Castle, Pennsylvania, but his family relocated 3,000 miles in the mid-1950s and found themselves across the street from the Wilsons – albeit in a different district.

'Our street was the border between Inglewood and Hawthorne, so there were all sorts of kid feuds, territorial things,' Marks remembered in 1980. 'Carl and Dennis were across the street, throwing trash over, that kind of thing. Then eventually Dennis and I got really tight and did all sorts of creepy kid things together – chopping down trees in the park, setting a drainage ditch full of dead grass on fire, everyday stuff, you know?'

As an eleven-year-old, Marks envied the way that Murry Wilson was always spoiling his kids with possessions (if not affection); there were telescopes in their bedrooms, go-karts in their yard. Plus, there was a piano and a Hammond organ in the Wilsons' living-room. It was there that David and thirteen-year-old Carl Wilson sat around after school, trying to emulate Ventures tunes on their guitars. Marks was still dropping by the house when the Beach Boys were being formed. Sometimes he would strum some guitar while they sang. In his head, he was almost a member of the band. 'I'd been practising with them, so when they snuck out that first single without me, I was really crushed.'

Marks was still on the outside when the group held a second session in February 1962, cutting a skeletal version of a new Wilson/Love song (or Love/Wilson, the way Mike remembered it) entitled 'Surfin' Safari'. With just four musicians, they sounded like any other garage band in small-town America: higher on hope than chops. But within two months, with David Marks filling out the instrumentation, they were a fully-fledged rock 'n' roll band, fronted by a singer with a hoodlum edge that suggested he might be after your wallet as well as your girlfriend. The way Marks remembered it, as a producer 'Brian was the lone guy in charge from the very start. Brian didn't become a dictator – we begged him to take control. We were his biggest fans … We'd all jump around and pound him on the back and say, "Wow, you're a genius, man!"'

With a minor hit already to the name, and a major label deal with Capitol Records, the Beach Boys were now recognised as chart contenders. 'Surfin' Safari' was even reviewed by *Billboard* magazine: 'The beach scene gets a rolling, rocking treatment on this side by the boys. Tune swings along neatly on lead singer's talent and support of the rest of the group.' It took a few weeks, but the single broke out in Detroit, 2,000 miles from the Pacific Ocean, and then had to wait another month before it made the Hot 100. Surfing wasn't the only safari in town: Billy Vaughn's band were offering 'A Swingin' Safari', while R&B sax player King Curtis was staging a 'Beach Party'. Having charted first in high summer, the Beach Boys' single didn't peak until mid-October, but Capitol's national distribution pushed it all the way to number fourteen.

Success had immediate repercussions. 'The hardest part was that our friends resented us,' David Marks recalled. 'All our buddies turned against us. It was hard for them to relate to someone who became famous overnight. They constantly made fun of us. There was fighting and constant threats. The surfers would come after us in the parking lot after the gig and try to beat us up.' As a result, David and Carl Wilson both had to switch schools from the public system to a private institution that hosted child actors and film-star offspring. Around the same time, Dennis Wilson was kicked out of school altogether for beating up another kid. Hawthorne was getting too hot for the Beach Boys. It was time for them to claim a much larger stage.

We Got Love

Profile #1: Mike Love

Why do people hate Mike Love? Let me count the ways.

They hate him because they detest his demeanour on stage. They don't like the way that he still acts out the lyrics to the Beach Boys' early hits as if he's performing to an audience of young children or idiots. They hate the way he ogles cheerleaders, or beauty queens, or any other young women visible from the stage. They hate his insistence on restricting the Beach Boys to their original sound and teenage themes – his concentration on surf, cars, girls and fun – at the expense of anything more adult. They hate him for telling Brian Wilson: 'Don't fuck with the formula'.

They hate his rant at the Rock & Roll Hall of Fame ceremony, when the induction of the Beach Boys was overshadowed by Love challenging the Rolling Stones to a battle. They hate his voice, his nasal sneer, the fact that, alone among the original group, he lacked vocal range and soul. They hate the fact that he has controlled the Beach Boys for the last forty years, steering them towards simple-minded nostalgia and allegiance with the Republican Party of Donald Trump. And they hate Transcendental Meditation, especially when Mike Love talks about it.

Most of all, they hate the way he has treated the other original members of the band. They hate the fact that he told Brian Wilson that *Pet Sounds* was 'music for dogs'; that he sabotaged the *SMiLE* project; that he undermined his cousin's sense of artistic integrity; that he sacked Brian from the Beach Boys after the 2012 reunion. They hate his persecution of Dennis Wilson; his refusal to admit Dennis's genius; the fact that his brother beat Dennis up; his lack of support for Dennis in his final descent into alcoholism. They hate the way that he has picked on his closest buddy in the band, Al Jardine, since Carl Wilson died in 1998; the way he launched lawsuits, shut down Al's bands, teased him and belittled him.

Basically, they hate Mike Love and they aren't afraid to let people know. Just look at any website that is open to comments, and they will be filled with hatred and contempt for the oldest, least talented, most bald and most nauseating man ever to find himself at the centre of a major pop band.

That is the case for the prosecution.

In the interests of fair play, not to mention factual reality, here is the case for the defence. Quite simply, there would have been no Beach Boys beyond 1962 if Mike Love had not existed. He was the only member of the band able to translate teenage California into words: to echo Chuck Berry by turning the minutiae of surf and school and teen romance into rock 'n' roll poetry. He was also the group's only obvious frontman: the only Beach Boy brave enough and charismatic enough to stand in front of a crowd, in 1962 or more than six decades later, and command them with ease. He's a consummate showman and so, like many entertainers, he can appear insincere or glib to people who prefer their artists to be, well, 'artistic'. But he is the Beach Boys' ultimate crowd-pleaser, the man who can channel a party spirit, a collective energy, a populist sense of humour and, when required, a wry sense of self-mockery, and combine them into something that delivers entertainment to arenas of any size. And there, in a nutshell, is the Beach Boys' dilemma: how do they operate as both an experimental studio product and a mass-market live attraction?

Mike Love has also retained a natural energy – through ego, TM, health foods or some contribution of all three – way beyond the lifespan of a rock 'n' roll star. Only Mick Jagger rivals him for irrepressible spirit and *joie de vivre* – and Mick takes years off between tours to work out at the gym. Mike Love has kept his hands on the wheel from the start and ensured that at least some form of Beach Boys would be ready to take the stage when the supposedly more talented or creative members simply weren't able or prepared to carry the weight. I'd never argue that he was the band's finest composer, or the most poetic lyricist to work with the Beach Boys, or their most mellifluous singer, or their most sympathetic personality. But none of those admirable qualities and attributes would have been enough to keep the Beach Boys alive. Only one factor has enabled that: Mike Love's determination.

What else can we say for Mike Love? He claims never to have told anyone, 'Don't fuck with the formula', and maybe he never did. He may have been initially sceptical about *Pet Sounds*, but he lent himself fully to completing and promoting the album and has been vocal about its strengths ever since. Likewise *SMiLE*: he might not have understood Van Dyke Parks' lyrics or felt that *SMiLE* was the best use of Brian Wilson's composing skills, but he turned up for the sessions, he sang the songs, and he would have sold that album with the shameless panache of Colonel Parker if it had been completed.

Mike didn't reject Dennis Wilson as a composer: instead, he assisted him, writing lyrics to some of his most powerful songs. He isn't ultimately responsible for the actions of his brothers, Stan and Steve, falling out with them both at various points of the family saga. If he lost patience with Dennis the alcoholic, the drummer who could no longer keep time – or, for that matter, stay behind the drum kit – but who would stumble across the stage sabotaging the band's performances, well, that's understandable. If he grew tired of Al Jardine, it was because he felt drained by Al's all-too-obvious loss of enthusiasm for life in the Beach Boys. If he undermined Brian at times, once again, he had been forced to apologise for Brian's lapses and make up for his absences and conceal his failings for too many decades – and, in any case, Brian was quite capable of demeaning Mike's singing and personality in interviews, though fans chose not to blame him for it the way they did with Mike.

I'm not a fan of Mike Love's performing persona; I'd rather the Beach Boys had never chosen to make teenage girls parade and dance on stage at their shows; I certainly don't share his politics; and some of his songs ('Sumahama', anyone?) make me feel slightly nauseous. But his contributions to the Beach Boys' success – his innate feel for pop commerciality, his command of an audience, his frat-guy drawl, his subtle bass harmonies, that boundless energy – should never be forgotten. I admire Mike Love, even if I don't always love him. And you can't remove him from the story of the Beach Boys without also deleting their existence as a functioning band. Go back to those comments sections if you want cheap jibes at the man, the ego and the voice.

Michael Edward Love was born on 15 March 1941, the oldest child of Milt Love (owner of the Love Sheet Metal business) and Glee, the wonderfully named sister of Murry Wilson. For much of his childhood, Mike was raised in the wealthy Baldwin Hills area of Los Angeles, in a virtual mansion on the corner of Mount Vernon and Fairway. (Brian Wilson would set a 'Fairytale' at precisely that location three decades later.)

For all that the US claims to be a classless society, there is still a gulf between a branch of a family that enjoys financial comfort and its poorer relation. Wealth conveys ease, confidence, plenty, safety, superiority. Kids feel it, even if they don't understand the details. No surprise, then, that as the oldest and most privileged of the Beach Boys' relations (at least until Love Sheet Metal ran into mid-'50s penury), Mike Love should possess a sense of belonging that his Wilson cousins lacked. Those months and years of seniority added to his status and made him the psychological leader of the group – even though it was his slightly younger cousin Brian who was awarded the title by the outside world.

More ways in which Mike stood out: he was sexually active before the others, married before the rest, likewise a father, likewise a divorcee. He was the group's resident bookworm, unlikely as that might sound, with an ear for the pre-modernist rhymes and rhythms of poetry and a penchant for classic fiction. He was the original Beach Boy most likely to be found admiring the architecture of the cities they visited, but also, alongside Dennis, the one who found it easiest to charm cheerleaders ('I even married one,' he sang in 'Brian's Back'), starlets and other passing beauties.

The Mike/Dennis hate/love dynamic kicked in early. 'We fight, we really do,' Mike explained in 1964. 'On one occasion, after we had done a month's tour, and had been living too close to one another all the time, our tempers got a bit frayed, and Dennis and I had a real set-to. A good fistfight, it was. When we got to the plane to fly home, it looked as if we had been in a war.' Two years later, at a show in Canada, 'Good Vibrations' warped into a screaming match between the two over errant harmonies and missed cues. And so it continued, right up until the end. (According to Carli Muñoz, a Beach Boys band member in the 1970s, the feud began for a reason. Mike once confessed to him: 'Dennis fucked my first wife'.)

If Dennis was the Beach Boy most likely to be mistaken for James Dean, Mike Love also aroused adult fury. The most aggressive write-up the young Beach Boys ever received came from Barry Robinson of the *Asbury Park Evening Press*. He attended their otherwise uneventful shows at the local Convention Hall in July 1965 and tore into the group for their 'skintight, white see-through pants' and 'guise of a James Cagney mobster'. (Yes, this is the Beach Boys he's talking about.)

'It's easy to see that Mike Love is the big man on the Beach Boys' campus,' he continued. 'He wears his shirt over his pants so its tails go flapping behind him, giving him the overall appearance of a beach bum rather than boy – at his age, he should be ashamed to be called a boy, anyway.' (Love was twenty-four.) 'He's the one who's up front, making audience contact, dancing a bit and gesticulating madly. In a less permissive age, some of his gestures and body movements would be considered on the verge of being obscene … his actions are such that they would be highly offensive to an adult audience.'

And this, Robinson concluded, was the secret to the Beach Boys' success: teenagers were rebellious and needed a way of thrusting their rebellion into the faces of their elders. 'What better way than a raunchy-looking, offensive-acting group? The Beach Boys are it! … They look tough, too … tougher than anyone else … the epitome of malcontent.' Their only rivals in these regards, according to Robinson, were inevitably the Rolling Stones.

No matter that other reporters reckoned that Mike was 'the most serious-minded of the group', 'the old man of the operation, a wizened 24', 'worldly, sarcastic, thoughtful', 'shrewd with money, immensely practical'. Early fans had recognised a teenage arrogance in Mike Love's vocal tonalities and now an experienced pressman saw him as a rebel occupying dubious territory on the verge of obscenity. Fortunately, neither supporters nor critics knew that, in Love's own words, he had an addictive personality: that might have prompted Barry Robinson to stage a citizen's arrest.

Something else that wasn't widely known in the early 1960s was that, for all his family's former wealth, Mike Love had missed out on the qualifications that might have offered him a different career path. Before the Beach Boys, 'I was a sheet metal apprentice, and gas/oil/check-the-tires attendant at a gas station. My dad asked me what I'd do if the group didn't work out. I told him I'd be back bending metal.' That threat fuelled the drive that propelled him forward through the 1960s and established the persona – no, more than that, the *personality* – that would prove so successful and would provoke so much disapproval from those who felt they understood the Beach Boys better than he did.

I Just Wasn't Made for These Times

Profile #2: Brian Wilson

He was the oldest son, born Brian Douglas Wilson on 20 June 1942. He grew up around music, which nurtured him before he was conscious of what it was and what it might turn out to mean. His mother Audree had a beautiful though untrained voice, which she turned casually towards the pop hits of the day, those by Doris Day and Rosemary Clooney, Helen Forrest and Mary Ford. His father Murry was a songwriter, often described as 'frustrated' in later years, but also determined to succeed and utterly incapable of backing down, either in an argument or in a battle for his songs to be heard. There was a piano at home, of course, and soon enough a Wurlitzer jukebox, which Murry stuffed with the pop (but definitely not R&B or rock 'n' roll) standards and novelties that he loved.

Brian grew up knowing that success in his father's eyes meant more than behaving at school and achieving good grades or helping around the house or lending a hand to his father's tool hire business at weekends. All those things were important, and Brian could be scolded (or worse) for neglecting any of them. But Brian also had a higher purpose: to repeat and possibly even (if such a thing were possible) surpass the musical excellence of his father. He was encouraged to learn accordion, but eventually drifted instinctively towards the piano, where he quickly discovered how to pick out tunes, then assemble chords, then delve into the mystical, hypnotic realms unveiled when notes chimed into harmony.

Before he entered his teens, Brian's parents noticed that he tended to talk out of one side of his mouth and would turn his head around to pick up sounds or voices that came from the opposite side of his head. Tests were carried out, and it was determined that he enjoyed less than 20 per cent hearing in his right ear. What was the cause? There is no definitive answer, but plenty of speculation.

In the 1991 autobiography that he certainly didn't write and perhaps never even read, 'Brian' recounted that Murry had 'dropped me in my infancy on the concrete sidewalk outside our apartment' and that as a result he might have suffered brain damage. 'Whether the deafness was a result of a birth defect or one of my dad's early beatings has been lost and buried among my family's many skeletons.' In subsequent interviews, Brian regularly put the entire blame on his father's violence. But in his more convincing 2016 memoir, he claimed that his hearing had been affected after a local kid called Seymour hit him over the head with a lead pipe. That's the story that Audree told in 1976, though she added: 'it's a damaged ninth nerve, so he could have been born that way'. In any case, the hearing loss was real enough and although there was a short period in 1967 when everyone in the Wilson family pretended that a recent ear operation had cured the problem, the consequences were unsatisfactory. His ability to hear increased, it's true, but so did his sensitivity to loud sounds and his tendency to experience tinnitus.

'I've always been afraid that as I grow older, I'll become a square,' Brian admitted shyly in 1964. That fear was partly spurred by the dread that he might mutate into his father. But it was also an accurate reflection of a young man whose instinctive musical tastes were exactly as 'square' as his father's had been. While brother Dennis loved the delinquent swagger of rock 'n' roll and Carl tuned his radio to catch the illicit thrill of rhythm and blues (both tastes shared by older cousin Mike), Brian couldn't tear himself away from music that was decidedly less confrontational. He adored the clean-cut, utterly conformist stylings of vocal groups such as the Hi-Lo's, the King Sisters and, above all, the kings of gently swinging harmonic blends, the Four Freshmen. He learned the art of phrasing and enunciation from Rosemary Clooney, the power of swing from Frank Sinatra, and the timeless appeal of novelty from the banal ditties that dominated the airwaves during the first half of the 1950s. (His father's compositions also provided a practical guide to that approach.) He began to explore the counterpoint between bass and melody in the piano pieces of Bach, and the majesty of Beethoven's dense, dramatic symphonic arrangements. From as far back as he could remember, he had been entranced by George Gershwin's blending of sweet jazz and classical stylings, exemplified by 'Rhapsody in Blue'. And he always tried to please his father, so he was readily available for party pieces and public exhibitions of his prodigal talent. He was usually able to bully his brothers and cousins into joining in: they bowed to his superior understanding of how music worked in all its constituent parts, while secretly wishing that they were singing R&B smashes by the Robins or Chuck Berry instead.

At the heart of the Beach Boys' formation myth is Brian's passion for the Four Freshmen. He was mysteriously thrilled by the precise, utterly polished way in which their quartet of voices combined. Harmonies could be found in all kinds of music, from church choirs to folk groups, but the way that the Four Freshmen formed ever-shifting chords with their voices opened up a panorama of musical possibilities for the young boy. At first, they sounded other-worldly; then he began to pick at the family piano and trace the way in which their different vocal parts soared and intertwined. He had a house full of lab rats with whom to practise: his parents, his brothers, school friends if necessary, maybe his Love cousins at Christmas or Easter. He became accomplished at handing out parts, teaching each of his vocal orchestra the exact notes he expected them to sing. It was soon apparent to Murry and Audree that their eldest son could conjure up musical combinations in his head before they were given physical life. Music became his language of choice, with which he was far more articulate than he ever was with words.

Unless you were present in the Wilsons' home, or exposed to one of his occasional recitals in school assembly or at a family gathering, it was easy to miss the fact that there was anything remarkable about Brian Wilson. His friend Rich Sloan, whom he met at the age of fourteen, recalled Brian's interest in baseball, football and cross-country running, though he was never one of the Hawthorne High sports heroes. 'He liked his music,' Sloan said, 'and he liked to entertain people so that they could find enjoyment in what he did. If his humour brought happiness to people, he liked that.' Sloan remembered occasions on which the pair of them might play practical jokes at Murry Wilson's expense, or take advantage of any serious, adult situation to inject some humour based on *Mad* magazine culture. 'He'd do those kinds of things to get people's reactions,' Sloan said.

Otherwise, the young man stood out for his poor driving, his beaten-up 1951 Mercury and his shyness around girls; he could talk to them but not ask them out on dates. 'If you had to ask our senior class who would be the most unlikely to succeed in anything serious, it would be Brian,' Sloan said. 'That was a shock to all.' Even his music teacher, Fred Morgan, failed to spot any genius in embryo. 'Brian was never a good piano player, not a very good musician to speak of. None of [the Beach Boys] were particularly gifted. If they sing by themselves, they're terrible.'

There was an innocence, a naïvety about the teenage Brian Wilson that must have been perceived as immaturity by his peers and observers. He didn't react to things the same way the other kids did. When he was eighteen, he recalled, he heard something that 'bent me out of shape a little bit'. It was the Christmas carol, 'Joy to the World' (not to be confused with the Three Dog Night pop hit). His memory was that the music touched him so deeply that he could only express his response in one way: he came home from college, he claimed, and cried for fifteen minutes. Outside of the Beach Boys' collective interest in Transcendental Meditation, religion was rarely something on which he expressed a public opinion. Something about 'Joy to the World' changed him profoundly, though. 'My whole life was given over to

God as soon as I heard that,' he admitted in his late fifties, 'so in a way I can't be blamed for being a little more sensitive than usual, because I gave half my life to God and the other half to try to be a human being, so it's been tough for me in that regard.' This perhaps explains why his *SMiLE* project, as reconstituted for an album in 2004, opened with the breathtaking wordless harmony exercise entitled 'Our Prayer'.

Inhabiting a world shaped by the music in his head, Brian might sound like an archetypal introvert. Everyone remembered him as shy. But when there was an opportunity to perform, even if it was only acting up in class to make girls laugh, he was happy to exhibit himself as a clown or a buffoon – or, if there was music to be made, a young man with an innate understanding of harmony and melody that was beyond the ken of his classmates. Remember that anxiety about becoming a square? Music freed him from that insecurity, as if it represented a higher calling than everyday existence. It was only when he was teased for his effortless ability to slide into a piercing falsetto – jarring, from his tall, stocky, somehow clumsy body – that his self-confidence was punctured. Nothing was worse for Brian than to be accused of being feminine, which was one of the perennial insults thrown his way by a father who thought men should be men and that men only came in one form: rugged, brutal, brusque, above all manly in all the predictable senses of the word.

Even though Murry adored his eldest son's musical talent, he couldn't let that show in public. Nothing his boys did was ever enough and, as (so it seemed) the son with the most potential, Brian was inevitably the most disappointing to his father. The other Beach Boys bowed to Brian's superiority but automatically rebelled when he tried to exert his authority. The group's 1960s session reels are filled with takes that begin with Brian begging the others, 'Come on, you guys', expressing the frustration of being the only man in the studio who knew what they were trying to achieve.

There was a brief period around 1965–66 when, under the influences of marijuana and an occasional acid trip, Brian Wilson was suddenly able to access extra powers of communication and unseen levels of being.

In early interviews, he had repeated the same slightly conservative clichés about contemporary music, sounding adult and faintly dull. Suddenly, in the right company, he became the mature philosopher of the California pop scene, with an artistic ethos to reveal.

Here he is in spring 1966, for example (and in heavily abbreviated form): 'I think that record production has definitely improved … First of all, there's a consciousness of the value of a good bass line, and records are being made so that they sound as though they were thought out … I'm trying to be as harmonic and as melodic as I can, and at the same time dynamic. I'm trying to use dynamics more effectively … I think that the melody is a thought in itself and it has body … I think harmonically, to begin with. Harmony inspires melody in me … I think any artistic endeavour – if it's really inspired – is something that only the person that's inspired knows, and to make that manifest – it's generally very individualistic how a person goes about making manifest what he conceives …' Somewhere, in another dimension, that speech is still in progress, as Brian teases out all the potential implications of the creative mind.

That was the same Brian who, as his wife Marilyn revealed later that year, was 'the most creative person I know. He never sits still. He's also a very spiritual person, who always wants to learn new things. He buys about ten books a week. And he believes very strongly in such things as astrology and numerology.' But that was in the 1960s, when Brian had everything to say and a universe to explore. Thirty years later, after lengthy treatment from Dr Eugene Landy, his conversation was reduced to monosyllables, and he admitted that he had stopped reading: 'I got bored with it'. Perhaps it would have been impossible for him to exist at the fever-pitch of creativity he reached in the era of *Pet Sounds* and *SMiLE*. But the loss of that joy for experimentation and exploration and discovery and growth and fulfilment: that was the cruellest ending of all.

Surf City, Drag City

The Beach Boys and teen culture

Surf music – not to be confused with beach music, which is something else entirely – defies definition. Or, at least, any single definition. It's either a style of guitar-led instrumentals pioneered by the likes of Dick Dale; or it's rock 'n' roll songs themed around the beach; or it's music that sounds like Jan & Dean and the Beach Boys, heavy on the harmonies and soaked in the California teenage experience. Most likely, it's a combination of all three. But purists will insist that only instrumentals count and that the Beach Boys' exercises in the genre were simply too juvenile to match up to the real exponents of the style, most of whom you will never have heard of.

Rely on Wikipedia for your knowledge and you'll be told that the best-selling surf album of all time is *Surfbeat* by the Challengers, which 'quickly went up the charts' – though not the national charts, where it didn't feature at all. That band's bassist, Randy Nauert, also reckoned that it was the first of its kind, which was news to Dick Dale, whose *Surfers' Choice* beat it into the shops by a full year. Where does that leave the Beach Boys? That depends on definitions, laced with snobbish disdain for anyone who succeeded in commercialising the genre. The facts are irrefutable, however. The Beach Boys mightn't have been the first surf group on record, or the toughest, or the most expert, but they were definitely the most popular. They also released the best-selling, highest-charting surf-themed album of all time, *Surfin' USA* in 1963. Case closed.

After 'Surfin' Safari' reached the US Top 10, the teenage nation demanded a follow-up. What they didn't want was a revamp of the dubious American folk lyric, 'Ten Little Indians', set to the same tune and rhythm as Bill Haley's version from 1954. But that was what Capitol released as the Beach Boys' third single. It would be another six years before a Beach Boys 45 sold so poorly again. No matter that 'Surfin' Safari' topped the charts in Sweden, where surfing was unknown, of more concern was the tepid reaction to the *Surfin' Safari* album in their homeland. Its quotient of novelty rhythm songs clearly failed to impress the media. To quote the *Daily Northwestern*: 'A new album by a group of pseudo-singers who should have stayed on the beach. They have reached success by using the following formula: LITTLE TALENT plus INFERIOR MATERIAL plus TASTELESS DJs equals BIG HIT.' The *Indianapolis Star* was more compact: 'one of the worst albums we've heard recently'.

It was obvious that what the Beach Boys needed was more surf songs and a more focused attitude to their repertoire. But music was not the group's only concern in the winter of 1962–63. Mike Love's first marriage was on the verge of collapse. He had also outraged his uncle Murry by swearing in the studio, with the result that the band's manager was now petitioning its ostensible producer (Nik Venet) to have its lead singer expelled. Maybe Murry was feeling emboldened by the banishment of Dennis Wilson from the family home for persistent bad conduct and lack of parental respect. Dennis was now room-sharing with writer/producer Gary Usher, whose creative partner, Brian Wilson, had also left his parents to live with his friend and occasional collaborator, Bob Norberg. Carl Wilson was marooned at home to soak up his father's resentment. Not content with outraging his dad, Dennis also threatened the group's short-term future early in 1963 by smashing his Jaguar XKE into a wall, causing injuries that forced them to replace him on a temporary basis with David Marks' young friend, Mark Groseclose. Not that Marks' position was safe: he was also upsetting Murry by behaving like a kid – which he was. He was gradually eased aside, threatening to leave so many times after arguments with Murry that eventually the manager said, 'OK, go'.

Amidst that family turmoil, Brian established two new writing partnerships, each of which would produce commercial material in the frenetic days of 1962 and 1963. Gary Usher was first on the scene: four years older than Brian, he was an aspiring singer with strong connections in the tight-knit Los Angeles recording scene. A few months later, Murry facilitated a meeting between Brian and Roger Christian, a local disc jockey and self-styled 'car poet'. Brian's first car song, '409', was co-written with Usher (and helped by uncredited additions from Mike Love), but it was with Christian that he composed the band's most enduring paeans to hot rod racing and the thrills of automobile ownership. Their first collaboration was 'Little Deuce Coupe', but the first to appear on record was 'Shut Down', an ultra-competitive anthem for the Californian boy racer.

It surfaced on the flipside of the Beach Boys' first single of 1963: 'Surfin' USA'. This was an anything but subtle rewrite of Chuck Berry's 1958 hit, 'Sweet Little Sixteen'. (Laughably, Brian's first autobiography pretended that 'there are plenty of musicologists who'd argue otherwise', proof that nobody who knew about music had anything to do with writing that book. The two songs are identical in melody. Meanwhile, Randy Nauert of Challengers fame insisted that it had been his idea first to supply new surf lyrics to existing songs, though there's no evidence he passed that concept to the Beach Boys.)

Jimmy Bowles, brother of Brian's on-off girlfriend Judy, supplied a list of surfing haunts, which Brian and Mike shaped to fit Chuck's song structure. Carl contributed the Berry-style guitar intro and solo, and Brian transferred the sessions from Capitol's own studio to Western Recorders, which became his preferred venue for the next few years. The sonic advantage of the switch was obvious. 'It was the first record we made that had rocking guitars,' Brian said. 'The overall effect was more electric.' Or, as Carl confirmed: 'It was the first time we were aware we could make a powerful record.'

'Surfin' USA' became the best-selling American single of 1963, in a world yet to discover that the Beatles existed on the other side of the Atlantic. It peaked at number two in the *Billboard* Hot 100 chart, which would have thrilled Murry Wilson if another surf single hadn't gone one place better in its wake. Worse still, the competitor was written by his son Brian for another act.

Jan Berry and Dean Torrence – alias Jan & Dean – were pioneers of the California combination of garage-rock with vocal harmonies. Barely older than Brian Wilson, they were still heroes by virtue of a run of minor hit singles. They crossed paths with the Beach Boys in August 1962, when the two acts briefly performed together at a summer carnival. The duo invited the Boys to support them in the studio when they cut their own versions of the band's first two singles. Brian carelessly demonstrated 'Surfin' USA' on the studio piano, leading Jan Berry to demand that he hand it over. Instead, Brian presented him with the bare bones of another surf-themed anthem and the pair fleshed it out into a chart-topping single, 'Surf City'. After that, Murry Wilson wouldn't speak to Jan, whom he called 'a pirate'.

To his father's horror, Brian was now spraying songs in all directions. Jan & Dean picked up 'She's My Summer Girl', 'Drag City', 'Dead Man's Curve' and 'Surf Route 101'; the Sunsets were given 'My Little Surfin' Woodie'; the Timers received 'No-Go Showboat' (one of the few giveaways recorded by the Beach Boys as well); and, in late 1963, Brian, Usher and Christian stayed up all night to concoct an entire soundtrack's worth of laughable new tunes for *Muscle Beach Party*, a teen movie starring Annette Funicello.

The most significant of Brian Wilson's donations involved a trio of teenage girls who called themselves the Honeys. Brian would ultimately fall in love with two of them (Marilyn, his future wife, and Diane Rovell), while also pining for their younger sister, Barbara. No surprise, then, that he appointed himself their producer and sometime songwriter, their early singles pitching the Honeys as female consorts to the Beach Boys' surfing gods.

Carl Wilson would complain a decade later that the Beach Boys had been awarded their surfing identity, not claimed it: 'Promoters created our surfer image. We were told how to dress, in the striped shirts and white pants. We were built up as big hot rodders, and the number one surf band, when we would really rather have been ourselves.' But it was Brian Wilson who crafted the songs that matched up to the image – many of which helped to fill out the *Surfin' USA* album. Not that the entire LP was riding the surf: alongside a clutch of guitar instrumentals, it included 'Farmer's Daughter', a faintly laughable but musically irresistible account of teenage romance, with Brian's falsetto at its most unaffected. The record also boasted one of the earliest Wilson/Usher collaborations, 'Lonely Sea', a timeless, eerie reflection of emotional devastation that should surely have found a place in a David Lynch movie.

The next beach-themed album, *Surfer Girl*, demonstrated Wilson's mastery of contemporary teen themes, from what one writer called 'a hymn of automotive braggadocio' ('Little Deuce Coupe') to the exhilaration of 'Catch a Wave'. But it was the ballads that hit hardest. Once again, Gary Usher enabled the birth of 'In My Room', a haunting evocation of adolescent alienation that presaged Brian's lifetime of turmoil ahead – in which the room would mutate from a refuge into a prison cell. Equally enduring was the title track, which Brian would always introduce on stage as 'the first song I ever wrote'. 'Surfer Girl', Carl Wilson reflected, 'has a real spiritual quality to it'; it also had the power to reduce his brother Dennis to tears.

Squeezed out between those two surfing albums was *Shut Down*, one of a pair of various-artists albums rushed out by Capitol to reflect current trends (the other being *Surfing's Greatest Hits*). As proof that a new craze was on hand, *Shut Down* reached the US Top 10. Capitol immediately prompted the Beach Boys to cash in. Precisely four weeks separated the release of *Surfer Girl* from *Little Deuce Coupe*. This auto-fuelled classic concealed just one interloper: the group's first version of 'Be True to Your School', which simply transferred the bragging from transmissions and polished chrome to the football field. The song was souped up a few weeks later with the addition of the Honeys, playing the role of school cheerleaders, and released as a single.

'There's something about that song that touches a common chord in millions and millions of people,' Mike Love declared in 1987. 'We sang songs about surfing, but only people in California surfed. We sang songs about cars, and a lot of people had cars. But just about everybody went to high school.' Only Americans chose to boast about it, though, until the US obsession with high-school proms and class presidents was exported to the rest of the world by teen-oriented TV series such as *Saved by the Bell* and *Sweet Valley High*.

That song didn't spark a wave of school-pride anthems. Cars, though, were soon rivalling surfing as a commercial brand. Syndicated columnist Jerry Shilan explained all in 1963: 'The lyrics change to fit the frame. They jack it up with automotive jargon so that the dragsters have something to identify with. Squealing tires and roaring engines must add to the effect. Promotion is moving at full throttle. Hot rod organisations and motor magazines are injecting fuel to the fad. Toy companies are making do-it-yourself kits of miniature models to be given with each album.' He concluded: 'Come on! Jump on the wagon! Let's all get taken for a ride!'

There was no shortage of takers. Messrs Usher and Christian were inevitably in the lead, creating such obvious exploitation fodder as the Competitors' *Hits of the Street and Strip* album. Jan & Dean scooped up Brian Wilson's leftovers, while the songs that escaped their net ended up with the likes of actor Paul Peterson ('She Rides with Me', produced by Brian) and 'Move Out, Little Mustang' by the Rally Packs. Among the outsiders who also seized the moment were Bruce Johnston and Terry Melcher, who took over an existing band called the Rip Chords for 'Hey Little Cobra' and a succession of soundalikes in its wake.

The hot rod craze stretched into 1964, before widening and dissipating as it encompassed motorcycles, beach buggies and ultimately skateboards. As proof that yesterday's surfer was today's drag racer, the Beach Boys and Dick Dale both appeared at the Winternationals Custom Auto Fair in February 1964. By the end of that year, even Murry Wilson was waking up to what had been happening, as he penned inane ditties such as 'Car Party' and 'Outta Gas'. And, as late as 1966, Dennis

Wilson was still thrilling interviewers with tales – some of which were true – about his exploits on the drag strip, where he claimed to hold numerous track records. His brother Carl, meanwhile, was said to be a demon behind the wheel of a go-kart, which somehow seemed a little less credible.

All the Beach Boys except Dennis looked ill at ease amidst an array of classic cars on the cover of the group's first album of 1964. Capitol had the bright idea of titling it *Shut Down Volume 2*, as if the first *Shut Down* set had been a Beach Boys album as well. It opened with a fabulous double-whammy: 'Fun, Fun, Fun', the group's finest updating of the Chuck Berry sound, followed by the wonderfully vulnerable ballad, 'Don't Worry Baby'. The latter might have become an international teen anthem if its theme of adolescent self-doubt hadn't been lumbered with car-themed lyrics by Roger Christian. But Brian Wilson's delivery was so poignant, so undeniably personal, that the emotional resonance wiped the context clean.

The rest of the album was a ragtag of utter throwaways (a laboured cover of 'Louie Louie', the embarrassing showcase 'Denny's Drums'), lame comedy (a 'humour' track that pitted cousins Brian and Mike against each other for the first time), effortlessly commercial car ditties – and one utterly devastating ballad. 'The Warmth of the Sun' was written either the night before or after the assassination of John F. Kennedy – co-writers Wilson and Love could never decide which. Either way, the sheer beauty of the melody, ably supported by Mike's most touching lyrical contributions, evoked a deep sadness that fitted perfectly with the national mood. Like 'Don't Worry Baby', the song hinted that its composer might be capable of touching raw nerves beyond the imagination of any of his teen-pop peers. What nobody knew, not even Brian Wilson, was exactly how raw those nerves would prove to be.

The Wanderer

Profile #3: Dennis Wilson

'Dennis is crazy and alive' was the judgement of Bruce Johnston in 1966. That much was true. But the second half of Johnston's character analysis was more open to debate: 'He has a real talent for living.'

This is where interpretation intervenes. If a real talent for living requires reckless daring, hunger for new (and preferably perilous) experience and an addiction to hedonism however it comes, Dennis Carl Wilson was the epitome of life. If that talent also entailed care for oneself and regard for the future, then Johnston's verdict seems a little less secure.

Born on 4 December 1944, Dennis was utterly opposed to discipline unless it was self-imposed. He could spend weeks ensconced in a recording studio, painstakingly dubbing his own voice over and over on tracks that were destined not to be released in his lifetime. He could fish in an ocean or a river and not require any company beyond the sky, the sea and his own capacity to dream. But present him with the banalities of everyday life – school assignments, speed limits, parental rules, shared responsibilities – and his instinct was to rebel. No wonder that he was the most frequent and vehement target for his father's notoriously short and violent temper. No wonder that he could infuriate his bandmates (or their siblings) to the point of anger and despair. No wonder that he was the first of the Beach Boys to die, which was the only possible outcome for a life spent defying the laws of mankind and the physical limits of human life.

The mystery is how he survived so long. Dennis Wilson didn't so much live in the fast lane, as the cliché has it, but lie down in the middle of it and wait to see what would happen next. Not that he had a death wish, as such, although occasionally he would talk about suicide as if it was never entirely absent as an option. But he had no terror of death; or, perhaps more accurately, no awareness that its oncoming arrival might have anything to do with him.

As soon as the Beach Boys began to gather media attention, Dennis was identified as 'soaring among the white caps', champion of the surfers, the quintessential beach bum without whom there would have been nothing to write or sing about. He was also the group's unchallenged (much as Mike Love tried) alpha male, the magnet for fans' attention, even though he claimed in 1965: 'I don't understand it. I think I'm the ugliest.' His obsessions were listed in teen zine profiles as cars, clothes and girls. He also identified himself as a jazz fan, in keeping with his beatnik lifestyle.

Perhaps inevitably, he became the group's focus for violence and injury, some of it self-inflicted. To choose some random examples: he was hit in the face by an object thrown from the crowd at a Kansas City show in July 1964 and had to be replaced by the drummer from the support group, the Kingsmen. In 1965, he and his family had to be rescued by a lifeboat when his 24-foot cabin cruiser broke down in thick fog between Santa Catalina Island and Redondo Beach Harbor. In 1966, he came off his motorcycle with passenger Terry Melcher on a mountain road, forcing him to play a subsequent British tour with heavily bandaged hands. A year earlier, he'd turned up for a California gig with his hands injured by a shotgun blast. In his spare time, he went drag racing and claimed to have set track records at several West Coast strips while competing under false names. Nothing was ever fast or dangerous enough for Dennis Wilson. And he played the drums the same way, as if he might take home a medal for thrashing them harder than anyone else.

But there was an alter ego which emerged in his music and, just occasionally, in his interviews. This was the Dennis Wilson who composed a long sequence of almost painfully romantic ballads; who turned his very limited vocal range into a tool for the most profound emotional expressions; who could not help but recount his love for his family and friends, and especially the songs composed by his brother Brian.

This incarnation was also prepared to own up to vulnerability, a quality belied by his physical exploits. Concert programmes labelled him as 'a complete outgoing extrovert ... the group's glad-hander, good-timer, max-mixer and sex-pot'. But he could also shed tears over the plight of the many animals he gathered around him or the sheer beauty of his children's existence.

Dennis found it difficult to forget how he had been treated in his hometown of Hawthorne, both by his abusive father and by the wider community who saw him as a bum who was destined to fail. When he acquired the trappings of success, he took flamboyant revenge. 'I like showing them that we've got a lot of cash,' he explained. 'When I visit my mother there, I drive my Ferrari down Hawthorne Boulevard, go home, drive the Cobra along the same street, and do the same thing with the Aston-Martin and my brother's old T-Bird.' Jim Stark, James Dean's character in *Rebel Without a Cause*, would have been proud of him.

Outwardly boisterous and macho, Dennis was also, by his own account, frail. 'I'm really a sick guy', he revealed to a student reporter from Harvard in 1965. He told her that he was suffering from 'cancerous arthritis' (he was only twenty years old) and that, unlike other members of the Beach Boys, he was not able to drink alcohol. 'I can't afford to,' he insisted. 'With everything that's wrong with me, I'd be dead in a year.'

His brother Brian compared him to the 'nature boy' of Nat King Cole's hit record, but also described Dennis as 'the most messed up person I know. He's too nervous. He has to keep moving all the time. If you want him to sit still for one second, he's yelling and screaming and ranting and raving.' (A generation later, he would have been raised on Ritalin.) Brian continued his diagnosis: 'It's like everyone else is on 33rpm and he's on 78rpm. I only hope he'll grow out of it as he gets older.'

One consequence of Dennis's personality was that he missed out on several key opportunities to be featured on classic Beach Boys songs: he'd become ill if he was told in advance that he'd be the lead vocalist, or he'd walk out of the session because he couldn't get it right on the first take, or he'd simply never show up at all. 'Good Vibrations' was merely the most famous of the songs that Brian tailored for his brother's voice, only for Dennis to sabotage his opportunity. Perhaps it was predestined that at the moment when his own distinctive talent as a songwriter began to blossom, Dennis Wilson would scar his enduring reputation by entrusting himself to a commune led by a man who became one of the most notorious American criminals of the 20th century.

Baby Let Your Hair Grow Long

Looking at the Beach Boys

Billboard magazine provided a spotter's guide to the surfer in 1963: 'hair bleached blond (to give one the sun-faded look) and white Levis cut off at the knee'. The first time that most fans saw the Beach Boys was on the cover of their debut album, *Surfin' Safari*. 'We weren't very creative,' Mike Love admitted later. 'We were actually wearing Pendletons with white T-shirts underneath and white jeans.' No cut-offs, but Dennis Wilson, heartthrob of the group, was distinctively blond and shaggy; likewise the uber-young David Marks, while Mike Love's haircut, though conventional (and already starting to recede), was at least fair. 'Everyone was bleaching their hair,' Carl Wilson recalled. 'Brian tried it, and it turned out an unnatural orange – very funny.'

Nobody would have mistaken the Beach Boys for fashion icons. Their plaid Pendleton shirts might have made them look rebellious, marginally, in 1962, but by 1964 they were straight as choirboys alongside the Rolling Stones or even the less confrontational Beatles. The Pendletons had vanished, but instead the Beach Boys had adopted something even more square: striped, short-sleeve shirts, a look that Love acknowledged they had stolen from Al Jardine's folk heroes, the Kingston Trio. 'We just picked up their laundry one day,' he said with more than a little self-deprecation. And the Kingston Trio were obedient schoolboys when compared to the real outliers of the folk scene such as Bob Dylan and Phil Ochs.

Future radio producer Jack Cheeseborough saw the Beach Boys at the Hollywood Bowl in 1964 and was impressed as much by their audience as the group themselves: 'The scene was fantastic ... the Bowl was packed with cool surfer kids. The guys were all sporting that kind of modified Kingston Trio look – button-down striped shirts with short sleeves that hung to elbow length. The Beach Boys had that look and so did their audience. And the girls were just incredible. They all had long, straight hair – I think it was the first place I saw the ironed hair look – beautiful tans and open-back dresses. It was a warm night, the air was fragrant, and I thought I'd found paradise.'

Look back, and the Beach Boys always seem to have been slightly out of step and out of time. They were still sporting those striped shirts in 1966, the year of military jackets, Carnaby Street and cravats. By 1968, they had gone 'mod' (or the American approximation of the same) – what we might call 'smart casual' today. But their rock peers were now dressing either like farm workers from the nineteenth century or drug-glazed beatniks, hair down to their navels. Mike Love flaunted a beard that year and let it grow, and by the early 1970s, the Beach Boys were, at last, interchangeable with the rest of the rock community: uniformly shaggy, bearded, denim-clad, counter-cultural. Not that they felt comfortable in that garb. As soon as possible, they veered into some of the more embarrassing avenues of 1970s leisure wear, from jumpsuits (which the plumper members of the band maintained well into the 1980s) to the ridiculous bathrobe that Brian Wilson adopted as stage fashion in 1978.

Back in 1962, however, the Beach Boys were presenting themselves as typical California teens, to the point that they were chosen that August to perform at a back-to-school fashion parade at the Hi-Deb department of the Van Nuys store, The Broadway. By the end of the year, they were letting their hair grow dangerously close to their eyebrows, especially Dennis Wilson and David Marks, who were the reason the group were dubbed both 'long-maned' and 'unkempt' by suspicious commentators.

Marks' time with the band was already running short, and his replacement, the returning Al Jardine, could not help but look respectable, even when he masqueraded as a hippie in the 1970s. But the 'shaggy haired' Dennis was the unchallenged target of female lust. His nearest Beach Boy rival was Mike Love, whose unbridled stage antics led some followers to dub him a 'beatnik'. A reporter in 1965 noted thankfully that Love had 'a normal haircut' compared to his colleagues and came over like the archetypal 'boy next door'.

But 1965 was also the year when Love took a long, hard look in the mirror and decided that whatever else a pop star could be in the 1960s, it wasn't bald. 'He appears to wonder whether teenagers can adore a man who doesn't have ringlets hanging all over his face', the *Los Angeles Times* noted with unwelcome honesty in 1966. His locks were vanishing too quickly for a combover to suffice (although he did attempt this tactic with varying degrees of desperation between 1968 and 1970), and to his credit he never opted for the hairpieces, transplants and other cunning subterfuges adopted by some of the world's leading rock stars in decades to come. Instead, he consolidated his off-beat, coffee-bar, college dropout appearance by wearing that most revolutionary of 1965 fashion statements: headgear.

Reporters would continue to poke fun at Love's receding-cum-disappearing hairline for years ahead, as if he was the only bald man of his generation. But the often-maligned singer should be congratulated for the sheer variety of his hats and head coverings during the next decade. He began with a blue cotton floppy hat borrowed from disc jockey Murray the K, and then graduated through caps, berets, Cossack hats, the trilby, the Panama, the beanie and, finally, the quite unique escape route of donning a turban. By then, Al Jardine had joined him at the hatter's store, while other band members employed a diverse array of hat designs to show off their bohemian credentials. Love's ever-changing beard, which left him in danger of being mistaken for an Indian mystic by 1968, helped to divert attention from any shortcomings elsewhere. ('I hate to shave,' he insisted when it first arrived on his face.) Throughout everything, Dennis Wilson kept his hair and the devotion of female fans without even having to try.

If the fluctuating waistlines and other weight-related crises demonstrated by both Brian and Carl Wilson were a constant source of comment and mockery, they were not the Beach Boys' only stylistic weaknesses. The uniforms were a constant bugbear, especially when they visited England in 1966. Pop commentator Anne Nightingale noted that she thought groups wearing matching outfits had gone out of style two years ago. It didn't help when they gave up the striped-shirt look and wound up instead in identical white suits – fine for cabaret, but unmistakeably unhip. As late as 1968, the *Los Angeles Times* could pair the conservatism of the group's look with their following, who were 'white, pubescent, clean-cut and squealingly reminiscent of rock 'n' roll audiences of the late 50s and early 60s'. The Beach Boys entered 1969 wearing mink ties and (Mike Love, of course) a mink hat, but their fans were still short-haired and well-scrubbed.

So it is easy to imagine the shock a couple of years later when the band was suddenly racially diversified, hirsute to the point of appearing dissolute, and boasted a most unusual creature on stage. Over to the correspondent of the *Ithaca Journal*: 'Wait a second, are you sure that's really them? Long hair, beards – what happened to the peach fuzz and matching striped shirts? And what's that – a black dude playing guitar and doing vocals? And that guy back there – is he Mexican or Puerto Rican or what? [No: South African.] And – hey, just a minute, isn't that going a bit too far – a CHICK, for crying out loud. [Toni Tennille, soon to become better known as half of Captain & Tennille.] And from that moment on, you somehow got the feeling that whatever you anticipated, you weren't quite going to get it.' [That was a compliment.]

That was the Beach Boys' moment of maximum identification with the hippie movement, the rock community, the revolution and any other counterculture clichés you care to mention. Fast forward four years and there's someone else on display: 'the huge, bearded figure in the bathrobe who sang off-key' and proved to be a very reluctant Brian Wilson, compelled back on stage by his therapist and his family in 1976. Mike Love, meanwhile, was apparently clad in 'a mirrored Arabian vest, turban and white gloves', as if he was modelling looks for Michael Jackson.

Two years later, the Beach Boys were in Hawaii, where the *Honolulu Star-Advertiser* sneered: 'Never has a rock group looked so badly on stage. Leader Brian Wilson showed up in an aloha shirt and terrycloth Bermuda shorts; Jardine sported a snazzy suit; and the others were casually attired … But paunches are setting in.' By 1981, Carl Wilson had fled for a solo career and the others were sinking fast. Dennis Wilson was too sick to make it to the stage in Salt Lake City (medicine overdose, presumably), while 'Brian Wilson looked more like a beached whale than a bleached blond' and was 'completely lifeless'. Mike Love merely 'looked ridiculous with greying beard, balding legs and OP [old person] shorts, singing "Be True to Your School"'. Other reporters claimed that Brian now resembled Mama Cass or simply looked pregnant. Even Mike Love had to concede in 1982 that Brian had been 'backsliding, getting fatter and more unhappy' while his brother Dennis was simply 'drunk'. And then Brian lost weight and the Beach Boys settled into comfortable middle-age, at least as far as their leisure wear was concerned, from Mike's permanent baseball cap downwards.

In the decades and, indeed, new century to come, Mike Love and Bruce Johnston would reliably wear the 'Hawaiian shirts and Bermuda shorts' that a journalist first noticed in 1987. Johnston, indeed, should qualify for a bravery award for donning shorts quite so skimpy so far into old age. It stopped mattering what the Beach Boys were wearing and how they looked at the same moment that they stopped functioning like a regular rock band who made albums and wrote songs. Ultimately, their lack of image became a style in itself: they were simply themselves, existing outside time and beyond the reach of fashion. Yes, they often looked ridiculous. But nobody much cared: it was only the Beach Boys, after all.

Bugged at My Old Man

Profile #4: Murry Wilson

When Murry Wilson died, on 4 June 1973, he was merely fifty-five years old. He still lived longer than two of the three sons he bullied and encouraged and hectored and, in his own peculiar way, loved – or so we must assume.

The Beach Boys' record company issued a tribute that was both revealing and tellingly unspecific. 'Murry Wilson was a hard, oyster shell of a man,' it began, 'aggressively masking a pushover softness which revealed itself at the sound of a beautiful chord or the thought of his wife and three sons.' He and his wife had been separated for several years, though she was with him at the end. Down the years that followed, his precious boys would expose his cruelty and affirm their love for the man who had driven them to success and scarred their lives.

Back to that corporate announcement: 'An unending source of high-powered energy, he could wear down the strongest souls just by explaining his thoughts in a telephone call. A jealous guardian of the incredible career he helped build for his sons, he was the enthusiastic champion of any who sought to help them, and the scourge of those who used the Wilson name for personal gain.' Sadly, he was also the scourge of those who used the Wilson name because they were born with it; or with the surname Love, as taken by his sister when she got married; or, for that matter, Marks and Jardine.

'His continuing pleasure for years was music,' the tribute added. 'He relished writing songs, anguished over lyrics and drove studio musicians like a construction foreman in his role as producer.'

There was more they could have said. It wasn't only studio musicians who were treated like a lazy work gang running two years behind schedule. First in the firing line were the young musicians who were both the joy and the bane of his life: the Beach Boys. For three formative years of their career, he acted as their manager, record producer, human cattle-prod and (much to their disgust) moral guardian. 'Brian and Michael, especially, wanted to not have my father involved because he screwed them up with chicks,' Carl admitted. 'We'd want to find a girl to be with, on the road, and he was really kind of prudish about it.' Or, as Murry saw it, 'When they are travelling, they find a father comes in handy, and I can also keep an eye on them.'

One thing is certain. Without his encouragement and goading, the Beach Boys would never have made a record, let alone become one of the most successful acts in the entire history of popular music. But without his bullying, the lives of his three sons would have been utterly different – less financially lucrative, perhaps, but also enormously less stressful.

So closely attached was Murry Wilson to the young Beach Boys that more than one early profile of the band assumed that he was an active member. His emotional distance from the music his sons made was illustrated when he was asked to describe their sound by the trade paper *Billboard*: 'The basis of surfing music is a rock 'n' roll bass beat figuration, coupled with a raunch-type, weird-sounding lead guitar, an electric guitar plus wailing saxes. Surfing music has to sound untrained with a certain rough flavor to appeal to the teenagers. As in the case of true country-western, when the music gets too good, and too polished, it isn't considered the real thing.'

If there was ever anyone connected with the Beach Boys who was obsessed with the idea of sticking to a formula, it was not Mike Love but his Uncle Murry. When they started out with rock 'n' roll, in the form of its surfing mutation, he wanted them to veer towards the kind of novelty pop songs or sentimental ballads that he had been crafting on a semi-professional basis since the late 1940s. When the hits started coming, he could only imagine repeating that 'gimmick' (as he saw it) until the world lost interest. He could never see the commercial sense in Brian Wilson opting for ever more sophisticated production techniques from 1964 onwards, nor for the group to be anything other than a clean-cut, smiling, morally pure hit machine. Yet, at the same time, he could recognise musical beauty (especially when created by his eldest son) and he came to appreciate that what came out of Brian's head was infinitely more innovative and influential than anything he could have concocted himself.

Unfortunately, this father figure became an insufferable ogre in the Beach Boys' lives, just as he had been a sadistic bully when the three Wilson boys were young, especially when they were teenagers. Brian Wilson once described the physical abuse in excruciating detail: 'He would take his belt and we would have to drop our pants and then bend over the bathtub, and he would whack the hell out of us. He'd start with me and then he'd go to Dennis and then he'd go to Carl. When it came to Dennis, he whacked the hell out of him. He whacked me real hard, but he killed Dennis, whacked him harder than us. He'd barely whack Carl. He hated Dennis the most, and he hated me second, and he hated Carl third. But once in a while he'd lay it on me strong and he'd take that strap and he'd whack the hell out of my ass and, man, it hurt, and I cried and I cried. The scenes in our house, they were so terrible and we couldn't do anything about it. We were all getting beat up and getting knocked around.'

Little wonder that Dennis rebelled, that Carl learned that the only way to survive in life was to be a peacemaker, and that Brian grew up looking as if he was always expecting to be hit, even when he was standing in front of an audience of adoring fans. Not surprising that, when Brian began to hear voices in his head – threatening, insulting, mocking him – they would often sound like his father. What's more shocking was that, in different ways and at different times, all three brothers publicly expressed their love for Murry while never denying the reality of what he had done to them as boys.

It transpired, when writers dug into the Wilson family history, that Murry himself had been bullied by his father and, like his own son Dennis, felt that the only way he could establish himself was to leave home. He could have learned from this experience, but instead he elected to repeat it.

Persistent like a preying mosquito, Murry infuriated everyone who had to face him as the Beach Boys' manager and taskmaster. Legend has it that engineers at Capitol Records set up a fake board in the studio control room, which they allowed Murry to 'operate' without making any difference to the group's sound. But when Brian wasn't recounting episodes of physical and psychological torment, he would sometimes concede that his dad was a talented mixer of their recordings, with a fine ear for what would be commercial. It was only when tapes of the group's early recording sessions leaked onto the black market that the full scale of Murry's interventions became apparent. Most notorious was the 1965 session at which the hapless Al Jardine was attempting to record his first lead vocal for a Beach Boys single, 'Help Me, Rhonda'. Murry arrived drunk and proceeded to ruin the session with his constant bickering and disparagement. Eventually, Brian threw him out of the studio and the group went home.

There was additional tension on that date, because it was only a few months since the group had officially fired Murry Wilson as their manager. Quizzed about the decision, Brian achieved an explanation worthy of a lifelong diplomat. 'We changed from our father to outside management basically because of the emotional strain we were under,' he said. 'We felt that even though my father had his heart behind it and had good intentions, because of the situation you get into between father and son, you just seem to go nowhere. It's an emotional struggle and that's more or less a crippled situation, so we eliminated it. It was done more or less maturely. Finally, we decided he is better as a father – not a manager.' Only the group knew what a barbed compliment that was.

Murry's sacking, said his wife Audree, 'destroyed him. That was a horrible time for me. He was just destroyed by that and yet he really wasn't up to it. He'd already had an ulcer and it was really too much for him; but he loved them so much, he was overly protective, really. He couldn't let them go. He couldn't stand seeing anybody else handling his kids. Those were terrible days, frankly, and he was angry with me. You always take it out on the closest one. He was angry at the whole world. He stayed in bed a lot.' And that was something else that Brian learned from his father.

Coping mechanisms weren't the only similarities between them. Brian was effectively deaf in one ear and, when British feature writer Maureen Cleave met Murry Wilson in 1964, she noted: 'He says he is deaf in one ear through applying it too much to the telephone.' (Another distressing physical similarity: Murry suffered from severe back problems in adult life. So did all three of his sons.) Cleave found Murry to be 'one of those charming, polite, generous Americans who loves to dispense things. He carries a bulging briefcase from which he dispenses bottles of scent, pictures of the Beach Boys, copies of the Beach Boys' songs, Life Savers [a popular American candy] and dollars.'

He was also keen to show off his own compositions. Even before he was fired by the Beach Boys, he was boasting that he had discovered another young band, for whom he was determined to write all their songs. After the sacking (which, by 1965, had turned in his head into a resignation on his part, because of his ulcer), the newly named Sunrays became his replacement sons and protégés. It was their misfortune to be forced to record such appallingly weak facsimiles of the Beach Boys' style as 'Outta Gas' and 'Car Party' (which even referred to his boys in the lyrics). Only when they removed their manager as chief songwriter did the Sunrays achieve success, with the Brian Wilson-inspired 'I Live for the Sun'.

As late as 1967, Murry still wielded sufficient influence with the Beach Boys' record label that he was able to sign a contract for what was effectively a solo album – even though he himself didn't play a note on the entirely instrumental *The Many Sides of Murry Wilson*. 'I've always written tunes,' he reassured the press, 'beautiful tunes. And this seemed to me to be just the right time to put some of them on record. I've seen the success of my boys and I figured that I should give them a little competition. I want them to realise that their dad is on the ball – it will encourage them to work harder. They'll say, "If dad can do it ...".' Murry wrote a handful of the songs, one of them in association with his wife, and was also proud to announce the discovery of a new songwriting talent, who bore the mysterious (pseudonymous?) name of Eck Kynor.

Murry didn't stray far from his family and friends in assembling this album of what, in a previous decade, would have been called 'good music': tuneful easy listening, in other words, with smooth, one-finger melody lines. Arranger Don Ralke, who had studied with classical modernist Arnold Schoenberg, did his best to supply novelty, altering the instrumental or tonal approach on almost every line. Murry composed five of the twelve attractively bland tunes, his melody lines often exuding a pretty (if conservative) air of slight melancholy. Ralke also wrote an orchestral setting for the Wilson/Love ballad, 'The Warmth of the Sun', and for an otherwise unknown Al Jardine offering, 'Italia', which might have been composed for a college assignment to stereotype a nation's musical culture within one simple tune.

One of Eck Kynor's compositions, with the unpromising title of 'The Plumber's Tune' (a nod to his day job), was chosen as the single. It may have opened briefly like a Nelson Riddle theme to a TV cop show, but the melody – inspired by the Jimmie Rodgers hit that Brian Wilson loved, 'Honeycomb' – was ultimately played on a piping electric organ. Eye always open for an angle, Murry announced a writing contest: anyone who could come up with a convincing lyric to accompany the banal melody should send it in and it might be recorded. The winner, he boasted, stood to make as much as $50,000 (considerably more than anyone can have earned from the entire album).

By the late 1960s, that sum was chickenfeed to Murry Wilson. In every interview, he boasted about how wealthy he was. The source of his income was his co-ownership of Sea of Tunes, the publishing company which handled most of the songs written by his son Brian. 'I am now a millionaire in my own right,' he bragged. But as his health declined, as if mimicking the Beach Boys' flagging US record sales, he decided to cash in his assets while he could. Documents for the sale of Sea of Tunes were drawn up and signed by both Murry and (supposedly) Brian – although in years to come, Brian would claim variously that his signature had been forged or that he had been in no fit mental state to make any kind of legally binding declaration. Irving Music Inc (in the person of Jerry Moss, co-founder of A&M Records) purchased the more than 400 songs in the catalogue for what would prove to be the knock-down price of $700,000.

By his own account, Brian registered the sale as a bereavement – and a statement that his father had lost faith in his future earnings power. It may not be coincidental that this proved to be the moment when Brian began to back out of songwriting as a regular activity. Yet there was little public awareness of the impact of Murry's decision, because neither Brian nor any of the other members of the Beach Boys spoke about it.

In an act of true paternal cruelty, one of the final songs written by Brian before the sale took place was 'Break Away' – on which Murry was a secret co-composer. Supporting him in the studio at one moment, selling off his nest egg behind his back at the next: Murry did not seem to know how not to hurt his sons. But in his final years, Murry and Brian continued to talk about songwriting, and Brian even promised that the Beach Boys would record a tune of Murry's entitled 'Lazaloo'. (They didn't.) Meanwhile Dennis, the son who Murry supposedly hated the most, became his sporting buddy. The pair would go fishing and watch boxing matches together on TV. Carl, a calming influence 'til the last, would pledge that he still loved his father and always had. And Brian, under the guidance of his therapist, continued to reiterate his father's cruelty as a simple explanation for everything he had ever suffered.

The most succinct summary of Murry Wilson's legacy came from his nephew, Mike Love: 'You know, there's a streak of insanity in that family. Their father was crazy, his father was crazy … but along with that streak, there's a real creativity.' Dennis Wilson stripped that theme to the bone: 'Our father beat the shit out of us; his punishments were outrageous. But one thing about my father – beautiful music would always melt my father's heart. You always wanted to sing to him. Dad was a frustrated songwriter, and I think Brian wrote his music through him.' Not that Brian saw it entirely that way: 'He was always telling me I couldn't do shit. So I'd go in the studio and prove him wrong.' One thing is certain: outdoing your father might not erase his cruelty, but it is certainly a satisfying form of revenge.

You're Welcome

Profile #5: Al Jardine

Even in 1985, by which time one Beach Boy had drowned in an alcoholic haze and another was under 24-hour psychiatric care from a therapist, Al Jardine was still starry-eyed. The Beach Boys, he declared that year, represented 'a vanguard of wholesome living … we are speaking to the child, the adolescent, the lover in all of us'.

Until the late 1990s, when disillusionment soured his enthusiasm, Alan Charles Jardine was the ultimate team player in the Beach Boys' ranks. He was indeed that 'vanguard of wholesome living': sober, moral, reliable and unfailingly available for whatever his service to the band required. He was never the most distinctive vocalist in the ranks, nor its most soulful. But his voice has survived the decades in remarkably pristine state and, in his early eighties (he was born on 3 September 1942), he is arguably the best-preserved rock singer of his generation.

His forte has always been his adaptability. He never boasted the ego nor the writing talent to be able to bend the Beach Boys into his shape, but he was always on hand to assist those who did. As Wilson brothers came and went from the touring line-up, he could take the lead on any of their hits at a moment's notice, offer a perfect facsimile of Brian's soaring falsetto when the original failed, or slip unobtrusively into the group's vocal blend as the bedrock of the harmony stack. Nobody ever left a Beach Boys concert disappointed because Al Jardine let them down, and when Brian Wilson's health dimmed in his final years on stage, Al was there again to convince the audience that, really, nothing was wrong, even while his supposed bandleader sat unmoving behind a silent keyboard.

It seems that Jardine has never forgotten that he owes his lifelong career path to the man he first heard sing at Hawthorne High School and then befriended at El Camino College. Between those two spells in Californian educational establishments, Al was taken away for a year to Michigan by his family to attend Ferris State College in Big Rapids, Michigan. The Beach Boys returned to his alma mater for a 1972 show, at which college employees turned the hall lights off and on at random intervals as if to discipline the audience. 'This is the first time I have ever seen so many adults treated so much like children,' Dennis Wilson remarked afterwards.

Jardine was happier to claim allegiance to the friendship with the Wilson brothers that developed back on the West Coast. The only fracture in their relationship came early, when Brian messed up a call on the football field and Al found himself under attack from a pack of rampaging opposition forwards. He emerged from the fracas with a broken leg and knew that he could always mention his injury if he wanted to score a point off his friend in the studio. Most of the time, though, Al was there at Brian's beck and call, even when (as during the *Pet Sounds/SMiLE* era) the composer sometimes changed more quickly than the sideman could comprehend.

At heart, Jardine's personal tastes have never wandered too far from the folk music he first heard (and played) as a child. 'My mother bought me a ukulele,' he recalled. 'I had a thing for melodies. I was known as quite a little balladeer.' When the Kingston Trio broke through with their slick harmonies on updated folk ballads in the late 1950s, Jardine was entranced. Musicologists have enjoyed tracing the roots of several of his own original compositions back to obscure Trio album tracks.

Al would have been quite happy singing 'Tom Dooley', 'Raspberries, Strawberries' and 'Seasons in the Sun' for his entire life. But his destiny changed when he first suggested to Brian Wilson that they should form a vocal group. His plan for a folk combo was quickly diverted into performing Wilson's original songs: 'it turned into surf music, which is a kind of folk music,' Al convinced himself. Not that he imagined, even after the Beach Boys released a single on which he played stand-up bass, that this diversion might conceivably become a professional career. Around the time that 'Surfin'' crawled to its eventual peak of number seventy-five on the national singles chart, he took the entirely adult decision to step away from music and pursue his studies in medicine, anticipating a career examining teeth.

His replacement, the very young David Marks, was a promising guitarist but nobody's idea of a singer. Brian Wilson could have chosen to forget his friend, but instead he jogged his memory constantly with tapes of new songs and excited reports from the road. Within a year, Jardine had been persuaded to put his studies on hold – where they remained forever. 'He saved me from a life of dentistry,' Al recalled. His return allowed Brian to concentrate on songwriting instead of touring, until pressure from Murry Wilson led David Marks to leave the group. Once again, the touring unit was reduced to a quartet, forcing Brian back onto the road.

By then, Jardine had wedded his first wife, Lynda, who would become the subject of a hit song fifteen years later, just as their marriage began to collapse. In the mid-1960s, she often toured with the group and the couple maintained the lifestyle of mature young adults while all around them could descend into debauchery. 'While the other Beach Boys have mastered every Berkeley variant of free speech,' the *LA Times* said euphemistically in 1965, 'Jardine still restrains his language.' Rather than bedding groupies, Al maintained 'a sort of father image to the teen chicks', as he put it.

His friend Brian said proudly that Al had 'the most sincere smile in the world'. Speaking in 1966, however, Wilson regretted that 'he keeps his opinions to himself the whole time. Not because they're not good, but you see he's not a member of the corporation. It makes him feel left out and not really a full member of the group, so he doesn't want to force himself or his opinions on us. But this feeling is only on his side … I wish we could convince him, but no matter what we say, he's always the same.' The following year, Jardine did become a fully incorporated member of the business, drawing this tribute from Brian: 'He is our anchor, his goodness and strength flow through the microphone, along the wires and onto the tapes.'

At the end of the 1960s, Al Jardine slowly began to make himself felt as a composer and arranger, responsible for a hit arrangement of 'Cottonfields' and the most commercial element of the 'California Saga' on *Holland*. A natural musical conservative, he found himself on Mike Love's side in any debates with the Wilson brothers, but his loyalty was spread evenly among them all. In a band riven by torment and acrimony, Al Jardine seemed to inhabit a different universe, one in which the Beach Boys' harmony merged with the collective ethos of the folk scene to create a brotherhood that transcended blood.

Spectre of the Studio

How Phil Spector haunted Brian Wilson

The American author Tom Wolfe dubbed him The First Tycoon of Teen. An American court condemned him as a murderer. His biography is filled with instances of spousal abuse, financial deceit, emotional control and every imaginable form of eccentricity. He was a monomaniac, a recluse, a wreck of a human being; yet also charismatic, inspirational and (within the limited framework that he allowed himself to command) a genius of a record producer.

Phil Spector lived in a mansion where he regularly locked in his guests and refused to let them leave until he had forced them to take part in shambolic jam sessions. In the end, he would trap an actress named Lana Clarkson and then kill her when she tried to escape before he was ready to say goodbye. Long before that, he loved nothing more than to juggle a handgun in someone's face, or let off a round during a recording session, or control the mind of anyone who fell under his spell to the point where they would lose sight of their own personality. He was also the mastermind behind many of the most astounding records of the 1960s and 1970s, from the wilfully naïve 'girl group' records by the Crystals and the Ronettes, through the mature pop gems of the Righteous Brothers and Ike & Tina Turner, to his collaborations with songwriters such as John Lennon, George Harrison and Leonard Cohen, for whom he was able to conjure up soundscapes that surpassed their own musical imaginations.

The madness, the capacity for violence, the psychological brutality of his relationships with women: little of that was apparent when Phil Spector first met a younger man whose genius would outshine his own, but who would also start to lose his own identity in his belief that Spector was controlling every aspect of his life, not least the workings of his mind.

For Brian Wilson, Phil Spector's much-vaunted 'Wall of Sound' was more than a production technique: it was an emotional weapon. Spector commandeered Gold Star Studio in Los Angeles, where he had learned the rudiments of producing a record from in-house engineer Stan Ross. It was there that Spector assembled the city's most prestigious session musicians, doubling or tripling orthodox instrumentation until he had built up a cacophonous wave of noise. Then he would add the voices of the (mostly) young black women signed to his label, delivering seductively innocent paeans of love and – in the case of Ronettes leader, Ronnie Bennett – lust. This sonic barrage was then mixed precisely to heighten its impact over the tinny speakers found in teenagers' car radios or portable transistors.

'Subtlety' was a word rarely applied to Spector's monstrous collages of sound, but it was the quality that Brian Wilson identified in his work, 'bringing in drums and saxes like nobody else had done'. Wilson set out to emulate the intensity of Spector's productions, 'where you hear something as a total unit, and eventually discover things in the record, which is a beautiful contribution to the business'. As Carl remembered, 'Brian just adored Phil; he couldn't get enough of him. Brian started going to Phil's sessions and it just blew him away. Phil would play things back so loud it was scary. I think the psychological and emotional impact of going in and hearing songs before they came out made him totally fascinated with Phil, under a spell, almost.'

Various Spector productions have been identified as triggering Wilson's fascination: 'He's Sure the Boy I Love' or 'Uptown' by the Crystals; 'Zip-A-Dee-Doo-Dah' by Bob B. Soxx, perhaps. But no other musical influence in Brian's life – not even George Gershwin's 'Rhapsody in Blue' – would prove to be as enduring, as pervasive and as ambiguous as the first single by the Ronettes: 'Be My Baby'. Though he would sometimes claim to have been present at Gold Star when the record was made, it is more likely that Brian first heard the single like most of its future purchasers: on his car radio. A majestic, soulful pop record, 'Be My Baby' can be dissected to discover its secrets: the opening tattoo of drums from Hal Blaine, who would play on dozens of Beach Boys sessions; the subtle impact of Spector's sonic wall; the fearless yet still vulnerable beauty of Ronnie Bennett's yearning lead vocal; the blinding adolescent need for love and security portrayed in Ellie Greenwich's lyrics. But even when combined to overwhelming effect, none of that can explain the way in which Brian Wilson's mind was thrilled, then hypnotised, and finally controlled by the experience of hearing that song.

He bought multiple copies so that one would always be within reach wherever he travelled. Every morning, he would rise from bed and play that solitary single, over and over again, way beyond the powers of endurance of his wife or anyone else in the vicinity. Placed at a piano, his fingers would automatically reproduce the song's chordal structure and melody. And this was not a passing infatuation: his devotion to 'Be My Baby' was unending, to the point where his fellow Beach Boys would laugh hysterically every time the record was mentioned, which was almost every occasion on which Brian attempted to explain himself to an interviewer or a new acquaintance. 'Every day, every morning,' admitted his second wife, Melinda. 'It kind of gets his soul going.' Year after year, decade after decade, it was 'Be My Baby', 'Be My Baby', 'Be My Baby'. Again and again and always, always again.

Inevitably, given the tight-knit nature of the Los Angeles record-making community, Spector and Wilson's paths would cross. They were employing the same musicians, often in the same studios, and the increasingly sophisticated productions of Beach Boys records from late 1963 onwards mirrored Brian's willingness to imitate and perhaps even surpass Spector's achievements.

No matter how dazzling his own productions, however, Wilson was relentlessly intimidated by Spector, his sound and his egotistical, manipulative personality. It didn't matter that Phil's career came to a standstill in the late 1960s, floundered for much of the 1970s, and then effectively died after 1981. For Brian Wilson, Phil Spector was still the touchstone; still the master; still, it seemed, the man who operated, shaped and ultimately steered his increasingly fragile psyche.

Twice, at least, Brian attempted to infiltrate Phil's world as an equal. He imagined his collaboration with Roger Christian, the divine 'Don't Worry Baby', as a sequel to 'Be My Baby', not realising (a) that Spector already had his own successor up his sleeve, in 'Baby I Love You', and (b) that Christian's car-themed lyrics were scarcely appropriate for Ronnie Bennett to sing. A year later, Wilson offered Spector another song, 'Don't Hurt My Little Sister', only for Phil to utilise the backing track for an entirely different song, 'Things Are Changing'. Maybe it was on that day, maybe earlier at one of the sessions for Spector's *Christmas Album*, but there was an occasion on which Phil instructed Brian to play piano at one of his sessions, then exiled him from the studio a few minutes later. It was like being rejected by God, and Brian's ego never recovered from this verdict, even though he felt he deserved nothing better than Spector's contempt. 'He was very egotistical, self-centred,' Brian would recall nearly forty years later, the wounds still raw, the intoxication still active. He had 'a very scary kind of talking style. Just a very scary person.'

Exactly how scary Brian perceived Spector to be became all too apparent by 1967, when his lifelong battle with mental illness was heightened by his intake of mind-altering substances. His friend, the journalist Jules Siegel, was with Brian at his house when he explained how he had been overwhelmed by paranoia when he went into a movie house to see *Seconds*, the John Frankenheimer thriller about adopting a new identity, only to hear the first line of dialogue apparently aimed precisely at him: 'Hello, Mr Wilson'. Within the context of the film, this was hardly surprising: Antiochus Wilson was the character played by its star, Rock Hudson. As Siegel reported, though, there was no room for coincidence in Wilson's imagination. 'What if it's real?', Brian pleaded to his friends. 'You know there's mind gangsters these days. There could be mind gangsters, couldn't there? I mean, look at Spector, he could be involved in it, couldn't he? He's going into films. How hard would it be for him to set up something like that?'

A few months later, another writer friend, David Dalton, attended a Beach Boys photo session at Zuma Beach and then joined the elite at Brian's home. There were drugs available on the tables, cans of nitrous oxide to inhale, hip chatter around the room. As Dalton recalled, 'Brian was (apparently) oblivious of everything swirling around him. He walked about his house with a child's cassette player in the shape of a yellow plastic duck, swinging it by the handle like a toddler. On it he played only one song, the Ronettes' 'Be My Baby' (and only the first four notes of that).'

As the evening progressed, Brian's interactions with Dalton became increasingly surreal, until the journalist realised that Brian was talking to him as if he was Phil Spector – in disguise, perhaps, or shapeshifting to fill any available human body. 'By this point,' Dalton wrote long afterwards, 'Brian was seeing Phil Spectors all over the place – especially where he wasn't. It was as if Phil's absence [he had apparently retired from the music business in 1967] had created an entity so pervasive and ubiquitous that he had become as menacing and spectral as his name.' Brian would come to believe that he had named the Beach Boys' most famous album *Pet Sounds* to reflect the initials of Spector's name – except when he credited someone else with inventing that theory, proving that he simply couldn't remember.

In later decades, Brian Wilson could sometimes refer to Spector as an equal, a fellow practitioner of the musical arts, someone to learn from and outdo. But he found it hard to disguise his obsession. 'We relied on Spector,' he admitted in 1987. 'We looked to him for assurance that our feelings could be turned into art. And he was also a dilemma, as we didn't know what to do after him.' At times he sounded like one of the disciples: 'I looked to Spector for inspiration. I wanted to take his ideas and make them known to the world through the Beach Boys.' Or he might reveal himself as one of Spector's victims: 'I was paralysed with fear,' he said at the end of 2001. 'I was afraid of Phil Spector. I thought he was going to kill me.' Or again as a helpless conduit for Spector's inspiration: asked whether he thought his music came from a mystical or spiritual source, Brian declared in 1999: 'Yeah, sometimes I think it's coming from Phil Spector.' Then he paused and rescued himself: 'But it's not.'

Given the extent of Spector's sway, it was not surprising that, as his own songwriting began to dry up, Brian would begin to imagine that Spector might offer a solution. He would drop hints that he was working on an album of Spector covers, or that he was about to lure Phil out of twenty-first-century retirement to produce him as a solo artist or with the Beach Boys. 'I don't know if it's possible,' he mused. 'I know I could, but I don't know if he could. He's supposed to be hard to work with.'

Perhaps Brian had forgotten that, in around 1985, Spector had contacted Brian's therapist, Eugene Landy, and invited the pair over to Phil's mansion, the Pyrenees Castle, in the Los Angeles suburb of Alhambra. On the agenda was a bold proposal: that Phil Spector should rekindle his dormant career by producing the Beach Boys. 'So we went over to his mansion,' Brian explained, 'and it was all dimly lit. We waited twenty minutes before he came into the room. I guess he wanted the tension to mount. We talked for a while and he said, "I'll produce you a record even the DJs now will play", and I said, "Great". He called a couple of days later, but he and Gene couldn't agree on the money side of it.' Or, more likely, Landy refused to countenance the project unless he would be credited and paid as co-producer. In Brian's world, his saviours were often as devious as his persecutors – although Eugene Landy never sparked anything as magnificent as 'Be My Baby' or as appalling as the murder of Lana Clarkson. Yet, as late as 2016, by which time Spector had been in prison for seven years, Wilson published his second, 'official' autobiography. There, on page two, a declaration of the soul, was this admission: 'Phil's voice is scary, always challenging me, always reminding me that he came first.' For Brian Wilson, escaping the curse of Phil proved to be even more difficult than escaping Phil's house had been for everyone else.

Let's Go Trippin'

The Beach Boys on stage

In 1962, even with a Top 20 single under their belt, the Beach Boys would sing anywhere for money. Take the last week of October that year, as 'Surfin' Safari' hit its chart peak. The group could be found at Taft High School, performing at assembly – but, interlopers please note, 'only for those who have purchased activity cards'. The Beach Boys set up in front of the basketball hoops, with a patriotic flag unfurled alongside David Marks' tiny guitar amp.

Three days later, they were lining up with an array of stars at the majestic Hollywood Bowl, as part of a YMCA celebration known as K Day. Then they were back to 'The Swinginest [sic] Coffee House in Town', better known as Pandora's Box on the Sunset Strip. (Four years later, the venue would become the centre of the so-called Sunset Strip riots, commemorated in Stephen Stills' song, 'For What It's Worth'.) And then November opened with a brace of appearances at newly opened branches of Leonard's department stores, where they were at least billed as 'Nationally Famous Capitol Recording Artists', even if the locale was anything but glamorous.

Ignominy was always possible, even close to home. In December 1962, the Beach Boys appeared at the Surf Fair in Santa Monica (also on the mono-themed bill: the Surfaris, the Surf Tones and the Surf Side Four). The promoter was one Louis Owen, who recalled the event in unflattering terms twenty-five years later: 'They played on a very, very small stage. They were so bad that the kids booed them and chased them off the stage. Then some of the kids in the audience came on stage, picked up the instruments and started playing them themselves.'

More hit records, together with a schedule filled with constant touring, expanded their reputation, their fan base and, most importantly, their ability. By the end of 1963, the Beach Boys were top of the bill on a return visit to K Day and were ready, four days before Christmas, to be recorded by Capitol Records in one of the band's favourite locations: Sacramento. Capitol also taped a return visit to the city the following August, the result being *Beach Boys Concert*, which became the only non-compilation album of their entire career to top the American charts.

'Here's your front-row-center seat at a screaming, wailing, rocking, way-out Beach Boys performance,' Capitol promised of the album. 'And, if you have ever attended a Beach Boys concert, you know how exciting that can be!' Even as they increasingly filled their studio albums with original material, the group relied heavily on borrowed showstoppers in their live shows, from Chuck Berry's 'Johnny B. Goode' to Boris Pickett's 'Monster Mash', which gave ham actor Mike Love the chance to titillate some pre-teen fans by masquerading as a Halloween ogre.

Fortunately for posterity, two of the Beach Boys' 1964 live appearances were filmed and preserved. That spring they visited NBC's Los Angeles studios for a concert in front of a small theatre audience, which was then screened around the nation as part of a closed-circuit event that also featured the Beatles on stage in Washington (the headline attraction), with the young Lesley Gore as the opening act.

The sound quality of the Beach Boys' set was risible, the twin guitars of David Marks and Carl Wilson lost under the vocals and screaming fans. But what became known as *The Lost Concert* (as it was titled for a 1990s DVD) offered an authentic taste of what the Beach Boys were offering their devoted admirers. The prime attraction, to judge from the volume emitted by over-excited adolescents, was the James Dean scowl of Dennis Wilson. He responded to their adulation by attacking his drum kit like a demolition man fuelled by amphetamines, each assault on his tom-toms being answered by a deafening volley of orgasmic yelps.

Second on the young girl's wish-list was zany frontman, Mike Love: the stranger and less cool his antics, the louder they screamed. Even funnier, for thirteen-year-old America, was Mike impersonating the densest of country yokels on 'Long Tall Texan'. Not that bandmate Brian Wilson was impressed: 'Mike's sharp', he muttered just out of microphone range, but very much on camera, to his brother Carl. Brian's tolerance for his cousin was noticeably short that evening. As Mike launched into what might have been a memorably crass introduction to 'Shut Down', Brian counted off the tune as cousin Love was still speaking.

Whether it was caused by the cameras or the time of man, Brian's nerves appeared to be shredded down to bare wires. He clutched his bass guitar across his chest like a missile defence system and stared out into the audience at his girlfriend Marilyn for constant reassurance. Occasionally a camera would pick her out as it panned the crowd. She was the teenager not screaming or lusting after Dennis, but sending gestures of calm mindfulness out to Brian, suggesting that he should smile during a song, and letting him know that he should keep his eyes fixed on her throughout. Did anyone notice back in 1964? Knowing what we would know soon enough, it is difficult not to feel the panic that seems to have been sending shockwaves through Brian Wilson's chest.

Come October 1964, and the Beach Boys' brief, explosive set for *The T.A.M.I.Show*, Brian was transformed into a natural entertainer, almost dancing on the spot as the band careered through 'Surfin' USA', 'I Get Around' and 'Dance, Dance, Dance'. Taking the lead on 'Surfer Girl', he luxuriated in the focus of the girls who whinnied every time he slid into his effortless falsetto. By the end, with Dennis thrashing his drums like a manic headmaster wielding a cane, Brian looked as if he was exactly where he wanted and deserved to be: in the spotlight. But that was October. By December – when *Beach Boys Concert* was the best-selling album in the nation all month – everything had changed.

You Need a Mess of Help

Brian Wilson's breakdown

Sometimes it seemed as if everyone in the 1960s pop world was having a breakdown or suffering exhaustion. The news pages of the British weekly music press kept score, as the likes of Dusty Springfield and Brian Jones competed to see whose fragile psyche would crack next. What had made this generation of young entertainers so vulnerable? It wasn't a lack of trigger warnings, but the sheer, grinding, unrelenting pressure of touring schedules and publicity requirements that laid them low. Concert dates were assembled to ensure maximum travel and minimum rest, with spare time divided between interviews, radio shows, TV cameos, sponsorship duties, possibly even recording sessions – anything to ensure that pop stars would implode into a tangle of frazzled nerves and wounded souls.

In isolation, Brian Wilson's breakdown on a December 1964 plane between Los Angeles and Houston was not a career-defining moment: in fact, it would have passed virtually unnoticed if he had followed the guidance offered to his peers, taken a few days' rest in a comfortable retreat and then picked up his burden where he had left it, never referring to his weakness in public again.

Two factors made that tactic impossible. The first was that Brian was choosing (though he didn't realise it) to hack out a path through a jungle of stress towards an oasis (or a mirage): a lifestyle that was both sustainable and creatively empowering. The Beatles and Bob Dylan would take similar decisions in 1966, stepping away from a punishing routine of live appearances and finding solace in seclusion and creative renewal. That was exactly the step that Brian Wilson chose to make at the start of 1965. It was courageous, unprecedented, utterly sensible for both artistic and personal reasons – and completely misunderstood by his family and friends. What he saw as salvation, they could only interpret as betrayal. In retrospect, all of them, even the most sceptical, would come to realise that Brian's decision was not a selfish whim, but a defiant declaration that he was first and foremost a creator, not a performing seal. But at the time? The rest of the Beach Boys were angry, panic-stricken and convinced that he was sabotaging everything they had built together. In the macho culture favoured by his father and his cousin, Brian was displaying that most despised male quality: human frailty. And that outweighed any idea that he might also be enabling himself to become the artist that only he could become.

The second factor was unique and entirely individual. It could have been avoided if anyone, Brian himself, his parents or the rest of the Beach Boys, had realised that he was already on the verge of displaying a personality disorder. It was exacerbated by pressure from outside and the brutal chaos he imposed upon his own psyche via his experiments with psychedelic drugs. Perhaps he would have begun to display symptoms of paranoia and schizophrenia without taking LSD/acid, but the drugs ensured that confusion would always win out over stability. At times, the post-acid Brian felt as if he was entering, as he proclaimed in 1966, a 'golden age'; and musically he was. But the ecstasy could not be maintained. He could touch heaven, only to find that it was on a fast track to hell.

None of that was apparent when Brian suffered an extreme panic attack on that plane to Houston. (It should be noted that his friend Lorren Daro once said that Brian had told him the 'nervous breakdown' was a ruse designed to get him off the treadmill of constant touring.) The teen magazine *Tiger Beat* printed a compelling account of what happened, told in Brian's own voice: 'I was run down mentally and emotionally, trying to be everything to everybody … I had no peace of mind, no chance to sit down and rest or think … After about five minutes in the air, I felt myself going to pieces and I turned to Al Jardine in the next seat to me and I said I was cracking up … I put a pillow over my face and began screaming … I was past help. The rubber band had stretched as far as it would go.' The next day, 'I felt I was going out of my mind. I must have cried about fifteen times that day … I was flipping out fast.' He flew back home, where only his mother could comfort him: 'I told her things I'd never told anyone in my life. Generally, I dumped all my lifelong hang-ups and she helped straighten me out as she always does.'

Brian continued the story: 'My old man said I'd be a traitor if I didn't travel one-nighters with the other guys. Everyone outside the group was giving me a lot of static, too.' But what about the rest of the Beach Boys? Mercifully, 'they didn't press [me] because they didn't want to bug me'. It's clear that they were waiting for the crisis to pass and normality to resume.

Instead, early in the sessions for *The Beach Boys Today!* in January 1965, 'I laid it on the line to the boys. I told them I wasn't going to ever travel or perform on the stage again. I said the Beach Boys could have a beautiful future if they did their job and I did mine. There would have to be a replacement for me on the road. Man, they all broke down. I'd already gone through my breakdown, now it was their turn.' Mike Love and Al Jardine cried, Dennis Wilson threatened random acts of violence and 'good old Carl was the only one who didn't get uptight'. And Brian won the day.

Even his father came to accept what his boy had done, even if he had to rewrite the story to conceal any hint of psychological weakness. 'Brian was suffering from the noise,' Murry recounted in 1967. 'His ears used to click for three or four hours after each concert. It was his own decision to quit appearing with the group and put a substitute in his place. His decision had a bad psychological effect on the group. They were crestfallen. Brian was their leader on stage and off, but they decided to go on and it was probably the best thing for them, because they were leaning on him too much.' Then a magnificent concession from a father who could be cruelly judgmental: 'Brian is happier the way things are now.'

And it was at this moment that the man who had been Brian's harshest critic and most authoritarian influence revealed his humanity – although only to an interviewer in London, not to his son's face. 'He's very shy, timid even,' Murry admitted. 'He'd be afraid to appear on a stage now. I think he'd be panic-stricken if he had to join the group again.'

Unfortunately, the rest of the Beach Boys weren't listening.

Let Him Run Wild

Growing up in public with the Beach Boys

It didn't matter who else was in the studio: as long as there was at least one Wilson brother in residence, their father Murry could ruin a recording session.

From 1964 until mid-1967, the majority of Beach Boys sessions featured seasoned studio players laying down the backing tracks, with occasional contributions from Brian or Carl Wilson. Once the tracks were set, Brian would call in the original members of the group to add their vocals.

April 2 1964 was the day when Brian conducted the so-called 'Wrecking Crew' of session hotshots through the rapid changes of a new rhythm track. 'We had no idea what the finished product would sound like,' said drummer Hal Blaine. 'Sometimes we would hear rough vocals in the studio, but the Beach Boys didn't really want anybody around when they did the finished vocals. Then we started hearing the records on the radio and realized what was going on. The combination of Brian's vision and the painstaking work on the songs created something that took pop music to a new level.'

Blaine was also witness to the father/son conflict that haunted the band. 'Murry Wilson was often at the dates and his presence caused a few clashes. Brian knew exactly what he was going for, but Murry was usually thinking in opposite terms.' That's exactly how it was in April 1964, with a drunken Murry mocking his son's instrumental framework for a new song. Various other members of the band were there to watch the session unfold, but it was Brian who was Murry's target. Eventually, the normally peaceable eldest son leaped out of his chair, slammed his father against the wall and told him to get out and not come back – with the reminder that he was no longer the Beach Boys' manager and that his musical advice was no longer required.

The song that Murry was so convinced was a loser? That turned out to be 'I Get Around', which prompted headlines that read 'Beach Boys Scuttle Beatles' as it reached the top of the American charts in June 1964. Feisty, sassy and utterly self-confident, it exuded street-level smarts and musical pizzazz from every bar. 'I Get Around' compressed the Beach Boys' entire repertoire of attitudes and hooks into little more than two minutes. Pop has rarely, if ever, sounded so perfect.

That diamond was the sparkling gem that made it impossible to ignore the group's first classic album. *All Summer Long* set two Beach Boys trains rolling. The first was a production express, which led to *Pet Sounds* and beyond. It proved to Brian Wilson, and to anyone paying close attention to his music, that he could extend his artistic spectrum by becoming ever more sophisticated in his approach to the recording studio. He could maintain the pop dynamism of the Beach Boys' early singles and extend it to encompass textures and tones, instruments and harmonies, far richer than teenage pop had ever considered before.

The second train was slower, like one of those endless American freight-wagon marathons that can keep you at the crossing gates for an afternoon. But it is still running to this day and, in the world of the Beach Boys, it has become probably the most important service of them all. It's the one that labels the Beach Boys as the gods of summer, the soundtrack for sunshine and waves and every other cliché of life on the beach.

They claimed that title with *All Summer Long*, defended it a year later with *Summer Days (And Summer Nights!!)*, and then let it slip for nearly a decade. Then there was *Endless Summer*, and an equally endless seam of nostalgia for the original West Coast sound, when summer meant fun and there were two girls for every boy. It was there every time that

Mike Love rhymed 'sun' with 'fun fun fun'; when 'summer' and 'some of' became interchangeable in a Beach Boys lyric; when it was always 'Almost Summer' and all that mattered was 'Keepin' the Summer Alive'. Ultimately it belittled the memory of the remarkable music that the group recorded between 1965 and 1973, the Beach Boys years when love wasn't always true, when water could be polluted as well as pure blue and when fleeting joy was always cloaked in the melancholy certainty that one day it would end. But it delighted an audience far wider than any number of repetitions of *Pet Sounds* and *Surf's Up* could have done, and it is the version of the Beach Boys that history is most likely to remember, no matter what those of us who care passionately would like to think. For the Beach Boys after 1977, every day has been summer, every road led to the beach and everyone could pretend they lived in the fantasy that would last all summer long.

Back in 1964, the title song of *All Summer Long* was an altogether more intimate affair – playful, flirtatious and slyly revealing in the way it acknowledged the soft-drink spillage that had made Brian's first meeting with his future wife so memorable. (In the lyric, she upsets Coke over her blouse; in real life, it was Brian who lived up to his reputation for clumsiness by covering her leg in hot chocolate.) The equally joyous 'Wendy' bequeathed its name to Brian and Marilyn's second daughter. More pertinently, 'We'll Run Away' captured the naïve impatience of a couple desperate for their parents' permission to marry. At the time it was recorded, Marilyn Rovell was just sixteen years and two months old.

These personal intimations weren't relevant to the Beach Boys' audience, who relished the authenticity of an album filled with teen trivia. There was a nostalgic nod to the long-lost rock 'n' roll days of just six years earlier in the historically inaccurate 'Do You Remember?' and a gloriously innocent revival of one of those golden oldies, the Mystics' luscious 'Hushabye'. 'Little Honda' tackled the latest teen vehicle for speed merchants, the compact motorcycle; 'Drive In' portrayed the ideal date night; 'Don't Back Down' summoned up the existential crisis of a kid afraid of crashing out in front of his friends. Even the utter throwaways hit the seam: every bedroom guitar player in the US reckoned they could match 'Carl's Big Chance', while 'Our Favorite Recording Sessions' showed that the Beach Boys were just goofballs at heart, like you and your classmates.

'We're just gonna stay on the life of the social teenager,' Brian promised later that year. This was true to the extent that he was still (and would remain) a teenager at heart and that it was his life and its attendant anxieties that would increasingly dominate the Beach Boys' agenda. We were still a long way from songs about how to drive to Brian's house and his recipes for healthy eating, let alone the psychodramas he would unveil in the late 1970s. But the move from the general to the specific – teenagers as a class to the teenager in Brian's psyche – had a quantifiable effect on the Beach Boys' record sales.

Exhibit One: an August 1964 single entitled 'When I Grow Up (To Be a Man)'. For the first time, it didn't celebrate the ideal youth that its potential buyers might enjoy, but mourned its inevitable corrosion. Nobody among the Beach Boys' fanbase wanted to ask, 'Will I dig the same things that turned me on as a kid?', let alone: 'Will I love my wife for the rest of my life?' Only brand loyalty and a cute numerical counterpoint carried this oddity into the Top 10.

There was little relief if you flipped the record over. 'She Knows Me Too Well' not only questioned the very nature of romance, but offered one of the strangest opening lines in pop history: 'Sometimes I have a weird way of showing my love'. That was true enough for Brian, but nobody else wanted to know about it. The fact that the track was a stunning development of 'Don't Worry Baby' was only evident in retrospect.

This commercial blip also tarnished their next single, 'Dance, Dance, Dance', an otherwise perfect jewel of pop ecstasy. When the group maintained its teen-party fixation with a Dennis Wilson revival of 'Do You Wanna Dance?', the Beach Boys seemed to be drifting slowly out of favour. But Brian had deeper issues to explore. 'I have lately become very aware of the spiritual side of life,' he revealed as he gathered up some of these singles for their next album. His work 'stimulates everything'; he relished 'the inner strength it's given me'.

Even though *The Beach Boys Today!* needed that exclamation mark to prove that it was still OK for their fans to have fun, its melange of insecurities and emotional accounting was a clear precursor towards a more adult sensibility to come. Its clearest evocation of the future, for Brian and the Beach Boys, was 'Please Let Me Wonder', which could have been saved for *Pet Sounds* without sounding out of place there. There was still room for romance, and its physical manifestations, on the joyous 'Kiss Me Baby', which inspired Brian to build cascading circles of harmonies around the melody line. More chilling for Marilyn Wilson, if she thought through its implications, was 'In the Back of My Mind'. It was a *cri de cœur* from her new husband, a frank admission that marriage had not provided the inevitable solace that 'We'll Run Away' had assumed.

Brian tried to distance himself from that revelation by casting his brother Dennis as the narrator of that song. But none of the Beach Boys, least of all Dennis, was prepared to front up to another song Brian composed in early 1965. Musically inspired by Phil Spector's work with the Righteous Brothers, 'Guess I'm Dumb' was a heartbreaking account of romantic alienation set to a melody that fluttered agonisingly and then stabbed like the staccato strings in the *Psycho* shower scene. Brian could, and should, have delivered it himself, but instead it was gifted to short-term replacement Beach Boy, Glen Campbell. It failed to revive his solo career, a task that would require more adult material from the likes of Jimmy Webb later in the decade.

Just four months after *The Beach Boys Today!* was released in March 1965, Brian had prepared another new album: *Summer Days (And Summer Nights!!)*. Its cover testified to the speed at which it was assembled, with the Capitol Records art department unable to postpone the photo session until Al Jardine could join the rest of the band. New recruit Bruce Johnston, who recalled that 'I just kind of floated into the band', wasn't featured in the pictures either, as he was still officially under contract to another label.

A week or two after the album appeared, Carl Wilson told a schoolgirl journalist in Charlotte that it 'has something of a new sound, mostly instrumental, a little bit "intellectual", mostly older'. He was from the same generation as them, more or less, but there were older, more jaded bodies in his band as well; one of them quizzed a pressman about where the local Playboy Club was, while another suggested that the writer should round up some suitable girls for their night's entertainment.

There was hedonism to be found on *Summer Days*, but it wasn't quite that blatant. For Carl, the album stood out amidst the mayhem of their touring schedule because his brother 'was getting into a very expansive stream of energy. We could see that he was opening up and making very serious music, and it was serious rock 'n' roll music, which made it complete.' As Brian passed middle age and began to obsess about the idea of making 'a real rock 'n' roll album' – sounding about nine years old every time he said it – he would single out *Summer Days* as the perfect example of what he meant.

It was also a conscious capitulation to the demands of his record company, who – certainly not for the last time – were asking what had happened to the carefree surfers of yesteryear. The new record exuded teen consciousness, with a particular fascination for the word 'girl'. There was one from New York City, more from Salt Lake City and one special mademoiselle who was addressed first-hand in 'Girl Don't Tell Me'. (The last of these songs featured the first major lead vocal performance by eighteen-year-old Carl Wilson, whose timbre and personality in front of the microphone would mature at dazzling speed over the next twelve months.)

Of all the girls on *Summer Days*, though, none would endure like 'California Girls'. It was the first Beach Boys song on which Bruce Johnston appeared, while Al Jardine concluded it was 'my concept of what most people feel the Beach Boys are or should be'. For Brian Wilson, it 'will probably be our most remembered record', because of Mike Love's voice and Carl Wilson's 12-string guitar. 'When I die, I want people to remember "California Girls",' Brian added. But on another occasion, asked to name one thing that he regretted from his long and troubled life, he did not mention divorce, mental breakdowns or drugs, but said: 'I would have made the rhythm of "California Girls" a little better. That is my only regret.'

The simplicity of the song, its instantly accessible melody, its playful assertion of West Coast pride, its rolling waves of chorus vocals: they added up to a hit record (although not enough to out-sell 'I Got You Babe', 'Help!' or 'Like a Rolling Stone' at the top of the charts). But what caught the ear of anyone plagued by the predictability of most pop records was the introduction, which seemed to have been beamed in from another planet. Composed (allegedly) during an early Brian Wilson acid trip, it repeated a descending 12-string phrase against a series of harmonic variations, with a sophistication worthy of a classical genius.

Equally daring, for a teen-pop album, was 'Summer Means New Love', Brian's first exercise in creating romance from purely instrumental (and orchestral) music. Another song on the record was given the working title 'I Hate Rock Music'; if Brian wasn't quite going that far, he was certainly serving notice that he would now be transcending the *lingua franca* of teenage rock 'n' roll. That track turned into 'Let Him Run Wild', a production extravaganza which out-Spectored Phil Spector for dynamic intensity. It pushed Brian's falsetto to its physical limit, causing him to curse it as a sign of effeminacy for the rest of his life. (In his second autobiography, he described his vocal as 'crapped-out' and 'an abortion'.)

Summer Days also included the group's second number-one single, 'Help Me, Rhonda' – an agile revamp of an album track ('Help Me, Ronda') from the *Today!* album. It afforded Al Jardine his first lead vocal on a hit, despite the best efforts of Murry Wilson to undermine him from the control room. Perhaps that was the moment in which Brian came up with the idea of immortalising his father's cruelty in song, with the purely comic 'I'm Bugged at My Ol' Man'. Eleven years later, in 1976, Brian, Carl and Dennis Wilson would revive this adolescent lament for a TV special, cracking each other up in a glorious display of brotherly love.

The entire band subjected themselves to self-mockery on the last album of this pre-*Pet Sounds* era. 'Capitol said they wanted a party album,' Bruce Johnston explained at the time, and *Beach Boys' Party!* was what they got. It sounded spontaneous and totally genuine, a bunch of extraordinarily talented kids attempting unplugged and sometimes only half-remembered versions of songs by Bob Dylan, the Beatles and some of their 1950s heroes. As a Brian Wilson production, of course, it was slightly more complex than that. It may have sounded like an audio-verité document of the gathering pictured on the album cover, but it was as carefully curated and edited as any of their records, with friends joining them in taping additional sounds of revelry to be added to the studio-based party music. The results still seemed spontaneous, even joyful in the innocence of their harmony singing.

Party yielded another hit single that would follow the group for the next sixty years: a chaotic revival of the Regents' late 1950s hit, 'Barbara Ann'. 'It wasn't even a produced record,' Brian complained when it hit the charts. 'We were just goofing around. Somebody in Boston started playing the track, and they had to put it out as a single. But that's not the Beach Boys. It's not where we're at.'

Not the Beach Boys? What Brian wasn't admitting, at least in 1966, was that the lead vocalist on 'Barbara Ann' was actually Dean Torrence of Jan & Dean fame. 'I was explicitly warned not to participate,' Torrence recalled. 'And I explicitly forgot the next day, went in and did it. I thought I was really going to get in trouble that time. I could see all my royalty cheques just flying out the window.'

What Brian meant, though, wasn't that 'Barbara Ann' wasn't a Beach Boys record, because it was – and it remains one of the two or three hit singles that they always, always have to perform, regardless of how many original members are on stage. No, his message was more subtle than that: he might have sung on 'Barbara Ann' and produced it insofar as it was produced at all, but it was not a Brian Wilson record. Or, at least, not the kind of Brian Wilson record that he wanted to make. What remained to be seen was whether it was possible for him to create a sound that belonged entirely to him and then smuggle it onto the market under the name of a group who were known for something utterly different.

Why Do Fools Fall in Love?

Sex, love and the Beach Boys

Kevin Bacon and Griffin Dunne were among the actors who cut their teeth in *Album*, a 1980 production by the Boston playwright David Rimmer. Nominated for a Pulitzer Prize, *Album* was an unsettling study of burgeoning sexuality in which two sets of teenagers played out their fantasies and fears against the backdrop of a 1960s pop soundtrack. At the heart of the play were the Beach Boys. The characters toyed with a game of strip poker and embarked on some exploratory kissing while 'Surfin' USA' played from the speakers. One of the girls, Trish, had taken over the family photo album, substituting pictures of the Beach Boys in place of her parents and scrawling the group's lyrics alongside them. No boy, she declares early in the piece, can ever measure up to the appeal of Brian Wilson, on whom she has an agonising crush. In fact, she says, she simply 'can't do anything sexy with a regular boy': only Brian will do.

What would Trish have made of the real Brian Wilson, the boy who concentrated his late-teens attention on much younger girls at school because they felt less threatening ('That way I could make sure they would look up to me') and who announced later in life that sex was much less interesting than music? 'Women come after the important stuff,' he declared in 1991. Or, as in 2015: 'I'm singing – and this may surprise you – with a subliminal sense of sexual tension. I think that frustration, that pent-up passion, can be felt in a lot of my songs. Critics haven't pointed that out, but then again critics often don't hear what the artist hears.'

Sexuality and romance are ambiguous grounds for any young man catapulted, at an age of immaturity and inexperience, into a position of power and opportunity over young fans. Two of the Beach Boys expressed quite openly how disturbed they felt by their transformation in fortunes. For Dennis, just seventeen years old when the group began to tour, the problem was the strict regime imposed by his manager-father, Murry. 'Can you imagine what it was like,' he complained years later, 'to have all these thousands of girls screaming at you during concerts and still be a virgin yourself?'

Three years older than his cousin, Mike Love was married, and the father of a baby girl, when the first Beach Boys single was released. While Dennis Wilson carried himself like James Dean, able to charm women with a contemptuous toss of his hair, Mike had to overcome his physical limitations. 'I was a skinny little guy with freckles,' he recalled of his teenage years. 'I was always chasing girls, with no success at all.' As his hair began to recede in his early twenties, he devised a persona built around a façade of absolute self-confidence, the frontman for whom every woman in the crowd was fair game for flirtation.

Perhaps lulled into a sense of security by talking to a small-town newspaper, Love let down his guard just once to reveal the insecurity beneath his arrogance. 'I was definitely no Don Juan,' he admitted to the *San Luis Obispo Tribune* in 1987. 'Regrettably, I was still a virgin when I graduated from high school.' He paused to reflect: 'It's funny, isn't it? You can do a lot of permanent damage to yourself in high school if you can't get a date. In a way, I think I'm still trying to prove myself because of that. That sort of thing puts a kink in your psyche that you find is still there when you're forty-six.' There it was, the secret lack of self-belief beneath the impeccable veneer of bravado.

In the 1980s, the Beach Boys compensated for their pronounced lack of new material, and draining sex appeal, by surrounding themselves on stage with cheerleaders in their teens or early twenties. In his most repellent public moments, Mike Love would refer to them as 'my babes' and himself as their 'lover boy'. Perhaps he was thinking back to 1961, when his cheerleader girlfriend became pregnant and the couple were forced by their families to marry. Or perhaps, as critics alleged, he was merely demonstrating middle-aged sexism: 'the bikinied schtick seems more and more ludicrous and lecherous each day Mike gets older. He's fifty-one; the girls keep staying eighteen.' This was in 1992, when comedian Woody Allen had just revealed his sexual relationship with his own partner's adopted stepdaughter. Love couldn't resist a wisecrack in his direction on stage in Minneapolis. Looking at the young women prancing around him, he drawled: 'They look so good that I don't know whether to propose or adopt them. Maybe I should ask Woody Allen what to do.' But in that 1987 interview, he admitted: 'I'll be standing there with the microphone in my hand singing "Be True to Your School", and I'll look all around me, and there will be these beautiful high-school cheerleaders in their sweaters and short skirts. And I'll sort of smile and think to myself, "Gee, where were you girls when I needed you?"'

Instead of cheerleaders, the Beach Boys were mobbed by packs of schoolgirls during their early tours. The guitarist David Marks, a temporary Beach Boy in 1962–63 and again many decades later, claimed in his memoir that the group were constantly being treated for venereal diseases during his original stint with the band, and that both he and Carl Wilson lost their virginity to prostitutes. Yet a psychiatrist who joined the Beach Boys at their final shows of 1964 was relieved to announce that rumours of 'sex orgies' after their shows were 'greatly exaggerated'. More typical, perhaps, was the reminiscence of fifteen-year-old fan Frances Driscoll, who visited the band backstage at the New Haven Arena in November 1964 on behalf of her high-school newspaper.

'Dennis sat at the end of the narrow room with a girl perched on each knee and two more draped over each shoulder,' Driscoll recalled. 'He was laughing, beautiful, blond and young.' She noted that 'pudgy youngest brother Carl was trying to get the attention of one – any one – of Dennis's groupies'. Unable to catch their eye and ask some innocuous questions, Driscoll was encouraged by a photographer to make a move on Dennis, 'but I made myself look busy. There was a lot of kissing going on at that end of the room. I was embarrassed and trying not to notice.'

During that leg of their endless 1964 tour, Brian Wilson quit the road as he was unable to cope with the pressure. Among his traumas was the fact that he missed his sixteen-year-old wife of two weeks' standing, Marilyn Rovell. She was the middle of three sisters and a member of the singing trio the Honeys alongside her elder sibling Diane and their cousin Ginger Blake. Brian's tangled relationship with the Rovell trinity would be the stuff of prime-time adult drama. He felt drawn to all three girls, especially the youngest, Barbara. But the Rovell parents assumed that he would partner Diane, with whom he ostensibly had the most in common (not least their musical tastes). Instead, he homed in on Marilyn, who long before they were married found herself acting as both lover and carer/mother-figure to the tragically fragile musician. The Rovell family clearly didn't regard Brian as a threat, as he was allowed to share a bedroom with the girls during his frequent stopovers. He would later admit that sometimes he would insinuate himself into Barbara's bed, although she refrained from letting him go too far. Even (or perhaps especially) after he had married Marilyn, he continued to carry a torch for both of her sisters, eventually becoming just a little too intimate with Diane. When he was forced back into the musical limelight in the late 1970s, Brian wrote songs for two of the three: the playful and child-like 'Marilyn Rovell' and the agonised romantic lament 'My Diane' (although he passed that vocal responsibility to his brother Dennis, perhaps in a desperate attempt at subterfuge). Soon afterwards, Brian and Marilyn would separate, although she remained a trusted confidante for many decades to come. Her tolerance levels were clearly epic: not only had she nursed him through a succession of severe breakdowns and chosen to ignore a succession of affairs, but she laughed her way through Brian's revelations about their sexual habits to the reporter writing a *Rolling Stone* cover story in 1976.

The entire subject of sexuality seemed to infantilise Brian, whose conduct and speech through the 1970s became ever more inappropriate. An earlier *Rolling Stone* piece had seen him discussing the way that one of his toddler daughters was playing experimentally with a baby male cousin in the bath. That was in 1971, when Brian declared to manager Jack Rieley that he wanted to write a song about a masseuse he was visiting regularly, called Marcella. Twenty-five years later, Rieley claimed to remember Brian showing off a dildo in front of his small girls. He had bought it, he said, to impress Marcella, because 'his dick was too small'. Rieley's account deteriorated from there: 'There came the day I was in his living room with [his daughters] Carnie and Wendy when Brian strode in, a huge dildo protruding from beneath his jeans. I was repulsed as Brian caused Carnie to come over to him while he talked about the dildo.' The anecdote ended with Brian supposedly telling the girls (perhaps four and two years old respectively): 'I'm not your father'. Brian apparently felt unmanly because he had only produced girls, while his two brothers and his father had all spawned boys.

That wasn't his only area of discontent with his masculinity. One of the key strengths of the young Beach Boys sound was Brian's magnificent, aching and apparently effortless falsetto voice. Early audiences would occasionally be so taken aback that they would laugh in shock – enough for him to regard this musical jewel as a crippling sign of weakness. He would describe that early vocal identity as 'effeminate' and apologise if he was going to employ it in public. As late as 1999, he introduced the gorgeous *Pet Sounds* ballad 'Caroline, No': 'I'm only going to sing one song like this. Like a girl.'

Rather than apologising for his voice, Brian should have reserved his regret for the troubling narratives of several songs he wrote in the late 1970s. He continued to inhabit the persona of a teenage boy in these pieces, which was fine (if slightly embarrassing) in a car song such as 'Honkin' Down the Highway'. But eyebrows were raised on the same 1977 album, *The Beach Boys Love You*, when he employed Dennis to growl his way through 'I Wanna Pick You Up'. The lyric was apparently a joyous celebration of his daughters – although Brian then revealed that 'it's a cute song about this guy who thinks this girl is still a baby even though she's grown up', in which case the chorus ('pat, pat, pat her on her butt') became decidedly awkward.

Worse was to come. In 1978, the group's *M.I.U. Album* featured 'Hey Little Tomboy', in which Mike Love and Brian addressed a girl who could have been anywhere between seventeen years old and seven. 'Sit here on my lap, I've got things I've got to tell you … Hey little tomboy, time to turn into a girl … I'm gonna teach you to kiss, you're gonna feel just like this.' Love was thirty-seven years old, Wilson thirty-six. Within a few years, an earlier mix of the song leaked onto the black market. It featured a section in which certain members of the Beach Boys acted out what sounded like a meeting of a grooming gang, as they instructed the 'little tomboy' how to please them in voices oozing equal parts lust and contempt: 'put on a little lipstick … shave your legs for the first time'.

But the most alarming expressions of desire on any Beach Boys songs came from two pieces written and mercifully held back from release around 1976. It was Brian, inevitably, who wrote and sang 'Lazy Lizzie'. The lyrics began in the familiar territory of Chuck Berry's 'School Days', with the 3.15 bell signalling the end of class. But for 'Lazy Lizzie', 'it's so hard to walk home/when you're walking alone'. And so Brian's narrator, a man of indeterminate age, cruised up the street behind her: 'I slow down in my car and pull up to the curb / Lazy Lizzie, I saw you walking alone.' Fortunately, what happened next was left to the imagination.

Dennis Wilson's 'School Girl' joined a long line of lustful hymns to teenagers that stretched back to the pre-war blues tune 'Good Morning, School Girl'. But soon after he recorded the song, the thirty-three-year-old Wilson was arrested following an April 1978 Beach Boys show in Tucson, Arizona. In the early hours of the morning, a sixteen-year-old high-school girl phoned her parents, saying that she was trapped in a room at the Plaza International Hotel. Her father contacted the hotel manager, while her mother called the police, and together these authorities broke into the room and discovered the teenager alongside the semi-conscious figure of the Beach Boys drummer. ('Empty beer bottles' were scattered around the room.) Dennis was arrested on the grounds of contributing to the delinquency of a minor, to which he pleaded innocent. He was released on bail but escaped prosecution when the girl and her family decided that they did not want to go through the ordeal of a court hearing. Carl Wilson asserted his brother's innocence: 'We have to keep our mouths shut,' he said later that year, 'but I don't like having my brother abused. The charges were dropped. There was nothing to settle, though they did get some dough.'

Weirdly, a similar outcome triggered an intense family saga stretching across almost two decades and involving the Beach Boys' two most openly lascivious members. In 1965, a twenty-three-year-old California secretary named Shannon Harris took Mike Love to court, alleging that he was the unacknowledged father of her toddler daughter, Shawn. A Superior Court judge ruled that there was insufficient evidence to prove the case and thus Mike Love was not the girl's legal father. But to make the issue go away and ensure that Ms Harris could not appeal, Mike agreed to make a one-off settlement of $9,500.

Fifteen years later, separated from his third wife and his subsequent partner, Christine McVie of Fleetwood Mac, Dennis Wilson was rooming with his teenage daughter in Venice, California. Among the party-loving kids who habituated the local bars was a girl of sixteen who approached him and said, 'You know my dad'. Dennis asked his name and was told 'Mike'. It took one more query to learn that his new acquaintance was Shawn Harris – or, as she insisted on calling herself, Shawn Love.

The rivalry and increasing antipathy between Dennis Wilson (unashamed hedonist) and Mike Love (egotistical frontman and strict adherent of Transcendental Meditation) had carved an unbridgeable chasm between the two first cousins. Dennis took devious pride in informing Love that he was now dating the singer's daughter. Just before her seventeenth birthday, Shawn became pregnant and, in 1982, gave birth to Dennis's youngest child: a son named Gage, after Murry Wilson's middle name. Shawn and Dennis's relationship was as chaotic and ultimately tragic as any of the drummer's previous liaisons: Dennis died at the age of thirty-nine; Shawn was diagnosed with cancer a few months later, but survived another nineteen years, dying at just thirty-eight years old.

Meanwhile, the Beach Boys continued to take the stage with cheerleaders dancing around them – and perhaps inevitably, having begun his sequence of wives with a cheerleader, Mike Love's final marriage was to a young woman he met when he was judging a bikini contest in Hawaii. Some things, and some people, never change.

Hold On Dear Brother

Profile #6: Carl Wilson

'I've always been the one who worked real closely with Brian,' his youngest brother Carl Wilson reflected in 1983. 'I was his sounding board. I was his underling. I always tagged along. In addition to being one of the players in the studio, I worked with him in the control room because he wanted my ear.'

It was in 1965, when he was eighteen, that Carl Dean Wilson (born 21 December 1946) began to appear alongside his brother at every studio session scheduled between the Beach Boys' live dates. His ambition then, he said, was to become as good a composer as Brian, or to work in movies somehow, maybe writing soundtrack scores, perhaps even directing. He had been studying his brother's music for as long as he could remember, always the first person that Brian dragooned into his impromptu family vocal experiments. As the youngest member of the family troupe, Carl prepared himself meticulously to ensure that his brother would always be satisfied. He maintained that ethos throughout his more than thirty-five years as a Beach Boy: planning plus ability equalled perfection, and perfection was what he came to expect from everyone. All too frequently, he would be disappointed.

As the kid of the Wilson family, Carl was used to being overlooked. He recalled that his brother Dennis suddenly stopped playing with him in public when he went to junior high, as it wasn't cool to be seen out on the street with someone so young. Brian had a natural penchant for younger kids, though, as Carl remembered. 'Even when he was a senior, he was always great to me. His girlfriends would talk to me and say, "Aw, ain't he cute?".' Brian's musical buddy Al was equally kind: 'Al didn't treat me like a little kid at all, so I thought he was the greatest guy in town.' Mercifully, Carl's father tended to ignore him, distracted as he was by his obsessive itch to discipline his two elder sons.

Carl was the ideal age to become a pre-teen rock 'n' roll fan, a passion he shared with his brother Dennis. But other family influences dug deep: his mother's lovely voice crooning ballads; his father's constant battle with the piano to produce an unforgettable melody; most of all, his eldest brother's relentless investigation of how harmony parts could be constructed and reproduced. Soon he was making music of his own. 'A friend of my parents, a fantastic guitarist, often stopped by to play and visit. Whenever he put the guitar down, I'd grab it and start messing around, looking for chords and melodies. My folks brought me a guitar when I was twelve. I took a few lessons from a teacher, but was soon bored and quit because he had me playing simple things like "Yankee Doodle Dandy", whereas I was already more advanced than that.'

Like his neighbour and friend David Marks, Carl wanted to learn rock 'n' roll guitar. The boys were taught riffs and runs by a young man named John Maus, who became a pop star a little later than the Beach Boys as a member of the Walker Brothers. Carl shared his first guitar hero with the likes of Keith Richards 6,000 miles away, almost religiously analysing Chuck Berry's distinctive solos and intros. The earliest demo recordings by the Beach Boys, made just before his fifteenth birthday, feature brief bursts of his surprisingly mature playing amidst the boyish harmonies. But it was only when they became a genuine garage rock band that his talent as a rock 'n' roll guitarist was recognised. Years after his musical tastes mellowed and matured, he would still mark the end of a Beach Boys concert by tearing into the opening barrage of 'Fun, Fun, Fun' with reckless teenage enthusiasm.

Of all the original Beach Boys, he was the last to register as an individual with the public, although when he did, it was as the achingly poignant lead vocalist on 'God Only Knows' and 'Good Vibrations'.

Both were recorded in 1966, which was also the year when he married sixteen-year-old Annie, sister of teen pop idol Billy Hinsche. Maybe marriage forced him to grow up fast, but his vocals soon became arguably the Beach Boys' most striking individual strength. He was peerless with a ballad, easing himself into the role which his eldest brother had originally held in the group. But soon he also revealed an unexpected aptitude for soul music, adding a rasping timbre to his voice that erased none of its preternatural sweetness and beauty.

'I can hardly express the great admiration I have for Carl,' Brian admitted as his brother emerged as a genuinely unique talent. 'He's the most truly religious person I know. He's completely at peace with himself and the world, and he radiates this. He can spot a rough situation and avert it before you knew it was there. He's also our best musician. He's starting to write songs and they sound good. I think he'll really expand as he grows older.'

Yet even after brother Dennis began to flourish as a composer in the late 1960s, and Brian eased himself aside to make room for the rest of the Beach Boys to grow, Carl Wilson seemed almost reticent to present himself as a songwriter. His role instead centred around production. He lacked Brian's madcap genius; in its place he substituted a flawless vision of artistic perfection, demonstrated when he transformed the Ronettes' forgotten single 'I Can Hear Music' into a gem of sophisticated adult pop. It was Carl who succeeded in transporting pieces such as 'Our Prayer' and 'Cabinessence' from the darkness of the *SMiLE* archive into the dazzling sunlight of the *20/20* album. By the time of *Sunflower* in 1970, Carl had become such a master of his brother's technique and sound that it was genuinely impossible to tell their voices and production touches apart.

None of that comprised an individual identity as an artist; it merely emphasised the immense skill required to facilitate the fulfilment of other people's ideas. For Carl Wilson to become a genuinely striking composer required the arrival of manager/adviser Jack Rieley. Hearing sketches of Carl's melodic ideas, Rieley pressed him to continue, before contributing sets of lyrics that carried Carl overnight from teenage pop into the vanguard of rock expressionism. 'Feel Flows' and 'Long Promised Road' on *Surf's Up* carried the Wilson/Rieley dual credit, as did the equally remarkable 'The Trader' from *Holland*. But after Rieley departed, so apparently did the impulse for Carl to continue pushing through and around barriers, and he stepped back into the vital but less creative role of ensuring that the Beach Boys continued to operate to a tolerably high standard of performance.

The creative urge that was briefly channelled into songwriting seemed, during the 1970s, to have been diverted towards spirituality. But for all his talent as a natural peacemaker, Carl came to seem an increasingly brooding presence on stage. Whenever he sang, he delivered, bringing pathos and sincerity to the most boorish of outdoor pleasure festivals. But he lacked the easy capacity for fun enjoyed by his cousin Mike Love – or, for that matter, the appetite for raucous extravagance that became a trademark of his brother Dennis. People started to complain that he was 'petulant' when he scolded his bandmates for mischievous behaviour in front of an audience. A typical moment was preserved on the wonderful *Beach Boys in Concert* album from 1973. Carl was about to slide into the most delicious reading imaginable of the *Pet Sounds* ballad, 'Caroline, No', but first he had to admonish those around him: 'Shut up, you guys'.

The irony was that if anyone shut up – shut up and shut off his own creativity, to be precise – in the 1970s Beach Boys, it was Carl Wilson. As with Mike Love, there would have been no live Beach Boy experience without him. The band needed his precision and tender care, the same way it required Mike's arrogant swagger; somehow those warring elements locked together as the pillars of a functioning band. But what was sacrificed and lost? Only Carl Wilson could have told us, and he chose to remain silent.

I Know There's an Answer

The making of *Pet Sounds*

'I used to think they were the best group in the world,' lamented former Beach Boys fan Keith Moon at the end of 1966, 'but I don't like their new stuff at all.' The new stuff was 'Good Vibrations' and *Pet Sounds*, each frequently cited as the greatest single/album of all time. But Keith Moon wasn't alone in his struggle to understand what had happened to the surfing kings of 1963. Reviewers reached in vain for a category to describe *Pet Sounds.* Was it swing music, in the ring-a-ding Sinatra style? Was it a tribute to the standards beloved by every mainstream entertainer? Was it teenage pop at all? One retailer in Kansas City focused on the cover and assumed that it must be the group's 'Special Salute to Pets'.

By 1972, when the original mono mix of *Pet Sounds* was sold with the new Beach Boys album, *Carl and the Passions – "So Tough"*, critical opinion had coalesced and solidified. Tom Nolan in *Rolling Stone* described it as 'Brian Wilson's evolutionary compositional masterpiece … the first rock record that can be considered a "concept album" … nobody was prepared for anything so soulful, so lovely, something one had to think about so much'. Within a year or two, the music press embarked on its apparently endless quest to identify the best albums of all time. Until a younger generation of critics tried to overthrow its elders by casting the debris of the 1960s aside, *Pet Sounds* was always cited amongst the top five or ten suggestions and was frequently named as number one. Once the passing trend to suggest that Radiohead and U2 were more significant than the Beatles, Stones and Dylan combined had subsided, twenty-first-century voters continued to voice their admiration for what was then routinely described as a song cycle, with Wilson cited as a composer to rival Mahler or Richard Strauss.

'He was really the first to make albums as a whole,' claimed Carl in 1983. *Pet Sounds* 'had rhythm and power in it, and yet the chords and constructions were starting to get classical'. The album's title was accurate, Carl added: 'his favourite sounds: his pet sounds'. But Carl couldn't forgive the way in which the Beach Boys' record label, Capitol, reacted when the album was delivered. 'They gave it a real lukewarm reception,' he recalled. 'That really worried Brian; it really bothered him. He'd put his heart and soul on the line.'

The dizzying shift in Brian's musical aspirations between 1964 and late 1965 took everyone by surprise. His decision to quit touring with the Beach Boys led him to explore two avenues of freedom: musical, within the boundless toybox of the recording studio, and psychological, sparked by his immersion in every available form of mind-altering drug. Within a year, each of these freedoms would have curdled and soured. But for one glorious spring and its aftermath, Brian's ambition was both limitless and tightly focused, his decision-making precise and instinctively correct.

On the day in July 1965 that 'California Girls' was released, while the touring Beach Boys were out of town, Brian took over Western Studios on Sunset Boulevard to cut a basic track for a pop arrangement of the calypso/folk song, 'Sloop John B'. It sat unfinished for five months until the group added vocals either side of Christmas. Before then, Brian had written and recorded, in some haste, a new Beach Boys single: 'The Little Girl I Once Knew'. Christmas releases aside, it proved to be their least successful offering since 'Ten Little Indians' back in 1962 – a chilling reminder of the expectations that Brian had to overcome if he wanted to refashion the Beach Boys brand.

What held it back? Disc jockeys were likely alarmed by the passages of total silence – two bars, eight beats – that separated the verse from the chorus. They would also have thrown any adolescent dancefloor into chaos. Was the record over? Had the power gone off?

But there was a deeper, less immediate problem with a record that was impeccably sung and arranged with the skill of a master painter. Its scenario focused not on the teenage girls who were the Beach Boys' natural audience, but on its narrator: a romantically uncertain and confused young man who was struggling to negotiate the etiquette of modern life and the unsettling fact that, as time passed, people changed. In other words, 'The Little Girl I Once Knew' was by, about and for Brian Douglas Wilson: the young man who was still unable to decide whether he desired his teenage wife more than her older or younger sisters.

It was this problem, among many, that Brian discussed with the advertising copywriter Tony Asher, whom he recruited as the lyricist who could help him create something entirely new: an album that charted the range of romantic dilemmas facing young Americans. To plunge deeper into his swirling emotions, Brian could not imagine any musical vehicle more appropriate than the orchestrated soundscapes created by arranger Nelson Riddle for a series of themed albums by the ultimate torch singer, Frank Sinatra.

Brian had already worked with former Four Freshmen arranger Dick Reynolds on *The Beach Boys' Christmas Album*. But now he was imagining musical juxtapositions and collisions beyond Reynolds' grasp. Brian's aim was to reach 'a new plateau for us. It will be the most carefully produced album ever made.' And already he was prepared for the fact that teen and pre-teen girls might find this territory hard to explore. His new market was young adults aged twenty to twenty-six, precisely the age range of Asher and the members of the Beach Boys. Once again, Brian was creating music for himself and hoping that the rest of the world would understand. When he boasted during the recording sessions that 'Personally, I think the group has evolved another 800 per cent in the past year,' the key word was 'personally': the development was coming entirely from him. And growing as an artist felt like the most natural thing in the world: 'It's like I'm right in the golden era of what it's all about. It's all just coming out like breathing now.'

In the autumn of 1965, Brian was creating melodies that captured the essence of longing, of loss, of hope for what might come, of nostalgia for what had gone, ultimately of fear that every dream he held might turn out to be an illusion. It was Tony Asher's task to translate those primal but still cloudy emotions into words that would speak for their composer yet still appeal to the world beyond Brian's music room. Themes and ideas were tossed back and forth for several months. It was only at the end of January 1966 that Brian felt confident enough to add voices to the music that expressed his soul.

He prepared for the ordeal ahead by conjuring up ever more subtle and complex instrumental tracks. The other Beach Boys were nowhere to be seen, although his brother Carl showed up whenever he was home from the road. Otherwise, it was just Brian, an engineer or two and the pick of Los Angeles session musicians. Gone were the days when it was enough to assemble a hand-picked rock 'n' roll line-up. Now Brian wanted to hear an oboe against a cello, or horns alongside vibes and xylophone, or a bass harmonica over an exotic rhythm track. He couldn't play most of these instruments or even speak their language, but his musical instincts were so finely tuned at this moment of his life that he could coax or direct these seasoned practitioners into creating the music he could hear in his mind. At first, this combination of experience and creative daring produced tracks that were destined never to carry anyone's words – complex amalgams of jazz and easy-listening and film soundtrack dynamics, such as 'Run, James, Run' (later renamed 'Pet Sounds') and 'Let's Go Away For a While'. But by late January, he was finally ready to lay down song skeletons for the Beach Boys to hear.

For most of that month, the rest of the group had been touring Japan. 'California Girls' aside, their repertoire was still rooted firmly in their garage band past, mixing surf anthems and hot rod tunes with covers of quintessential American rock standards. Then they relaxed for a few days, some of them in Hong Kong, the rest in Hawaii, where they regrouped for one more show. During this tour, Brian had been playing his instrumental tracks down the phone to Carl, who kept telling Bruce Johnston that he had to hear them as soon as they got home.

'I paid attention and made myself available,' Bruce remembered, thereby making himself the most receptive of the non-Wilson members to Brian's experiments. Brian remembered that when it came to adding vocals, he and Carl 'prayed every night for about a month. It showed up in the harmonies and the love that came across in our voices.'

That was the *Pet Sounds* adventure as an idyll. But there was an alternative scenario which came more quickly to Brian's wounded memory. 'The band didn't like it,' he claimed in 2016 when looking back at the song cycle he and Tony Asher had written. 'They thought it wasn't very commercial. But about a month later, they all decided they liked it.' As ever with Brian and the past, however, the details altered sharply in each new telling.

Al Jardine remembered that the band travelled straight to the studio from the airport and arrived severely jet-lagged. This was not an ideal way of coming to terms with Brian's reinvention. 'It was quite a big deal, because we had never been involved with music of that kind, so it took us a while to adjust to the new realities. But we dug in … We had a lot of adjusting to do, physically, emotionally, mentally, musically.' In one retelling, Brian claimed: 'Carl and Al were yelling at me like, "Why the heck don't you want me to be on the album? … It doesn't sound like the Beach Boys anymore."' But 'they understood, finally. They got the message.'

In Brian's mind, the identities of the heroes and villains altered, often within a matter of weeks. His 2016 autobiography, *I Am Brian Wilson*, saw him asserting that the least supportive Beach Boys on the *Pet Sounds* project were his cousin Mike and his brother Dennis. Interviewed to promote the book, however, he insisted that it had been Dennis and Carl who had helped him most. Inevitably, as in most stories pertaining to the Beach Boys, there was a villain on hand. His name was Mike Love.

During the long period in the early twenty-first century when he and Love were lobbing lawsuits at each other like tennis opponents, Al Jardine said definitively: 'Michael hated *Pet Sounds*. He didn't have anything to do with the writing and didn't understand the lyrics.' To prove his case, he recounted the tale of the song 'Hang on to Your Ego', co-written by Brian and road manager Terry Sachen. Mike scoffed, accurately enough, that it was self-indulgent and pretentious, and went away to concoct a set of lyrics that the public could understand: 'I Know There's an Answer'. Steven Gaines' muckraking biography of the band claimed that Mike 'reportedly' described the entire project as 'Brian's "ego" music', an accusation that was picked up and repeated as irrefutable fact thereafter.

Like many of the group, Mike was certainly abashed by his cousin's perfectionism during the *Pet Sounds* sessions. He told Gaines that during one night of endless takes and retakes, he said to Brian: 'Who's gonna hear this? The ears of a dog?' But, he added, 'Brian had those kind of ears, so I said, "OK, we'll do it another time". Every voice in its resonance and tonality and timbre had to be right. Then the next day he might throw it out and have us do it again.' (By the time that this story made it to the *Dallas Morning News* in 2000, 'Who's gonna hear this shit?' – note the added expletive – had become Mike's verdict on the entire *Pet Sounds* project, rather than a single late-night expression of frustration.)

Did Love's lack of enthusiasm stall Brian Wilson's progress on *Pet Sounds*? He admitted that he had been dubious about the melancholy atmosphere of the album. 'Some of what Brian did back then kind of got away from what the Beach Boys did best, which is positive songs that people can relate to.' But he vehemently denied that he hadn't co-operated on the project, or that being sidelined as Brian's lyricist had upset him: 'I worked very hard on the *Pet Sounds* album. How could you be negative about any of those songs? Tony Asher did a fantastic job, I thought.'

Mike wasn't alone in finding Brian's demands overwhelming. Al Jardine recalled the *Pet Sounds*-era Brian as 'a real dictator. We were at his beck and call. We would go out and work our tails off, we would finance the project with our touring … Sure, we got really ticked off.' But it was worth it. '*Pet Sounds* is the most creative statement the man has ever made … the most creative album I was involved in.' It just wasn't

Al's *favourite* album, because his memories of the pressure the group had been under during the sessions were still so vivid.

From the start, Brian was adamant that each track was equally important: there were none of the customary throwaways designed to fill out a long-playing record. 'I'm trying to be as harmonic and as melodic as I can,' he explained as he was assembling the final running order, 'and at the same time dynamic. I'm experimenting with sound combinations, with combinations of instruments which aren't generally associated with the rock 'n' roll business.' *Pet Sounds*, he said, was 'a collection of art pieces, each designed to stand alone yet which belong together'. And 'Let's Go Away for A While' was 'the finest piece of art I've ever made', regardless of the fact that not a single Beach Boy voice was to be heard. (Its closest precursor outside the classical repertoire was probably 'Sleepy Village' from the *Concert Jazz* album by the Sauter-Finegan Orchestra.)

The two instrumentals were not the most troubling songs for Brian to complete. Closest of all to his heart, perhaps, was 'Caroline, No', yet another elegy for lost love and the inevitable changes wrought by time. Perhaps inspired by his bandmates' initial lack of enthusiasm for the project, he pushed Capitol to allow him to release it as a single under his name alone – although not before his father had encouraged him to speed up the tape and raise the track a semi-tone, accentuating the youthfulness of his voice. The first solo release by any Beach Boy appeared in early March, at which point more than half the album tracks still required vocal embellishment. 'Caroline, No' was entirely lacking in Beach Boys energy or effervescence, which sapped its commercial potential and hampered airplay. It climbed into the Top 40 and then vanished from the US chart. We are left to ponder an alternative version of history, in which that single reached number one, prompting Brian to reclaim *Pet Sounds* as his own and abandon the other Beach Boys to performing 'Johnny B. Goode' and 'Papa-Oom-Mow-Mow' for eternity.

'Caroline, No' was not the only confessional rendered for Brian in Tony Asher's words. The starkest and also most self-revealing statement on *Pet Sounds* was 'I Just Wasn't Made for These Times'. (No wonder that Brian tried to convince Dennis to sing it, as a method of distancing himself from its adolescent agonies.) 'That's a strange cut,' he remembered more than three decades later. 'It's too close to home.'

Another form of expression worried Brian as he came to complete *Pet Sounds*: the lyrical content of a song that Bruce Johnston called 'the best song we ever recorded', only to be trumped by Paul McCartney, who once said it was the greatest song ever written. There were two issues with 'God Only Knows' as far as its composer was concerned. The first was the opening line, 'I may not always love you'. It was explained and softened by what came next, but by anyone's account, it was an unusual opening for an expression of love. Even more controversial was the title itself; any mention of 'God' in a popular song risked accusations of sickliness at one extreme and blasphemy at the other. British listeners were unabashed. Issued as a single, 'God Only Knows' reached number two, out-sold only by the Beatles. But at home it was decided to sneak the song onto the B-side of 'Wouldn't It Be Nice'. Even some UK reviewers questioned its lyrics: Maureen Cleave in the *London Evening Standard* found the track 'faintly comic', while the *Bristol Evening Post* declared that Asher's words were 'a load of old junk'.

A final controversy was kept strictly within the group. It concerned a track that had been completed in time for inclusion on the album, only for Brian Wilson to sideline it at the last minute. 'We should have put "Good Vibrations" on *Pet Sounds*,' Al Jardine insisted forty years later. 'I told Brian. We all told him.' But this was not 'Good Vibrations' as we know it today: the original version had lyrics by Tony Asher and lacked the repeated chorus lines contributed later by Mike Love. It carried a distinct rhythm-and-blues feel, as if it had been recorded at Motown's studio in Detroit – which was perhaps why Brian toyed with passing the song to someone like Wilson Pickett or Marvin Gaye. Fortunately for the Beach Boys, he decided to keep it for them instead.

Two frequent complaints about the final presentation of *Pet Sounds* have long been laid at the door of Capitol Records. The first was that this apparent concept album, which (if you try hard enough) you can track as the story of a doomed love affair, was interrupted midway through by the single issued by the Beach Boys during the final sessions:

'Sloop John B'. 'Capitol forced them to do it,' say the critics, 'and they ruined the album.' Al Jardine agreed – with the verdict at least: 'the biggest mistake we made,' he lamented. But the truth was that Capitol did not insist that the single was included: indeed, they might have preferred to reserve it for a later, more teen-oriented collection. The choice was Brian Wilson's alone.

That wasn't the case with another common bugbear: the cover artwork. Brian picked the title of *Pet Sounds* and Capitol's art director ran with it, sending the group to San Diego Zoo for a photo shoot. Rather than cuddling kittens or puppies, the five Beach Boys (Bruce Johnston had to keep out of shot for contractual reasons) were required to wrestle with an uncooperative pen of goats. The zoo's publicity director was outraged by their behaviour (the band, not the goats). 'First off, one of them bounced a carrot off the head of one of our tigers. Another tried to stick the head of an antelope through some iron bars. Then they went around handling puppies and baby chicks, putting them down in the open and walking off. A few young girls who saw the Beach Boys acting like this were certainly disillusioned.' Dennis Wilson was even said to have punched a goat in the head. But, as Bruce Johnston explained, 'the goats were terrible. They jump all over you and bite. One of them ate my radio. The zoo said we were torturing the animals – they should have seen what *we* had to go through. We were doing all the suffering.'

The suffering continued when it was time to deliver the completed album to Capitol's A&R department. Brian and Mike attended the initial playback and were horrified when the executives said, 'Well, this is great, but where are the surfing songs?'. 'They wanted *Shut Down Volume Six*, or something,' Mike recalled. 'They didn't get it at first, because of all the unusual instruments, all these incredible, beautiful, intricate, complex orchestrations and harmonies.' As Bruce Johnston noted, 'they said it wasn't commercial and people wouldn't understand it.' And he said it was no coincidence that Capitol rushed out *The Best of the Beach Boys* just six weeks after *Pet Sounds* reached the shops, Bruce calling it 'the first "I guess your career's over" greatest hits album'. By that point, Brian had become so disillusioned by Capitol's attitude towards his music that he turned up for one publicity meeting with a set of printed cards that bore messages such as 'Yes', 'No', 'I don't know' and 'That's a good idea', raising the appropriate card each time he was asked a question. Not a word came out of his mouth.

The label's response was a savage blow to the album's chief creator. 'I think it killed about 99 per cent of Brian's inspiration,' Johnston reflected. Brian's wife Marilyn said that he 'couldn't understand it' when the album wasn't a hit: 'I think that had a lot to do with slowing him down.' But the myth that Capitol killed *Pet Sounds* isn't strictly true. Whatever they said in a boardroom, Capitol serviced and promoted the record in exactly the way as they had the previous Beach Boys records. Yes, the *Best Of* album might have distracted buyers, but the Beatles had proved in 1964 that it was quite possible for an act to score two (or more) hit albums simultaneously. *Pet Sounds* only reached number ten on the US charts for one simple reason: it wasn't aimed at the very young fanbase who had lapped up their earlier releases. In Britain, where the album soared to number two, it was judged more on its own merits, as the Beach Boys hadn't enjoyed the same run of teen-oriented hit singles. It didn't hurt that the cream of British pop talent, from the Beatles downwards (though not Keith Moon), competed to praise *Pet Sounds* and acknowledge its innovative genius.

For Brian, success in Britain was only mild consolation for feeling rejected at home. Looking back, Al Jardine believed that 'Brian just lost faith in the whole process and started taking drugs in an even greater amount, and kind of blew himself out, and it was very difficult for him to complete things'. Rather than taking pleasure in its enduring reputation, Brian came to regard *Pet Sounds* as an embarrassment. Under therapy in 1976, he grimaced and judged the album to be 'too artistic for comfort. I don't want to be that vulnerable.' Back under Dr Landy's care fifteen years later, he made a direct connection between the music and the evil narcotics that had helped to inspire it. 'I was smoking marijuana the whole time I made this. Drugs helped me create, but then they made things worse.'

Pet Sounds continued to endure a dual existence in the decades after its release: an object of adulation among fans and critics, and a source of frustration and disagreement for the Beach Boys. The more often Mike Love had to read that he was supposedly responsible for sabotaging *Pet Sounds*, the less he wanted to hear about the album. Bruce Johnston, who had undertaken a solo publicity tour to England before the album was released, continued to fly the flag – suggesting, for example, that Brian and the group should remake the album in the 1990s with conductor Simon Rattle and the Birmingham Symphony Orchestra, hiring guest soloists.

Meanwhile, a new generation of Capitol Records executives struggled to bring *Pet Sounds* into the digital age, with warring Beach Boys factions holding them back. The initial CD package escaped in Japan, but was delayed elsewhere because various members of the group objected to the bonus tracks. Then the planned thirtieth anniversary box set release in 1996 was cancelled at the last moment, after the touring band (everyone but Brian, in other words) discovered that they barely merited a mention in the accompanying booklet. As the group's in-house diplomat, Bruce Johnston spelled out the problem: 'In Brian's heart, it is absolutely his creation. But the other guys are trying to remind everybody that the other Beach Boys had a lot of input and that was overlooked in the liner notes ... I think the band might've felt they were treated like they were just backing vocalists.'

Suitably amended, *The Pet Sounds Sessions* was released in 1997 to ecstatic reviews; the package was duly nominated for a Grammy Award as Best Historical Album (it lost out to a Hank Williams collection). And, in January 2002, Brian travelled to Europe and Britain for a series of concerts in which he and his meticulous, highly skilled band performed the entire *Pet Sounds* album. For the first time, Brian Wilson was forced to confront the confusing reality that *Pet Sounds* was loved, adored, worshipped even, despite everything he remembered and believed. In 2016, he celebrated the album's fiftieth anniversary with another tour, on which he was joined by two other Beach Boys survivors:

Al Jardine and Blondie Chaplin. The 1997 box set was revamped and reissued, and the entertainment world joined in the celebrations. 'People love *Pet Sounds* wherever we go,' Brian said. It had taken fifty years, but at last he sounded as if he believed it.

Gettin' in Over My Head

Demolishing the popular song with Brian Wilson

If *Pet Sounds* represented the pinnacle of the popular love song, what could possibly come next? The melodies composed by Brian Wilson represented the ultimate pop expression of the romantic ideal that had emerged through poetry and classical music in the late eighteenth century. They were intensely personal, rooted in emotion and organically whole, despite their musical complexity. Yet their creator was scarcely able to pause long enough to reflect upon his achievement. By the time the album was released in May 1966, his imagination was being stimulated in entirely different ways, under the influence of intense creative urges and chemical experiments that altered the way in which his brain processed and translated ideas into physical form.

Without having any knowledge of developments in early twentieth-century art and literature, Wilson had accelerated his way from classic songwriting techniques into a modernist approach within a matter of months. In musical terms, he was no longer satisfied by the restrictions of the traditional popular song, with its verse, chorus and middle section format. Just as LSD shattered the orthodox levels of consciousness, his shift into modernism (no matter how unknowingly) saw him abandoning existing formulas in favour of a new way of writing. For the next year, his songs would be built not on a melody that ran through the piece, but on a collage of fragments. These might be repeated, like a normal chorus, or they could be juxtaposed with other sounds or interpolations that would disrupt the listener's expectations.

Brian had a pet name for these pieces of melody: they were feels. As he explained in May 1966, 'feels are brief note sequences, fragments of ideas. Once they're out of my head and into the open air, I can see them and touch them firmly.' It would be quite possible to use a 'feel' as the launch pad for a traditional melody. But Brian's imagination no longer worked that way. Feels seemed to come to him automatically, a gift of God or a route of access to a fresh layer of consciousness. The challenge would now be to control those feels, bring them together, shape them into something that could function as a piece of music that could be recorded and performed.

By the time he acknowledged the existence of feels, he already knew that his initial, *Pet Sounds*-era attempt at 'Good Vibrations' was not satisfactory. Instead, he returned to the studio in May to re-record the skeleton of the song, followed by an initial pass of a collage to which he had already given the title 'Heroes and Villains'. He had a feel that fitted those three words perfectly, but nothing else – though the full extent of the song at this stage is impossible to gauge, as the May 1966 session tape has been lost. All that remains is a log of participants in the session and engineer Chuck Britz's memory that the piece was overwhelmingly powerful in its scope and tonalities.

This was still an era when artists were expected to complete a song in a session or two: as an example, it took three days for the Beatles to record 'Paperback Writer' and 'Rain', which made up the two sides of their most complex single to date. Yet the two songs that Brian Wilson had conceived by May 1966 would preoccupy and tantalise him for more than a year. Both ultimately emerged as Beach Boys singles. 'Good Vibrations' has often been described as the greatest recording in pop history, while 'Heroes and Villains' escaped its maker's grasp and marked the moment when the Beach Boys began a calamitous commercial decline.

This process had hardly started when Brian admitted that he

had 'tried to make a pocket symphony' out of 'Good Vibrations'. In November 1966, there was finally a record to fulfil expectations and Brian used statistics to describe the complexity of the process: 'This took ninety hours in four studios over a period of six months. We made tape after tape, and at one time I was so disheartened by not getting the new sound we were striving for that I scrapped it all for three months. I even considered making it completely on my own.' Here it was again: the rumbling belief that the only thing standing between creative effort and triumph was the Beach Boys.

It was easy to see where this suggestion came from. Mike Love never doubted his cousin's powers of musical invention, but he was puzzled by the lyrical and conceptual approach on Brian's initial attempts at the song. Mike recalled: 'When I heard "Good Vibrations" for the first time, I said, "Wow, how is anybody going to relate to this?" Because the whole world wasn't smoking pot, just Brian and his buddies, taking acid and stuff. So I wrote it from the standpoint of a boy-girl attraction that people can relate to ... I always tried to find the bridge between Brian's spontaneous brilliance and the masses.' Tony Asher's original lyrics weren't entirely removed from that boy-girl attraction, but they described a state of confusion rather than romantic engagement. Mike achieved perfectly what he set out to do: he cut the narrative voice back to a single, ecstatic romance and then added the 'vibrations/excitations' chant that became part of the track's main lyrical hook.

'Michael didn't write the [verse] lyrics until the very last minute,' Carl Wilson remembered. By then, Brian and the group had already spent session after session dubbing vocal parts to the segmented rhythm track recorded across Los Angeles. 'We'd double or triple or quadruple the exact same part, so it would sound like twenty voices,' Carl said. 'It was pretty daring back them to record a section and see if it would fit in later.' His brother Dennis denied that Brian's work was too complex for the average listener: 'I don't call it complicated, I call it fun'. But their father – the voice of pre-acid, pre-rock tradition in the music business – fretted that the various shifts of tempo would make the second half of the record too difficult for kids to dance to.

By this point, everyone was making suggestions. Bruce Johnston sheepishly remembered a session in which he insisted that the middle of 'Good Vibrations' could be improved by adding the reverberations of a large gong. They rolled tape and, as Bruce admitted, 'the needles in the control panel went crazy. So – no gong. Guess we had enough vibrations already.' Another less conventional addition to the sound spectrum made it to the finished record, however: the electro-theremin designed and played by Paul Tanner. That had already been used subtly on 'I Just Wasn't Made for These Times' to mimic the singer's sense of dislocation from the rest of the world. On 'Good Vibrations', it was given the more central role of bringing the whole concept of vibrations to startling sonic life. (On tour, the Beach Boys later employed a more practical substitute, the Melsinar built by synthesiser pioneer Robert Moog. They visited his offices towards the end of a November 1966 tour on which Mike Love had been given the stiff task of wrestling vaguely appropriate sounds out of Tanner's instrument.)

By the end of the sessions, Brian Wilson supposedly admitted that 'I was so excited, I hid the master tape away and couldn't remember where. My house was torn apart in the search and I was almost suicidal until it was found behind the fridge.' (Am I alone in hearing a publicist's imagination at work in this quote?) But his excitement wasn't a private affair. As Mike Love said, 'everyone blew their minds' over the record in Britain, even if they couldn't understand it. Old-school singles reviewer Derek Johnson of the *New Musical Express* made a valiant attempt to describe its sound: 'Tempo varies between a vigorous surf-shake with tambourine, and a slow drag pace with organ and weird oscillations. Colourful lyrics; highly electronic.' Beatles publicist Tony Barrow, writing under a pseudonym in the *Liverpool Echo*, concentrated on the impact rather than what had caused it: 'Good Vibrations,' he said, was 'not so much a record, more an Audio Happening'.

The single quickly became a top-five hit in most territories that kept track of these things; more importantly, it topped both the UK and US charts. Since 1966, it has been performed at Beach Boys concerts more than any other song. Indeed, has there been a show since then that hasn't included it? 'Good Vibrations' was nominated for four Grammy awards in 1967, though it lost in every category. (The Best Contemporary Song of that year? 'Winchester Cathedral' by the New Vaudeville Band, of course. Best Group Vocal Performance? 'A Man and A Woman' by the Anita Kerr Singers. It's worth a listen to this record, just to hear the context in which Brian Wilson's feels were being created.) But the Beach Boys' track was incorporated into the Grammy Hall of Fame many years later, whatever that was worth.

Unfortunately, by then 'Good Vibrations' had joined the catalogue of Beach Boys recordings that caused their composer pain. As early as 1974, Brian stepped outside of the studio to avoid hearing 'Good Vibrations' during an otherwise amicable live radio interview. Much later, he would describe it as 'a scary record, very scary', a verdict he explained like this: 'It's too weird for me. To hear it now shakes me up too much. I've done my good vibrations. I'm through with it.' But inevitably he was forced to perform it whenever he appeared in concert, with or without the Beach Boys.

Brian was very much alone in his agony with 'Good Vibrations'. Its successor – supposedly due for release just eight weeks later, but eventually delayed for a further six months while Brian battled against the monster to which he felt forced to give birth – well, that was a different story.

'Heroes and Villains' sounded so simple at first. Brian described it in November 1966 as 'a three-minute musical comedy'. As such, it would be part of an album that 'will contain lots of humour … It won't be like a comedy LP, but someone might say something in between verses.' Anything might happen, in fact, which was precisely the problem: for this was the song on which everything did happen, to the point that Brian was no longer able to recognise what constituted a song.

From what we know (very little) about the mysterious May 1966 recording of the song, it came in at less than three minutes and had a recognisable shape: verses filled with long, descending melody lines, followed by a chorus in which the phrase 'heroes and villains' made perfect metrical sense. Then it was put aside (or lost) for several months, only to be picked up in earnest towards the end of the year. It was supposedly finished in January 1967, or in February, or in March, at which point the only issue preventing its release was the Beach Boys' ill-timed dispute with Capitol Records. By April, Brian had utterly lost faith in the recording, or the song, or himself, and the entire thing was scrapped. Then it was reborn in June and July, at which point a confused-sounding Bruce Johnston revealed that 'there are about six different tapes of this number about and now it is just a matter of selecting the right one'.

The decision was not as simple as that might sound. Consider a comparison: the Beatles' equally experimental 'Strawberry Fields Forever'. Early in the process of creating that masterpiece, the group knew exactly what constituted the song; the complication was choosing which of two contrasting arrangements, in different keys and tempos, they preferred. (Famously, their producer George Martin was able to combine the superior moments of both versions into a coherent whole.)

If Brian Wilson had originally known what 'Heroes and Villains' was meant to be, that certainty had been lost by the early months of 1967. In fact, the struggle with this song was a microcosm of the entire saga surrounding the non-completion of the *SMiLE* album. But that challenge should not have held back the completion of the single. It was just that Brian couldn't decide whether 'Heroes and Villains' was three minutes long, or four, or seven; whether it filled one side of a single or both; or even whether it was a potential single at all.

The Beach Boys' mid-1960s publicist, the charming and impeccably astute Derek Taylor, was as vital as anyone in maintaining Brian's morale – or at least the public perception of the same – during this torturous period. But an innocent anecdote he related in a British music paper in March 1967 inadvertently revealed how mercurial his client had become.

'At any time, Wilson may have a change of mind, or ear,' he explained. 'One such happened a couple of weeks ago when he was called from a cinema to be told that two men had been caught robbing his Rolls-Royce in the car park. At the police station later he watched with quiet dismay the heroes and villains scene played out with real heroes and villains, real cops and robbers. And as a result, he completely reshaped one section of the song and had it re-recorded. I have heard several of the sections and ultimately they will become a masterly whole. But only when they're totally related and correctly shaped.'

There's a well-reported story that when Brian finally mastered a fresh version of 'Heroes and Villains' ready to offer to the world, chaos ensued. Legend has it that he and his posse arrived at a Los Angeles radio station, only for the DJ to say that he couldn't grant listeners an exclusive preview of this long-awaited gem because the song wasn't on his playlist. Karl Engemann, Capitol's A&R director, experienced this event from the other end, after he was invited to Brian's house for his own first hearing: 'I arrived and no one was there. Brian had gotten so excited with the finished tape that he had taken it to KHJ so he could hear it on the radio.' Then Brian apparently took copies to several other stations, all of which began playing it. Not only did Capitol not have any records for the public to sell, but they still hadn't settled their contractual dispute with the Beach Boys.

Bruce Johnston also had an unsettling 'Heroes and Villains' experience to report that month. He was at a hip English discotheque, where 'the announcer said they were going to play a brand-new Beach Boys record. So they played "Heroes and Villains" and everybody flipped out dancing – and then the tempo changed, and I knew it was a stiff.' As Al Jardine noted much later, 'it should have been a hit, if it wasn't so esoteric. We started out with a pretty good track and we "devolved" it.'

If dancers were thrown by the fragmented nature of the song, reviewers were equally puzzled. Privileged insiders had been previewing 'Heroes and Villains' for months as a breakthrough in the history of the popular song. But the jewel-like surface of the single failed to crack open to yield such obvious treasure. Back to Tony Barrow in Liverpool: 'I am left with the impression that somewhere along the way, something failed to click into place. I'm sure Brian Wilson himself had hoped for much more.' Searching for comparisons again, writers claimed that the melody line sounded like Chuck Berry's 'You Never Can Tell' or Mitchell Torok's 'When Mexico Gave Up the Rhumba'. The song's lyricist, Van Dyke Parks, said it made him think of the Marty Robbins hit, 'El Paso'. Even the Beach Boys faced a dilemma with the song: they valiantly attempted it at two concerts in Hawaii while it was still in the charts, but then dropped it from their setlists for several years because it was too difficult to perform.

And Brian Wilson? He knew that he had let a gem slip through his fingers. Jack Rieley, the Beach Boys' 'career adviser' in the early 1970s, remembered a telling conversation with him during that period. 'Brian blurted it out one evening,' he explained, 'and later spoke about it several times in agonising detail. He had expected that "Heroes" would be greeted by Capitol as the work which put the Beach Boys on a creative par with the Beatles. All the adoration and promotional back-up Capitol was giving the Beatles would also flow to his music because of "Heroes", he thought. And the public? It would greet "Heroes" with the same level of overwhelming enthusiasm that the Beatles got with record after record. As it was, Capitol execs were divided about "Heroes". Some loved it, but others castigated the track, longing instead for more surfing/car songs. The public bought the record in respectable but surely not wowie zowie numbers. For Brian, this was the ultimate failure.' And it directly led, Rieley contended, to Wilson becoming a recluse.

Insiders later admitted that Brian had suffered bouts of nervous exhaustion – breakdowns, in other words – during the months of creating that single. The first was in March 1967 and prompted him to abandon the track for a while; a second followed its comparatively poor public reception. It still peaked at number twelve on the US chart, but only one new Beach Boys composition would enjoy success on that scale in the future – and that was 'Kokomo'. 'Heroes and Villains' punctured the Beach Boys' mid-1960s image of musical invincibility. They were pop superheroes who had suddenly lost their powers and their once-loyal audience couldn't help but pick up the scent of failure. But by then, the group were already having to deal with an even more disastrous sequence of events: the non-appearance of the album confidently predicted to be the greatest pop record of all time.

Words We Both Could Say

Writing lyrics for the Beach Boys

As far as Brian Wilson was concerned, 'kids in the States buy a sound. Whatever the lyrics are about doesn't matter.' Not true, countered his college friend Al Jardine. 'The lyrics are about what kids are doing today. Lyrics of the standard songs don't tell the story our audiences want to hear.'

For Wilson, at least in 1964, lyrics were primarily a vehicle: the tools with which he could construct breathtaking combinations of voices in harmony. Or, for the wider cause of the Beach Boys, they were a way of attracting an audience, of staking a claim to a subculture of West Coast teenage life, of marking themselves out against their more amorphous peers.

When it came to expressions of teen sentiment, Brian had a choice of skilled collaborators. Roger Christian was the self-confessed 'car poet'; Jan Berry of Jan & Dean could handle themes of surf and speed; and, closest to home, Brian's cousin Mike Love became a master of squeezing the iconography of American youth into tightly constructed lines that scanned and rhymed. He was also adept at coining a phrase, even the most banal of constructions, that would define and identify a song – like his idea that they should open the automotive tribute '409' with a chant of 'giddy-up 409'. Simplistic but right.

In Mike Love's fantasy life of the Beach Boys, the Wilson/Love combination would have run smoothly for eternity – the only difference being that publisher Murry Wilson would have awarded Mike the credit he deserved, for songs on which Brian ended up being credited alone. But getting your name on the record and your hands on the royalties were not the only lyrical issues to cause rampant dissension. Lyric-writing would become a Beach Boys battleground for eight years, the period when the band journeyed furthest from their original incarnation as the sirens of surf and hot rod racing.

By 1965, when the Wilson/Love team came apart for a couple of years, Brian was increasingly struggling to express deep emotional needs: romantic confusion, alienation from his surroundings, even at times existential despair. Mike could write about love, but his words tended either to sentimentalise the emotion or to recount it in purely adolescent terms – first-date crushes and high-school proms. So when Brian wanted to explore in song why marriage had not automatically made him happy, why he felt increasingly at odds with his surroundings or and how experiments with chemicals and other illegal substances had altered his psyche, well, Mike Love was not the poet he needed.

Brian lacked what John Lennon and Paul McCartney relished, at least for most of the 1960s: a songwriting partner whom he regarded as an equal and who was undergoing similar changes of habitat, perspective and philosophy. Nor was he a Bob Dylan or Paul Simon, capable of verbal insight and dexterity, who could find the words to match every subtle alteration in outlook and experience. He could throw out ideas, but found it hard to crystallise and shape them – which put him at a lyrical disadvantage, to say the least, in the creative pop ferment of the mid-1960s. As Mick Jagger complained in 1966, 'it's all soft. He writes lyrics that are unbelievable – they are so naïve.'

What Brian needed was an interpreter: someone who could understand and relate his confusion and uncertainties; someone who could give him the words that were just out of reach; someone who could match the dizzying complexity of his new music. Working at a studio down the hall from a Beach Boys session was part-time songwriter/full-time advertising copywriter, Tony Asher. He sidled into the room where Brian was working and they exchanged song ideas. When Brian later discovered that Asher was a mutual friend of promo man and scene-maker Loren Schwartz, he phoned the ad man out of the blue and suggested that they should write together.

Asher was steeped in showbusiness, from his previous role as a talent agent at GAC to his parents' movie heritage: his mother had been a silent-film star; his father a producer. Tony, who had been playing piano since he was twelve, had already composed a tune for surf instrumentalists the Chantays, of 'Pipeline' fame. But as befitted a UCLA graduate in journalism, words were his forte.

Three years older than Brian, Asher proved to be not only a superb lyricist for the *Pet Sounds* album, but also an ideal emotional sounding-board for Brian's romantic and existential tribulations. To his surprise, Brian was willing to allow his co-writer to reshape the music he had written, accepting a suggestion, for example, that a line might work better with an upward rather than downward deflection. Asher's most enduring contribution to *Pet Sounds*, however, was his ability to capture teenage and post-teenage emotions in the raw. The two men shared their intimate histories of romantic failure and connection, to the point that their experiences became intertwined. For once, Brian was able to work with words that were entirely open, not merely descriptive (like Roger Christian's car lyricism) or coated in a young man's protective ego (as with Mike Love).

Neither Asher nor Wilson felt that Tony's original lyric for 'Good Vibrations' matched the song's musical potential. It is impossible to judge the commercial impact of Mike Love's insistence that the lyrics should be centred around romance rather than psychological ambiguity, but it certainly didn't hurt. By the time that single was a worldwide hit, though, Brian had already plunged deep into arguably the most profound and undoubtedly the most controversial writing partnership of his entire career.

Child actor, musical prodigy, unashamedly intellectual, major in classical piano and musical composition: Van Dyke Parks was the unlikeliest of folk guitarists. But it was in that guise that he first surfaced on the California music scene in the early 1960s, working in such combos as the Steeltown Two Plus One, the Brandywine Singers and the Greenwood County Singers. Then, as the nylon-stringed acoustic guitar became as passé as the crew cut, he switched attention to his first love, the piano.

He rapidly fell into the company of musicians such as the Byrds (with whom he recorded) and Buffalo Springfield (whom he named). He formed a folk-rock band called the Van Dyke Parks with Stephen Stills, before realising that he lacked the physical stamina or patience for the life of a pop star. He could never have been accused of thinking small: his first single was nothing less than a pop interpretation of the key movement from Beethoven's ninth symphony, called inevitably 'Number Nine'. He too was a friend of Loren Schwartz. He was destined to collide with Brian Wilson when the Beach Boy's brain was at its most responsive to being stimulated and expanded by a superior mind.

Perhaps only Van Dyke Parks, of all the people Brian had met so far, could have withstood the challenge of Brian's erratic, fragmented, driven and mercurial approach to composing. Quizzed later about the complexity of his lyrics, not least by Mike Love, Van Dyke Parks asked that musical context should be taken fully into consideration. 'You must remember that the words chased the music,' he explained. 'Brian made music requiring a certain number of syllables. If you think the lyrics are dense in "Heroes and Villains", what would you do with those syllables? You either tell the man to stop playing like that or you follow suit with the devotion of a dog, and I did.' Parks elected to match the fearless experimentalism of Brian's music with words that would convey impressions rather than rigid narratives or facts. Hence Mike Love's sarcastic complaint that Parks 'writes vague, alliterative prose and lyrics, but I can't understand that stuff. Too simple-minded, I guess.' More pertinent, perhaps, was Bruce Johnston's response, which began by following Love ('The lyrics didn't make sense') and then offered an important addendum: 'I couldn't relate to them – not as a Beach Boy, anyway. Maybe I could on some other level.'

Even Love would sometimes concede that although 'sometimes people get too far out with their lyrical imagery', it's 'an art form' – just one that he didn't understand and couldn't ever have mastered. In the hands of Van Dyke Parks, song lyrics were no longer a means of literal communication between pop star and teenage audience. But they were, unmistakeably, art and as such they sat perfectly in sonic terms on top of Brian's equally abstruse melodies and arrangements. They sounded (and sang) beautiful, expressive and artistic, but they couldn't be boiled down into a slogan for a greetings card.

Acutely aware that many of the Beach Boys did not appreciate his writing, Van Dyke Parks eased out of the process of creating *SMiLE* a few weeks before Brian too abandoned hope. His reward was a credit on some of the most beautiful songs ever written and a reputation for brilliant difficulty (or perhaps difficult brilliance) that would fuel a cult recording career while cutting him off from any chance of mainstream acceptance.*

Parks' departure for a solo career left Mike Love in prime position to reclaim his role as Brian's chief lyricist. Yet there were songs recorded by the Beach Boys in the late 1960s that – regardless of their credits – seemed to have sprung fully grown from Brian's head alone. One hundred and seventy years earlier, the poet Coleridge invented a new style of blank verse which has passed into literary history as conversational poetry. As its name suggests, this technique suggests that the poet is chatting casually and intimately to the listener, rather than offering a formal recitation.

Brian's writing between 1967 and 1969 seemed to represent a stoned, almost anti-poetic approach to the same destination. Take, for example, 'I'd Love Just Once to See You' from the *Wild Honey* album. (The unmentioned words that complete the title are 'in the nude'.) Brian delivers this slice-of-life vignette with a sly naïvety that does its best to

* Regardless, the man is still a genius, as a composer, singer-songwriter and arranger. One recommendation for something that you have probably never heard: his collaboration with Inara George on her 2008 album, *An Invitation*.

disguise his adulterous preoccupations: 'I wouldn't mind if I could get with you right away.' By the end of the song, though, he is equally hopeful that the unnamed woman might arrive in time to help him dry the dishes – and, hey, any chance you might cook me a pie?

Having burst open the notion of a Beach Boys song, Brian became even more confessional on 'Busy Doin' Nothin'' (issued on the *Friends* album). Over a seductive, lazy samba beat, he sings the same way he might have chatted on the phone to a friend, before reeling off a set of directions to his house (although he omits to tell us precisely where the journey should begin). And by the end, everything is revealed: he is about to write the very letter that he has just translated into song. Having discovered how much fun these tunes were to write, and sing, he kept drawing from the same well. 'Games Two Can Play' mixed sexual innuendo with candid self-analysis; 'H.E.L.P. is on the Way' coupled the joys of health food with an invitation to visit his store. But, by now, the Beach Boys were wise to his tricks; neither of those charming but utterly self-indulgent tunes was included on a contemporary album.

Just when it seemed that Wilson had chosen to employ lyrics solely as an escape from responsibility, he was able to compose arguably the two most remarkable songs of his post-*SMiLE* career. 'This Whole World' from *Sunflower* was a work of harmonic and melodic wonder, shifting key signature in almost every phrase. Equally stunning were its words, a simple but still somehow desolate hymn of universal love. A few months later, ''Til I Die' (released on *Surf's Up*) inverted that mode. In the briefest of phrases, Brian employed images of the natural world to convey utter despair – almost as if he was conducting a funeral rite for his own creativity. None of his collaborators could have written something so stark, so personal. And when he returned to solo writing in the late 1970s, he was never quite able to match the devastating beauty of that most revealing of farewells.

The Smile You Send Out ...

The Great Lost Beach Boys Album – was it ever found?

After books and box sets and almost six decades of mythology, is there anything left to say about *SMiLE*? Bruce Johnston told me in 1990 that the best possible outcome for the Beach Boys was that people would keep talking about *SMiLE* but never hear it: it kept the legend alive, without any fear that reality would prove to be a disappointment. But the Beach Boys' archives have always been the leakiest of safe-houses and, from the early 1980s onwards, fragments of what might have been *SMiLE* began to escape into the arms of eager collectors, first in tantalisingly short elements but eventually in a virtual torrent. By the 1990s, bootleggers were competing to assemble the 'ultimate' *SMiLE*, a task as tantalising as assembling the True Cross from the fragments that churches around the world claimed as holy relics.

A brief recap, for anyone who has managed to avoid the drama of *SMiLE* over the past sixty years ... Thanks to his friends, admirers and publicists cleverly dropping hints in the media, everyone who followed the rapid development of pop in 1966–67 knew that Brian Wilson was taking music into realms that nobody else had ever imagined. 'Good Vibrations' hinted at what might be possible within the confines of a pop single, but the album that Brian was concocting now would blow all his competitors out of the water. As the single was released, Dennis Wilson confided that the best was yet to come in the shape of Brian's indescribable new music. 'In my opinion, it makes *Pet Sounds* stink,' he claimed. 'That's how good it is.' As anticipation built, Bruce Johnston stoked the fire: the next album will 'blow your mind', he promised. 'All the ideas are new.'

A few weeks before the end of 1966, Brian submitted a provisional list of *SMiLE* song titles to Capitol Records. The company took that as a final decision, but what's obvious in retrospect is not just that the track listing was in constant flux, but that the actual identity of individual pieces of music also changed from day to day. No matter: believing the Beach Boys when they said that the record would be ready for release in January 1967, Capitol scheduled a publicity campaign worthy of pop's most progressive act. The first advertisements were placed at the end of the month. They promised that the album would be 'Brian, Dennis, Carl, Al and Mike's best ever! Contains Good Vibrations ... AND an exciting full-color sketchbook – look inside the world of Brian Wilson!'

That world was mercurial, magical, confusing and wildly over-ambitious. At its heart was a man who was working at maximum creativity, under maximum artistic and chemical stimulation. Like Mike Love, Tony Asher had been cast aside in favour of the novelty of a fresh collaborator: wordsmith par excellence, Van Dyke Parks. He was perhaps the only man in Los Angeles capable of writing lyrics as rich and multi-faceted as Brian's latest collages of feels. He not only kept pace with the composer, but inspired him to think more conceptually and on a more profound, more extended scale. It was Parks who dismissed Wilson's original album title, *Dumb Angel*, as being unsuitable for musical experiments so exploratory and joyous. Instead, he told Brian, the album should be called *Smile* (or, as the projected cover artwork had it, *SMiLE*).

It was Van Dyke Parks too who put Brian Wilson in touch with the designer and illustrator Frank Holmes. Holmes rapidly assembled a cover design that reflected the child-like nature of Brian's innocent genius. He also sketched visual accompaniments for many of the musical ingredients, which were combined into an album-sized colour booklet.

Holmes recalled that Capitol were so convinced *SMiLE* would be a smash that they printed up half-a-million copies of the cardboard sleeve and the booklet. They were only waiting for one thing: the music.

Several full-length books, countless long-form essays and hundreds of speculative articles have been devoted to collating and analysing the *SMiLE* saga in all its chaotic, traumatic detail. Brian's bandleader, Darian Sahanaja, encouraged him and Van Dyke Parks to return to the songs, fragments, drafts and dreams of 1966–67 to assemble a 'definitive', album-length version of *SMiLE*, which was performed live by Wilson and his touring musicians in 2004, and also recorded for CD release. In 2011, Capitol Records fulfilled decades of fandom fantasies by unleashing an epic Beach Boys box set devoted to *The Smile Sessions*. It contained five full-length CDs (one of them filled with nothing but working versions of 'Good Vibrations'), two vinyl singles, and printed material that explained and enhanced the remarkable music it accompanied.

So the problem is not what to say, but what to leave out. Scour the internet and you will find hundreds of experts and fanatics who have trawled through all the available documentation and music to determine exactly what would have appeared on *SMiLE*, in what order and under what titles. Many of them have made convincing arguments for their theories, but nobody knows what Brian Wilson wanted *SMiLE* to be, because that was a riddle that he never solved to his own satisfaction. Recording *Pet Sounds* had been an epic musical adventure, but it was never an existential crisis, for the simple reason that Wilson knew clearly what songs should appear on the record and how they should sound. *SMiLE* was something else entirely.

Two small vignettes from the final weeks of 1966, when Wilson's imagination was running free and wild and completion still seemed possible, hint at both the range and the dilemma of *SMiLE*. Carl Wilson explained its inspiration like this: 'God is love – God is you – God is me – God is everything right here in this room. It's a spiritual concept which inspires a great deal of our music.' Brian agreed, absolutely, but at the same time he was declaring that the album would be filled with 'children's songs' or 'little musicals'. To satisfy his inner child, he had already placed his grand piano in a giant sandbox in his home, so that he could feel the sand between his toes. He was also buying toys with the hysterical glee of a child let loose in a store: he had a room filled with silly putty and battery-powered police cars and a 'monster robot' that could speak and a toy boat and much, much more – and he was the only child in his house. 'I think that buying these toys represents some fantasy of childhood that we are trying to relive,' he mused.

That was just the Wilson brothers. Van Dyke Parks could have offered an entirely different perspective: as far as he was concerned, *SMiLE* was not just a musical playground but an exploration of seminal American themes, involving humanity and nature, pilgrims and native Americans, industry and the land, the American republic's sense of manifest destiny and (of course) heroes and villains. Aware that he was adorning music rather than writing a thesis, though, Parks explored those themes and more in verbal imagery that was impressionistic, suggestive rather than descriptive, opaque rather than facile. Notoriously, Mike Love – the Beach Boys' bard of teenage scenarios – challenged Parks during the sessions to explain some of his more obscure phrases. He refused, on the grounds that his writings were designed to be interpreted afresh by each listener. That confrontation highlighted the gulf between two active visions of what the Beach Boys could be: either a vehicle for exploring the nation's most profound philosophical issues or a pop band aiming to reach the widest possible audience of American teens. It polarised two men who were ostensibly working towards the same ideal – of completing *SMiLE* – and has allowed subsequent generations of commentators to label Love or Parks hero or villain, depending on their taste. Most have chosen to identify Love as the man who failed to comprehend Wilson and Parks' vision, but they have forgotten one thing: he was the man who was fronting the Beach Boys on the road, where they came closest to their audience. Brian was composing for himself and his equally turned-on, daredevil posse of friends; Mike was puzzled to know how he could sell artistic utopia to halls full of teenage girls.

The lyrical divide between singer and writer was far from being the major crisis point in the *SMiLE* saga. In retrospect, Brian clearly began to lose control of his creations: it was like the fable of the sorcerer's apprentice, only with the songs seizing power and asserting their independence, with catastrophic consequences. His 'feels' mutated and cross-fertilised; his concepts sprouted tendrils which tangled and knotted themselves together; his musical maze trapped him in its centre with no route map home.

One song encapsulated Wilson's conundrum. 'Heroes and Villains' was already proving impossible to tailor into the concise form required for a hit single; now it threatened to take over the entire album. With no definitive shape, no certainty about which fragments belonged to the song and which elsewhere, and a chorus segment that lent itself to being added to several other works in progress, 'Heroes and Villains' was a musical soup that Brian was trying to force into a sandwich. I wonder now, with almost sixty years' hindsight, whether the only conceivable way of making sense of 'Heroes and Villains' would have been to transform it from a song into a suite, its key motifs repeated throughout and acting as a wrap for all the other fragments it could contain and enhance. It could easily have filled one side of a vinyl album, thereby becoming the most ambitious long-form pop composition written to that point. But that wasn't what Brian Wilson wanted – or rather, he knew that he didn't want *that*, but he couldn't decide what he *did* want.

Other legendary compositions would become congealed in the 'Heroes and Villains' morass or seep across their own conceptual borders. 'Do You Like Worms?', for example, which Al Jardine still insists was once an entirely different song, not actually recorded during the *SMiLE* sessions. Or the legendary 'Elements' suite, which would conjure up the spirits of air, earth, fire and water, although in proportions that were not always easy to measure or describe. Brian's wife Marilyn said prophetically of her husband during the sessions that 'when he gets home, he won't be satisfied. He's never satisfied.' That was a truism, which became a curse. Mike Love revealed in early 1967 that the group was going for 'a perfectionist thing', but not even Brian's bandmates realised the toll that this quest was exerting on his psyche.

Some songs were finished; others existed only as mosaics, shattered pieces of a once coherent vision. Amidst the gems, none sparkled more brightly or concealed more depth than 'Surf's Up', which Brian debuted solo at the piano for a suitably pretentious TV documentary about modern pop, fronted by Leonard Bernstein. 'Our Prayer' was a self-explanatory exercise in vocal harmony which erased all musical borders between pop and mediaeval choral music; eleventh-century monks probably didn't have a leader who interrupted their singing to ask, 'Denny, do you have any hash joints left?' and 'You guys feeling the acid yet?'. 'Vega-Tables' hymned the benefits of a healthy diet, inspired by Brian stumbling across the radio proselytising of health evangelist Curtis Howe Springer. 'Wonderful' was a paean to beauty with a melody that would have delighted Schubert. All these tracks were effectively complete or could easily have become so, but they became mired in the same confusion as 'Heroes and Villains'.

After lengthy delays and prolonged struggles with his mental health, Brian didn't so much admit defeat as abandon the struggle. Derek Taylor announced the apparent cancellation of *SMiLE* in May 1967, hinting for the first time that the session tapes might not just have been shelved but even destroyed. Brian could have gone into seclusion, but instead he had an eight-track studio installed in his newly acquired mansion on Bellagio Drive, which would become the Beach Boys' recording centre for the next three years. There, in a matter of a few weeks, he led the group through uncluttered but undeniably stoned renditions of some of the *SMiLE* songs, alongside fresh pieces rich in hipster comedy, to create a rush-released album entitled *Smiley Smile*. Carl Wilson would famously reflect that this record was 'a bunt instead of a grand slam', bunt being the baseball equivalent of tip-and-run. That verdict has passed into history as a denunciation, but there are times in a ball game where a bunt is precisely the most rewarding tactic to employ – and this was definitely one of those moments in the Beach Boys' career. 'We had to sit back and mark time,' Bruce Johnston declared, though he absented himself from most of the *Smiley Smile* sessions. 'We were getting too far ahead of the audience.'

The trouble was that the world was expecting nirvana, not what sounded like the soundtrack of an afternoon in a psychedelic play-pen. Most reviews were viciously negative: the *London Evening Standard* complained that 'hardly a track isn't marred by cerebral haemorrhage-inducing *Dr Who* electronic effects'. But the fledging rock press was more encouraging, *Cheetah* magazine going so far as to suggest that *Smiley Smile* was 'the most beautiful rock album ever recorded in this country'. Brian's peer group knew better, however: they had heard the almost completed remnants of *SMiLE*. David Anderle could only suggest that 'Brian Wilson got bored. That's why we got *Smiley Smile* instead of the original *SMiLE* – which was a mindblower.'

In the absence of the album, which was presumed deceased, a post-mortem dragged on for decades afterwards. At first, the group gathered forces around Brian. 'We decided not to have a complicated album this time,' Carl Wilson explained. 'We didn't scrap [the tapes]. We just haven't used them yet.' Mike Love added that he trusted Brian's decision-making and that music he set aside often returned in more magnificent form later. Dennis Wilson shared the decision to end the project among them all: 'We got very paranoid about losing our public. We were getting loaded, taking acid, and we made a whole album which we scrapped.'

It was the stuff of legend, which quickly inflated until it overshadowed everything the Beach Boys did in its stead. Unable to release *SMiLE*, they raided its vaults for songs. Elements of what might have been surfaced on a series of subsequent albums: *Smiley Smile*, of course, but also *Wild Honey* (the closing feel of the 'Mama Says' chant); *Friends* (a small section of 'Little Bird'); *20/20* ('Our Prayer', 'Cabinessence' and the final 'Workshop' sound effects on 'Do It Again'); *Sunflower* ('Cool, Cool Water'); and *Surf's Up* (resting place at last for the title track in a medley with 'Child is Father of the Man').

In several cases, Brian was vehemently opposed to retrieving these songs from the *SMiLE* tapes, but the group overruled him. Then, after the release of *Surf's Up*, Carl held a press conference to announce that he and the band's career adviser, Jack Rieley, had rescued the *SMiLE* tapes and were putting together a finished version of the mythical album alongside the band's next studio set, *Carl and the Passions*. 'Carl and I got Brian's explicit support to remove the originals from the vault and take them to Carl's place,' Rieley recalled, 'where the two of us listened to songs and snippets, full works and outtakes, night after night. Without even an engineer around, we tried mending and splicing the brittle multitrack recordings. Sometimes we succeeded. With the 'Fire' tapes, which were there but damaged (and not by fire), we had to settle for long passages and short gaps.' Ultimately, though, the project proved to be beyond them: it required active participation from Brian, not just tacit approval.

In its absence, explanations were required for *SMiLE*'s refusal to be tamed. There were endless theories: that Capitol had rejected the album; that Mike Love had somehow sabotaged the project with his supposedly perennial war-cry of 'Don't fuck with the formula' (a popular one, this, with Wilson aficionados); that Brian had been over-awed by hearing the Beatles' latest recordings; that he had retreated into a drug-addled stupor. This last idea was given voice by Mike in 1975: 'What happened is that Brian took some acid or something. It blew his mind. He never really totally recovered from it.' More diplomatically, Carl described the entire episode as 'a rather painful experience, especially for Brian ... But the pressure got too much for us and the people around us were taking the whole thing too seriously.'

Brian toed the Love line in 1976–77, before deciding that he couldn't remember what had happened. In the final months of 1977, Dennis dragged the *SMiLE* tapes out of the group's archives one more time and excitedly played them to Brian. Dennis said that his brother 'curled up, put his hands over his head and started to cry'. Then Brian said he wanted to remix them for the group's next album. Classic Brian ...

It was Carl in 1983 who offered a more cogent and informed explanation for the demise of *SMiLE*: 'Brian just couldn't thread it together. He couldn't make that full cycle and tie it all together. If people heard the *SMiLE* tapes today, they'd hear a lot of themes that keep cycling back on each other. A lot of tunes were interchangeable. You could take a section out of one and put it in another. To get that album out, someone would have needed willingness and perseverance to corral all of us.'

By the late 1980s, it was obvious that popular demand was eventually going to require that some kind of *SMiLE* release be prepared for the burgeoning market in CD repackages. The ever-avaricious Eugene Landy dragooned Brian into the studio with the original tapes in 1988, eager to claim a credit for himself as co-producer of this legendary album. 'We're going to fix up *SMiLE* so that it's in the right sequence,' Brian conceded. 'We're going to release it as sessions, not as an album.' His memory of the project had become blurred, to the point where he believed that there were 'only a couple of cuts where the [other Beach Boys] sang', which simply wasn't true. He claimed that the music was magnificent, then in the next breath that '*SMiLE* doesn't strike me as being that great'. Producer/composer Andy Paley was pulled in to help complete the project, insisting that Brian actively wanted to pass all the session tapes to the public so that they could construct their own versions of the album. But once again the idea faded away.

By the mid-1990s, when Wilson and Van Dyke Parks had been reunited for the *Orange Crate Art* album, the lyricist was adamant that 'only greed or vanity would lead to the reissue of this reckless rehash of work that we almost completed thirty years ago'. In any case, he insisted, *Orange Crate Art* was a more interesting album. Brian Wilson was soon heard to say that he wished they had burned the *SMiLE* tapes in 1967, as legend insisted. Then he decided that he actually *had* burned them, which is why the album hadn't come out. By 1999, he delivered his definitive opinion on the subject: 'I hate that fucking album. I don't like where it's coming from. It was a bad time and it's not something I'm especially proud of. It's really a drag of an album and it's a drag that people ask about it all the time.' But did anyone care what he felt? The myth of *SMiLE* had become self-generating – and eventually it dragged the reluctant Brian Wilson back into its grasp.

Let it Be?

The Beach Boys and the Beatles

First, the Beach Boys made a record. Then they heard it on the radio, which made fifteen-year-old Carl Wilson so excited that he stuffed himself with burgers and threw up. After that, it was a process of vanquishing their heroes and rivals, as one by one they out-sold and out-manoeuvred Dick Dale, Jan & Dean, and the Four Seasons. By the end of 1963, they began to accept that they might be the hottest rock 'n' roll band in the US – and wasn't the US the world?

Then, to keep the narrative fresh and the Beach Boys firmly in their place, four English musicians flew into New York, took *The Ed Sullivan Show* by storm and, within a few weeks, had notched up the top five singles on the national chart. 'The mystique of the English groups distracted everybody's attention,' Al Jardine reflected. Worse still, the Beatles were on the same record label as the Beach Boys (in the US and Canada, at least). The single that the Beach Boys felt was their most commercial to date, 'Fun, Fun, Fun', roared into the Top 10 – and hit a Liverpudlian wall. As Brian Wilson noted in summer 1964, 'anybody singing today who says they're NOT afraid of the Beatles is a liar!'.

Looking back, he admitted that 'the Beatles sensation made me a little bit jealous and uncertain for the Beach Boys' well-being and our future, but after about a year of surviving the Beatles, I realised that we could stand on our own'. Yet as Mike Love recalled when the US celebrated the twentieth anniversary of the Fab Four's arrival, 'the Beatles showed our band different ways of doing harmonies. Their albums, particularly *Sgt. Pepper* and *Rubber Soul*, were green lights to all musicians. These records said it's alright to push your talent. I don't think the Beach Boys would have had the confidence to have made "Good Vibrations" without the influence of the Beatles.'

Capitol Records did their best to assure fans that the groups' relationship was entirely cordial. A telephone conversation was staged, allowing fans to hear Brian Wilson admiring the Beatles' haircuts ('they look great') and quizzing John Lennon: 'Is it true that you guys have your own private barber?' 'No, it's a dirty rumour,' Lennon replied with his trademark wit. 'We cut it ourselves.'

But musicians everywhere had to respond to the threat posed by the Beatles, and for Brian it became a deeply psychological battle; he carried the creative burden of matching the Beatles' progress. The challenge sparked his competitive instincts to the full, but added further weight to the mental strain of matching the production extravaganzas being concocted by Phil Spector.

The battleground wasn't confined to the airwaves and sales charts. At stake in 1964 was a more intimate terrain: the romantic longings of the two groups' teenage and pre-teen audiences. Comparisons were inevitable, and not always flattering on either side. In mid-March 1964, the Beach Boys had to take second billing on a closed-circuit TV event aimed specifically at young girls across North America. After a brief showcase for the proto-feminist pop singer, Lesley Gore, a film of the Californian quintet was broadcast to cinema-loads of crazed fans, primed for the opportunity to see the Beatles. 'Moans of disappointment' greeted the arrival not of four identically coiffured English boys, but an assorted quintet of Americans who ranged from 'a clean-cut, virile, un-Beatle-like drummer' to [look away, Michael Love] a singer who 'was about 37 years old' (he was actually twenty-three). Despite not being John, Paul, George and Ringo, the Beach Boys did manage to evoke a volley of screams, especially when young Dennis Wilson was on screen. ('I had this mop four years before the Beatles,' the drummer assured his American fans.) The girls, one reporter claimed, sounded 'something like a dozen pigs with their tails tied together'.

Over the next year, journalists continued to quiz compliant teenagers about the competing attractions of the two outfits. Beatles fans dismissed all rivals as an irrelevance, but some American youngsters remained unswayed. 'Compared to the Beach Boys,' one girl insisted, 'the Beatles are just punks with long hair.' Male admirers were more likely to applaud the Beach Boys for their short hair and the fact that 'they like surfing, motorcycles and American pastimes'. Ultimately, one ten-year-old boy in Philadelphia declared that the Beach Boys would endure longer. 'The Beatles are getting old,' he claimed. 'They've been around a while.' But reporters judged that the response to the Beatles was altogether more hysterical (and female) than that aroused by the Beach Boys. Three times more security staff were required to police a Beatles performance, it transpired.

After he absented himself from the road, Brian Wilson only cared about the relative musical performances of the two groups. Starting work on *Pet Sounds* in late 1965, he credited the Beatles with potential staying power beyond the lifetime of a mere pop phenomenon. 'I think the Beatles' influence is so far-reaching that it is hard to say what their influence is up to date. I think it'll show up even in the next five years.' His touring replacement, Bruce Johnston, praised the Beatles' 'great harmonic ability', but loyally stated that Brian's skill was in combining that quality with the rhythmic impact of the Rolling Stones.

The creative advances apparent on *Pet Sounds* and the subsequent 'Good Vibrations' single cast the Beatles' innate sense of superiority into doubt. Johnston took it upon himself to mount a one-man publicity campaign for the album in Britain, which prompted Capitol to accelerate its release there. He astutely infiltrated the upper echelons of London's music community and left them to spread the word. George Harrison was his first conquest; passing that test allowed him access to Lennon and McCartney. Bruce recalled a fervent debate between McCartney and Rolling Stones manager Andrew Oldham, the two Englishmen discussing which of Brian Wilson's innovations each group should copy.

There was a brief media drama in August 1966 when 'God Only Knows' coincided with the aftermath of John Lennon's controversial comments about the relative popularity of the Beatles and Jesus in *Datebook* magazine. Mike Love slightly misread Lennon's intentions: 'They're trying to put everybody on.' He subsequently introduced 'God Only Knows' at a San Francisco concert by criticising the Beatles' motives, prompting a pioneering rock critic to complain that the Beach Boys song was 'frightful in its pseudo-sanctity'. And a reviewer in Omaha upset Beach Boys fans by suggesting that the group had deliberately concocted a song with 'God' in the title to capitalise on the Lennon furore.

Brian had already moved on, seeking to trump the Beatles' experiments on their *Revolver* album with his gargantuan vision of *SMiLE*. Although the public heard nothing from this project in 1966 beyond 'Good Vibrations', extracts from the session tapes must have made their way across the Atlantic by January 1967. The following month, pianist Dudley Moore and his comedy partner Peter Cook released a single entitled 'The L.S. Bumble Bee', a savagely enjoyable satire on the new strain of psychedelic pop. The record has passed into history as an imitation of the Beatles, even appearing under their name on underground albums in the early 1970s. But Moore's musical collage sounds like nothing so much as a ragbag of leftovers from Brian's sessions for songs such as 'Heroes and Villains' and 'Do You Like Worms?'.

The shift in power, short-lived as it was, had been confirmed on 3 December 1966, with the announcement that the readers of Britain's best-selling pop weekly, *New Musical Express*, had voted the Beach Boys rather than the Beatles as the World's Top Group. 'Show business will vibrate with the sensational news,' the paper trumpeted, but they were underplaying the story, which was soon reported around the world. Soon afterwards, the *NME*'s rival paper, *Melody Maker*, heralded the same result from their slightly older readership.

What none of those voters knew was that the Beach Boys' triumph was premature. Their crowning as World's Top Group came just as their campaign to outclass the Beatles with the quintessential pop album was in the process of disintegration. The long delay of their 'Heroes and Villains' single, and the non-arrival for another few decades of *SMiLE*, marked a concession of defeat on Brian Wilson's part. There have been rumours that he was deflated by the release of 'Penny Lane' and 'Strawberry Fields' in February 1967; or, less convincingly, that the final blow was delivered by *Sgt. Pepper* and 'All You Need Is Love' in June. Wilson's collaborator on *SMiLE*, Van Dyke Parks, recalled that the Beach Boys 'were tremendously concerned about their position vis-à-vis the Beatles, who were the only other act in town'.

With *SMiLE* abandoned, the Beach Boys were left to be judged by the material they *did* release. In 1965, that had included *Beach Boys' Party!*, an amusing and sometimes joyous contract-filler of an album that featured playful cover versions of three Beatles songs. One of those, 'You've Got to Hide Your Love Away', was even added to their live repertoire, though on the album, singer Dennis Wilson's painful sincerity was undercut by the sarcastic interventions of his bandmates. Three years later, the semi-detached Beach Boy, Bruce Johnston, prepared a bland version of 'With a Little Help From My Friends' as a possible solo single. Rightly convinced that it didn't work, he rethought the song, only to be overtaken before he could return it to the studio. 'When I heard Joe Cocker's version, I just died, because it was so close to the one I was going to do. I think that's groovy, because it just proves I was right.'

The shocking collapse of the Beach Boys' commercial profile between 1967 and 1969 was epitomised by their disastrous tour with the Maharishi Mahesh Yogi – timed perfectly to catch the backlash as the Beatles disavowed their spiritual mentor. In the days before that coincidence, rumours spread across the British pop world that not only were the Beatles about to launch their Apple Corps enterprise, but they were planning to invite the Beach Boys to become their business partners. 'The result may be the setting up of a new record company by the two groups,' one report asserted, 'and experiments with new electronic sounds and instruments.' The source of the rumour? Mike Love, drawing upon vague conversations he had shared with the Beatles in India and unaware that their enthusiasm for the idea had merely been polite.

After the break-up of the Beatles, there was no longer a reason for journalists, lazy or otherwise, to waste copy on the respective merits of the Liverpudlians and the Californians. But one man at least kept the lines of communication between the two groups open. In November 1970, Paul McCartney attended one of the Beach Boys' critically acclaimed shows at the Whisky a Go Go in Los Angeles. He was in the middle of the sessions for his album *Ram*, which included a majestic recreation of Brian Wilson's mid-1960s production sound on the song 'The Back Seat of My Car'. Over the subsequent decade, he attempted to maintain a friendship with Brian, attending his birthday party in 1976, although on several occasions Wilson fled in terror rather than confront the reality of one of the men he had failed to topple a decade earlier. Unperturbed, McCartney regularly cited 'God Only Knows' as the greatest song ever written and claimed to have forced each of his children to listen to *Pet Sounds* when they were teenagers.

Aside from Bruce Johnston, the most vocal champion of *Pet Sounds* at the time of its release had been Derek Taylor, whose move from handling the Beatles' publicity in London to Los Angeles introduced him to both the Byrds and the Beach Boys at their early creative peaks. Urbane, civilised, charming and peerless as a pop commentator, Taylor was the first to dub Brian Wilson a 'genius' as he chronicled his journey towards *SMiLE*. His praise added inadvertently to the burden of Wilson's daily struggle with his muse.

Several years later, Beach Boys' manager Jack Rieley interrogated Brian about this period of creative adventure stymied by self-doubt. Rieley's verdict was that Wilson's efforts had been undermined by a lack of corporate and family solidarity. 'The Beatles were focused, strategic, professional and well-led during the years of their mounting ascendency,' he explained many years later. 'During that same period, the Beach Boys were divided, unprofessional and horrendously led … There was no career direction to speak of and chaos reigned.'

There was an additional factor that may have been exacerbated by 'chaos' but certainly wasn't caused by it: Brian Wilson's declining mental health. As decades passed, it became apparent that the Beatles, particularly Paul McCartney and specifically his song 'Let It Be', had become a focal point for Brian's instability. Millions have been able to relish the song for its spirituality and sense of peace, but for Wilson it represented something much more troubling.

In a brutally frank 1983 interview, Brian admitted: 'I've been crazy for a long time. I've seen some awesome things in this world. I've gone through what I'd call intimidation. Sometimes I lay in bed, afraid, and the words to the Beatles song "Let It Be" come to me. I get these rushes, that things aren't going to be fine, and sure enough, that lyric comes to me.' Years later, he conceded that 'I used to rely on that [song] to help me live my life'. But now, sadly, 'I can't listen to it anymore. It's too scary, or too powerful, or too whatever. When "Let It Be" comes on now, I turn it off.' And that was why, despite numerous instances on which he had expressed a desire to record with McCartney beyond their solitary duet on his *Gettin' in Over My Head* album, Brian had to admit that McCartney still 'scared' him. Asked why, he could only say: 'He's the guy who wrote "Let It Be". I still can't figure out what it means.'

Mike Love was more certain of what he thought. From the vantage point of 1984, he declared that the Beatles were 'fools. They went from something brilliant [in *Sgt. Pepper*] to the *Magical Mystery Tour*. They became the un-Beatles.' Not that this prevented Love from performing 'Back in the USSR' with the Beach Boys (the original inspiration for the song), or paying tribute to John Lennon with 'Imagine', or inviting Ringo Starr up to perform at a giant July 4th gathering. Stridently confident in himself and what he had helped to create, Love was not going to let something as epic as the Beatles' reputation get him down. Brian may have been overawed by the Beatles, but Mike saw them simply as one more act that the Beach Boys had equalled – and then outlasted.

The Walrus was Brian

Paul is dead: the ultimate '60s myth

Ask any Beatles fan.

There is one indisputable fact about the hash-glazed, acid-crazed days of the late 1960s and it is this: Paul McCartney was killed in 1966. His fatal car accident was kept secret from the public, for fear of undermining the British economy, but his fellow Beatles planted a series of ever more obvious clues to the tragedy on their records over the next three years.

The news was confirmed in October 1969 by Michigan disc jockey Russ Gibb, who hosted a phone-in so callers could discuss the significance of their findings. The Beatles album *Abbey Road* had just been released and the lookalike recruited to replace McCartney was pictured barefoot on the front cover, in front of a car with the registration plate 28IF. Here was confirmation, it appeared, that McCartney would have been twenty-eight years old – IF he had lived. (The reality was that he would not have turned twenty-eight until June 1970, but such petty details were forgotten in the wake of this momentous story.)

Over the weeks to come, this intriguing but clearly ridiculous story spread around the world. To this day, there are still those who claim that a Liverpool lad named Billy Campbell was substituted for the fallen McCartney at the end of 1966. YouTube is full of videos that compare the shape of McCartney's features pre- and post-accident to prove their case. There again, even more people are prepared to believe that NASA never reached the Moon in 1969; the difference being that Stanley Kubrick wasn't employed to disguise the identity of the new 'McCartney'.

What few people realise today is that the Beach Boys were at the heart of the 'Paul-is-dead' saga – or so another participant in the original hoax would have had us believe. Fred LaBour, of the student newspaper the *Michigan Daily*, responded to Russ Gibb's broadcast by penning a satirical review of *Abbey Road*, built around the clues that listeners had unearthed. It was LaBour who invented and named the McCartney substitute, William Campbell. And LaBour widened his theory to include another of the era's musical mysteries: the non-appearance of the Beach Boys album, *SMiLE*.

As LaBour told the story, *SMiLE* was initially a Beatles project, stalled when it became 'bogged down in intra-group squabbles and bickering' and then torpedoed when McCartney met his untimely end. Eventually, LaBour wrote, *SMiLE* was 'picked up by Brian Wilson, who attempted to salvage it but couldn't. He was allowed to work on *SMiLE* because the Beatles, especially Paul, had enjoyed "Good Vibrations" to a high degree and respected Wilson's ability immensely. *SMiLE* was finally thrown away' – this much of the story was true, or so it seemed in 1969 – 'and Capitol Records, ignorant of the whole plot, sued Wilson. Brian later paid tribute to Paul with *Smiley Smile*.' LaBour left his readers to puzzle over which *Smiley Smile* song might contain a concealed eulogy for the Beatles' bass guitarist. ('She's Goin' Bald', maybe?)

There was one last twist in LaBour's tale. Ever since 1968, Mike Love has believed that his presence alongside the Beatles at the Maharishi's meditation camp provided the inspiration for their song, 'Back in the USSR'. Not so, the *Michigan Daily* claimed: the opening track to the Beatles' 'White Album' sounded like the Beach Boys for a very different reason. The song was actually 'a thank-you note from the Beatles to Brian Wilson for his work on *SMiLE* and his cover-up job involving where the tapes originated'. All of this explains why Brian would later find it so difficult to be in Paul McCartney's company: he couldn't convincingly pretend that he thought Paul was still alive.

Hang on to Your Ego

Brian Wilson's adventures with mind expansion

'I think there will be more and more adventures into spiritual music,' Brian Wilson predicted in late summer 1966. 'Chants, choral prayers, hymns and all that.' To another reporter, he admitted: 'I have lately become very aware of the spiritual side of life.' His brother Carl was of similar mind: 'We believe in God as a kind of universal consciousness.' And music, Brian explained, 'is the deepest expression of my soul. I do not think there could be a more beautiful way of communication.'

The Beach Boys were not alone in their spiritual quest; the Beatles were becoming increasingly fascinated by realms beyond the everyday. These parallel lines of exploration emerged out of similar influences. In June 1967, Paul McCartney became the first of the Beatles to admit that he had taken LSD, the hallucinogenic chemical concoction also known as 'acid'. His baptism into the acid experience came many months after two of his bandmates had first been dosed. But his willingness to talk about the drug aroused enormous controversy in Britain.

Seven months earlier, Tom Nolan had surveyed the California music community in the *Los Angeles Times*. Brian Wilson, described as 'a 23-year-old cherub', was one of those he interviewed. Brian repeated his religious prophecy, before tracing the impulse to its source. 'About a year ago, I had what I consider a very religious experience,' he said. 'I took LSD, a full dose of LSD, and later, another time, I took a smaller dose. And I learned a lot of things, like patience, understanding.

I can't teach you, or tell you, what I learned from taking it. But I consider it a very religious experience.' Nolan reassured his readers that Wilson would never take the drug again – 'because that would be pointless, wouldn't it?'

Acid became a dividing line in both Brian's life and his music. To anyone who followed the Beatles, it was obvious that there were changes in style and stance between *Beatles for Sale* and *Help!* in 1964–65, and the trilogy of *Rubber Soul/Revolver/Sgt. Pepper* in 1965–67. Doors of perception had been opened; visions had been sparked and allowed to run free; barriers had been broken. And, as the Beatles soon revealed, their bodies and psyches had abandoned the era of alcohol and amphetamines in favour of experimenting with cannabis and then LSD.

With Brian, the before-and-after identities were equally recognisable in his music, for which a succession of lyricists (Mike Love, Terry Sachen, Tony Asher, Van Dyke Parks) supplied suitable words. First to change was the richness and texture of his arrangements and productions, a shift towards sophistication that reached its pinnacle on *Pet Sounds*. Then, with the same abruptness that acid could fracture perceptions of the outside world and inner horizons, he exploded the traditional song format into brilliant fragments, on 'Good Vibrations' and then the ill-fated *SMiLE*.

As the music changed, the personality altered with it, eventually warping to the point that it could no longer be restored to any kind of normality. And as Brian's mental disorders began to be recognised as a life sentence rather than a transitory side-effect, it was easy for those around him to single out a culprit: acid, and the people who had supplied it to him.

'I could kill the guy that gave him acid,' said his first wife Marilyn in 1976. 'Really, that was the worst experience for him to go through.' As she described it further, though, the nightmare seemed to dissolve into dream. 'Brian's trip happened to be a very outrageous one. It was a beautiful experience for him and yet, being so naïve and pure, I just don't think he was ready for it.' Mike Love agreed: 'it blew his mind,' he declared in 1975. 'He never really totally recovered from it. Instead of being his normally productive and aggressive self, the way he used to be, he became totally withdrawn and introverted, even more than before, and he was plenty introverted before.'

Other witnesses were happy to agree. Carl Wilson reckoned that Brian 'was just the wrong person to go popping LSD', that it was his biggest mistake 'and it almost destroyed him', that 'all these pressures and the chemicals took Brian apart'. Al Jardine conceded that Brian 'had some very bad experiences with acid. No one should experiment with these things unless they are very, very in tune with themselves.' And Brian insisted in a 1989 affidavit that his life had been ruined by the LSD he had been given, by an unnamed representative of the William Morris publicity and promotion agency.

Who was this man who had ruined Brian Wilson's life and mind? The West Coast promo man from the Morris agency was Loren Schwartz or, as he preferred to be called after consulting a numerologist in the 1970s, Lorren Daro. Decades after he had first been named and shamed as the villain of Brian's tragic saga, Daro set out the case for his defence in a 2012 blog posting, 'Brian and LSD'. He subsequently shared more candid reminiscences of his involvement with Brian on the SmileySmile.net message board, in which he singled out the four people whom he believed had exerted the most harmful influences on Brian's life: Murry Wilson, Mike Love, Eugene Landy (so far, so predictable) and, to many people's surprise, Marilyn Wilson. (He condemned her for failing to understand her husband and for failing to understand that perhaps she was not equipped to understand him.)

According to Daro's account, Brian hounded him for months around 1963 to hand over some marijuana cigarettes. Daro explained that he ran a 'salon' of enlightened and stimulating minds, at which 'almost everyone smoked marijuana except Brian. I would not allow him to.' It was only after a year that Daro let Wilson experiment a little, noticing that the joints seemed to have an entirely positive effect on his mind and music.

Next, Brian began to demand LSD which, in Daro's version, he had first been offered by a family acquaintance and Beach Boys employee, Terry Sachen. To avoid Brian being exposed to chemicals that might not be pure, in surroundings that might not be conducive to a good trip, Daro gave Brian one dose of '125mcg of genuine Owsley, a clean, pure and correct dose from the best source known. This happened in 1964. LSD was not declared illegal until 1966.' Daro claimed to have been the most sensitive guide possible, knowing how much one's milieu and companionship could taint the acid immersion. If Daro's chronology was accurate, then Brian's 'breakdown' in December 1964 might have been directly triggered by his experience of acid, as the likes of Marilyn Wilson have claimed.

Challenged by fans and scholars on a Beach Boys message board, Daro dug down in his own defence. 'Please remember that the three years following [Brian's] LSD experience were the most creative of his entire artistic life,' he insisted. 'After that, the bullshit he got from that list of true villains finally got to him, plus the bad drugs, the food, the conflicts with his wife, the problems with his ideas for new albums, and a host of other issues. I was long gone by then.' He claimed that he had left Brian's assembly of friends early in the process of creating *SMiLE* to work on the road with other artists. Before then, he said, he fed Brian books on metaphysics, starting with popular introductions to the subject and getting deeper as Brian's passion grew. 'I helped him apply those ideas of universal love, logic and justice to his frustrations,' Daro wrote, 'and a lot of it worked for him. He began to see things in a larger way.'

But there is a chasm, of course, between this beatific vision of Brian Wilson opening his heart to the whole universe in 1965 and 1966, and the Brian Wilson of 1967 and 1968, plummeting from one breakdown to the next, struggling to maintain his sanity while answering his creative urges. For that change, Daro needed to identify someone to blame and his target was Terry Sachen (who had conveniently died in 1994). In Daro's narrative, Sachen 'fed Brian coke, speed, meth, hash, LSD and anything else he could get his hands on and did more to set Brian on the wrong road than any other person, including Eugene Landy'. But Sachen was not around to take the blame or mount his own defence.

All of which assumed, of course, that Brian was an adult man with the instincts of a child, who was unable to exert any control over any aspect of his life except one: his music. And there were those around Brian who seemed to have viewed him in exactly that way. In an anonymous article that was probably written in 1967 by the Beach Boys' press agent Derek Taylor, it was stated that youngest brother Carl 'feels a strangely paternal protective thing towards Brian – a need to shield him from realities; and to put up this barrier against the world, Carl will employ soothing white lies'.

After which it is sobering, and somewhat of a relief, to hear Brian's own voice. At the start of 1968, he was recorded in a free-flowing conversation with the journalist J. Marks (who operated for many years under the fictional identity of Jamake Highwater, a Cherokee native). This Brian is articulate, calm, open, chilled, both warm- and light-hearted. 'I started to feel really conscious of the power of love,' he explained when describing his experiences of recent years. 'So many things started happening at one time, I blew my mind. Completely blew it. And ever since I blew my mind, everything has just been so groovy.' He admitted that he was running dry on ideas 'in the conventional sense', but he did not sound concerned. Instead, he said, 'we'd like to pull out of conventional sound-making and try to get into sounds that have never been made before'.

It was a utopia that Brian was destined never to reach. Within months, he would become a father for the first time and would then be consigned to a mental hospital when his baby was only a few weeks old. There he was prescribed psychotropic drugs for the first time, which bent his mind into different dimensions from those he had discovered on acid.

After this, nothing was ever the same again.

When I Grow Up

Carl Wilson refuses the draft

In the highlights reel of the decades after the Second World War, two celebrities always face the challenge of being called up by the American armed forces. Under the Selective Service system in place since the war, all American males were required to register for a national database once they reached their eighteenth birthday. Any of those young men might be required to step forward and serve their country before they reached twenty-five.

Rock 'n' roll icon Elvis Presley did his patriotic duty, widened his popular appeal and effectively redirected his subsequent career by answering Uncle Sam's call in 1958. Footage of his military haircut and his initial appearances on parade filled newsreels and TV bulletins. Nearly a decade later, heavyweight boxing champion Muhammad Ali became a pariah for many white Americans, but would pass into history as a hero for refusing to sign up for military service in Vietnam.

Remarkably few of the era's most rebellious rock performers were called up for the Vietnam War, as potential exemptions were available to those who were married (such as Mike Love), in college, unfit in some medical or psychological sense, or could afford lawyers prepared to battle the US Army into a state of exhaustion. Beyond that, some potential inductees used their imagination to escape an unwanted trip to south-east Asia.

Future Beach Boys member Bruce Johnston took a popular, if risky, route by feigning femininity. He reported for his draft board wearing foundation make-up, heavy perfume and flamboyant clothes, before informing his inquisitors that his great wish in life was to become a dancer. He was ruled '4F' – unsuitable for military service. Had he received the call, there is no doubt that Brian Wilson would also have failed his examination, on grounds of his erratic mental health.

One of his brothers evaded the draft for similar reasons. Dennis Wilson presented his board with a bulging folder of medical evidence declaring that he was suffering from stomach complaints and arthritis. But he only convinced them that he wasn't military material when he swore that he would kill himself if he was forced to serve. Not that this represented any commitment to peace: 'I'd clear all American soldiers out of Vietnam,' he stated in 1965. 'Then I'd send a note to Red China saying, "You've got twenty minutes. The bombs are on their way."'

Dennis's threat of self-harm didn't end his obligation but merely postponed it. Two years later, his attitude to the military had matured: 'I would not be drafted if they called me. I'd serve my time in jail if necessary, but I'd never have anything to do with killing. There is no reason for anyone to be connected with anything that could kill someone.'

By then, he had an example to follow: his younger brother, Carl. On 3 January 1967, while eldest sibling Brian continued his months-long struggle with the creation of 'Heroes and Villains', Carl refused to accept the draft board's command to join the military. As he neared his eighteenth birthday in 1965, Carl had filled out the government's questionnaire, registering him for the draft. The form allowed him to declare himself a conscientious objector on religious grounds, but he left that box unchecked. A year later, his moral horizons expanding as he matured, he belatedly filled out a second application, asking to be exempted on religious grounds. But his request was refused.

Officially, then, Carl Wilson had no coherent grounds for refusing the draft and had to be regarded as a potential criminal. A federal grand jury was assembled in Los Angeles to investigate his case and an indictment was issued on 5 April 1967 for his arrest, on the basis that he had violated the Selective Service Act. The machinery of justice clanked into action and the FBI were deputed to find Carl and bring him before a court. But it was another three weeks before he was confronted after the Beach Boys had appeared at the Long Island Arena in Commack, New York. Agents escorted him away from the complex and whisked him in front of a US commissioner, who had the authority to transport him back to California. Carl declared that he wished to be granted bail so that he could tour Europe with the Beach Boys a week hence. The commissioner gave him until the following morning to find a lawyer and then appear before a judge.

Carl was freed to complete the current touring sweep along the East Coast, before flying back to California for the hearing that would determine his immediate fate, on 1 May. Meanwhile, the remainder of the Beach Boys touring group, now reduced to four members, were jetting in the opposite direction, from New York to Dublin, where their European tour would begin the next day.

In Los Angeles, Carl explained afterwards, 'I spent a day in jail. It wasn't too bad, really. Peaceful.' Before the judge, his attorney asserted that although his client did not profess to belong to any specific religious group, he was morally opposed to all wars. 'My duty to God is far greater than any mortal demand,' Carl contended. The judge imposed a hefty bail tariff, then freed Carl to join the group in Dublin, with two provisos: he should maintain regular contact with the Beach Boys' attorney, Howard Smith, who could vouch for Carl's whereabouts, and he should return to court in late June to face trial. But while Carl was en route to Ireland, the Beach Boys quartet was forced to take the stage of the Dublin Adelphi without him. 'They seemed at a complete loss,' journalist B.P. Fallon reported, 'like some amateur group struck with stage fright at the local talent contest.' Bruce Johnston was allotted the role of lead vocalist on 'God Only Knows' and forgot the words. 'Sloop John B' proved so disastrous that many members of the audience fled the theatre demanding their money back, while those who remained launched a volley of boos at the Beach Boys for their apparent incompetence.

Three hours later, it was time for the second house. The group delayed its entry as long as was feasible, before Al Jardine led them into a defiant but ragged 'Help Me, Rhonda'. Then, as the opening chords of 'I Get Around' were heard, Carl was ushered onto the stage in his travelling clothes and the group's morale immediately revived.

Back in California, the unashamedly patriotic Murry Wilson was required to defend his son. He credited himself and the boys' mother for hammering the Ten Commandments into their three sons and inculcating a deep respect for life. But Murry admitted that he hoped that Carl would agree to join the military in a non-combatant role, which his son had already ruled out.

At the subsequent trial, Carl was happy to declare that 'I want to do something good' – work in a hospital, perhaps, but not as a member of the armed forces. 'We were put here to live,' he told the court. 'Killing is very evil and destructive and results in human suffering. I love my country very much, but I won't take part in the destruction of people.' His moral principles were not decisive in the proceedings. Instead, he was acquitted on an obscure technicality, after his lawyer unearthed a tiny irregularity in the way that his induction papers had been signed by the board. 'I am not going to find a man guilty of a felony when the board does a thing like this,' the judge grumbled.

After the trial was over, Wilson's attorney filed yet another statement of conscientious objection and this time his status was accepted. He was ordered to report for work as 'an institutional worker for the county Department of Charities'. That was in late 1967, but the paperwork crawled its way through the system and was then ignored – by Carl, perhaps, or by the Beach Boys office – when his assignment was set in stone. He failed to report for his charitable work and, once again, he was under federal indictment. This time there was no exemption for morals and, early in 1970, Carl was found guilty after the jury deliberated for a whole fifteen minutes. He faced a potential sentence of five years' imprisonment and a $10,000 fine. But the judge was lenient, placing Wilson on probation for three years and insisting that he should carry out work at hospitals.

In the true spirit of the American legal system, even this decision turned out to be provisional. There were more hearings until, in September 1971, approaching the fifth anniversary of Carl's original refusal, he was granted dispensation to avoid hospital service and instead appear with the Beach Boys, free of charge, at prisons, orphanages and hospitals. 'I feel this is an opportunity to do something I can do well,' he announced. He promised to devote at least forty hours a week to this work, which he would perform 'diligently and faithfully'. But the Beach Boys were in the final stages of recording their *Surf's Up* album, which postponed any benefit concerts for several months and, when touring resumed, they made fewer charitable appearances than they had in the years preceding Carl's sentence. But by then, even justice no longer had the energy or enthusiasm to prolong this protracted Californian legal saga.

Time to Get Alone

Making sense of the late 1960s

'I think, basically, the Beach Boys are squares,' Brian Wilson declared in August 1967. 'We're not happening … we're not a hip group.' As for Brian himself, 'I'm running out of ideas'. And the group? 'I'd say we have between three and five more years of Beach Boying to go.'

He was speaking in Honolulu, where he was about to join the group on stage for the first time in nearly three years. 'I'm actually nervous,' he admitted. 'I'm doing it because we're cutting this live album. We're calling it *Lei'd in Hawaii*. It will be out on Brother Records, our new label.'

Having installed an eight-track studio in his Bellagio Drive home, Brian arranged for two similar machines to capture a pair of shows at Honolulu's HIC Arena. Although Bruce Johnston flew with the group to Hawaii, he did not perform with them, choosing instead to take a connecting flight to London, where he planned to set up his own production company. It was the original five-man group who took to the stage, Brian preferring to lurk behind his triple-decker Baldwin organ rather than stand centre-stage as of old. (He later confided that he associated the Baldwin sound, central to the Beach Boys sound in 1967, with death.) The organ wasn't the only break from the past: before at least one of the shows, Brian encouraged his brothers to join him in dropping acid.

One way or another, Brian's presence introduced chaos to the Beach Boys' touring routine. He threw out their familiar introductions and endings, and insisted that they should tackle new material such as 'Heroes and Villains' and 'Getting Hungry'. He even attempted to revisit their complex *a capella* arrangement of 'The Lord's Prayer', which they hadn't sung in four years, until his colleagues demonstrated that they no longer remembered their parts. The shows were shambolic, as if the audience had paid to attend a lazy rehearsal. As one local reviewer gently put it, the Beach Boys 'will probably have to do a lot of studio editing'. Instead, the band re-recorded the entire show in Brian's home a couple of weeks later, with the idea of substituting a couple of 'fake' cuts in place of their live equivalents. That ploy was abandoned when he realised that nothing on the authentic Honolulu tapes deserved to make the grade. There was only one positive outcome from the Hawaii trip: Marilyn Wilson became pregnant there. She gave birth to daughter Carnie exactly nine months later.

The Hawaii visit sparked a period of recording activity so manic that it was almost as if Brian knew that his artistic coherence was running out. Having taped *Smiley Smile* in July 1967, and the fake live album two months later, the Beach Boys went straight into sessions that ensured *Wild Honey* would be rushed into stores before Christmas. There was barely time for the group to visit Europe, and meet the Maharishi, before they launched into the recording of *Friends*. That was completed in time for Carnie's arrival, but within another month, there began an epic sequence of recording sessions that were eventually channelled into another album, *20/20*. Along the way, Mike Love's son Christian (a future touring Beach Boy) was born and Love's marriage subsequently collapsed, while Dennis made friends with a budding songwriter and hardened criminal with a penchant for collecting stray, vulnerable young women. Oh ... and Brian was held in a mental hospital for several weeks, receiving treatment that altered the subsequent course of his life – and not for the better.

Wild Honey lasted fewer than twenty-four minutes in total, one of the shortest pop albums of all time. Aside from a Stevie Wonder cover and a rowdy group collaboration, it was entirely composed by Brian with assistance from Mike Love. But when it came to production, even in a studio built in his own house, Brian stepped back from full responsibility. 'Brian asked me to get more involved in the recording end,' Carl explained. 'He wanted a break. He was tired. He had been doing it all too long.' This was both true and a subterfuge, as Brian was producing music during that period – but not for the Beach Boys.

While the *Wild Honey* sessions continued, Brian decided to focus on another vocal combo: a trio provisionally dubbed Redwood, who later became more successful as Three Dog Night. Their leader was Danny Hutton, who became one of Brian's stalwart companions over the next decade. Brian prepared backing tracks for two new songs, the blue-eyed soul tune 'Darlin'' (which is what Hutton called everybody he met) and a confessional waltz, 'Time to Get Alone'. Redwood duly added their voices, but then commercial realities intervened in the shape of Carl and Murry, with Brian 'persuaded' (or compelled) to give both songs to the Beach Boys. That made artistic sense: Carl's raucous vocal on 'Darlin'' outstripped Hutton's attempt, while 'Time to Get Alone' was too baroque to fit the Redwood style. But Brian saw it as a personal betrayal. 'I understand,' Hutton said generously. 'The Beach Boys were gods and here was Brian futzing around with these three unknown guys. It was a sad time. Very dark days.'

By now, Brian was so impatient that he insisted 'Darlin'' should be rush-released as a Beach Boys single, even while 'Wild Honey' was still climbing the charts. With 'Getting Hungry' from *Smiley Smile* also issued as a Brian and Mike duet 45, four singles had emerged from the Beach Boys in fewer than five months. Album buyers were equally confused. In the same short period, *Smiley Smile* and *Wild Honey* were released alongside a second *Best Of* package and a *Beach Boys Deluxe* reissue of their three previous albums. Brian had also begun work on an album of Beach Boys instrumental backings, stripped of the vocals, which was issued as a proto-karaoke album, *Stack-O-Tracks*, in 1968.

Nor was that all. Leftovers were piling up in the studio cupboards. Some of them were ephemeral, such as the remakes of recent hits by the Box Tops and Wayne Fontana. Others were more substantial: Brian briefly revisited 'Surf's Up', no doubt aware that it was the most regrettable casualty of the *SMiLE* era, and also diverted part of the fabled 'Elements' suite into a track that became 'Cool, Cool Water'.

To prove that the experimentation of the previous winter had not been forgotten, Brian embarked on another series of endurance-sapping sessions to rival those that had spawned 'Good Vibrations' and 'Heroes and Villains'. The focus this time was a song – or more accurately a set of *SMiLE*-style feels – entitled either 'Can't Wait Too Long' or 'Been Way Too Long'. It was as hypnotic as anything from his collaboration with Van Dyke Parks, building its circular magic with dazzling variations and harmonies. Brian toyed with it and returned to it and worried about it for the best part of a year, but in true *SMiLE* tradition, he never quite succeeded in isolating exactly what the track was supposed to be. It certainly wouldn't have fitted alongside the crisp R&B and pop tunes on *Wild Honey*, nor indeed the eccentric fare offered on *Friends* a few months later.

Of all the strangenesses and vagaries offered by the Beach Boys in the 1960s, nothing was quite as unusual, or as charming in its idiosyncrasy, as *Friends*. It was another ultra-short record, stretched to twenty-five minutes only by including an instrumental Hawaiian travelogue entitled 'Diamond Head'. Mike Love was absent on meditative business for most of the sessions, removing Brian's most immediate collaborator from the creative process. Instead, he welcomed suggestions from anyone in the vicinity, with the result that 'When a Man Needs a Woman', barely two minutes long, listed no fewer than six co-writers, two of whom weren't in the Beach Boys. (The song was an oddity in any case, as it proudly celebrated the birth of a son who, a few weeks later, turned out to be Brian's daughter Carnie.)

Friends also celebrated a fresh writing talent: Dennis Wilson, who composed the deliciously simple 'Little Bird' and 'Be Still' with poet Steve Kalinich. In fact, all the Beach Boys (except Bruce Johnston) were credited for a set of songs that seemed almost wilfully unhip. They celebrated teenage crushes rather than the sexual frenzy of Janis Joplin or Jimi Hendrix, and prioritised simple friendship over the revolutionary collectivism that was the prevailing anthem of contemporary rock. Whenever Brian was audible behind the controls, the results were equally weird, whether it was his instruction guide to visiting his house, 'Busy Doin' Nothin', or the deliberately cacophonous 'Transcendental Meditation'. Brian would subsequently claim on multiple occasions that *Friends* was his favourite Beach Boys album. But the wider world of 1968 chose to ignore it. From being the world's leading group eighteen months earlier, the Beach Boys seemed to have decided to be forgotten.

Just before the *Friends* sessions began, a remarkably calm and articulate Brian had laid bare his current state of mind to Jamake Highwater. He repeated a familiar claim that he had exhausted his creative stock, while simultaneously announcing plans for fresh work: 'We'd like to pull out of conventional sound-making and try to get into sounds that have never been made before.' The reason, he explained, was that he had pushed himself too hard in the past. 'We pulled out of that production pace really because I was about ready to die, I was trying so hard. All of a sudden, I decided not to try anymore ... not such big things.'

But what else could he do? Rather than concentrating on raising his first child, Brian decided to fill the house with music once again. He attempted about a dozen tunes over a five-week period, which ranged from 'Rendezvous' (soon retitled 'Do It Again' and an obvious hit single) and the airy 'Sail Plane Song' (later to become 'Loop De Loop' in Al Jardine's hands) to what promised to be exquisite arrangements of 'Walk On By' and 'Ol' Man River'. He also continued to play with 'Can't Wait Too Long'.

Once again, Brian struggled to complete any of these projects, symbolic of the moment when he no longer felt in control of his life. Precise details are sparse, but around July or August 1968, he was hospitalised for several weeks, apparently diagnosed as suffering from a severe anxiety disorder; for the first time, psychiatrists began to throw around words such as 'psychosis' and 'schizophrenia' while discussing his case. The result was that his psyche was barraged with several simultaneous forms of 'cure', which ranged from psychoanalysis to electro-convulsive therapy and heavy doses of a drug called Thorazine. Several of its physical side-effects were visible in Brian's everyday life over the months to come:

sleepiness bordering on narcolepsy; pronounced weight gain; awkward physical movement. It was the kind of drug that triggered as many problems as it tackled, leaving one to wonder how Brian's life might have proceeded if it had never been forced upon him at all.

In his absence, the Beach Boys grew up as artists. It's true that, to fill out the *20/20* album, they had to reach back into the stockpile of *SMiLE* material to borrow 'Our Prayer' and 'Cabinessence'. But in other ways they successfully obscured Brian's withdrawal. Carl assembled a shimmering cover of the Ronettes' 'I Can Hear Music'; Dennis transformed a Charles Manson tune into the haunting 'Never Learn Not to Love'; Bruce Johnston handed over a reworked 1950s hit 'Bluebirds Over the Mountain', which he had intended as a solo single, and also prepared a piece of instrumental 'good music' entitled 'The Nearest Faraway Place', which must have appealed to Murry Wilson. Brian had insisted on preparing only mono mixes of all the earlier Beach Boys albums, because of his semi-deafness, but now they were able to employ full stereo effects on a record for the first time. Just audible in the mix of the libidinous 'All I Want to Do' was a personal touch from Dennis, in more ways than one: the sound of a female prostitute stimulated to the point of orgasm by a Beach Boy who considered himself a master of the art. Sadly, Murry Wilson's thoughts on that piece of production expertise were not recorded.

Jai Guru Dev

Meditation, the Maharishi and the Beach Boys

'I was really freaked out on astronomy when I was a kid,' Brian Wilson confided to his friend Jules Siegel in 1967. 'Baseball, too. I guess I went through a lot of phases ... The whole spiritual thing is very physical.' His beliefs were changeable, his methodology confused, but his goals remained the same: growth, fulfilment, creativity, belonging, truth and, if you like, transcendence.

Among his many paths, which ranged from the obsessive replaying of a Phil Spector single to experimentation with hallucinogenic drugs, was an openness to spiritual and mental development. He was ripe for a man who, visiting California in October 1966, promised 'a way to educate man to apply his inner potential. Man becomes more capable on all levels of life, free from stress and strain.' For someone already struggling with his mental health, under severe pressure from himself and his milieu to achieve artistic miracles, words like these represented a form of nirvana. Brian was still an equal-opportunity enthusiast at this moment in his life, but the pronouncements of the Maharishi Mahesh Yogi, the proselytiser of Transcendental Meditation, chimed with the chords already running through his soul. Soon after that ambassadorial trip by the guru, Wilson was inducted into the philosophy and practice of TM.

Wilson had been introduced to TM several months before the Beatles, who claimed the (sometimes dubious) credit for popularising the Maharishi and his techniques among Western youth. The English group attended a lecture by the guru in London and then travelled to North Wales in late August 1967 for a weekend conference. Aware that their sponsorship of his work could be both spiritually and financially lucrative, the Maharishi took every opportunity he could to exploit his links with the Beatles.

On 15 December, he invited them to accompany him to Paris, where he was taking part in a fundraising concert for the UN's children's charity, UNICEF. John Lennon, George Harrison and their wives took up the offer. At the afternoon rehearsal, the Maharishi was introduced to some American guests: the Beach Boys. He immediately invited the group to join him at his hotel, where he led them in an informal discussion, impressing them – as Mike Love explained – 'with his warmth and gentleness. We talked about being initiated into the Transcendental Meditation movement.'

The following morning, Love flew to London to meet friends, but no sooner had he arrived than he was contacted by Dennis, who told him: 'You've gotta come back to Paris. We want Maharishi to initiate us!' Love maintained that he was 'still sceptical', but he joined the group in seeking out the objects they had been requested to bring to the ceremony: fruit, flowers and a handkerchief. 'We found the flowers and the fruit,' he recalled, 'but we went all over Paris to find the handkerchief. It was Sunday and nothing was open.'

Love had a vivid memory of what happened next. 'We went into the room with Maharishi and he led us in meditation. It was so simple and I felt immediate peace of body and mind. When we opened our eyes, we all laughed. Maharishi knew we felt happy and he laughed too. That afternoon we had a second meditation after which he gave a lecture – a kind of intellectual explanation of the process which made some profound things very clear.' Love's philosophy and daily practice of life were changed forever. And he was not alone. Carl Wilson declared that the Maharishi was 'the purest, most honest human being I've ever met'. Two days into the routine of meditation, Carl was 'completely convinced that it is a good and constructive thing ... I'm sure he has the answer – it may not be the only one, but it is an answer.'

The following month, the Maharishi came to New York, where his progress was handled by a leading public relations agency. Having already captured the Beatles, he was happy to show off his intimacy with the nearest American equivalent. Brian accompanied the other members of the band to a meeting with their new guru, after which the Maharishi announced their enthusiastic support of TM to a conference of cynical journalists. They groaned when the Beach Boys' name was mentioned and demanded that he explain why, if he was so spiritual, he needed their support. 'They inspire the young to meditate,' the Maharishi said simply. 'All the singers want the audience to float in waves of happiness.' He announced that the Beatles would shortly be travelling to his Indian ashram at Rishikesh for a prolonged study of meditation. 'I told him I wanted to come,' said Mike Love, 'and he said that would be fine.'

Love joined a select group that, besides the Beatles, included folk singer Donovan and actress Mia Farrow. Although Paul McCartney complained, many years later, that Love seemed to be preoccupied in selling his fellow celebrities cans of Coke and other Western treats, Mike viewed his weeks at the meditation camp as a formative spiritual experience. Music was a unifying factor: 'We made up songs and sang them together, people of all ages singing after the tea was served … We sang the new and the old. It was funny to see an elderly lady joining in on "Heartbreak Hotel". But in the ashram age becomes unimportant. Time is only change.' That change is measured in human terms by birthdays, and Love celebrated the twenty-fifth anniversary of George Harrison's birth by composing a song about Transcendental Meditation. Two weeks later, the Beatles reciprocated, wishing Mike Love a happy twenty-seventh birthday with a ditty about spiritual regeneration.

Soon afterwards, Love left India and returned to Los Angeles in time to add his voice to the Beach Boys' *Friends* album. He was preceded by rumours that the Beatles were planning to make a film about the Maharishi, which would also involve the Beach Boys, and by the definite news that the Beach Boys would be accompanying the Maharishi on a joint lecture/concert tour of American colleges during May 1968. Arriving home, Love happily spread the word that this unique marriage of music and meditation would only be the opening act to a lavish global scheme for a Festival of Peace. The Maharishi's spokesman explained that 'it would be a festival of music and culture that would tour the world from city to city, drawing in artists of all nations' – led, of course, by the Beach Boys and the Beatles.

Days later, Paul McCartney flew home to London and was quizzed about this extravagant proposal. 'It is the idea of one of the Beach Boys, Mike Love,' he said carefully. 'We have merely said that if it gets off the ground it would be a great idea. There are no details worked out so far.' Two weeks later, his colleagues Lennon and Harrison left the Maharishi's camp in high dudgeon, having been convinced that their guru was more interested in earthly (and, indeed, erotic) pleasure than the divine. With their public disillusionment, plans for joint ventures with the Beach Boys were abandoned. More troublingly, the Beatles' decision to distance themselves from the Maharishi reframed the Beach Boys' imminent concert tour. For a moment, it seemed as if they had seized the cultural zeitgeist of young America. Now they were inexorably linked to a man, and a cause, that the Beatles had renounced. The icons of the age had damned the crusade to sell Transcendental Meditation to the US.

The publicity machine continued to roll forward as if triumph was inevitable, with Mike Love taking the central role. 'The Maharishi got our vibrations,' he proclaimed. 'He wants to get his message across to American youth. His meditation will do a lot of good by getting kids away from LSD, pot, booze and speed, because you really don't need it if you understand what the Maharishi is saying.' A reporter noted cynically that Love concluded his remarks by 'downing a noonday Bloody Mary'.

Before American youth could be transformed, however, they had to be enticed into the theatres. The original intention had been to target American colleges, but the promoters – perhaps the Beach Boys, too – grew greedy, even though profits from the performances were earmarked for the TM movement. Large arenas were added to the datebook and no fewer than thirty shows were concertinaed into a nineteen-day schedule. Advertisements promised 'The Event of the Decade', but they also made clear that spirituality ranked more highly than entertainment. Top of the bill was 'MAHARISHI MAHESH YOGI Speaking on Transcendental Meditation'. Filling out the programme were 'His Devotees, THE BEACH BOYS', though they were also billed beneath another guaranteed attraction: 'World Peace'.

The initial show in Washington DC set the tone, with a near sell-out audience at the Coliseum. Publicity agents claimed that the Beach Boys would be unveiling a new style of 'tranquil music', and Mike Love took the stage sporting a prophet's white robe and flowing red beard. But old habits were hard to shake and the mostly pre-college audiences vocalised their desire to hear the surfing hits of five years ago. The band obliged, with Love reverting to the childish jokes and hand signals that had long been standard Beach Boys fare.

All too soon, after maybe thirty-five or forty minutes of music, it was intermission, the show resuming with the stage set for spiritual devotion. Clad in brilliant white like his disciple, the elderly figure of the Maharishi walked slowly in front of the crowd, bowed his head and began to speak. Without a microphone. His thin, piping, giggling voice barely reached beyond the front few rows and, within a few minutes, many of the fans left, while others booed or shouted out insults and complaints. The same day's show in nearby Baltimore was even more disastrous: the Maharishi's name was spelled wrongly outside the theatre and fewer than one in five seats were filled. Those who remained laughed aloud when they first heard the guru's voice, while provocateurs interrupted his speech with profanities. But reporters admired the Maharishi's determination to prevail without raising his voice against the opposition. 'Glad you are in a happy mood,' he replied as the insults continued, and the bulk of those still in the hall applauded him.

It was immediately obvious that the tour was headed for financial disaster, regardless of its spiritual impact. Three shows were scheduled for the second day, but the first and potentially most lucrative, at a stadium in New York, was cancelled a few minutes before its advertised start time when only 5 per cent of seats were filled. In Westchester, Mike Love had to return to the stage during the Maharishi's speech to beg fans to give the guru a hearing. The audience was no more respectful during the evening concert in Philadelphia, where fully half of the 6,000 left during the interval before the Maharishi even appeared before them. Those who remained found his voice drowned out by the venue's air-conditioning system. 'The music, the air-conditioning, the stage – it all produced the wrong vibrations,' a fan said afterwards.

The third day began in Hartford, Connecticut, where comparative order and respect reigned, but although the entourage was supposed to travel on to Rhode Island for the evening show, the venue in Providence received a phone call from the Beach Boys' manager to say that the Maharishi had decided to end the tour and that the musicians would not be appearing either. And that was it: despite vague promises of a resumption later in the month, the marriage of music and meditation collapsed after just five concerts, with a further twenty-four cancelled.

Where did the Maharishi go? A local paper was told that he had left 'to meditate with moviemakers in parts unknown'. Another journal reckoned that he had travelled to Israel. The *Los Angeles Times* claimed he had caught 'a mild case of pneumonia'. But the same outlet dug deeper the next day and noted that financial problems may well have forced the cancellations. The guru was now said to be 'resting in Santa Barbara', having been well enough to fly 3,000 miles away from the sites of his recent disasters.

The Beach Boys collected the bills, both monetary and reputational. The group, said the *Ottawa Journal*, 'are rapidly sinking. After reaching a high with "Good Vibrations", the unit has been going slowly downhill on record. Their last three discs have failed to make noise and their current offering, "Friends", is having trouble getting airplay in their hometown of Los Angeles.' Despite his lack of involvement in the concert tour, Brian Wilson battled to find a positive interpretation of the Maharishi's reception by their fans: 'He expected it. He felt that if even one per cent of our audiences listened to him, that would be good. But with his health at stake, we just didn't feel it was worth it, so we cancelled out.' Carl was more realistic: 'I don't think we should have got involved with him. It was a mistake.' Their collective losses were put at anywhere between $250,000 and $400,000, but the blow to their morale was even more significant. Far from leading a spiritual youth revolution, the Beach Boys resumed their touring obligations in July – not with a global guru, but with Gary Puckett & the Union Gap. And their support act proceeded to win better reviews than them.

Critics complained that regardless of how experimental and artistic their records continued to be, the Beach Boys' live shows had not kept pace with the changing times. Their audiences were also reluctant to grow with them. The group, alleged the *Chicago Tribune*, 'are a bit like circus dogs who keep wagging their tails (and making their feeble jokes) long after the crowd has tired of their single trick'. Already, fewer than seven years into their professional career, they were being held back by the past. No wonder that some of them continued to rely on meditation to retain their equilibrium, that Dennis Wilson traded in the Maharishi for an altogether more disturbing guru, and that brother Brian, as Johnston admitted with grave humour, 'has trouble getting out of his house'. Two years before, they had rivalled the Beatles as the world's most successful pop act. Now they struggled to fill the front rows of halls that had once been standing room only. And it was at this moment that the Beach Boys elected to build a business empire that would rival the Beatles' Apple corporation for extravagant expense. If only a guru had been available to warn them about building office complexes on sandy ground.

Seventeen Girls for Every Boy

Dennis Wilson and Charles Manson

After Charles Manson was convicted of murder, the Beach Boys felt the need to explain how his life had managed to collide with theirs. Their individual accounts varied in small details down the years, but basically ran like this.

In March or maybe April 1968, free-living, free-loving Beach Boys drummer Dennis Wilson picks up two young female hitchhikers and invites them back to his home at 14400 Sunset Boulevard. Either he has sex with both girls, or else one of them is heavily pregnant and is presumably excused from some of Dennis's preferred leisure options. Then he picks them up again – and maybe the pregnant woman has had her baby, or maybe there was never a baby at all … or maybe there was only one hike, one ride, one visit to Sunset Boulevard. The story is nothing if not ambiguous, from start to finish.

After a Beach Boys recording session, which some accounts date as 11 April 1968, Wilson drives home late at night and discovers his house is filled with semi-naked young women. He is met in his driveway by a slim, wild-haired, slightly older, more than slightly wizened man with electric eyes. Dennis asks defensively: 'Are you going to hurt me?' The intruder bows down before him, kisses his feet and invites him inside his own home to share women and drugs and whatever else the roaming commune has to offer.

The man and his almost entirely female following having set up home with Dennis; the drummer discovers that they are impossible to dislodge. Fortunately, he is only the tenant, not the owner of the property, and so he simply abandons the house to his turbulent new friends. Instead, he camps out in the basement of the home where his friend, occasional songwriting partner and (Dennis's word) 'house-boy', Gregg Jakobson, has set up residence. Dennis makes a public show of casting off his celebrity trappings in favour of an authentically hippie vibe. 'I'm a drop-out and I'll tell my kids to drop out,' he tells a reporter in July.

Before then, his Sunset house guest has revealed some idiosyncratic but genuine talent for free-form poetry set to semi-improvised music. The Beach Boys have open access at any hour to the recording studio set up in Brian's home on Bellagio Drive and to the resident (and superbly talented) studio engineer, Steve Desper. On (perhaps) 3 June 1968, at Dennis's request, Desper produces a solo demo session by the unorthodox singer-songwriter, with a view to signing him to the almost empty roster of the Beach Boys' recording company, Brother Records.

The songwriter's alarming demeanour and faintly aggressive behaviour leads Desper to tell Dennis that he never wants to work with the newcomer again. All talk of the Brother signing is dropped, but instead Dennis reworks one of his friend's songs, 'Cease to Exist', with the help of Jakobson. By September, it is ready to be recorded by the Beach Boys as 'Never Learn Not to Love'. The track is released as the flipside to a single, 'Bluebirds Over the Mountain', that November; and is also included on the Beach Boys' *20/20* album in February 1969. Songwriting credit for the song is claimed by Wilson and Jakobson, although Dennis's friend receives a one-off cash payment in return for signing over his rights.

Fast-forward to August 1969, when one of the most notorious murder sprees in American history takes place in two locations – one of which is the home of Hollywood actress Sharon Tate. Meanwhile, Dennis receives occasional threatening visits and messages from his one-time friend and his associates: reportedly a bullet is left at his new house, as a sign that his first wife's son Scott (subsequently adopted by Dennis) might be in danger.

It is only in early December 1969 that Dennis and the rest of the extended Beach Boys family discover the awful truth, that the perpetrators of the August murders were several of the commune whom he had met twenty months earlier – inspired by the rhetoric of his friend and potential recording artist, Charles Manson. Dennis is appalled, refuses to testify at Manson's trial and rarely, if ever, discusses his experiences in public or with a journalist again. (As Carl described it, 'Dennis went through a lot of personal hell over that, he felt mortified and humiliated'.) His name is constantly being raised at the Manson Family's trial – at around the same time as Carl is on trial for failing to fulfil his assignments as a conscientious objector, and then his cousin Mike is arrested for driving erratically while under the influence of extreme fasting – but somehow this combination of unfortunate events does not tarnish the Beach Boys irreparably, in the way that the Rolling Stones had to shoulder the burden of the debacle of Altamont, an outdoor concert where four audience members died. (With perfect end-of-an-era symmetry, the Altamont concert was staged in the same week that Manson Family members were arrested on murder charges.) In fact, the Beach Boys are able to sign a new record deal just two months after the Manson/Wilson connection is made public.

Underlying the official story, as promoted by everyone with the Beach Boys' interests at heart, is an admission and a parallel denial. Yes, it is impossible to evade the fact that Dennis Wilson was briefly associated with the Manson Family, and that he enabled Manson himself to take part in a speculative recording session at his brother's house. But no, Dennis did not have any connection with the Manson commune after the summer of 1968. In fact, so the tale always unfolds, he did his best to distance himself from them entirely.

Unfortunately for Dennis, he had already offered a very different account to several journalists in 1968 and 1969. To judge from his own reported words, the drummer was not only in regular contact with

Manson and his so-called Family until at least the summer of 1969, he was still viewing the future instigator of two sets of murders as a potential recording artist as late as that June, just two months before the killings that sent fear through the Los Angeles entertainment community.

Wilson's earliest account of his encounter with the Manson commune came in a syndicated column by Californian journalist Gene Hurley in July 1968. He interviewed the Beach Boys at their business headquarters just off Hollywood Boulevard and witnessed a heated debate about the value or otherwise of education between Dennis and Al Jardine. Wilson declared that education was 'a big nothing'; Jardine expressed his desire to work for a charity that might help persuade teenagers to stay in school. This would enable them to earn a decent living in the future.

'There you go again,' Dennis retorted, 'talking about material things. I'm rich, sure, but I sleep under the trees in the hills. The best food I ever tasted, some flat-broke kids made for me out of garbage cans. And honest, it was delicious.' Who were these 'flat-broke kids'? The members of Manson's commune, who raided dumpsters outside restaurants and supermarkets in search of free food. As Sandra 'Blue' Good recalled at Manson's trial, family members once undertook one of these missions from Dennis's Rolls-Royce. 'We did a garbage run and it was really funny,' she told the court. 'He [Dennis] was happy to have us bring the stuff back, as Dennis ate pills all the time and he was glad to have home cooking for a change.'

Making that connection with Manson in 1968 would have required some detailed knowledge of the Family's habits and morals. But over the next year, Dennis cast all discretion to the winds and openly discussed his relationship with Manson and his followers. More unsettling still was the fact that he began to preach elements of the Manson gospel as if it were his own. In fact, during 1968 and 1969, Wilson and Manson almost seemed to merge or even exchange their personalities. Once Manson was arrested, several witnesses came forward to testify that he had 'told them he was a songwriter and drummer for the Beach Boys rock group'. Meanwhile, Wilson talked as if he was the Family's prime mover – not a passing associate of Manson but an equal partner in his experiment in collective living.

Central to the Manson credo was the complete demolition of all sexual boundaries and possessiveness. Anyone who wanted to live in his commune had to take part in group orgies, regardless of their conventional sexual preferences. Manson had a hypnotic hold over many of the young converts to his Family; Dennis's celebrity and rugged physical appeal undoubtedly attracted and held many young people who might not have been entranced by Manson alone. Indeed, as Dennis admitted one drug-hazed night in 1976 to journalist Joel Selvin: 'me and Charlie, we founded the Family'. Dennis would also hint, in a late 1970s interview, that he had indulged in homosexual intercourse, perhaps with Manson himself, during a Family orgy.

In his 1969 court battle with his wife Carol, meant to determine how much alimony he should pay her while their divorce was settled, Dennis pleaded poverty. He claimed that he had been so badly affected by 'heavy taxes and expenses' in 1968 that he was reduced to living 'in a small room in a friend's cellar' – presumably the friend was Gregg Jakobson. Describing the room to British reporter Keith Altham in a June 1969 interview, Dennis said: 'I look at it as my mind. There's a piano in there and a bed, and that's all I need. I've tried living in luxury, living in the mountains, living with my family, and my favourite place is that room.'

Other reports from that period told a different story. The British pop weekly *Record Mirror* procured the two most remarkable interviews of Wilson's career – carried out by David Griffiths in December 1968 and Lon Goddard in May or June 1969 – in which he was allowed to speak at length and free from restraint about anything that came into his mind. So taken aback was Griffiths by some of Dennis's revelations that he admitted he had been dubious about committing them to print. Taken together, the two pieces painted a vivid portrait of how Wilson encountered the Manson Family and the extent to which they had become an active part of his life, long after the point at which he is supposed to have cut off contact from them and their guru-cum-leader.

'I went up into the mountains with my houseboy to take a LSD trip,' Dennis said of his initial meeting. 'We met two girls hitch-hiking. One of them was pregnant. We gave them a lift and a purse was left in the car. About a month later, near Malibu, I saw the pregnant girl again, only this time she'd had her baby. I was overjoyed for her, and it was through her that I met all the other girls. I told them about our [the Beach Boys'] involvement with the Maharishi, and they told me they too had a guru, a guy named Charlie who'd recently come out of jail after twelve years. His mother was a hooker, his father was a gangster, he'd drifted into crime.'

This is where he should have been recounting the way in which his house had been over-run and how he had been forced to escape the Manson commune's grasping lifestyle. But, instead, he explained: 'The house was in Pacific Palisades' (so this was the Sunset Boulevard address), 'but there were hordes of people with binoculars, and the police got the idea that it was an orgy and drug scene. We were on that [scene] to start with, but we soon got wise. Too many people – mostly girls – got on to it, and we had to move.'

As a result, he recounted in December 1968, 'I'm now experimenting with tribal living. I live in the woods in California, near Death Valley, with seventeen girls.' (Hence the *Record Mirror*'s shock headline for this piece: 'Dennis Wilson: I Live With 17 Girls'.) 'They're space ladies,' he continued. 'And they'd make a great group. I'm thinking of launching them as the Family Gems.' To avoid the retrospective speculation that this was not connected with Manson, Dennis described the two men's relationship: 'When I met him, I found he had great musical ideas. We're writing together now.' Again, this is months after the supposed date for Manson's audition at Brian Wilson's home studio and the Beach Boys' recording of 'Never Learn Not to Love'.

Six months later, the location had changed, but the personnel were exactly the same. 'Now we have an old movie lot owned by a blind man who lets us run the place,' Dennis declared. This was clearly the Spahn ranch, a Manson location which supposedly post-dated his involvement with Wilson. As Dennis laid out the commune's philosophy, he was unconsciously prefiguring everything that the Manson Family members would come to say about their life on the ranch. And, please note, there is never a moment where Dennis distances himself from his tale, or talks about 'they' and 'he': everything is 'we'.

Here is Dennis's account of Family life: 'We try to make it productive by helping anyone we can who looks like they need it. In the beginning, there were just a few girls living there besides myself and the other guys. We'd make love and discuss things while contributing to one purpose – to help others. The girls would go out on the streets and beg money from those that looked like they could afford it, then bring it back. I'd say [that's Wilson, not Manson, though he could have spoken the same words], go out and don't come back until you have five dollars. Later, I might say, do you love me? They might say yes, and I'd say, then go out and bring back another woman. Soon there were large numbers living there. We'd all combine efforts as if we were all writing a poem. We'd get the good and the bad from everybody until the end product was fantastic. I gave all I had to bring this about. We would make clothes for those who needed them or give the money to charity. We had complete freedom. We might decide to do all our talking by singing to one another for a day. All of us gave what we had and had a good time. There is so much in the power of love.' And this was the commune containing the people who, within three months of this interview, would commit two brutal sets of murders at Manson's instruction.

There is no hint in Wilson's descriptions of the commune that violence might be a necessary or pleasurable tool. In fact, Dennis claimed that his experiences had quelled his natural disposition for expressing himself with his fists. 'I used to go around punching people in the mouth and knocking out teeth,' he admitted. 'Now I am totally apart from violence.' And he entered into a long philosophical rant about love and sainthood and the purpose of life, which reporter Lon Goddard summed up like this: 'The man's personal point in life is to do that which feels good; he is in love with the man standing next to him; he thought he was Christ for a year.'

At times, Wilson sounded like a random nonsense generator of new-age clichés: 'We are the Bible of now … Plant the seeds of love and fullness … Your lungs make a decision every time you breathe.' But there were also hints of the old hedonism, topped with Manson-style carelessness: 'If I want to make love to a bunch of fifteen-year-old girls, I will … Do what makes you feel right.' And at a July 1969 press conference, Dennis feigned total indifference to human suffering: 'I could pass a car wreck and see bodies all torn up and blood all over the place and everything, and I just wouldn't let it bother me … It's all in the mind.'

This takes us back to the June 1969 interview with Keith Altham, to Wilson's most famous quote about his soon-to-be-notorious friend: 'Fear is nothing but awareness. I was only frightened as a child because I didn't understand fear – the dark, being lost, what was under the bed! It came from within. Sometimes the Wizard frightens me – Charlie Manson, who is another friend of mine who says he is God and the Devil! He sings, plays and writes poetry and may be another artist for Brother Records.' ('Another' not because of the young women he wanted to call the Family Gems, but because of a presumably more legitimate singer/guitarist named Medulla for whom he had apparently produced an entire album.)

So Charlie Manson was being considered for Brother Records and, at the end of 1968, he and Dennis were 'writing together now'. (Manson's perspective was that 'he and I worked on several songs together, two of which made it onto an album the Beach Boys recorded'. The second has never been identified, though 'Be with Me' sounds like a possible contender.) Both Manson and fellow Family member Bobby Beausoleil quoted Dennis Wilson's old Sunset Boulevard address as their home when they were arrested in 1969. Manson also claimed that he had been offered a $20,000 recording deal, presumably by Brother. Various associates or passing acquaintances of the Manson tribe ended up in possession of gold disc awards for Beach Boys albums, which had been given to Manson by Dennis, presumably in the spirit of freeing himself from the weight of possessions. Yet we are supposed to believe that the Wilson/Manson relationship ended in the summer of 1968, and that Dennis's only contact with the Family after that point was when he or his family were being threatened. (Mike Love claimed in his 2016 autobiography that Dennis had been scared away from the Family after he saw Manson commit a murder and dispose of the body down a well.)

Dennis's close-knit ties to Manson were overshadowed at the subsequent murder trials by another celebrity acolyte of the singer/songwriter and cult leader: Terry Melcher. The son of singer/actress Doris Day, Melcher produced the early albums by the Byrds and a string of pop hits by Paul Revere & the Raiders, and was the musical/production partner of Bruce Johnston (who claimed to have been involved with the Byrds assignment in a 1965 interview). More pertinently, Melcher was another Los Angeles music luminary who auditioned Charles Manson on several occasions and who subsequently sued any journalist or author who had the effrontery to suggest he had ever had sexual relations with any of Manson's disciples. (Libel lawyers please note: Melcher died in 2004.) Worst of all, for Melcher at least, until shortly before the murders, he had been living at the Cielo Drive address where Sharon Tate and her friends were killed.

There has long been speculation (indeed, it was raised at the trial) that Manson ordered people to be slain at that address as a message to Melcher that he had better give the Wizard a record deal. Likewise, revenge and/or frustration is supposed to have spurred Manson and his followers to make threats against Dennis and his young son, Scott. But what's apparent from Manson's statements immediately after his arrest is that he believed he had already been promised a recording contract, with that $20,000 advance.

Was that with the Beach Boys? There is no evidence to prove that it was. The group and their management closed ranks after the murders and admitted that although they did indeed hold one or more tapes of Manson's music in their vaults, they would never under any circumstances be released. June 1968 emerged as the preferred date when Steve Desper was asked to engineer at least one session, perhaps more, with Manson at Brian Wilson's house. Members of the Family certainly visited the home and the studio, as Brian's wife Marilyn insisted on having the toilets chemically cleaned after one visit to prevent anyone in her household catching sexually transmitted diseases from the visitors.

The most commonly cited date for a Manson tape to have been made – 3 June 1968 – sits in the middle of a long run of Beach Boys sessions staged at the same address. On that day, in fact, Dennis was in residence, and for many years Manson's online followers claimed that the cult leader had played guitar on Wilson's song, 'You Know I Knew'. (Apparently this is not true.) The Beach Boys as a corporate entity would like the world to think that there was just one Manson session before he was banished. But their former manager Nick Grillo once said that there were 'hundreds of hours' of music by Manson and his family in the Brother Records vaults. Moreover, engineer Steve Desper has claimed that he recorded Manson with none of the Beach Boys present (making that 3 June date less likely) and, more importantly, that his sessions with Manson actually took place just a few weeks before the murders, which shifts the date into 1969. If 3 June is carried forward a year, then the Beach Boys (Brian Wilson aside) were actually in Europe, which would tally with Desper's recollection that they were not at the Manson sessions.

There is one last, intriguing strand to this most unfortunate of Beach Boys liaisons, and that involves Manson's trial. Why did the prosecution not require Dennis Wilson to take the stand and give evidence about his involvement with the Family? Why was there not even an official police interview with Dennis, although his then-separated wife Carol was quizzed by detectives? Melcher's explanation, to investigator and author Tom O'Neill, was both stark and savage: apparently the police 'thought [Dennis] was nuts, and by that time he was. He had a hard time separating reality from fantasy, really.' Instead, Wilson maintained a steely silence, although his songwriting partner Gregg Jakobson did provide evidence during the legal proceedings. And there is one more mystery that has yet to be solved: who paid Charles Manson's legal expenses at his murder trial? O'Neill tracked down his defence attorney, Irving Kanarek, who said he was unable to name Manson's benefactor, although 'it would be big news. It might surprise you.'

At which point, heartless scandalmongers might want to suggest some (conveniently deceased) names: Terry Melcher, perhaps? Dennis Wilson? Could assistance of this kind have bought their safety from the remaining Family members after Manson was arrested? Speculation, of course, for which there is no evidence.

The possible connections seem to be endless. In October 1969, someone claiming to be 'Dennis Willson [sic]', once again giving the Sunset Boulevard address, was arrested by police in the hills above Los Angeles, on suspicion of having stolen a handgun from a car. On that day, the real Dennis Wilson was in his brother's recording studio, supervising the taping of his song 'Slip on Through'. Was this suspect a Family member relying on the trusted Palisades address used by Manson and Beausoleil?

More than ten years later, Dennis – who by then had an unfortunate knack of finding himself in perilous situations – claimed to have driven his camper van into a parking site in the California countryside and then been woken at night by people pounding on the door. He asked who they were, was told it was the police, and opened up. As a local paper reported, 'he was pulled from the vehicle and severely beaten by an unidentified police officer. His brutal beating was so severe that he blacked out.' Police claimed that, purely by chance, Wilson had chosen to park up at a campsite near a town where Charles Manson had once been arrested. In fact, the paper claimed, 'Wilson believes that someone there has a grudge against him because he once knew Manson'.

Even more speculative is a claim made by Manson in old age, during one of the countless interviews he gave from his prison cell to journalists and admirers. The 2010 book *Charles Manson Now* had the imprisoned cult leader stating that 'the drummer of the Beach Boys was in my band, the Milkey Way'. More bizarrely, Manson was now claiming that Dennis's death was a revenge attack from one of his followers, after Wilson refused to pay him money that Charlie felt he was owed: 'Do you remember how Dennis Wilson dived down in the water, and somebody grabbed his legs, and he couldn't come up and disappeared under the water?' Utterly ridiculous, of course: one of Wilson's companions on the boat would surely have noticed a stranger emerging from the water immediately after Dennis had vanished. But perhaps it was no more ridiculous than the fact that a member of a pop group with a squeaky-clean reputation and an impeccably polished sound should have been at the heart of one of the United States' most disturbing crime sagas.

Which Side Are You On?

Playing politics with the Beach Boys

The prevailing current was left; until it turned right, and then it rarely if ever looked back.

Folk was the music of protest in the early 1960s, as the American civil rights movement intensified its activities and prompted a violent backlash. By the middle of the decade, the threat of being drafted into the army and sent to fight in Vietnam haunted young American men, several members of the Beach Boys among them. But until the second half of the 1960s, when radical politics and the burgeoning rock music community collided, pop remained a refuge from social strife and political infighting.

Even within the California music scene, the original Beach Boys showed few signs of sparking rebellion. Parents might detest their haircuts, but the group's songs professed nothing more outlandish than swimming, surfing and (of course) remaining true to one's school. (This was a theme that did not have quite the same resonance in those countries, such as Britain, where revealing any attachment to one's educational establishment was inviting ridicule, bullying or worse from one's peers.) So important was school to Californian youth, in fact, that the Beach Boys lent themselves to a 'stay in school' programme, whereby the local school that enjoyed the best attendance record would be rewarded by a Beach Boys concert. Dennis Wilson and Mike Love might lower the tone in an interview by showing off the speeding violations and parking tickets the group had accumulated, but this was dismissed as the natural exuberance of the young rather than a concerted threat to the civilised order.

Proof that the Beach Boys were not secretly fomenting a revolution was provided by a 1966 survey of young male fans in *GQ Scene* magazine. While followers of the Rolling Stones preferred the comparative radicalism of JFK's younger brother, Robert Kennedy, those whose tastes ran to the Beach Boys preferred either the elderly president, Lyndon Johnson, or the Republican Party's defeated candidate from 1964, Barry Goldwater.

Even after the Vietnam conflict impinged on the group when its youngest member, Carl Wilson, came into dispute with his draft board, the Beach Boys continued to toe a respectable political line. They were approached in 1968 to tour US Army bases in South Vietnam and refused only (they said) because the army were insisting that their tour had to last at least seventeen days, which would eat into their orthodox concert schedule. Rock performers joined forces with student radicals at a succession of demonstrations and riots in 1968; it was also when the Beatles recorded 'Revolution' and the Rolling Stones relayed the experiences of a 'Street Fighting Man'. But the Beach Boys had nothing more counter-cultural in their touring routine than an occasional benefit concert at a prison, along with a youth decency rally designed 'to show that not all teenagers support the protest movements popular with some youths today'.

The single event that forced the Beach Boys to confront political realities was not an anti-war march or a Yippie protest or a civil rights demonstration or a rally to demand free speech on campus. It came instead during their summer 1969 tour of Europe. 'We plan to visit Moscow and other Communist countries,' an unnamed member of the group explained. 'We don't care about politics – we just sing to the people.' Moscow remained off limits, but the Beach Boys did become the first American pop or rock band to venture behind the so-called

Iron Curtain into the Communist bloc. (The Beach Boys made another attempt to perform in the Soviet Union a decade later, but the planned festival was abandoned.)

One show was booked just across the border into East Berlin, followed by three concerts in Czechoslovakia. The country had suffered an invasion by Soviet troops the previous year, designed to reassert Communist orthodoxy after a period of relative liberalism. The Czech leader Alexander Dubček had clung on to power until a few weeks before the Beach Boys' arrival, which sparked a frenzied reaction from the country's music-starved youth. When Mike Love dared to dedicate a song to Dubček, for the first time he experienced the performer's power to influence and inspire an audience with political rhetoric. 'They just whistled, stomped, clapped and screamed. It was deafening,' he explained a decade later. 'I guess we represented America and freedom, and consequently the reception was pretty thunderous.' Having discovered that technique of manipulating a crowd, he could never forget it, and although his own preoccupation was meditation rather than political debate, it was Love who became the Beach Boys' most noticeable (and unlikely) voice of political dissent.

That spirit of rebellion was maintained at home, as Love took the mid-'50s R&B hit by the Robins, 'Riot in Cell Block #9', and refashioned it for the era of Kent State and other crimes of the Nixon presidency. The rewritten song – credited entirely to Love, until the composers of the original heard what he'd done – was titled 'Student Demonstration Time'. With his voice miked to sound as if it was crackling from a megaphone, Love spat out a litany of establishment murders and assaults. Some of the rhetoric was clumsy, but no more so than in contemporaneous anthems from John Lennon or Jefferson Airplane. But what distinguished the Beach Boys from their radical-chic peers was the pay-off line: not a call for Marxist revolution, but a recommendation to 'stay away when there's a riot going on'. Nixon must have been quaking in his Hush Puppies.

No matter: it was quite possible to hear the song, respond to the namechecks for Kent State and Jackson State, relish the sonic landscape (scything guitar solos, police sirens, a pack of righteous horn players) and miss the moral entirely. 'Student Demonstration Time' dated faster than anything in the Beach Boys' catalogue – except perhaps their 1974 Christmas single, issued too late for Christmas – and it was bizarrely placed on the *Surf's Up* album after Bruce Johnston's deliciously soporific 'Disney Girls'. But it briefly placed the band among the surging elite of revolutionary rockers, with Mike Love in the vanguard, waving the red flag. The same album proclaimed their environmental ideals, most obviously on the opening cut, 'Don't Go Near the Water'.

For the first half of the 1970s, indeed, it was quite possible to believe that the Beach Boys were political radicals. They were encouraged in this direction by their new (self-styled) career director, Jack Rieley. Not that he was a fan of 'Student Demonstration Time', which, he said, 'had Carl and I blushing with embarrassment and which thoroughly disgusted Dennis'. But it was Rieley who suggested that they could consolidate their appeal to an older audience by taking part in rallies and demonstrations.

On 1 May 1971, the Beach Boys performed at a Potomac Park rally in the nation's capital, as part of a week of anti-war protests. They took their place on the bill alongside Charlie Mingus, Phil Ochs and Linda Ronstadt, and reportedly received a standing ovation. Ten days later, they participated in a benefit concert for the Berrigan Defense Fund at a college hall in Syracuse. Radical priests and brothers Daniel and Philip Berrigan had both been imprisoned as members of the so-called Catonsville Nine after they destroyed draft cards with napalm in 1968 – a symbolic echo of US bombing in Vietnam. Philip was subsequently charged again as a member of another 'conspiracy', known as the Harrisburg Seven. A reporter for the news agency UPI filed a scornful account of the benefit, describing the Beach Boys as 'a singing group popular about ten years ago'.

It wasn't just their attendance at rallies that identified the Beach Boys with the counterculture, but their racial make-up. In 1972, they widened their ranks to include what the Associated Press called two South African 'nonwhites': one 'South African Asian' and one 'colored'. A few months earlier, Bruce Johnston had declared that 'we're the only rock group left that plays white music'. Now the headlines read, 'Beach Boys to Desegregate' and 'Beach Boys Break Color Barrier'. The band briefly toyed with the idea of visiting South Africa at the very start of 1973, but only if they could perform to mixed-race, unsegregated audiences. The apartheid government would also have to overlook its policy of not allowing different races to mix, otherwise the band's new recruits would not have been allowed to socialise with the original members off stage. (New drummer Ricky Fataar was also barred from bringing his wife into his homeland, because she was a white American.)

The Beach Boys launched voter registration drives at their concerts and, as part of Carl's penance for refusing the draft, they played occasional shows at prisons. In Jessup, Maryland, they performed for an almost entirely black prison population. 'It took us a while, until the second show, to find out what they wanted,' Carl said, which was 'more rhythm and body stuff, more sensual stuff'. Their other South African member, Blondie Chaplin, drew the most enthusiastic response for his soul-brother screams on 'Wild Honey', so they performed it again as an encore. By then, Bruce Johnston had left the stage to sit with the prisoners. 'Most of these guys here are black and most of us are white,' he commented after their performances. 'I'm sure they would much rather hear Ike and Tina Turner.'

The band's radical image was not spotless during this period. The journalist Margaret Doris planned to interview them after a November 1972 performance at Ithaca College, but she was so revolted by their onstage demeanour that she left without meeting them. 'When it comes to the point that one of the leading rock groups in the country can stand on a public stage and solicit women,' she wrote, 'no matter how much in jest, for the purpose of sexually abusing them, and when it comes to a point where a crowd of 8,000 people will sit and listen to that and do nothing but laugh, as happened at last Friday's Beach Boys concert, then the time has come for a few choice words to be said.' Feminism and the Beach Boys were never natural bedfellows.

For probably the only time in his life, Mike Love was accused of being a Communist sympathiser after he participated in a May 1974 event entitled An Evening with Salvador Allende. The name was both ironic and commemorative, as the show at Felt Forum in the Madison Square Garden complex marked the overthrow the previous year of the left-wing government of Chile by a military coup sponsored by the CIA. Far from appearing in New York, Allende had been murdered as the troops took control. Right-wing church organisations in the US claimed that the entire concert was a show of Marxist propaganda.

On behalf of the Friends of Chile, Phil Ochs was responsible for organising the event, which sold out only when Bob Dylan announced a day before that he would take part. Sadly, Dylan took the stage in a state of advanced drunkenness, but expectation of his arrival ensured that every other performer was greeted by a disappointed groan when they proved not to be the legend himself. It took showmanship and radical credentials for the likes of Arlo Guthrie to quieten the crowd. After he left the stage, Ochs announced 'an experiment in aesthetics and politics' and introduced 'Mike Love of the Beach Boys' to a mixture of excitement and bewilderment. Love requested audience participation and launched into a brief rendition of that radical pop classic, 'California Girls'. Some people clapped, many joined in, as requested, and others laughed, catcalled or, at the end, booed, though they were drowned out by the applause. 'Alright', Love muttered in a wounded voice as he closed out his three-minute set. (He was clearly in an experimental mood in 1974, however: a couple of months later, he reprised the song on a TV show called *Speakeasy*, supported by jazz-rock guitarist John McLaughlin and flautist Charles Lloyd. Love managed to stay on course throughout the song, despite Lloyd's wildly free-form accompaniment, which seemed to be designed to disguise both the melody and the rhythm.)

That was the last occasion when any of the Beach Boys appeared on a platform that could be described even remotely as left-wing. The US was preparing for a national celebration in 1976 to mark the bicentennial of its independence and Mike Love intended that his band would take centre-stage. 'We are so mid-stream, mid-America,' he declared in June 1975. 'No other group typifies that as much as we do, I think. I want to make a bicentennial album. I want us to sing "America the Beautiful" *a capella*, in four-part harmony.' The Beach Boys, he revealed, had already recorded the 'Battle Hymn of the Republic' (the patriotic song better known outside the US in a version called 'John Brown's Body'). Almost fifty years later, the track was dumped onto the internet as part of a copyright protection release. It revealed why this performance wasn't issued at the time: it was ponderously slow, seemed to last for at least an hour and was utterly lacking in any dynamics, arranging skills or indeed human interest. Love might have claimed in 1975 that its words were 'almost psychedelic', but the aural effect was entirely sedative.

The 1970s began with the Beach Boys supporting radical critics of a Republican president and ended with them raising funds for another Republican candidate for the same position. It was the era when American musicians were commonly lending their names and time to campaigns by Democrat politicians: Governor Jerry Brown of California was running for the 1980 ticket and proudly advertised the support of the Eagles, Linda Ronstadt and the Beach Boys' close musical friends, Chicago. But only country musicians came out for the Republicans.

That changed in November 1979. Bill Nicholson was a member of the campaign team assembled by the CIA Director, George Bush, who wanted to become president. And Nicholson was also a friend of (who else?) Mike Love. He sold the Beach Boy on Bush's merits as a candidate and introduced him to the entire group (not including Dennis Wilson, who might have proved to be a disruptive element in the room, politically or otherwise). The Beach Boys had now completely distanced themselves from the counter-culture values they had embraced just a few years earlier. 'He seemed to us to be a forthright man,' Love said of the candidate, 'a very good man to represent us.' Bush's son Jeb declared that the band and the man 'shared the same concerns about the course of our country'. The following February, the Bush campaign announced that the Beach Boys would be performing a fundraiser before the Florida primary.

Bush was already struggling to attract enthusiasm for his cause, with media and public excitement focused on one of his opponents, Ronald

Reagan. The Beach Boys' show did little to boost morale. The band were well received, but any time that they or the warm-up comedian mentioned Bush, the crowd booed. In any case, a spokesman for the Bush people complained afterwards that most of the audience were 'teenyboppers' who were too young to vote. Bush lost the primary race to Reagan, who later appointed him vice-president, and the Beach Boys were given the role of honorary entertainment chairmen for Bush's celebratory cocktail party after the election. They also took part in Reagan's inauguration ball.

The group's drift away from radical ideals gathered pace that year. They celebrated Christmas and New Year by breaking a United Nations cultural boycott on performing in apartheid South Africa. They were hardly the first pop stars to appear at the Sun City holiday complex in a supposedly independent 'homeland'; they subsequently joined the likes of Frank Sinatra and Queen on a UN blacklist. Al Jardine justified the concerts by claiming that 'you can't really judge a country without going there. I really had to see it myself. I think it's important that we don't turn our backs on anybody.' The money wasn't a contributing factor, of course. 'I don't think the Beach Boys themselves have any political identity,' he concluded.

Events in spring 1983 almost seemed to support him. James Watt, the secretary of the interior, suddenly announced a ban on any rock groups taking part in the July 4th celebrations set for Washington DC. They would attract 'undesirable elements', he insisted. Though he didn't mention them by name, he seemed to be targeting the Beach Boys, who had been invited to stage a giant outdoor event in the city. There was immediate outrage, not least from Watt's boss, President Reagan. Watt quickly had to change his tune: 'The President is a friend of the Beach Boys,' he insisted, 'and I'm sure when I get to meet them, I'll like them.' It transpired that Watt's staff had to explain to him who the Beach Boys were after the furore erupted.

'When I caught the headline on news-stands, I almost fainted, I was so elated,' said Al Jardine, who realised that the promotional value of the fracas was incalculably high. Watt resigned and the Beach Boys lapped up the publicity for years to come. 'Now they are OK with the over-40 crowd,' announced their manager, Tom Hulett. 'They're OK with the corporate people. They're even OK with my mother.' When the Beach Boys duly performed in front of the Washington Monument on 4 July 1984, Mike Love greeted the crowd: 'Hello, all you undesirable elements'. He also claimed to be writing a song called 'Watt's Not Happening'.

'The whole thing has stimulated me,' Love explained as the scandal played out. 'It has given me a chance to use our "celebrity" to express some of my ideas on things other than music – the way we're screwing up the coastline with all the offshore drilling and the way we let millions of pounds of grain rot while people are starving around the world.' His imagination took flight: 'I see this as the start of a whole new movement. There's the Republican Party, and the Democratic Party, and we're going to come out with the California Beach Party. I'd like to do a series of free shows up and down the California coast, have a million people out there having a good time. Then we could take that same spirit and concert across the country.' The idea lived and died in the same interview.

As the 1984 election loomed, Bruce Johnston insisted that 'the Beach Boys have never supported a political candidate and never will'. But they still attended the inauguration ceremonies when the Reagan/Bush ticket was re-elected, having performed in August 1984 for attendees at the Republican National Convention in Dallas. This led to one of the more bizarre Beach Boys misadventures of the decade. The following day, Brian Wilson and two employees of his therapist Eugene Landy were arrested and charged with criminal trespass, having been discovered wandering around the Convention Center without credentials. The employees were also caught with large quantities of prescription drugs, which they were apparently holding for Brian. The trespass charges were soon dropped and the drugs case seems to have been quietly abandoned. The Beach Boys' image survived unscarred.

The group did not always toe the party line. For Mike Love, the quest for peace outweighed the needs of the state machine. The US, he proclaimed in 1985, 'needs an image in the world other than that of a monolithic corporate structure, waging economic war and carrying out military deployments'. He recalled how difficult it had been for the Beach Boys to remain apolitical in the 1960s, when young men 'were being marched by the American military-industrial complex right into the incinerator'. But in the same year, Love made a public donation to the Parents' Music Resource Center, an organisation led by political wives who wanted to prevent provocative albums from falling into the hands of vulnerable kids by introducing a record rating system, like that which regulated movies. Carl Wilson declared that he did not support the donation or the PMRC, and even the more conservative Bruce Johnston admitted: 'I hate to say I disagree with Mike, but yeah, I disagree with Mike. I don't believe in censorship.'

Despite this disagreement, Johnston joined Mike Love on the campaign trail as their man George Bush prepared to succeed Ronald Reagan as president. They even reshaped the lyrics of 'Good Vibrations' for the occasion: 'I'm picking up Bush vibrations / He's the best guy to lead the nation.' Bush duly won the 1988 election and Mike described him as 'such a cool, very straightforward person, a really nice guy'. He insisted that 'the Beach Boys have caring mentalities and hearts', but that financial probity outweighed everything else and 'the Republican Party has been known for being more sound fiscally'. The entire group joined President Bush's Points of Light campaign in 1990 to boost community service, performing 'Kokomo' and (for Bush's wife Barbara) 'Barbara Ann' at the White House. Mike Love was quite prepared to tease the boss: 'We came here to the White House when the former occupants still lived here. And after a benefit we went to a birthday bash at the vice-president's house. We have a videotape of us trying to teach George Bush to sing "Barbara Ann". It was a great moment in history.' He paused, like a practised comedian, and then drawled: 'You don't have to be a rocket scientist to sing this song.'

By the end of the Bush presidency, however, Love had distanced himself from the Republican Party for the first time in more than a decade. The group had travelled to the 1992 Earth Summit in Rio de Janeiro and were profoundly affected by what they heard. They left with what Bruce Johnston called 'a renewed commitment' to 'raising ecological awareness'. This mission chimed with the intent of their new *Summer in Paradise* album, although for once Mike Love wasn't being a PR man. What broke his links with the Republicans was the comment by Vice-President Dan Quayle, who attacked Democratic politician Al Gore for writing a book about the environment. His words, Mike said, 'were just so insulting to anyone and everyone who has an appreciation for nature and life and the environment'. He admired Gore, who was running with Bill Clinton on the Democratic presidential ticket, but he didn't feel able to step right across the political divide. Instead, he described himself as a 'humanist' and said that he would be voting for the Maharishi-inspired Natural Law Party – backed by ex-Beatle George Harrison in the recent British general election.

For another decade or more, Love seems to have remained sceptical about the power of politics and the usefulness of politicians. 'That whole mess of everybody being tied into the military-industrial complex, I think it's pretty tough to overcome that,' he reflected in 2006. 'There are people who want peace [his new solo project at the time was called *Mike Love Not War*] and there are people who absolutely do not want peace because they're making so much money off of war and the machinery of war.' He even seemed to align himself with the conspiracy theory of modern US history: 'Kennedy was elected in the early '60s, but they took care of him, didn't they?', 'they' being the warmongers. For a moment, he was sounding like the radical who had written 'Student Demonstration Time'. But reality intervened. 'I think it's sad, but unfortunately, I don't think rock songs are necessarily going to change an election. However, I do think it's good because it makes people think.'

As they aged and became the remaining standard-bearers of the Beach Boys, it was perhaps not surprising that Bruce Johnston and Mike Love, naturally the most conservative members of the original band, should slip back into the Republicans' cosy embrace. Johnston began to use the word 'liberal' as an all-purpose insult – applying it, for example, to the people around Brian Wilson who were claiming that the troubled musician had been cast down by the rest of the group. Meanwhile, celebrities congregated together like positive and negative particles. And long before he launched his political career, no American celebrity was as self-seeking and publicity hungry as Donald Trump.

Supposedly a Beach Boys fan since the age of eighteen, Trump relished the opportunity to book the band into his hotels and casinos. They signed for a run of shows at the Trump Castle in Atlantic City during July 1995, preceded by an elite show at the Philadelphia Art Museum, where Trump was seen to shut his eyes and sing along to 'In My Room'. He and the equally boosterish Mike Love were a perfect temperamental fit, and backstage at one of the Castle shows, the two men jousted over potential engagements in 1996. Trump demanded that the group should return to Atlantic City on July 4th and offered the band a free weekend to enjoy themselves at his Mar-a-Lago resort in Florida (the group duly performed there in March 1996). Love countered that the group already had a July 4th booking, but agreed that they would perform at Trump's fiftieth birthday party in the Etess Arena, part of his Trump Taj Mahal complex. They opened their 1997 touring schedule at Mar-a-Lago, while Love's spin-off group, the California Beach Band, returned a year later in the wake of Carl Wilson's death. The venue's hospitality was as brazen as its owner: a ticket to the first 1997 show included, as a reviewer noted, 'a poolside pre-show Hawaiian dinner, replete with steaming plates of poi, a man strolling from table to table twisting balloons into outrageous animal shapes and a 10-piece band playing Don Ho fare. There was even an ice sculpture in the shape of an electric guitar.'

Weeks of wrangling over the Beach Boys' future direction (and line-up) were solved in time for the new 'official' group – inevitably led by Mike Love – to return to the road on 4 July 1998 at (where else?) the Trump Marina Casino in Atlantic City. But in the twenty-first century, corporate relations cooled: other venues paid more (and much more punctually), and the Trump name vanished from the group's booking sheets.

When Trump upgraded his status from controversial entrepreneur to even more controversial president, the Beach Boys were among the acts he solicited for his inauguration celebrations. Tipped to perform at the main ball, the Beach Boys headlined the inauguration-eve Black Tie & Boots event run by the Texas State Society. After that, Mike Love was a regular attendee at Trump events, from a convention of the hateful trophy hunting organisation, the Safari Club (a favourite of Trump's eldest son, Donald Jr), to a Trump for President fundraiser in 2020. Both events sparked an angry response from his former bandmates Brian Wilson and Al Jardine, who publicly distanced themselves from endorsing Trump. Not that Mike Love was remotely abashed: come 2024 and another Trump victory, there he was, the solitary original member of the band, leading the Beach Boys at a post-Christmas celebration at Mar-a-Lago – the place where egotism, right-wing politics and celebrity were always destined to meet.

Add Some Music?

The triumph and disaster of *Sunflower*

Only the Beach Boys could achieve this. They signed a 'landmark' recording deal with the most artist-friendly record company in the US. All six active members were writing and singing to the peak of their ability. Their harmonies were arguably the richest of their entire career; likewise their soundscapes, courtesy of a studio engineer pioneering advanced stereo techniques of recording. They emerged with an album that one member of the band still regards as their finest and that all his colleagues agreed was a Beach Boys masterpiece. And yet it became, at that point, the worst selling record they had ever made.

The record in question was *Sunflower*, issued to a chorus of praise that has endured to this day. Bruce Johnston remains the album's in-house publicist. He told me that if *Pet Sounds* was the pinnacle of Brian Wilson's career, then *Sunflower* was the group's equivalent. He has continued to name it as his favourite Beach Boys record ever since. Carl Wilson rated it as 'one of our really good records' and said that it represented his brother Dennis 'at the very height of his creativity'. But the highest that *Sunflower* reached in the *Billboard* charts was number 151, at which point it was being outsold by such albums as Dean Martin's *My Woman, My Woman, My Wife* and a satire on Richard Nixon narrated by Orson Welles. (In the interests of accuracy, the less prestigious *Record World* chart saw *Sunflower* crawl all the way to number sixty-eight, which didn't make it any more of a 'landmark'.)

The Beach Boys' relationship with Capitol Records had begun to corrode in 1966: first, because of the label's lack of enthusiasm for *Pet Sounds*; second, because of a dispute over late or erroneous royalty payments which ran for another three years. The group attempted to strike out on their own with Brother Records the following year, but their contractual obligations entailed that Capitol remained their distributor, so it was a fragile grasp at independence.

Rightly convinced that their recent sales did not reflect the quality of their work, the group negotiated a fresh deal with Mo Ostin, the revered head of Warner-Reprise Records. This stable was renowned for its faith in its artists, valuing their creative ambitions over petty commercial concerns. In turn, Ostin's company was repaid by the loyalty of hip record-buyers, who recognised its logos as trademarks of integrity.

It was in that spirit that the Beach Boys' signing was announced in late January 1970. Ostin's official statement cited Brian Wilson's 'genius' and concluded: 'The Beach Boys are among the major figures in the history of American popular music. Their level of creativity and artistry has risen steadily during the last decade, and we believe that they will continue to influence the shape of contemporary music for years to come.'

If Mo Ostin believed in omens, then there were immediately signs and wonders to make him question the basis of his enthusiasm. 'Genius' or not, Brian Wilson was not the all-powerful master of the Beach Boys' destiny. (Warners must have realised something was up when Brian attended the signing ceremony with his face covered in green paint.) The group were frequently being mentioned in the press, but only because of Dennis Wilson's links to the Manson Family. Warners rushed their initial Beach Boys single into the shops, whereupon the group's frontman, Mike Love, was arrested and then hospitalised while he recovered from the effects of extreme fasting. The band had no sooner submitted 'Add Some Music to Your Day' as their debut 45 than they decided they didn't like the mix and weren't shy of saying so in public. The record proved to be anything but the smash hit that Warners might have been expecting. It was a perfect demonstration of their vocal prowess, a paean to the joy of song on which no fewer than five members of the band were spotlighted individually. But it fell between two audiences, being too complex for the easy listening market and too mellifluous for hip rock fans.

In Britain, the single wasn't even released – and if it had been, it would have been swamped by a re-recording of 'Cottonfields', a folk-song adaptation from their previous album. Neither did the follow-up make it beyond North America: the urgent Dennis Wilson rocker, 'Slip on Through'. Disc jockeys in the States decided that, despite its joyous arrangement and emotional commitment, it didn't sound like the Beach Boys, so they didn't play it. Soon afterwards, an unspoken consensus emerged that even those records that *did* sound like the Beach Boys were too outdated to appeal to a contemporary radio audience, and the group were effectively exiled from widespread US airplay. Capitol Records might have wielded the financial power to insist that the group appeared on station playlists. Warners had critical appeal, but nothing like the same sway over the Top 40 mindset.

Understandably, the company were pernickety when it came to their first Beach Boys album. Carl Wilson handed over an initial running order for *Sunflower* in February 1970, at which point Warners were still feeling optimistic. When 'Add Some Music' flopped, they listened again and heard flaws where there had once been charm. At the same time, Capitol Records hinted to the group that they were also owed a Beach Boys album, so it was Carl's melancholy task to assemble a record that would not damage their reputation nor annoy Warners. By May, the first *Sunflower* had been rejected, but Capitol had also recanted and decided that they didn't need another Beach Boys record after all. Several cuts from that initial *Sunflower* were cast aside, to be replaced by the best material from the Capitol submission. And, almost inevitably, Carl delved back into the *SMiLE* archive to unearth and then update part of the 'Elements' suite, 'Cool, Cool Water'. The retooled *Sunflower* was briefly retitled as well, to match the first Warners single, before the label reconsidered on the grounds that the US public had already elected not to add that particular piece of music to their day.

Sunflower emerged blinking innocently into the sunshine in August 1970 and was greeted by ecstatic reviews, which compared it to *Pet Sounds* and 'Good Vibrations'. But hardly anyone in the US bought it. Even in Britain, where the Beach Boys had still been assured of a hit single with almost every release, the album was a commercial disappointment: their first LP for many years not to reach the Top 20. Once again, the failure was a portent: the years of guaranteed UK hits were over.

In later years, Bruce Johnston attempted to rationalise the failure of *Sunflower*. 'It wasn't really fashionable to sing about staying healthy, getting through college, gaining a benefit from your job and supporting a family. It seemed more important to have hair down to your ankles and experiment with drugs.' But Mike Love's hair on the album cover did almost reach his ankles, Brian Wilson had been open about his family's experimental drug use, and Dennis Wilson's rebel persona had been consolidated by the Manson fracas. There was obviously something other than image that was hampering the Beach Boys' progress.

Perhaps the issue was public perception. People were prepared to accept the lushest of soft-pop confections from new acts such as Bread, the Carpenters and the Poppy Family. But the Beach Boys? Listeners old and new assumed they were an oldies act, in ways that the Beatles and the Rolling Stones clearly weren't. The group seemed too jaded to reach a teenage audience entranced by Bobby Sherman and (very soon) the Osmonds. But they didn't exude enough spirit of rock 'n' roll to excite those who were buying Led Zeppelin or Grand Funk Railroad. For that crossover to occur, it would require a total rebranding exercise – one that their new manager would soon inspire.

Where did that leave *Sunflower*? As an ageless, effortless, peerless collection of musical delights: pop production at its most delicious; harmony singing so richly layered that it was like the cake of everyone's childhood fantasies; songs that were intensely romantic and yet tinged in the realities of adult life. Engineer Steve Desper delivered the purest recorded sound of the Beach Boys' career: listening to *Sunflower* is like bathing in the group's exquisite voices. And the songs matched the sound, from Dennis's most poignant confession of love, 'Forever', to the Carl/Brian collaboration 'Our Sweet Love' and Bruce Johnston's unashamedly sentimental 'Tears in the Morning' (some fans hate it, I know, but I'll defend it to the hilt). Johnston also composed the effervescent, lush 'Deirdre', on which Brian received a co-writing credit. 'I gave him 50 per cent of the song,' Bruce lamented twenty years later, 'but it should have been 5 per cent. He came up with two lines, that was it. When the money arrived, I said, "That's all I get?" He was suggesting lines like, "My friend Bob/He has a job", and I was saying [sighing], "No, Brian". I was kinda disappointed – but maybe I sang flat once, and he was disappointed with me. Who knows?'

Even if Johnston's confections were too candied for your taste, *Sunflower* offered a cornucopia of Beach Boys magic. For sheer sonic brilliance, it's difficult to top 'All I Wanna Do', with its phased, delayed-echo vocals from Mike Love (try this one on headphones) – unless, of course, it's the hypnotic rounds of 'Cool, Cool Water'. Soaring beyond everything else was Brian's 'This Whole World'. It not only boasts one of Carl's most perfect lead vocals, but also offers an utterly unpredictable but never artificial tour through an endless variety of key signatures and harmonic phrases. It might be the finest recording of the entire Beach Boys catalogue, a lifetime's brilliance compressed into 116 seconds.

Other albums may be grittier, more direct, more obviously commercial, more adult, more teenage, more eccentric, more stacked with hits (the list goes on). But *Sunflower* is the place to go if you simply want to luxuriate in the fathomless depth, ecstatic comfort and sheer joy of the Beach Boys' vocal harmonies. For the last time, all six of the band were working in an atmosphere of mutual trust, and the sense of brotherhood beams out of every song. The strength of their collective creativity at this moment is demonstrated by the dozen or so absolute gems that were left over from the sessions. As an assembly of individual writers, the Beach Boys would never be so prolific again, or as sure-footed in the studio. But what does it mean when you fulfil your artistic dreams and your audience rejects you?

Superman Comes to the Supermarket

Profile #7: Jack Rieley

One of the most poignant moments of *Long Promised Road*, the 2021 Brian Wilson documentary, was when Brian was told that the Beach Boys' former manager, Jack Rieley, had died several years earlier. The news 'broke my heart', Brian said – although his own Twitter feed had announced Rieley's passing back in 2015.

Confusion, ambiguity and misinformation dogged Rieley's life. Multiple sources have asserted that Rieley claimed in his late twenties to have won both a Pulitzer Prize for journalism and a Peabody Award for newsworthy radio broadcasting: neither was true. Decades later, Rieley's partner gave an interview about their work together, in which he stated that Rieley had 'produced a number of Prince albums'. Jack hurriedly had to correct this misstatement. This penchant for exaggeration-cum-subterfuge supposedly inspired Brian Wilson to compose an early 1970s song entitled 'Is Jack Rieley Really Superman?' (although this might be as much of a myth as Rieley's awards history; certainly, such a song was never recorded).

Yet there was a real Jack Rieley beyond all these outlandish tales who, during his little more than three years of involvement with the Beach Boys, enabled them to make by far the most dramatic artistic shift in their entire career: from the sirens of surf and sun into an entirely contemporary, fully adult rock band who could boast seven active singer-composers in their midst. His jurisdiction encompassed three albums: *Surf's Up*, *Carl & the Passions – "So Tough"* and *Holland*. And as someone whose passion for the group began during that brief era of musical excellence, I can testify that this slender body of work rivalled anything being recorded at that time, for its sophistication, soulfulness and style.

In other ways, the impact of Jack Rieley on the long arc of the Beach Boys' career appeared to have been minimal. Before he took the managerial reins, they were struggling to assert their independence from the increasingly erratic Brian and were leaning massively on the back catalogue Brian had fashioned. Afterwards, they exchanged creative experimentation for the security of their vintage hits and settled for existence as an oldies-but-goldies act. What few acknowledged, then or since, was that Jack Rieley had pulled them out of a depressing cycle of dwindling attendances and transformed them into an outfit who could fill arenas and even stadiums with ease. Maybe Jack Rieley was Superman, after all.

Amidst all the resume-enhancing and invention, John Frank Rieley III did genuinely work in the fields of communications before meeting the Beach Boys. He was twenty years old in 1963 when he began to serve as a radio news reporter in Ohio. Three years later, he moved to Puerto Rico, which is where he claimed he won the first of his prizes, as a reporter and newscaster. Within twelve months, he was a news producer at station KYW in Philadelphia, from which he was poached by the local branch of the Democratic Party to become a media consultant. Radical politics remained a constant passion in his life. After 9/11, he contributed a series of increasingly left-wing columns for his local paper in Vermont, railing against President Bush's war in Iraq, nuclear power and fascist tendencies in Europe. (His first piece, reacting to the felling of the World Trade Center, was titled 'Colonnaded Ruins Domino' after a phrase from the Beach Boys' song, 'Surf's Up'.)

By his own account, Rieley was a Beach Boys fan from the start, though he remembered being disillusioned by their October 1968 show at the Fillmore East. He recalled that they were 'wearing identical striped shirts, did twenty-five minutes of hits, then left'. (Not strictly true: they were in white suits and performing a set that included some relatively obscure offerings from their new *Friends* album.)

July 1970 found him working for the Los Angeles station KPFK, part of the radical Radio Pacifica network. To his amazement, his request for an interview with the Beach Boys brought Mike Love, Bruce Johnston and Brian Wilson to his station. They were in the final throes of assembling the *Sunflower* album and clearly regarded the late-night chat as more of a 'rap' (in the parlance of the time) than an official PR outing. The three musicians were candid about their reputation: this is when Bruce made his notorious comment that the Beach Boys were now seen as 'surfing Doris Days', while Brian complained that what he called 'the clean American thing' was hampering their image.

They were flattered that Rieley knew and cared about their career, and were prepared to listen when he penned a six-page memorandum detailing how the Beach Boys could salvage their career. His advice seems obvious in retrospect: at the height of the counterculture and the hippie vibe, the Beach Boys should aim themselves at that potentially vast audience, rather than the teenagers who had been their original market. They should update their image; grow their hair; wear street clothes, not suits; extend their live sets to match the gigs being staged by hipper contemporaries; and compose material that reflected the underground zeitgeist of the age, not the surfing milieu of the early 1960s. So receptive were the Beach Boys that they followed Rieley's entire script for their future and appointed him as their manager/adviser. (This was not his first adventure in this direction: back in Puerto Rico, he had managed the Living End, a band featuring future Beach Boys keyboardist Carli Muñoz.)

The first public evidence of their strategic and philosophical shift came when the group appeared at the Big Sur Festival in early October 1970. They were walking in large shoes: the previous year's event had been dominated by Crosby, Stills, Nash & Young, the epitome of the contemporary rock ethos. The Beach Boys were also haunted by their failure to appear at the 1967 Monterey Pop Festival, a mishap that seemed to have punctured any hope they might be accepted as a relevant, modern act. Big Sur proved to be a triumph, however. Robert Hilburn in the *LA Times* highlighted one change, the foot-long red beard now being sported by Mike Love, and listened as the singer spelled out the new, Rieley-inspired credo. 'I look at us as a whole new group starting up again. We do things now that we never did before. Much of the audience will be hearing some of the things for the first time. We're just as much part of the times now as we were in 1963. There's more creativity, more maturity.'

Their 1971 album *Surf's Up* was a proud symbol of the revitalised Beach Boys. Its songs ranged from political anger to environmental concern to spiritual growth. It also boasted a new name among the writing credits: one Jack Rieley, listed as lyricist on songs composed by both Carl and Brian Wilson. Though it wasn't apparent on this record, Rieley was also collaborating with the third brother, Dennis. This, to him, was the key creative axis within the band. The other side, the Love/Jardine/Johnston triad, he regarded as insubstantial and frankly inferior. And, within a year, Bruce Johnston had left the band. The official story was that he wanted more room to compose but, as Brian recounted in 1973, 'he got into a horrible fight with Jack Rieley. Some dispute – and they got into a horrible fight, and the next day Bruce was gone.'

Though he wasn't credited as a performer on the album, Rieley also appeared on *Surf's Up* as the lead vocalist on 'A Day in the Life of a Tree' – tricked into the role by Brian. On 3 December 1971, the Beach Boys celebrated their tenth anniversary at Long Beach Arena. Even the normally recalcitrant Brian was persuaded to take the stage briefly, where he sat behind an organ and introduced Rieley to sing the next song. The manager had no choice but to walk into the spotlight and grope his way through 'Life of a Tree'. Some of the crowd laughed at his hound-like tones, especially when he forgot the words and had to ask the front rows for a prompt. Others hushed them impatiently. Was Brian celebrating their manager's active involvement in their music or satirising it? Nobody was quite sure.

Carl was much clearer about Rieley's impact. The youngest of the Beach Boys, he had played the role of apprentice to his eldest brother without having stamped his own creative mark upon the group. Now, co-writing with Rieley, he composed the three most significant songs of his entire career in little more than eighteen months: 'Long Promised Road', 'Feel Flows' and 'The Trader'. If their lyrical scope was expansive, from the workings of human consciousness to the sorry history of slavery, so was their musical invention. But one of Rieley's strengths was his ability to bend to each Wilson brother's requirements. With Dennis, he explored primal expressions of emotion in keeping with the drummer's deep and troubled soul; with Brian he was more playful, employing tricksy wordplay in such songs as 'You Need a Mess of Help to Stand Alone' and 'Funky Pretty'. He even facilitated the completion of the 'Fairy Tale' that Brian had begun to concoct for the *Holland* album, acting as both narrator and emergency story-weaver.

It was Jack Rieley who encouraged Carl to invite two young South African musicians to join the band, following through with a plan – sadly never fulfilled – that would have seen the Beach Boys visiting the apartheid-afflicted land as ambassadors of social change. Rieley's most enduring legacy, however, was persuading the entire group to relocate to Holland in 1972. (Only later did it emerge that during a Beach Boys European tour that year, Rieley had fallen in love with a young man who became his partner.) If his plan had stuck (and maybe if the resulting *Holland* album had sold better), both the band and their adviser would have made the move permanent, with unforeseeable consequences for their future.

When the Beach Boys decided that they were still Californians at heart, Rieley remained behind. For a while, he attempted to maintain his guiding role in their career but, removed from the heart of the band's eternal conflicts and machinations, his influence dwindled and then died. By then, even the newest members of the band were starting to have misgivings about his managerial techniques. As drummer Ricky Fataar recalled, Rieley 'was a divide-and-conquer kind of guy, playing us all off against each other … he was very much part of manipulating all the different people, starting stories and telling tales. Eventually all of that came to light, and he had to be let go.' One of the consequences of that atmosphere was what Fataar called 'a moving, shifting, liquid situation. One never quite knew where one stood, who was in whose camp and who wasn't talking to whom. It was all, "I'm not coming down to the studio because so-and-so is there".'

This sounds like a damning verdict on Rieley's methods – unless dividing the band was his intention from the start. In 1996, after years of silence on the subject of the Beach Boys, Jack was persuaded to answer questions on the online *Pet Sounds* message board. Over a period of almost a month, he penned what was effectively a manifesto for managing the Beach Boys, or at least that half of the Beach Boys that he viewed as important. His reminiscences were explosive, outspoken, often exaggerated and sometimes downright wrong. But he had the advantage over his detractors of having been in the room and having stirred up the band's perpetual hornet's nest.

Here's his account of the warring factions: 'Brian Wilson, Dennis Wilson and Carl Wilson represented the creative side; the appeal to musical beauty and romance and funk and get down and freakz/fanz; Love, Jardine and Johnston represented unbridled commercialism and power.' He said he 'encouraged the Wilsons to act as a unit', which meant that after Johnston's departure, they could win any show of hands in band meetings. In return, he claimed that private detectives were employed by the Beach Boys' pre-existing advisers to 'follow my car, check up on my friends and dig into my private life. I felt violated. The joy of music was being eclipsed by stench from the swine.'

Other claims from Rieley: it was his decision to make 'Surf's Up' the focus of the first album under his direction. (Note, though, that in a 1971 interview, he said that 'Surf's Up' was his least favourite track on the album, because it was pretentious.) He suggested that he was responsible for the newly written lyrics at the end of the song (a view with which Van Dyke Parks did not agree). He insisted that 'Feel Flows', arguably the highlight of Carl Wilson's composing career, was created 'under seriously powdered conditions' and that his lyrics had been designed to represent the experience of orgasm (as testified, he said, by multiple women). He said that he originally intended *Surf's Up* to be split into two sides, one with Wilson/Rieley songs, the other bearing the material by the lesser half of the band. And he told a story of Mike Love confronting him and shouting: 'I AM the Beach Boys!'

As Rieley saw it, 'upon my departure, the Wilsons went back to disarray. Carl was going through terrible domestic problems. Dennis was having a divorce. Brian adjusted poorly back to life in Bel Air after his highly creative, physically positive – he rode a bicycle daily and lost weight – stay in the Netherlands. Love and Jardine saw the hole in their armour and rammed through to renewed supremacy. Their musical/ideological vision of the Beach Boys was totally different from that represented during my period there. Love's bitter resentment of Brian's musical genius and his newly re-won power meant that it was back to shuck and jive. Within a year the Beach Boys had returned to the state they were in before I came along.'

All of this is contestable, of course, but there are some truths that need to be told. Certainly, Carl Wilson never found as adventurous a co-writer as Jack Rieley in his subsequent career. By contrast, Dennis maintained constant creativity until the end of the 1970s. Brian reverted from composing adult rock songs to concocting distorted mirrors of the teenage anthems he had fashioned with ease in the early 1960s. Most importantly, the Beach Boys completely abandoned the political, environmental and poetic route that they had followed under Rieley. They made two further attempts at 'adult' LPs, with the *L.A. (Light Album)* and the eponymous project with Steve Levine that was released in 1985. But both were 'adult contemporary' rather than 'grown-up', and neither of them touched on the progressive, radical themes they'd tackled happily enough in the early 1970s.

What of Jack Rieley, meanwhile? He stayed in the Netherlands, where he and his friend Machiel Botman composed and recorded a 1974 album which continued the themes explored on *Surf's Up* and *Holland*. Titled *Western Justice (Excerpts from a Diary)*, the record and its accompanying text portrayed a scenario in which Europe and North America were suffering famine and climate catastrophe. Meanwhile, the so-called Third World treated the old powerhouses with the same disdain that the West had once reserved for its former colonies. Rieley composed the bulk of the album, which opened with the majestic 'America' – rich and exploratory, as if Randy Newman and Dennis Wilson had been merged into a single creative soul. The rest of the album touched on musical themes that Rieley had learned from the Beach Boys: vocal rounds and tags, layering of harmonies, even Brian's startling collisions of naïvety and adult insight. *Western Justice* wasn't as accessible as the Beach Boys records on which Rieley collaborated. But, fifty years on, it represents the missing link between *Holland* and *Pacific Ocean Blue*, leading anyone who loved those records to wonder what might have happened if Rieley had opted for California rather than Europe after the Dutch adventure was over.

Instead, he relocated to Berlin, where he dabbled with local artists. Not that his creative urges ended there. He collaborated in the 1990s with his close friend, the rap/rock performer Jaye Muller, and then pulled off his most unlikely coup when he and Muller were awarded the patent in 1997 for an electronic invention that would transfer fax and phone messages from one network to another. It would have allowed people to receive the information from a fax without being present alongside their fax machines. Sadly, rapid advances in digital communications rendered this invention out-of-date almost as soon as the patent had been registered.

This leaves music as Jack Rieley's most enduring legacy: some of the most adventurous songs in the Beach Boys' entire catalogue, touching lyrical themes and musical styles that they might never have approached under any other circumstances. Plus, the memory of a tantalisingly brief golden age in their career and the fantasy of what might have been if the progressive ethos of 1971–1973 could have been extended into an imaginary future. Perhaps 1974 would have been the year of Wilson–Rieley: the trio of Carl, Dennis and Jack free to pursue songwriting as an adult artform, while the eternal teenagers of the Beach Boys (with or without their help) continued to frolic in the surf.

Make it Good

The Beach Boys grow up and grow beards

It might have been planned to mark the transition of eras. In November 1970, Brian Wilson was persuaded to join the Beach Boys for a run of shows at the Whisky a Go Go on Sunset Boulevard. He made it through both houses on the first night, but during the early show on the second day, he ran off stage in panic, his hands grinding into his ears as if he was trying to exorcise demons. He complained of extreme ear pain and dizziness, and was taken to hospital, where he remained for several days, 'resting but still very uncomfortable'. No doubt his discomfort was real enough, but Brian was also making a symbolic break from the Beach Boys.

The support act at those shows was a South African band named Flame, comprising three brothers from the Fataar family, plus singer/guitarist Blondie Chaplin. They had recently recorded their first American album, after a run of R&B releases in their native land. It was titled *Flame*, obviously enough, produced by Carl Wilson and released on the Beach Boys' own label, Brother Records. 'We actually recorded that album at Brian Wilson's house, which was interesting,' drummer Ricky Fataar told me. 'That was rather a fallow period for Brian. He'd wander in every now and then in his bathrobe and have a listen, then wander off again. He wasn't doing much.'

For Al Jardine, signing Flame was a declaration that the Beach Boys were now hipper than they seemed. 'We're trying to rub some of the plastic off our image. The Flame [sic] had been around in London for a while and both the Beatles and the Rolling Stones were interested in recording them, but they didn't feel they were ready. By the time we got to them, they were.' Not that *Flame* was a particularly distinctive record: it resembled a slightly more soulful pastiche of Badfinger, a band with its own superstar connection as part of the Beatles' stable. But Flame's 'See the Light' single did flirt with the US Hot 100 chart, which is more than recent Beach Boys 45s had achieved.

Under the guidance of Jack Rieley, the Beach Boys were endeavouring to reposition themselves as a contemporary rock band rather than a vintage pop group ('vintage' being a status awarded all too quickly in the 1960s). They were now touring with a vibrant horn section – hardly hip, as individually they were rooted in the post-war big band and jazz scene, but at least they widened the Beach Boys' palette. More effective as a marketing tool was an April 1971 show at Bill Graham's Fillmore East theatre in New York. Top of the bill were the Grateful Dead, who surprised and then thrilled their audience by inviting the Beach Boys out to jam. It was a brief but triumphant performance, seen by only a few thousand people, but the reverberations spread through the rock community and magically seemed to transform the Beach Boys' image. As Bruce Johnston explained a couple of months later, 'recently people have rediscovered us. In New York, they've been calling us Beach. Just Beach, like a hip term.' Years later, band members would deride this potential name change as a ridiculous suggestion by Jack Rieley. It has since been claimed that Brian Wilson drew up paperwork to make the transformation official. He presented it to the rest of the band, who set it aside and waited for Brian to forget about it, which he soon did.

Also in the air at the same time: the idea that George Harrison – fresh from his global success with *All Things Must Pass* – would produce a Beach Boys album; or that he might tour with them; or that Keith Moon, long a devotee of the Beach Boys, would quit the Who to replace the recently injured Dennis Wilson. None of it was remotely true, but all this speculation evidenced the band's sudden rise in prestige during 1971.

That was consolidated in August by the release of the Beach Boys album that, more than any other, won universal critical acclaim: *Surf's Up*. It was the perfect record at the optimum time, bridging the immaculate harmonies of their earlier albums with an overtly environmental theme. Naming the record after a legendary lost song from the *SMiLE* project helped, of course: Mike Love celebrated the moment by naming 'Surf's Up' as 'the most important piece of music we've done'. His own 'Student Demonstration Time', for all its political naïvety, placed the Beach Boys on the ideologically correct side of the culture vs counterculture debate. Carl Wilson blossomed under the encouragement of Jack Rieley, creating perhaps the richest music of his entire career, 'Long Promised Road' and 'Feel Flows'. 'Carl is the heavy on this album,' Rieley asserted. 'His two songs are introspective wanderings that pulsate.' Smoking the best stuff probably helped make more sense of that description.

Bruce Johnston contributed his most popular Beach Boys song, the winsome 'Disney Girls (1957)' – a rejection of the hippie movement, although nobody realised that at the time. But it was Brian Wilson whose songs proved to be the most enduring and the most subtle. 'Surf's Up' was almost five years old, of course, but 'Til I Die', a stark, heartbreaking evocation of existential doubt, was new and just as beautiful. (Someone in the band encouraged Brian to make the lyrics more positive; fortunately, he overruled them.) 'A Day in the Life of a Tree' took longer to settle – it was maybe twenty years before I realised that it was a masterpiece, a fact that was perhaps disguised by Jack Rieley's mysteriously awkward lead vocal. All that was missing from an otherwise superlative collection was any contribution from Dennis Wilson. Again, only the passage of time offered an explanation. He had submitted three songs for *Surf's Up* ('Barnyard Blues', '4th of July' and the song he intended as the album's finale, 'Wouldn't It Be Nice to Live Again'), but fell out with Carl about the sequencing. Displaying the same impetuosity that impelled him around this time to put his fist through a plate of glass, he declared that if he didn't get his way, he would take his songs back – and so *Surf's Up* appeared without them. Ultimately, Dennis was the loser.

The album proved to be their best seller since 1967, though it's uncertain that its success was heightened by a Warner Brothers marketing stunt. Remember that Beach rumour? 'It is Reprise–Brother Records' feeling that – by their name alone – the Beach Boys are doomed in today's record market,' the ad copy declared. 'So there's a mighty big PR job to do ... to convince the Northern Hemisphere that the Beach Boys can again be called your contemporaries.' Their solution? Readers should mail in a copy of the *Surfin' Safari* album from 1962, plus a dollar, and they would receive *Surf's Up* in return. Like Warners' equally outspoken ads for artists such as Van Dyke Parks and Joni Mitchell in the late 1960s, the promo campaign seemed more likely to insult the artist than sell records.

This was the moment for the Beach Boys to strike: to create something else that would consolidate the progress of *Surf's Up* and establish them as front-runners in the 1970s rock revolution. It didn't work out that way. In February 1972, the band held a press conference in London to make two announcements. The first was that two members of Flame, Ricky Fataar and Blondie Chaplin, had become fully-fledged Beach Boys. 'We were joining a band that had been together for a decade,' Fataar explained to me. 'We were treated fairly on a business level. But family is family – it's blood, you know. In a sense, it was inevitable that we would always be on the outside. While we were in the band, though, we were always welcomed and made to feel like we were part of what was going on.' The other declaration, made by Carl, was that he was finally completing work on the long-delayed *SMiLE* album – and maybe it would be released in a couple of months alongside the band's new record.

Carl and the Passions – "So Tough" (a Wilson family in-joke, lost on the public) was duly released in May 1972. But in place of *SMiLE*, it was packaged (in the US) with a reissue of *Pet Sounds*. In Britain and Europe, it was left to stand alone. The reviews were overwhelmingly negative; in retrospect, the band would have done better to leak the eight-song package onto the black market as a bootleg, where it would at least have enjoyed some kudos. It was divided equally into four parts:

lavishly (over-)orchestrated ballads from Dennis; anonymous blues-rock from the Flame refugees; spiritual material from the Love/Jardine TM axis; and two hard-edged rock tunes composed by Brian. 'Marcella' was the obvious hit, so of course the Beach Boys released 'You Need a Mess of Help to Stand Alone' first. This rough-hewed country-rock tune would have fitted perfectly onto an album by The Band, but it was never a commercial option for the Beach Boys (or even for Beach). All the momentum propelled by *Surf's Up* was lost in an instant. Also vanished was Bruce Johnston, exiled from the band without any explanations.

There was another album from the Beach Boys camp a few weeks later, though its commercial impact was minimal. During the 1960s, Brian had produced a run of singles by the Honeys: his wife Marilyn, her sister Diane and their cousin Ginger. Now the Honeys had become Spring (or, outside North America, American Spring). A young Brian Wilson protégé named David Sandler acted as producer for their debut album, although Brian was also credited, despite the fact his main contribution was arrangements. It was a low-key, often deliciously naïve album; much of it forgettable, though rarely less than pleasant. Its obvious highlights were a remake of the Beach Boys' 'This Whole World', with extra segments and a delightfully oblique instrumental pay-off, and 'Sweet Mountain', a hypnotic Wilson/Sandler creation on which Brian could be heard intoning a maudlin refrain.

Before that was released, the Beach Boys made for Amsterdam, where Jack Rieley had fallen in love and the band hoped to find fresh impetus away from their homes. 'It was the first occasion that people took a studio somewhere else and recorded in a different environment,' Fataar recalled. 'It was a little chaotic. While we were recording, we could only use certain parts of the mixing desk, because it was actually being built as we were recording. There always seemed to be a pair of legs sticking out under the console, wiring something up in the middle of a take.'

Much of the record was completed later in California, but *Holland* was retained as its title. Early in the sessions, Mike Love was promising that he would soon record 'a large, classical work' under the name 'Atlantis Rising'. That didn't feature on *Holland*, but the Love/Jardine wing of the band excelled themselves with 'California Saga', a three-song suite that moved from an evocation of 'Big Sur' (where Al would relocate several years later) to a setting of a Robinson Jeffers poem named 'The Beaks of Eagles', climaxing with an updated anthem in the classic Beach Boys style, named simply 'California'. Fataar and Chaplin offered a beautiful, soulful ballad named 'Leaving This Town', which found its nirvana on the road when keyboardist Carli Muñoz would weave ecstatic, magical solos. (Muñoz recalled that the song 'felt different every time we played it, each time taking it to the next blissful level'.) Carl Wilson collaborated with Rieley on a two-part evocation of slavery, 'The Trader', and took the lead on two aching Dennis Wilson ballads. Brian emerged briefly to guide the band through the quirky rounds and wordplay of 'Funky Pretty', although most of his Dutch time was given over to the creation of a strange children's 'Fairy Tale'. He left it unfinished, passing Jack Rieley the responsibility of completing and narrating the story, which was added to the album as a bonus single. (Inadvertently, Brian came up with the sound of the *South Park* cartoon character, Cartman, nearly thirty years too early, when he was voicing the role of the mysterious Pied Piper.)

Warners listened to the final running order and said that they couldn't hear a single – although I could have picked out 'California' for them if they'd asked. Not for the last time, they demanded more from Brian. A convoluted process of co-writing and retrieving and rewriting resulted in 'Sail on Sailor', with five men credited as composers, among them the emotive names of Brian Wilson and Van Dyke Parks. Blondie Chaplin delivered the vocal with righteous fervour, ensuring his place in Beach Boys history. (An earlier, alternative set of lyrics for the song was unveiled on the debut album by the supergroup KGB, written and sung by Ray Kennedy. A sample line that the Beach Boys rejected: 'Lord, it's frightening when you're coked out'. Just a little too close to the bone, perhaps.)

Holland was released just after New Year 1973 and Richard Williams's review in *Melody Maker* was ecstatic, helping to drive the album into the UK Top 20. The *Los Angeles Times* was equally effusive, but sadly their review didn't appear until almost three months after the album. Otherwise, the North American press was almost universally dismissive of a set that I would still rate among my favourite records by any artist. The *Montreal Star* went to town: *Holland* was 'gibberish', 'pretentious', 'humourless' and, for good measure, exhibited signs of 'Neo-Nazism'. The underground *LA Free Press* focused on 'Fairy Tale' which, they claimed, 'proves conclusively that Brian Wilson is really crazy'.

On stage, the Beach Boys were now arguably at some kind of peak, able to span their entire history with artistic care (for the 1966–73 material) and affectionate nostalgia (for the real oldies). To prove the point, they put together an *In Concert* album: a single disc, assembled in January 1973. 'I heard it,' Brian Wilson revealed, 'and said, "Don't release that, don't!" And they said, "We're gonna!" I just didn't think it was that good. But they really like it.' Perhaps inevitably, Warners shared Brian's opinion. Carl Wilson supervised the taping of another thirteen shows later in the year and assembled a double-album – again titled *In Concert* – that Warners agreed to release. Though I'm sure it was mildly sweetened in the studio, it sounded authentically live – rugged and righteous in perfect combination. Its only flaw was an omission: the front cover portrayed just a solitary Beach Boy, Dennis, whose voice was impossible to locate on the album.

After that, everything Carl and Dennis had imagined for the band slowly slipped away. Mike Love might proclaim, as he did in September 1973, 'we do concept albums now. We try to make certain all our songs have meaning.' But at the same time, Brian was obsessed with the utterly ridiculous chant, 'Ding Dang', and almost the entire band aside from Dennis seemed to have stopped writing. Blondie Chaplin left at the end of 1973: 'somehow he ended up having a fight with Mike Love's brother, Steve, and suddenly he wasn't there anymore', as Ricky Fataar explained. He added: 'I stayed on for another six months, but everything was so dislocated and floundering by that time – that's why I took up the offer to go and play with Joe Walsh.'

What else changed? Jack Rieley was gone; Brian entered a period of profound mental instability; Carl seemed to forget how to compose;

most importantly, perhaps, in 1974 Capitol issued an oldies album entitled *Endless Summer*, and the Beach Boys' efforts to outrun their past ended in failure. In truth, they had already stopped trying. There was just one significant recording in their adult style during 1973: a Chicago single, 'Wishing You Were Here', on which Carl, Dennis and Al Jardine were persuaded to add harmonies. It prefigured a long history of touring adventures between the two bands, but it would only be in the final years of his life that Carl decided to collaborate more intensively with Chicago member Robert Lamm – and, by then, any progressive urge in either man had gone. During the 1973–75 period, various Beach Boys tried to suggest that the band had an album almost ready for release, but they were lying. Dennis had completed several songs, but tunes from the other guys amounted to nothing more than fragments or backing tracks. When they did finally return to the studio, it was as if the tide that carried them from *Surf's Up* to *Holland* had been a strange mirage – one that they could never quite remember how to recognise again.

Let Us Go on This Way

Endlessly reliving the Beach Boys' past

The release of Capitol's *Endless Summer* compilation in 1974 pigeonholed the Beach Boys as the standard-bearers of summer, surf and nostalgia. At the precise moment their collective songwriting energies had effectively expired, it refocused public attention on their early 1960s hits. It also suffocated the band's attempts to escape their past – a weight that would hang over them for decades to come.

'When I first heard that Capitol was going to put out an album of old songs, I wasn't that crazy about it,' Mike Love admitted. 'Then I got the idea to make it an anthology of sorts, but Warners wouldn't co-operate', ensuring that nothing on the collection could post-date 1966. 'So Capitol did the best they could and I think it worked out pretty good' – which was an understatement for the group's first US number one album since *Beach Boys Concert* a decade earlier.

Mike's most profound contribution to the release was its title, borrowed from Bruce Brown's archetypal surfing documentary film. (He presumably didn't have a veto over the artwork, which employed unrecognisable caricatures of the mid-'70s Beach Boys, rather than anything more nostalgic.) In due course, he would form a Beach Boys offshoot called the Endless Summer Beach Band; in the late 1980s, *Endless Summer* also gave its name to a Beach Boys TV series, enlivened by its 'campfire' sequences of the band reminiscing with the aid of acoustic guitars.

Endless Summer became a brand, then, which revitalised the Beach Boys' status as a touring band. But it was also a curse. Here, in their own words, are the individual Beach Boys' responses to being typecast as the eternal denizens of a California beach …

> 'The surfing sound has been dead for three-and-a-half-years. It's like telling the same joke over and over again.' (Bruce Johnston, August 1968)
>
> 'We are a bit fed up with our own act of going out there, standing and singing all our hits, then walking off again.' (Mike Love, December 1969)
>
> 'If people in the audience yell for a particular song, we'll do it. But we don't do any of the really early stuff unless somebody wants us to do it.' (Carl Wilson, March 1971)
>
> 'We do the old stuff as encores. If that would have to be the main part of our show, I don't think we'd go on the road anymore. We know where that's at. That's dying.' (Bruce Johnston, May 1971)
>
> 'If we played just our old hits, then we wouldn't be popular on campuses. We would have to just play in Las Vegas like some of the older groups do.' (Bruce Johnston, March 1972)
>
> 'I enjoy doing the old ones. But if we were only to do old things, we'd get tired.' (Mike Love, September 1973)
>
> 'You want us to progress, but how can we when all you want to hear is the old stuff?' (Mike Love on stage in Ottawa, June 1974)
>
> 'Our only problem is the segment of our fans that only wants to hear our early songs in exclusion of anything else.' (Mike Love, December 1974)
>
> 'We're nostalgia now. We kinda have a thing about the past and so do our fans.' (Carl Wilson, March 1975)

'We could easily have wound up an oldies but goodies act.' (Mike Love, March 1975)

'When you think of the Beach Boys, you think of "California Girls", those type of records, those type of ideas. It's summertime now and I think we'd be fools to neglect that aspect. I mean, they're gold, they're sheer gold, and these are the kinds of things we should stick with.' (Brian Wilson, June 1976)

'We've stopped resisting our past. The people enjoy our old stuff, and we enjoy doing it.' (Carl Wilson, January 1977)

'What worried us the most about touring was the fear of eventually discovering that we were becoming a kind of nostalgia band.' (Carl Wilson, December 1980)

'It ends up being a show of meat and potatoes, just the hits, and the audiences love it. But I think there's a danger of really going to sleep on your talent. It almost gets down to going through the motions.' (Carl Wilson, July 1981)

'I disagree with what Carl says about the band. I think that people that come to see the Beach Boys want to hear our old stuff.' (Mike Love, September 1981)

'The audiences have locked us into a time warp. We have become the victims of our own success.' (Bruce Johnston, October 1981)

'We have to keep playing. There's no way out of it – it's like a freight train.' (Al Jardine, December 1981)

'It gets wearisome sometimes. I suppose it's kind of like the boxer who has a twenty-year career, but I don't have any brain damage yet.' (Al Jardine, May 1984)

'In order to have old music, we'd better make some new music. I don't want to be an equivalent of the actor who's been on Broadway, and he can only go out on a road show to do something he did eighteen years ago. We have another chance at making new music that will become old and go on our pile of hits. What's the point to being one of the most successful re-runs in show business?' (Bruce Johnston, May 1984)

'I guess we feel semi-boxed in. The artist always wants to do something a certain way, but that's not what the audience wants to hear. We've got some songs that are art treasures, but if we want to play something like "Caroline, No" or "This Whole World", we have to sneak them in sideways, play them between big hits. There's nothing worse than trying to play something very fragile and seeing people go to the bathroom.' (Bruce Johnston, January 1989)

'I don't want the Beach Boys to be the futile, endless road show of *The King and I*, or *I Love Lucy* re-runs. It's records that matter. There's no point touring without new records. We've got to be better than that.' (Bruce Johnston, May 1989)

'We can be a life raft for people who don't understand Guns N' Roses or are too young for Glenn Miller.' (Al Jardine, May 1989)

'We try to do all our Top 10 hits. We won't play obscure cuts.' (Mike Love, July 1989)

'I take the money, but somewhere along the way, the Beach Boys lost the will to make satisfying records and drifted into a prosperous funk. When we were young, the idea of an oldies band was, like, Squaresville! We've become that oldies band.' (Bruce Johnston, June 1993)

'I would like to do like Rocky Marciano did and retire undefeated. I'd like to do a planned series of farewell concerts that conclude our touring way of life and maybe fall back to Hawaii and have people come and see us. That would be a way to go out. Maybe it would take over the next two years to do that – go to London, have Elton John and Paul McCartney

> help us retire, and tell the folks that it will be the last time you'll hear "Good Vibrations" in England. That gives it an element of drama, of focus, of finality. I think people would bring their kids. It would be more special that way than just atrophying.' (Mike Love, November 1993)

Mike Love's dream of something 'special', of sparking that 'element of drama, of focus, of finality' – well, that gradually slipped away. More than thirty years later, Love and Bruce Johnston were still on the road with the Beach Boys, keeping alive those summer dreams of sun, surf, hot rods and girls. And people still flock to see them, all over the world. This is the global entertainment brand that Love has fashioned, almost single-handedly, out of the songs that his cousin composed. It is his natural milieu – and it has made him exceedingly rich. But it's hard not to wonder whether, in the reaches of the night, he is not occasionally troubled by the paths he might have followed: the ones that could have allowed the Beach Boys to continue as a creative force, rather than as a vehicle for lucrative but ultimately deadening repetition.

They Say Brian is Back

The (supposed) rebirth of Brian Wilson

Nobody ever suggested that Brian Wilson wasn't eccentric. In 1971, a year when respectable newspapers happily described him as a 'mad genius' or 'the mad scientist' of rock 'n' roll, he created some of the most beautiful music of his life. At the same time, his behaviour was so unorthodox that it was often impossible for those around him to decide whether he was insane, disturbed, mischievously playful or some surreal combination of all three.

After a lengthy session at his home studio for the *Surf's Up* album, Brian drove into the centre of Los Angeles to meet his wife. But he was tired, so he pulled up at a public park, lay down on a bench and went to sleep for a couple of hours. When he woke up, he got back in his car to look for a telephone so he could explain to Marilyn what had happened. Instead, he fell asleep at the wheel and ran into two other cars. Luckily no one was injured, but Brian was shaken up by the collision. He did the only thing he could imagine that would settle his nerves: he went back behind the wheel and set off on a random drive across the city. As the Beach Boys' adviser Jack Rieley said, 'That's Brian'. Or, as Mike Love explained: 'He's a very spacy person, and if he just drives down the road, he's liable to crash because he's off into something. He's just that kind of mind.'

Rieley had another story. He recounted how he had received an emergency phone call from Marilyn, saying that she desperately needed his help with Brian. He arrived to find Wilson in his back garden, no doubt covered in dirt, standing alongside a large hole he had just dug, the size of a grave. 'I'm pissed off!', Brian shouted when he saw Rieley. 'I've been digging for hours, trying to get it just right. But you know what? Fucking Mare [Marilyn] refuses to cover me up with dirt when I get in!' Rieley said that Brian looked genuinely furious, while he was horror-struck by the implications of what his client was saying. Then Brian dissolved into hysterical laughter, Rieley heard giggling from Marilyn behind him and realised that this was an elaborate set-up for the ultimate Brian Wilson practical joke.

When Brian was unreliable, or obtuse, or downright obstructive, or didn't react the way that a normal human might, it was impossible to tell whether he was insane or not. But the possibility was out there. And between 1973 and 1975, evidence for the prosecution began to mount.

Sometimes it came from within, as when Mike Love described his cousin as 'the Howard Hughes of music. He's a recluse.' And sane was never the first word employed when Hughes was under the microscope. Carl rushed to his brother's defence, suggesting that because he kept being called mad, 'he figured, "Well, I'll just be funny, put them on". He's aware of a lot of jive. He's just not ready to be part of it.' Was it jive when Brian went on the radio after his father died and complained that Carl wouldn't work with him in the studio? 'He won't let me,' he said. 'If I walk in the studio, he raps, you know? He just wants to work alone.' To which his sister-in-law Diane Rovell scolded him: 'Brian, you know that's not true! You work with Carl.' As far as Mike was concerned, the issue was that Brian 'only wants to be left alone'.

Of course, there was madness and madness. In April 1974, Mike Love and Dennis Wilson both took their clothes off and streaked across the stage in the middle of a Beach Boys show. Whereas Brian Wilson … well, he went with Todd Rundgren to watch jazz guitarist Larry Coryell support Leo Sayer at the Troubadour. Brian, who was wearing a white dressing gown, leaped onto the stage during one of Coryell's long, complex solos and began to sing the Gene Vincent rock 'n' roll classic, 'Be-Bop-A-Lula'. Was he improvising, performing a subtle act of musical criticism or losing his mind? Opinion leaned towards the last option – both then and when he wore the same bathrobe a few months later to Keith Moon's birthday party at the Beverly Wilshire hotel.

Session drummer Hal Blaine was in the studio when Brian was invited to produce a track for Bruce Johnston and Terry Melcher. 'It was more therapeutic than creative,' he recalled, 'just to see how Brian would react.' As Blaine told it, 'he acted strange and kept shaking his head, as if a nervous tick had overtaken him … He kept looking around the room at other people. They were all old friends, but he was squinting at them as if they were strangers. He got up after a few minutes and walked out. We were all speechless. Brian had really hit bottom.'

This was also the era when Brian's musical 'feels' mutated from moments of inspiration into manic forms of obsession. He became utterly fixated on particular riffs and songs, which he would churn out at the piano for hours at a time. Roger McGuinn recalled a drunken late-night jam at his house where the two men concocted a throwaway ditty entitled 'Ding Dang': one endlessly repeated riff, a chant and a couple of lines of lyrics. Eventually, McGuinn crashed in his room. He woke in the morning to discover that Wilson was still hammering away at 'Ding Dang', eight hours later. Even more persistent was the American folk song 'Shortnin' Bread', which Brian forced everyone around him to sing, and sing again, and keep singing, until they could take it no longer and left the room. Even recording it with the Beach Boys (more than once) didn't scratch the itch: he continued to cram the same piano riff into other songs for decades to come.

Mike Love knew Brian as well as anybody and he kept coming back to the word 'eccentric'. 'He's brilliant when he wants to be and a total dunce when he wants,' Mike said of his cousin in February 1975. This was just a few weeks after Brian had produced an eccentric (no other word fits) Christmas single too late to catch the seasonal market, but insisted on releasing it anyway. (It's called 'Child of Winter' and if you hear it, you'll understand why it never gets revived when December comes around.) 'He's just a far-out person,' Mike continued. 'He's one of the funniest people I've ever met. I'll walk into a room where he is and just start laughing.' This was what struck Marilyn Wilson when she first met her future husband: 'Everything he did was funny. The way he lifted a fork was funny! He'd ride a motorcycle in Gold Star recording studios. I couldn't believe him!'

Yet 1975 was also the year when Brian stayed in bed, stopped washing, stopped communicating, stopped relating to his wife and kids, stopped doing everything apart from eating and drinking and taking the drugs which mysteriously found their way into his mailbox. It was the year when his wife and youngest brother decided that the only way to save him from himself – to preserve him as a husband, a father, a musician, a functioning human being – was to put him under the radical care of a therapist named Eugene Landy.

Within a few weeks of Landy's enforced appearance in Brian's life, the one-time 'mad genius' was being encouraged to remember the 'genius' part of that tag. The truth was that although the Beach Boys couldn't be collectively diagnosed as 'mad', they were effectively non-functioning as a creative unit. Between 1969 and 1972, they had recorded some of the most adventurous music of their entire career and only a minority of those recordings had any assistance from Brian. The *Holland* album seemed to offer them a rich future without depending on their elusive former leader: every other member of the band was writing and the results were reassuringly beautiful and mature (as in 'adult' instead of 'teenage').

But instead of a fertile new direction, *Holland* proved to be a dead end. Between 1973 and 1976, just one new studio track emerged under the Beach Boys' name and that was the 'Child of Winter' single. Members of the Beach Boys not called Brian Wilson were quite capable of telling journalists that they were recording regularly, that they had a deep and wide seam of songs from which to choose, that they were exploring material that was maybe more environmental or more spiritual than in the past. But all of it was wishes, and very little of it was on tape (the exceptions being songs stockpiled by Dennis Wilson for a solo record).

In his role as Beach Boys' manager, Steve Love needed straws to clutch and Brian's apparent renaissance was the most obvious one within reach. And thus a publicity campaign was born: a hype that became an act of collective self-hypnosis and ultimately a curse for all those who had believed in it. The story was this: Brian Wilson was back.

Nothing made the other Beach Boys feel as safe as the idea that Brian would once again become their creative supremo, so his brothers, cousins and friends were eager to spread the gospel. Carl explained that Brian was 'in a funky sort of bag – very subtle rock in a cool way … very brilliant, very natural like a growing tree, not prefabricated in any way'. Maybe that was based on hearing his latest adaptation of 'Back Home', first attempted by the Beach Boys in 1963, then again in 1970, and revived in late 1975 as a good-time country boogie, sung by Brian in an alarmingly jagged growl.

As 1976 began, two things became apparent to the Beach Boys before anyone else: that the growl was here to stay, as Brian's voice had been sacrificed to his 100-a-day cigarette habit; and that the great songwriter of the past didn't have much to offer. Among his songs were a comedy skit with a minute-long ode to TM tagged on the end; a strange (of course) history of music entitled 'That Same Song', which was at least amusing; a near-vintage summertime romp entitled 'It's OK' (self-fulfilling title), written in 1974; and a tune he'd once given his wife to sing, called 'Had to Phone Ya'. Plus, of course, the inescapable 'Ding Dang', mercifully cut short from eight hours long, or whatever it could have been, to less than a minute. None of this added up to the new *Pet Sounds*.

What kept Brian interested was cutting rock 'n' roll oldies, arranged with varying degrees of skill and novelty. The Beach Boys agreed to a plan, or a choice of plans: they could either issue an oldies album and then follow through almost immediately with a set of new material, or they could combine the two projects into a double album. 'People will say the group copped out of the writing derby,' Brian conceded in

April 1976. 'But we make up for it in performance.' Carl had stopped raving about Brian's 'funky sort of bag' and was reduced to saying, 'our music will sound like whatever it sounds like'. Al Jardine insisted that Brian really had written lots of new songs, 'whether he admits it or not'. But Brian preferred not to.

The magazine *Modern Recording* was given exclusive access to the potential genius at work and what was expected to be the fulfilment of the 'Brian's back' myth. Dennis set them up: 'I know it's weird talking about a brother like that, but he's a fucking genius.' When it came to the sessions, however, what the *Modern Recording* reporter mostly saw was Dennis working on his solo material. After cutting a cover of 'Chapel of Love', the group suddenly stopped turning up at the studio. 'The Beach Boys may be rolling again tomorrow, or it may never happen again,' the magazine concluded, their exclusives restricted to the news that Brian preferred working with a string machine to using a live string section and was also experimenting with synthesisers for the first time.

Somehow, out of this indecision and lack of enthusiasm, an album was born. It was given the squirm-inducing title of *15 Big Ones* (fifteen years, fifteen tracks – you see?) and housed in a cover that looked more like a wanted poster than a marketing device. Joel Selvin in the *San Francisco Examiner* claimed that it was 'the most fully realized Beach Boys album since *Wild Honey* … daring and richly satisfying', but nobody who heard it believed him. The vocal arrangements were clumsy and simplistic, where Brian had once achieved effortless beauty; the song selection was banal; the performances forced and unsatisfying. It was as if the group had aged several decades while reverting to childhood. It sounded mystifying – but still somehow fun, if you dismissed all expectations based on what they had done in the past. In the US, it also proved to be the most commercial music they had released in a decade: their stodgy, misfiring cover of Chuck Berry's 'Rock and Roll Music' was even a Top 10 hit.

No sooner had the album been released, however, than elements of the group began to disown it. Dennis was the most vocal: 'I was unhappy with the oldies, absolutely. The album should have been

100 per cent original … Carl and I were really upset.' Carl was more diplomatic, describing it as a warm-up for his out-of-sorts eldest brother. But he had to admit that after they had cut the oldies, Brian had said: 'Well, I've recorded enough. I don't want to record any longer and the album's finished.'

A few months later, Brian would claim that they had somehow 'run out' of oldies to record and that everything was Mike Love's fault because he 'decided to make the record half old and half new. He literally forced us to do it his way. I resented that.' In fact, Brian had stepped away from the sessions, leaving the others to piece together the best of what was finished. Mike did his best to sound excited about the results: 'Each song is different and that's really far-out.' But he too was soon forced to concede that *15 Big Ones* was no more than a try-out, a way for Brian to get used to recording again. Unfortunately, he didn't tell record buyers that until it was too late.

Ultimately, it didn't matter whether *15 Big Ones* was a great album: the important thing, according to the advertising campaign prepared by ace publicists Rogers & Cowan, was that 'Brian's back'. Now it was time for the public to see this comeback in the flesh.

On 2 July 1976, Brian was driven to the backstage area of the outdoor Oakland Coliseum, arriving late to avoid the crowds. The Beach Boys were already on stage, uncertain whether Brian would agree to come. But he crept almost surreptitiously into their midst, stared goggle-eyed at the crowd and then planted himself behind a piano. Occasionally, he played along for a few bars or muttered a line or two of backing vocals. After a while, he obeyed the cue to sing something from the new album: 'Back Home'. Fans held up 'Welcome back' placards; Brian raised his hands like a small child in acknowledgement. He made it through two shows, then sat out seven weeks of the tour before he reappeared for another pair of concerts in Washington.

So 'Brian's back' was a hype after all? Of course it was: a sickening exploitation of an obviously disturbed man for the purposes of commercial greed. But Brian himself had other ideas. Maybe the Brian of 1966 had gone forever, but there was a new mad genius in town.

And just when everyone had written him off, he reinvented himself as a different form of genius, leaving the rest of the world to decide exactly where he belonged on the spectrum that spanned joyous eccentricity and sweet insanity.

Too Much Sugar

The Beach Boys' strange obsession with food

Has any other Grammy-winning composer devoted as much time to the universal topic of food? Or owned a health-food store? Or become so addicted to junk food that their continued existence was called into peril?

Whether it was for sustenance or pleasure, food seems to have been a perennial preoccupation for the Beach Boys. At various points of their career, two of their members were clinically obese, one of them addicted to the point of mental illness. The third Wilson brother went to the other extreme, claiming that food upset his delicate constitution and eventually preferring to ingest most of his calories in liquid – alcoholic liquid – form. (This was Dennis Wilson, who in later life would face stomach surgery to treat a tumour.) Another Beach Boys member was a fair-weather vegetarian, until he grew tired of having to ask exactly what was in every meal. And the last of the original five Beach Boys became so obsessed with what should enter his stomach that he wound up in hospital, and almost in jail. Raise a hand, then, to more-often-than-not Beach Boy Bruce Johnston, who seems to have stayed healthy and slim across more than six decades in the entertainment business without ever becoming unduly hung up about food (or indeed anything else).

No doubt to his profound embarrassment, Carl Wilson was enduring the extremes of puppy fat when he was thrust into the public eye. Journalists in those less aware times frequently dismissed him as 'porky' or 'a balloon'. The *Los Angeles Times* described his diet in 1966, by which time he was merely overweight: 'All the Beach Boys eat as if famine has been declared; you grab your meals when time allows. But Carl eats better than the rest. On the first day of their Oregon tour, he shoved four square meals into his rounding frame': airport breakfast, heavy airplane lunch, late afternoon dinner and midnight supper. In England, the other Beach Boys apparently described Carl as having 'the biggest appetite since Charles Laughton played Henry VIII'.

Back in California, Brian Wilson's appetites were equally huge, but altogether healthier than his brother's. 'He goes into phases,' his wife Marilyn explained. 'Right now, he's on a vegetable kick and loves asparagus. You should see what I have to cook for him.' Brian confirmed that the couple were devouring carrots, radishes, celery, lettuce, tomatoes, potatoes; 'vegetables are the best thing in the world for you,' he declared with the passion of a new convert. Not that cooking them was exactly his scene. He complained that, with carrots, 'first of all, you have to peel them, and I don't care for that. But if you peel them, I'll eat them.' So passionate was his devotion to the cause that he concocted a Beach Boys song, 'Vega-Tables', which almost became their first single of 1967. As released later that year on *Smiley Smile*, it ended with a heartfelt appeal for listeners to 'tell us the name of your favourite vegetables'. [Vegetables were in season that winter: the Mothers of Invention recorded Frank Zappa's 'Call Any Vegetable' around the same time. Van Dyke Parks' first wife, Durrie, has suggested that he might have been the unwitting conduit between the two vegephile songs.]

Carrots, spinach and the inevitable radish also featured in a mysterious short story published under Brian's name. It featured a character named Brian Gemini jousting with Michael Spinach-Glob (alias Mike Vosse) and David Carrot (aka David Anderle). I don't believe for a second that Brian composed this by himself: more likely it was a stoned group effort, published as a Wilson creation for maximum exposure.

But the dialogue attributed to Brian Gemini sounds weird enough to be his: 'We've got to get *out* of this tomato!'

By 1969, Brian had chosen to invest (with a friend and a cousin) in a health food store in Los Angeles. The Radiant Radish was situated on the corner of Melrose and N San Vicente Boulevard, and, according to a 1971 profile in *Rolling Stone* magazine, Brian could sometimes be found behind the counter, wearing his customary bathrobe, playing at shopkeeper. Around the time that piece appeared, however, the Radish attracted its last customer and the store declared bankruptcy. Brian subsequently blamed himself for having ordered too much stock in his zealous quest for fitness and health.

Unfortunately, his culinary progress from 1967 to 1969 was not as healthy as his rhetoric. His songwriting during this period became disarmingly personal, as if he were having a conversation with an old friend. 'When's the last time you baked me a pie?', he asked the subject of 'I'd Love Just Once to See You' – and there was no demand for carrots to be part of the recipe. By 1969, in 'Games Two Can Play', he was lamenting: 'I'm fat as a cow, how'd I ever get this way?' The following year, 'H.E.L.P. is on the Way' laid out his true confession: 'Seems lately all I've eaten's sugar and fat / It's getting obvious that's not where it's at'. He claimed to have been restored to the path of health when 'I read a book on organic foods' and demanded, 'Hamburgers and hot dogs, throw 'em all out'. The song ended with the Beach Boys plugging the Radiant Radish, which might have been helpful if the track had been released while the store was still in business.

Meanwhile, the touring band pledged allegiance to their own health food diets or, as Al Jardine explained, 'honey, milk and bran' if the real stuff wasn't available. They supposedly moved around the US on a private plane equipped with a forty-gallon tank of fortified apple juice, while Bruce Johnston for one kept his pockets stuffed with 'twelve different kinds of vitamins'. Al Jardine boasted that he'd written a song for the *Surf's Up* album while sitting in a health food restaurant, examining the leaflet that came with his new pair of sandals: the new-age lifestyle compressed into one anecdote. But he gradually felt forced to abandon his strict vegetarian regimen because sourcing appropriate snacks had become 'a big pain … I spent half my time talking about food' to determine whether he was allowed to eat it.

Mike Love decided to streamline his decision making in the early weeks of 1970 by banishing food entirely. 'I wanted to purge all the evil from my system,' he revealed in his autobiography – referring to everything that dogged his life at that point, from the Charles Manson scandal to the collapse of his latest marriage. 'I thought I could do that by going on a fast … For three weeks, all I consumed was juice, tea and water.' This purging of toxins from his body, he discovered afterwards, 'can also impair your brain and nervous system'. On 20 February, he cruised around the streets of Hollywood in his Rolls-Royce, which wouldn't have attracted any attention had he been travelling at more than 5 mph. A line of cars queued up on the late-night streets to overtake him and, soon enough, he caught the eye of a passing police car. Convinced Love must be drunk, the officers signalled him to stop with everything at their disposal: their horn, lights and finally their siren. But Love's car continued its labyrinthine progress through the Hollywood streets, its driver apparently unaware of his surroundings. Eventually, a sports car intervened to nudge the Rolls-Royce to the side of the road and the slowest auto chase in LA police history glided to an end.

Love, by now on the verge of drifting into a coma, was arrested, then bailed out by the Beach Boys' manager, Nick Grillo. His father and brother Stephen tried to take him home but, as Mike confessed, 'I bit Stephen and he yelled, "I thought you were a vegetarian!"' Next stop was a psychiatric hospital, where Love's depleted system reacted to medication as if it was poison and his mental condition deteriorated further. The Beach Boys faced a run of shows in the Pacific northwest, for which Brian had to be dragged out of retirement to sit behind a piano, while Carl took over the burden of lead vocals on almost every song. Mike's absence was, according to one reviewer, 'conspicuous'.

For future episodes of fasting, Love ensured that he was always under medical or dietary supervision. Within the Beach Boys, though, his controlled eating and Dennis's preference for downing his calories in alcoholic form aroused less concern than the relentless self-harm of Brian. He spent months at a time in the early 1970s refusing to leave his bedroom, while downing epic quantities of illegal drugs, alcohol and (inevitably) junk food, topped up with cigarettes and occasional madcap escapades in the public eye, fuelled by cocaine. The Beach Boys' future biographer, Timothy White, reported that Brian was 'subsisting on candy bars and milkshakes'. Brian's memory was that 'I got scared and I got lost, and I was eating caramel sundaes for breakfast'. His weight soared and, even after several months of Dr Eugene Landy's regime of enforced fitness and sociability, it was still an unrecognisably gargantuan figure who returned to the Beach Boys for sporadic concerts in 1976. Landy's role as Brian's guardian-cum-jailer was taken over by Mike's brother Stan Love in 1977 and, by spring that year, Wilson was noticeably thinner, though his conduct remained highly erratic.

Between Landy's departure from Brian's milieu in 1977 and his return five years later, Wilson's physical condition worsened substantially – with the substance all too visible on his frame, as his weight neared 350 pounds. 'His diet is all messed up,' Mike Love conceded in late 1982. 'He doesn't eat well and, well, he's emotionally weird sometimes.' Part of that weirdness was manifested in his obsessive behaviour, which would range from binge-eating giant steaks (four at a sitting was a regular Wilson meal) to that binge-performing of the folk song 'Shortnin' Bread'. Landy's return provided years of sternly enforced meal plans and another compulsory timetable of physical fitness.

Landy boasted about what he called 'the Brian Wilson Diet', which reduced his subject's weight almost by half. 'He couldn't see his feet, he couldn't tie his shoes,' Landy told a reporter with scant regard for his client's pride. 'You can take an obese person and reduce him rapidly if it's accompanied by intravenous vitamins. He received multivitamin shots six times a day, fortifying him physically to deal with a tremendous weight loss. For the first two weeks, he ate nothing but fruit juices – from carrots to cantaloupe, if you could put it in a juicer, we juiced it. From then on, he went on an 800-to-1000-calorie-per-day diet, with no fat, high carbohydrates and a rigorous routine of exercise.' The Landy programme also involved basic education about etiquette that Wilson had somehow forgotten. 'He's taught me things like manners,' Brian explained in 1985. 'I never realised that I used to rush through my meals. He's taught me to eat slower and enjoy them.'

By 1988, when his career as a solo recording artist began, Brian felt able to issue health advice to his fans: 'Stop eating red meat. Stop eating sugar. And exercise every day.' Inevitably, he channelled this advice into a song, 'Too Much Sugar', which was as naïve as it was informative. 'Too much sugar and too much cake,' he pronounced in a voice that sounded like a newly educated eight-year-old, 'You end up with a belly ache.' Another piece of Wilson wisdom: 'Stuff you eat can poison you'. Once control of his daily life passed from Landy to Brian's second wife, Melinda, and her staff, food began to assume a more orthodox role in his life, and the days of bingeing on cocaine and caramel were over. Or were they? Sean O'Hagan, leader of the High Llamas, met Brian around 1997 to discuss producing the Beach Boys. O'Hagan recalled: 'All he wanted to do was eat ice cream. He was just sitting there in his baseball cap while all these discussions were going on, going "Munch, munch, munch". He loves eating. He'd agree to anything as long as he can eat.'

Some obsessions never die. Early in the twenty-first century, Brian was asked to consider what he liked best about modern life. He thought for a while and then said: 'My favourite thing is going out to eat in a restaurant. It never ceases to amaze me. You sit there and all of a sudden there's food before you! It blows my mind. It just does.'

Forget Him, He's Crazy

Brian Wilson and Eugene Landy, part 1

The trouble with egomaniacs is that they don't know when to stop. George Benson was a ten-year-old blues/jazz prodigy when he was taken to New York by his agent, Eugene Ellsworth Landy. The agent seemed like a man to the kid, but he was only nineteen years old. He could talk, though, which is how the young Benson won his first, albeit short-lived, record deal. And he could flirt, which is why Benson remembered that Landy seemed to have girlfriends of all ages, arriving and departing on schedule to avoid bumping into each other.

That would have been enough to boast about for a man who had acquired wealth and a reputation in a field entirely removed from the music business. But Eugene Landy had to embellish it. It was true that in his mid-twenties, he had acted as producer for one folk album and two spoken-word records on tiny Los Angeles labels. That wasn't the way that Landy wanted to be seen, however. He needed bigger names on his resume, which is how he started to claim that he had produced a hit single for Frankie Avalon, despite no evidence to support his tale, and later that he had also been responsible for Barry McGuire's 1965 folk-rock number one 'Eve of Destruction' (Landy connection? Zero).

In pre-internet days, it was easier to exaggerate than to fact-check. Landy had the advantages of charisma, drive and an innate talent for making things happen. Having dropped out of school because of undiagnosed dyslexia, he explored not only the record business but also the world of hipsters and deadbeats. 'I first smoked grass on the streets,' he claimed in 1972. 'And I did LSD when everybody thought it was a law degree.'

By then, he was into his late thirties and had two other strings to his bow. He was the author of a successful reference work called *The Underground Dictionary* – the prosaic equivalent, perhaps, of one of Brian Wilson's favourite comedy albums, *How to Speak Hip*. He hit upon the idea when treating a twenty-five-year-old drug addict whose vocabulary he could barely understand. At the start of the 1970s, he briefly became the media expert on interpreting the underground milieu for the straight world. He was also by then a well-qualified psychologist, who specialised in helping those struggling with addiction by offering them round-the-clock care. His professional titles were certainly impressive: by 1972, he was the executive director of the Center for Adjunctive Therapeutic Activity and the founder of the FREE Foundation (FREE stood for Foundation for Rechannelling Emotions and Education). Though FREE operated as a non-profit, he also handled private clients; in Los Angeles, that meant wealthy celebrities. He continued to do free and high-paying work: $200 an hour by 1980.

Drugs was the prevalent problem of the age, he believed. 'This is a lost generation we're dealing with now,' he explained in 1972. 'Dopers are usually people who don't succeed at anything, so what we do is make him obtain success. We build success upon success, and slowly start integrating him back into the community.' As the decade progressed, his client list became more impressive: fewer twenty-five-year-old junkies, more film stars and rock 'n' roll icons, such as Rod Steiger, Alice Cooper … and Brian Wilson.

'Steiger couldn't even brush his teeth. Alice Cooper wouldn't eat.' That was Eugene Landy in 1980, displaying his customary after-care for his clients. He was no more discreet about Brian Wilson. 'What I saw was a man who was very frightened, scared and hiding in his room,' Landy revealed in 1983. 'He did not wish to talk to anybody. He did not want to have any demands placed on him. He had regressed to an infantile kind of state.' And he confessed that people had told him Brian was beyond even his help. 'They said, "Forget him, he's crazy".'

Brian had no wish to be treated by anyone. 'I was hiding in my bedroom from the world,' he admitted in 1976. 'I was out of it. I was unhealthy, I was overweight, I was totally a vegetable. In other words, my life got all screwed up. I started taking a lot of cocaine and a lot of drugs, and it threw me inward: it made an implosion, I withdrew from society.' Struggling with two young daughters and a man-child who rarely left his room except to procure drugs, Marilyn Wilson consulted with her brother-in-law Carl and made the decision to hire a therapist who claimed he could transform her husband's life. If Brian was indeed 'infantile', Landy's therapy would first accept that state and then try to change it. His work comprised two controversial tactics: total control of the client for as many hours per day as they could afford; and what has come to be known as reparenting – in other words, replacing a damaged parent/child relationship in a client's psyche with a healthier alternative. In effect, Landy explained, he was providing basic life lessons that his clients had somehow missed in their own childhoods. 'We teach people to be self-sufficient, to be vulnerable, that nothing's wrong with fear, that no one's perfect.'

Landy's first tactic in autumn 1975 involved provoking Brian's curiosity. Wilson refused to allow Landy in his room and would not come out to meet him. But he could hear Landy talking at great length with Marilyn and, after several visits, he emerged to find out what he was missing. Even in a state of extreme psychological distress, Wilson had been able to manipulate people into believing that he was about to change. But Landy offered him no alternative. Change wasn't restricted to the hours when Landy was by his side, but became an all-day and (if necessary) all-night affair, with assistants acting as Landy's surrogates. Their role was to watch Brian constantly and control what he did, who he saw and what he ingested. In place of drugs, cakes and burgers, Landy's team substituted health foods and exercise. Rather than staying in bed, Wilson was spurred into sitting at the piano and attempting to write songs.

Within nine months, Brian had taken part in a Beach Boys anniversary TV special (over which Landy demanded editorial control); completed an album; returned to live performance; and consented to agonisingly intimate interviews. He was forced to confront his fears and his failings in public, to recite his sins like a victim of the Maoist regime of self-criticism. Suddenly the recluse was everywhere: making embarrassing appearances on live TV, where he was cued to 'smile' with cards held up by Landy's aides; greeting stadium crowds like a small child being encouraged to wave at a train driver; even revealing the intimate details of his sex life in magazines that were sold on every news-stand. But at least he was alive, and (sort of) functioning. As he admitted, if Landy hadn't intervened, 'I'd have been a goner. I'd have been in the hospital by now.' Instead, he was writing and recording as if it was 1964 again and his record label were demanding four new albums a year.

Not that the patient was cured. The idea of therapy presupposes that the desired outcome is a change of habits and an improvement in the subject's life, psyche and health. Landy's tactic of surrounding Brian with minders made it physically difficult for him to stray, but it did little to remove the temptation. And Brian could not stop talking about it. A reporter from the *Washington Post* asked him if he was still taking drugs. Brian turned to Landy and said: 'Is marijuana a drug?'. Soon he appeared on Mike Douglas's TV chat show and waxed so lyrically on the joys of 'toking' that sections of the conversation had to be censored before it could be broadcast. Brian told David Felton of *Rolling Stone* that he was hoping he would start taking 'uppers' again, as they would help his songwriting. And, inevitably, he asked Felton if he had a drug connection he could recommend.

The most damning, pathetic, poignant of these late 1976 confessionals was carried out by David Rensin for *Oui* magazine. Brian asked him the same old question: 'Do you have any uppers?' Rensin pushed his subject further.

'If cocaine were offered to you, would you use it again?'

'Oh yes,' Wilson replied. 'I would use it if I were around it, yes.'

'Doesn't that imply a lack of self-discipline?'

'Yes, it does, but I would go back to it in a minute.'

Brian also cast a depressing verdict on the experience of living in Landy's therapeutic realm: 'I feel like a prisoner, and I don't know when it's going to end … he'd put the police on me if I took off, and he'd put me in the funny farm.' A minute later, Wilson was telling Rensin that he planned to start a new career as a professional athlete: 'I don't think I'm too old … Can you get me some uppers now?'

Dennis Wilson confided that Brian's agonies and struggles were all he could think about. 'I would give up my total career, everything, just for Brian to be OK,' he admitted. But what was OK? And whose right was it to decide Brian's fate? With costs of the therapy rocketing, and Brian sufficiently 'cured' to appear on television, the Beach Boys' management decided to intervene. Landy was fired, not for therapeutic reasons but because of money. 'Brian was just getting back on his feet,' Carl complained. 'He had been with Gene for more than a year. He was becoming a lot more productive. It was part of his therapy to make music. But Gene and Stan Love disagreed a lot about what Brian should do. Gene was doing it from a therapeutic angle, and Steve [Love] had business considerations. So Steve terminated Gene. It was really a shame, because Brian regressed pretty much after that.'

The Love brothers, of course, were Brian's cousins, but they were also employed by the Beach Boys and all they could see was an expensive stranger bleeding the corporate finances dry. (To be fair to the Love family, Brian was reportedly outraged when he discovered how much Landy was being paid and apparently punched his therapist in the face shortly before their relationship was terminated.) Once more, Brian was treated like a child. His business 'parents' switched him from one therapist to a cheaper one, who apparently died only a few weeks into their work together. After that, he was back under the tough love of cousin Stan and his new sidekick, Rocky Pamplin. Inevitably, their lack of therapeutic knowledge proved to be hopelessly counter-productive. Eugene Landy's motives might have been questionable – it's true that, as Carl said, 'he was fascinated by' Brian, though I can't help thinking of the way that a snake might be fascinated by a mouse – but the new/

old regime hadn't worked the first time, and it didn't work again. Brian might not have been functioning as an adult, but he knew how to be devious and he was famous enough to be able to obtain drugs whenever he wanted them, which was almost every waking hour. As he recalled in 1983, 'I started taking drugs again because I couldn't handle the freedom that I had all of a sudden'. His enforced withdrawal from Landy's care almost proved to be fatal.

By the end of 1982, Brian was six years distant from Landy and in a worse position than he had been in 1975. Massively obese, he was existing in a house with Carolyn Williams, an older woman who had started as his carer and then become his 'romantic' partner. Chaotic to work with and utterly unproductive, he pushed his bandmates to the point that they agreed to fire him from the Beach Boys, a ruse to force him to confront his demons. As Mike Love explained, 'he was too self-destructive, too difficult to deal with. He needed to get some help.'

Within a matter of weeks, Carl, Brian's now separated wife Marilyn and the band's manager, Tom Hulett, collectively decided that only one man could save Brian: Eugene Landy. 'I told the other guys in the band that, if we didn't do something, Brian was going to be the next headline in *Billboard*,' Hulett said, drawing on his memories of working with Elvis Presley during his twilight years.

The intervention was swift and dramatic. Landy installed Brian in a Los Angeles hospital for an urgent detox and full health check. 'His lung capacity was down to 40 per cent', Landy reported. 'He was smoking four packets of cigarettes a day. His system was full of toxic chemicals.' In fact, the therapist admitted, Brian would have been dead within two years without his intervention. From the hospital, Wilson was flown to Hawaii and Carolyn Williams was sent a legal letter explaining that her boyfriend was 'leaving town on a retreat for health reasons'. Moreover, she was ordered to quit the Wilson house. Having not heard from Brian himself, she stayed put; a month later, she received a telegram from Hawaii which read like a desperate message from a hostage: 'I will be back as soon as I can get away. They forced me to come … Please help me get home to you.' The press printed her allegations that Brian had been kidnapped. Landy and Hulett staged an impromptu press conference in Hawaii, at which a dazed-looking, distracted but undeniably slimmer Wilson mumbled non sequiturs, but turned down the chance to phone Williams in front of reporters. Later that day, he appeared on stage with the Beach Boys, still looking confused but at least functioning. Once more Brian was back – and so was Eugene Landy. This time he intended to stay around.

Adult Child

Running wild with Brian Wilson

Was Brian Wilson an adult or a child? Or a perennial anxious teenager, unable to grow beyond his feud with his father and his sexual insecurity? These were among the issues that Eugene Landy raised with his superstar client during his first year of therapeutic intervention. Even when Landy was fired, Brian never forgot about that adult/child duality – a particularly stark divide in the turbulent psyche of Brian Douglas Wilson.

Though *15 Big Ones* had been a false start, it had the desired effect of sparking Brian's creativity into life. But his ferocious work rate aroused problems. No record company could release material as fast as Brian was writing and recording it. Much of what he was creating did not fit the other Beach Boys' conflicting visions of what their band should be. And some of it was downright unsettling: proof of psychological turmoil, at least, and perhaps something more sinister.

In the summer of 1976, the Beach Boys were high in the American charts with their first new Top 10 album in a decade. In Britain, where the reaction to *15 Big Ones* was more ambivalent, the best-selling album of the sunshine months was a TV-advertised Beach Boys compilation entitled *20 Golden Greats*. The ground was prepared for a classic Beach Boys album from the pen of Brian Wilson. Speaking that August, Mike Love promised that Brian was already hard at work: 'He's got some heavy songs in the bunch. They'll flip ya out.' He presumably wasn't talking about 'Lazy Lizzie', Brian's song about stalking a schoolgirl, or the equally perverse 'Hey Little Tomboy' – or even 'Marilyn Rovell', a charming love song to his wife that had little resonance outside the extended Beach Boys family. What else was he working on? He had exhumed a 1965 leftover and added a fresh 1976 vocal to emerge with 'Sherry She Needs Me'; plus he was, of course, indulging himself with cover versions, from 'Ruby Baby' (gruff, spirited) to his one-man reincarnation of 'You've Lost That Lovin' Feelin'' (epic, strange).

Mike Love had already heard Brian demonstrating other new songs, however, and had reacted with wild glee when he heard 'I'll Bet He's Nice'. 'That is a motherfucker!', Mike yelled as Brian finished. Then Mike went down with hepatitis, leaving Brian to his own peculiar devices. In the final three months of 1976, Brian staged an intensive set of recording sessions pursuing a unique sound. Synthesised keyboards, replacing a bass guitar, were his latest sonic joy, pre-empting the New Romantic movement of the early 1980s. His two brothers were constantly on hand to fill out the instrumentation, but mostly these were one-man creations, with the other Beach Boys called in for vocal assignments. The working title of this very personal opus? *Brian Loves You.*

The whole band was behind that title, he assured DJ Dave Herman in an interview early in 1977. But the album that emerged that spring was called *The Beach Boys Love You.* Not that it could ever have been mistaken for anything other than a Brian Wilson creation. It was full of magical pop hooks, idiosyncratic chord changes, bizarre lyrics (including a song about a roller-skating teenager, of course), adolescent romantic conceits and less than a minute of the infernal 'Ding Dang', about as appropriate as a pie in the face during a royal funeral. What else made it so quintessentially Brian? The reference to Phil Spector in 'Mona'; the surreal lyrics to 'Solar System', inspired by a quick course in astronomy; the duet with the ever-patient Mrs Wilson on 'Let's Put Our Hearts Together'; and, perhaps best of all, the utterly strange and wonderful tribute to 'Johnny Carson'. (The late-night TV host seems to have been as bewildered by the song as most reviewers were. 'It was *not* a work of art,' he declared.)

With Dr Landy banished in late 1976, Brian had nothing to restrain him from his obsessions. One of them, fortunately, was writing songs, although he didn't describe the process the way anyone else did. It was 'just sitting down at the piano and pounding and getting rhythm patterns, and then later I add on the melody. It's almost like breathing to me, it's as basic as that. The only hard part is building up to it, going through the suffering until you have that need to start writing and then you just vomit the music out.'

Another Wilson fascination in the early months of 1977 was self-hypnosis. He'd come across Pat Collins, who billed herself as 'the Hip Hypnotist', on television; he attended three of her public classes and then had a private consultation. She was certainly a surreal enough character for Brian, looking like a gothic Tammy Wynette with plunging neckline, bangles and lots of black lace. The Beach Boys were lucky that Brian didn't decide to collaborate with her and add to her discography, which already included *Sleep with Pat Collins!* and *Turn On! The Power of the Mind*.

Such was Brian's passion that he celebrated the completion of *Love You* by immediately making another album, *Adult/Child* (Landy must have smiled). Brian had already retrieved one *Sunflower* out-take, 'Good Time', for *Love You*, and now he reached back for two more, 'Games Two Can Play' and 'Help is on the Way'. Other songs were more contemporary but from the same pool of eccentricity, including 'Everybody Wants to Live', which began by describing how a cigarette butt sounds when you drop it in the toilet pan, and 'It's Trying to Say', an on-the-spot account of a baseball game. And then there were four tunes that inhabited an entirely different dimension – and decade.

'I would love to do a crooner album,' Brian explained that spring, referencing Frank Sinatra's *Only the Lonely* as his template. In another interview, he claimed that 'I've been experimenting with adult music, something adults can get into and not just kids' – not apparently realising that the adults of 1977 were just as likely to be listening to the Beatles and Simon & Garfunkel as Ol' Blue Eyes and his Rat Pack chums. Brian's old idol Dick Reynolds, last heard on the 1964 *Christmas Album*, was called back to work up some arrangements, as Brian revisited the standard tune 'Deep Purple', forced Carl beyond the top of his range on the swing tune 'Life is for the Living', and then composed two of the most painfully poignant ballads of his entire career. 'It's Over Now' portrayed romantic disappointment, for which the only cure was to 'put a Frank Sinatra album on', while 'Still I Dream of It' dove deeper, down into the depths of existential anguish. It was the late-'70s equivalent of 'I Just Wasn't Made for These Times', haunted by another decade of psychological anguish. In his fantasies, Brian imagined that Sinatra might cover it – or if he turned it down (and he did), maybe Elton John or Stevie Wonder. But this was a confession only one man could own.

The Wilson brothers loved *Adult/Child*. But, as Brian recalled a decade later, 'there was a problem with Mike. [It should be pointed out that Mike was not in the country when the album was recorded.] He told me I was fucking around, that I wasn't serious. I cut a track with swing music and he got mad. He said, "What are you doing, messing around for?". I said, "I'm just trying to do what I like, what I think is right for today's times."' But there are two sides to that final line: *Adult/Child* was undoubtedly what Brian liked, but not necessarily appropriate for the pop market of 1977.

By then, it was a moot point. Brian excitedly announced *Love You* as 'the best album since *Pet Sounds*', explaining: 'I was in a much better frame of mind than I'd been in a long time.' Even Landy's departure was smoothed over. 'I do feel more like a member of the group again. It's a little easier to cope now.'

Then reality stepped in. Just as Warners were about to release *Love You*, they learned that the Beach Boys had decided to sign with their arch-rival, Columbia Records. Short-term gain might still have fired up the Warners marketing department if the reviews had been favourable but, almost without exception, North American critics were baffled or appalled. The *Miami Herald* called *Love You* 'a lyrical disaster' and said 'any actual 16-year-old could have written better lyrics'. The *Montreal Star* found 'abysmal songs that communicate nothing at all' and concluded that Brian had 'ceased to be an artist, and no one has yet given him the news'. And so the critics continued: 'one of the more woeful sessions of music to come along', 'the weakest album I've heard this year', 'a piece of trash', 'probably the worst album I've ever reviewed'. Only one paper got it right, the *Ottawa Citizen*: 'Like some of the best Beach Boy music, on the surface it's garbage but if you let it get to you, it's absolutely great … Wilson maintains his strange mix of genius and silliness, fluctuating between brilliant pretension and happy parody.' The strange mix of genius and silliness: that was absolutely perfect, both for *Love You* and for Brian Wilson in 1977.

TM in the A.M.

The spiritual Beach Boys

Maybe he guessed what would happen. Brian Wilson completed the basic work on the group's 1968 album *Friends* just before the ill-fated Maharishi tour and it was released to the public a few weeks after that venture's ignominious demise.

The album ended with a statement: a short song entitled 'Transcendental Meditation'. Mike Love and Al Jardine, the Beach Boys' most committed meditators, supplied the explanatory lyrics, Wilson the wilfully minimalist melody. Brian scrapped the initial attempt at the song – an entirely in-house and conventional piece of spiritual pop-art – and concocted a replacement without the band. The common decencies of pop arranging were set aside as he accompanied the song with nothing other than drums (played by the future matricide, Jim Gordon), electric bass and no fewer than ten saxophonists. Over the top (a phrase chosen wisely), Wilson dubbed all the vocal parts himself, sounding like banshees fleeing an Irish wake. It was cacophonous, confrontational and maybe cathartic if you were struggling with evil spirits or voices telling you that you were about to die, and it captured absolutely nothing of the inner peace promised by the Maharishi and his disciples.

Eight years later, Brian made his second attempt to capture the meditation experience: 'The TM Song' on the ragamuffin *15 Big Ones* album. 'I wrote the song for the Maharishi,' he explained, 'and I hope he hears it. His method for cultivating the mind is so advanced, it merited at least a couple of songs.' His verdict would have sounded more convincing if he hadn't already damned 'The TM Song' as 'corny' in *Rolling Stone* magazine.

Asked in the late 1970s what he found funny, Brian's answer was oddball but apparently sincere: 'arguments'. He'd already staged mock-confrontations during the *SMiLE* sessions, with session drummer Hal Blaine inhabiting the role of a bad-tempered storekeeper. Now he revived the technique, devoting almost a quarter of the track's minimal duration to a rowdy dispute between neighbours. The only solution? Seventy-five seconds of delicious Brian Wilson tunefulness, made up of four separate melodic segments that comprised an adult child's-eye view of meditation in action. It was infinitely preferable to the same album's other TM offering, Mike Love's 'Everyone's in Love with You', a sugar-sweet adoration of the Maharishi.

By 1976, the Beach Boys' most profound and moving expressions of TM consciousness were already in the past. 'All This is That' had been a secret highlight of the fragmentary *Carl and the Passions* album – secret in plain sight, that is, although its mellow harmonies and chanted lyrics seemed designed not to catch the ear. It took me several decades to realise that what had sounded bland and ignorable in my teens was actually a landscape of vocal beauty, uniting the Wilson brothers' perfectionism with the trance-like devotion to the Maharishi's teaching embodied by Love and Al Jardine.

Equally divine was a little-noticed collaboration between members of the Beach Boys and a fellow meditation devotee, jazz flautist Charles Lloyd, on his early 1973 album *Waves*. 'TM' is perhaps the ultimate Beach Boys-connected earworm, rolling through its circular chord changes like one of the wordless harmony masterpieces from David Crosby's first solo album. It features three Beach Boys (Mike, Al and Carl), one auxiliary Beach Boy (Billy Hinsche) and Pamela Polland, the former vocalist from the soft-pop band, the Gentle Soul, creating rich, repetitive harmonic phrases that dissolve into a heartfelt pronouncement of 'Jai guru dev' – exactly the same message (roughly speaking, 'hail the great teacher') that brought both 'All This is That' and the Beatles'

'Across the Universe' to their beatific close. *Waves* also included a brief Lloyd/Love duet entitled 'Rishikesh', based on a self-penned poem that Love took to reciting as part of the Beach Boys' live shows in the early 1970s. He couldn't help boasting that 'a University of California professor has told me it is one of the best classical poems he has ever seen'. He planned to publish it in a 1975 collection of his Beach Boys lyrics, but the book never appeared. (Neither did the photo biography of the group that Love was said to be assembling in 1976.)

Love has been accused of many things in his lifetime, but his devotion to the Maharishi and the practice of Transcendental Meditation has been utterly faithful. Beach Boys fans might not always want to hear it, but Love is convinced of TM's life-altering properties and has seen it as his mission to spread the gospel of meditation to everyone around him. For many years, the group were entirely supportive of his crusade: they opened their 1969 European tour, for example, with a show at the Brighton Dome, from which all profits were earmarked for a local meditation centre. (Mike had to reassure a scoop-hungry British newspaper that he had no romantic designs on the young woman running the centre, Viggie Litchfield, whom he had met in India.) In August 1971, Love and Jardine took an intensive TM teacher training course in Arcata, California, with the result that the group were unable to tour until several weeks after their *Surf's Up* album had been released. They continued their studies in spring 1972. 'We've found it to be really helpful in our music,' Love insisted, 'and also in maintaining harmony among the group members.'

Later, however, he revealed that he had found the return to the Beach Boys environment so jarring that he nearly left the band. 'One night I walked into a dressing room littered with cigarettes of various kinds and liquor bottles,' he recalled. 'I decided that if this was the way it had to be, then I would quit and let them get on with it. But I spoke to the Maharishi and he told me I should continue with the band and carry on doing my own thing at the same time. At that time, it was people outside the actual Beach Boys who were, in my opinion, flagrantly abusing alcohol and drugs. Eventually they had to go. It was either them or me, and I decided it made more sense if they left.' As late as May 1974, he was confiding – to a journalist, no less – that he wanted to leave the group and enrol as a student in TM.

By the late 1970s, the divide between those Beach Boys who had remained faithful to the tenets of the Maharishi's teaching and those pursuing hedonism and oblivion in varying proportions had cracked open to reveal a spiritual chasm. The artistic and psychological disappointment the group suffered after the *15 Big Ones* album heightened Love's awareness of the split. He would attempt to lecture the Beach Boys' audiences about the joys of TM and then lose his temper when they talked over him or jeered him. The stress took its toll on his body, as he was stricken with hepatitis in January 1977, but he had already arranged a temporary escape. Although *The Beach Boys Love You* was set for release in April, he informed the group that he would be unavailable for the next six months as he was heading to Switzerland to study with the Maharishi. (He had undergone training in the same location in 1975.) Brian Wilson's response was to beg the guru to send his cousin home, a sentiment he channelled into a song entitled 'Mike Come Back to L.A.'.

On his return, Love hatched a plan to rescue the Beach Boys from their perilous flirtations with rock star excess, while reinforcing a project he had been supporting individually for several years: the Maharishi International University in Fairfield, Iowa, deep in the Midwest and 1,800 miles from the California surf. At the same time, he put together a musical group outside the Beach Boys' jurisdiction: a band initially called Making Waves, then just Waves (after the TM-inspired album by Charles Lloyd, one of the participants) and eventually Celebration. They took up residence in Fairfield and Love's offshoot continued to operate on the fringes of the Beach Boys for the next year. At MIU, Love recorded with both outfits in the final weeks of 1977 – although, ironically, there was virtually no mention of spirituality, and none of the Maharishi, in the woeful albums that resulted from this intensive period of studio work.

Relocating the site of Beach Boys activity to Iowa rather than their home state did nothing to prove the healing powers of TM. Instead, the sojourn almost broke the group in half, with neither Carl nor Dennis keen to spend more than a few days at the sessions. Love took this opportunity to fire many of the band's stalwart support musicians and replace them with fellow TM adherents. (One of them was keyboardist Ron Altbach. Carl welcomed him at his first rehearsal by telling him to 'fuck off'.) It was effectively a coup, although Love held back from applying the final thrust of the blade and firing the two unrepentant Wilson brothers. They expressed their disdain for their cousin by walking off stage as soon as he mentioned meditation during their disastrous early 1978 tour of Australia. Within a few weeks, the group's studio facility in Fairfield had been dismantled and the Beach Boys were once more a California band, albeit a highly conflicted one.

Mike Love remained a zealot of clean living and spiritual clarity. On stage, he might lecture the Beach Boys audience about the way in which they could use meditation to 'maximise energy and creativity' – to which Brian responded, one night in Albuquerque, by pointedly leaving the stage while his cousin was speaking, claiming he needed to rest. The members of Celebration were now based in Love's Santa Barbara home, which they rebranded as a TM centre of meditation and health. Mike had formed an independent production company designed to handle artists who displayed positive life values (in other words, they meditated). It was inevitably called LoveSongs Inc. Soon afterwards, he added a charitable institution to his business roster: the Love Foundation, which raised funds for a variety of good causes, many of which proved to have links to the Maharishi.

So advanced was Love's practice of TM by 1978 that he had apparently mastered the Maharishi's Sidhi programme. It promised to revolutionise the relationship between the mind and body to the point that it could inspire the art of levitation. Indeed, Love 'is said to have succeeded in getting off the ground', a reporter was told. (Disappointingly, online videos of the 'levitation' technique involve a series of cross-legged bounces, rather than the more impressive trick of floating in the air – although TM masters can supposedly achieve that when the cameras are turned off. It was reported that Mike had a room in his Santa Barbara home insulated with five-inch-thick foam rubber to make his bouncing more comfortable.) Love's development didn't end there; in 1979, he claimed that he had now learned how to dematerialise and reappear at will while employing TM techniques.

He was not the Beach Boys' only spiritual adventurer. Carl Wilson may have been battling severe back pain and flirtations with cocaine and heroin in the late 1970s, but he had not neglected his soul and his psyche. Back in 1974, he had experienced weekends with the organisation 'est', run by the controversial 'trainer', Werner Erhard. His courses were confrontational, physically and psychologically taxing, and often described as a cult – to the extent that 'est' was discontinued in 1984 and relaunched in a more relaxed form as the Forum (later the Landmark Forum). Carl admitted that he had been 'scared' during his training, but he also declared that 'the people who complained were donkeys' and that 'est' had made it easier for him to remain positive in stressful situations. Carl persuaded his brother Dennis to undergo the same experience, alongside their mother and several other members of the Beach Boys' entourage.

By the time of MIU, Carl had shifted allegiance to another organisation, with whom he remained involved for the rest of his life. This was the Movement of Spiritual Inner Awareness, which in time would also be dismissed as a cult. 'I spend an hour praying,' he would explain. 'The spiritual experiences have a real balancing effect. I was into insight training and it really took off like a rocket. It was beautiful, man.' Lawyers for Brian would later use Carl's time with the Movement as proof that he was 'easily intimidated or controlled' (unlike Brian with Dr Landy, of course). Carl remained loyal to the cause: 'It's like surrendering yourself to who you really were before everything else changed you.'

Meanwhile, Mike Love remained the loyal disciple of Transcendental Meditation, constantly seeking to access the 'field of energy, intelligence and creativity within'. As the decades passed, he would note that strict adherence to the Maharishi's principles could halt or even reverse the ravages of age (although the guru himself left this physical realm in 2008, at an unknown age but probably in his nineties).

Mike credited TM for his eternal youthfulness. 'I tell people I may be forty-six years old,' he joked in 1987, 'but I have the body of an eighteen-year-old Adonis'. The following year, he stripped down to his underpants and enjoyed a massage in front of journalists so that they could testify to his remarkable physical condition. 'Rather than just accepting the norm of aging, deterioration, disease and death ultimately,' he pronounced in 1993, 'you can reverse the aging process and live a longer life in perfect health in the direction of immortality. There are people on the Earth now who will live to be a couple of hundred years old, people who are alive this minute.' If Mike Love turns out not to be one of those pioneers, he will have to settle for another form of immortality, outlived by the music he has helped to create.

Holy Man

How Dennis Wilson found his voice

In the summer of 1969, singer-songwriter James Taylor raced a stolen motorcycle off-road in Martha's Vineyard, unaware that the brakes didn't work and the throttle sometimes stuck open. He found out when he drove into a clump of trees, breaking bones in all four limbs.

Just less than two years later, singer-songwriter Dennis Wilson – no stranger to wrecking his own bikes and cars – injured his hand so severely when he stuck it through a pane of glass that he would have died from loss of blood if his wife had not immediately secured a tourniquet around his wrist.

In the summer between those death-defying mishaps, Taylor and Wilson spent six weeks together, filming their only acting roles. Monte Hellman's *Two-Lane Blacktop* was hyped as the natural successor to *Easy Rider*, but its featureless plot and anti-acting from its supposed stars condemned it to cult appeal. Taylor's moody silence was charismatic for a tortured rock star with a history of heroin abuse, but it did not translate onto the big screen. Wilson's carefree normality was only marginally more compelling to watch. The two men bickered on set, as Dennis kept blowing takes by screwing up his lines. But, as Monte Hellman recalled, he had a naturalistic style in the film that was innate rather than studied. 'He was so totally un-self-conscious,' Hellman recalled many decades later, 'to the point where he literally forgot there was a camera, and he got caught up in just watching what was going on. It's an amazing thing to see and I've never experienced that before.'

Neither Taylor nor Wilson was troubled with further movie offers. Taylor moved forward into superstardom; Wilson on a path to self-destruction that began with that June 1971 accident. The particulars have never been clear: at various times, Wilson's injury was attributed to a DIY repair gone wrong; a simple misjudging of distance between body and glass; a fight with his second wife, Barbara; or (most likely) a burst of drunken rage. Previous self-inflicted disasters had kept the drummer off the road for, at most, a few weeks, but this was altogether more serious, requiring lengthy and complex surgery, followed by years of recovery and rehabilitation as nerves and sinews slowly reconnected.

In a single moment, Dennis had sabotaged his status as the Beach Boys' drummer: it would be more than three years before he returned to the drum kit. Also halted was his exploration of a solo career, which had been launched almost imperceptibly in 1970 with a haunting British single, 'Sound of Free'. Having convinced himself that he could maintain an artistic voice beyond the group, he had begun to assemble his first solo album, supposedly given the working title of *Poops* or *Hubba Hubba*. But that project was torpedoed by his accident.

The most enduring aftermath of his injury was the damage to his sense of self-worth. Perhaps, like Brian, he could hear his father's voice deriding him for ruining his career. Or perhaps he had been using his drums as a form of catharsis, to hold frustration and depression at bay, and that relief had now been removed. Whatever the precise psychological cause, Dennis slid immediately into a level of alcohol abuse that was a serious barrier to his future as a functioning adult, let alone a creative artist.

In concert, Dennis was now restricted to playing piano (one-handed for the first few months) and singing. To fill the long gaps between these contributions, he drank, drank some more and then fell over, or picked fights with his bandmates, or abused the audience, or some combination of these vices and more. Dennis loved (*almost*) nothing more than performing with the Beach Boys, but once he was barred from the drums, he felt purposeless in front of a crowd. Sporadic incidents during late 1971 and 1972 mutated into constant misbehaviour in 1973, when critics frequently noted that he appeared to be utterly disconnected from what was going on.

Somehow, amidst this chaos, he continued to compose songs – agonisingly slow romantic ballads for the most part, which chronicled both his obsessive love for Barbara and the anguish of jeopardising her devoted attention. There was still a Dennis Wilson who loved rhythm and blues and could growl oldies such as 'Sea Cruise'. But his authentic voice was that of the star-crossed lover man, seductive, tender and ultimately doomed.

After the '*Poops*' project collapsed towards the end of 1971, there was a pause of almost two years before Dennis was able to resume any kind of coherent recording schedule. The tune that signposted his return as a creative force (and should have laid out a path for his colleagues to follow) was 'River Song'. It began to appear in the Beach Boys' live set in the summer of 1973, as a rolling epic that captured the awesome power of water (and the group's equally majestic harmonies). He and Carl began work on a recording later that year and, in a kinder, more productive world, it would have built the foundation for a true successor to the *Holland* album: adult, emotionally driven, fired by a personal connection to the environment. But nobody else in the Beach Boys was ready to make that record. Instead, Dennis accumulated songs for his own purposes: 'Rainbows', 'Holy Man', 'Friday Night', 'My Love Lives On' and 'Pacific Ocean Blues' (with lyrics of environmental concern provided by cousin Mike Love) in 1974 alone. If his name had been Brian, the band would happily have let him mastermind a Beach Boys record containing nothing but his compositions. But Dennis? He was just the drummer, the alcoholic, the screw-up. The fact that he was by far the most adventurous and coherent songwriter in the group for the next five years was treated as an irrelevance.

Also in 1974, R&B/gospel singer/organist Billy Preston issued an album entitled *The Kids & Me*, which included an attractive and lusciously arranged soul ballad, 'You Are So Beautiful'. The song was covered by Joe Cocker, whose version became a US Top 10 hit. The following summer, Dennis Wilson began to sing it with the Beach Boys, usually coming out alone at the start of the encores to stand centre stage and break the audience's collective heart. He never made the claim in public, but he told friends that he had co-written the song during a drinking session, though he wasn't one of the listed composers. He certainly made it his own, even into the early 1980s, by which point his voice had disintegrated into a gravelly croak, as if a giant toad was having its throat squeezed. (Wilson never explained the precise circumstances, but he is believed to have suffered permanent impairment to his vocal cords after a drunken brawl around 1973. Despite many claims to the contrary, the injury was not caused by the later assault he endured from Rocky Pamplin and Stan Love. Whoever the culprit was, they transformed an already gruff voice into a painful, though still affecting, growl. Addictions and prolonged throat strain did the rest of the damage.)

Like his brother Carl, Dennis never claimed to be a lyricist, though his music often spoke more potently than words. He would sometimes collaborate with Mike Love, despite the unbridgeable gorge between their respective lifestyles. During the late 1960s, he had begun to write with Gregg Jakobson, and that relationship continued through the 1970s, until Dennis's involvement with heroin drove Jakobson away. Steve Kalinich was another occasional helpmate, as was Carl. And, from 1975 onwards, he would occasionally seek lyrical inspiration from his new actress girlfriend, Karen Lamm. Over the next few years, she would become both his third – and fourth – wife, as Dennis finally met a woman who was equally as wild as he was.

Born Barbara Karen Perk, she had moved from Indiana to California in 1970. She met Chicago keyboardist Robert Lamm at the Whisky a Go Go and married him a few weeks later when she was still only eighteen. In what would become a pattern, they were divorced the following year, but Robert and Karen remained close, which is why she was in the entourage when Chicago and the Beach Boys were on the road together in 1974. By then, she was picking up regular work as a model and actress, although rarely in a major role. She began a tempestuous relationship with Dennis, which hit the headlines when he was arrested in January 1976. Precise details were lost amidst their joint alcohol abuse, but during a domestic incident they argued, he hit her, she reached for a loaded pistol and he drove off with it. She called the police, who charged Dennis with battery and grand theft. The following day, Karen sobered up and withdrew all the allegations. The couple married just less than four months later. After fifteen months, they were divorced; ten months later, they remarried, before divorcing for the final time in May 1980. There were complications along the way: at one point, they had a seventeen-year-old staying in their house who stole a diamond ring worth $25,000 from them, only to return it a few days later. Chaos became their normality and their stimulation.

Karen was intensely supportive of Dennis's music, sometimes supplying lyrics – at least, during the periods when the couple weren't fighting just as intensely. No wonder that all the brushstrokes of his creativity became more passionate, more desperate, more extreme during their relationship – the tumultuous emotional landscape of their union was transferred directly into his work. Not one to hide her light, Karen proclaimed that Dennis would never have completed a solo album if it wasn't for the loyalty of two people: his lyrical collaborator, Gregg Jakobson, and, of course, Karen herself.

From 1974 to 1978, Dennis camped out at the band's Brother Studios facility while taping dozens of musical fragments and epic romantic ballads. But it was only in 1976 that he was awarded a recording contract in his own right by Caribou boss, and sometime Beach Boys manager/bassist, James William Guercio. Company executives did not want Dennis to produce 'just another Beach Boys album'. Guercio recognised that the drummer-turned-keyboardist had a unique voice, physically and as a composer, and did not want that to be softened or commercialised by the rest of the band. Mike Love and Carl Wilson did offer lyrical assistance, of course, and Carl also lent closet instrumental support. So did a host of other names from the Beach Boys' milieu, Bruce Johnston (then still in exile from the band), Billy Hinsche, Carli Muñoz, Ed Carter and Bobby Figueroa among them. But the lavish, dense, overwhelming emotive tapestries of sound came from the imagination of one man – an impulsive, hyperactive drinker who found the patience to spend countless hours overdubbing dozens of keyboard parts and multi-tracked harmony vocals.

As Gregg Jakobson explained, 'Dennis comes into the studio in the morning and stays until he's tired'. Dennis called his approach 'self-indulgence', but he was being too harsh on himself. His fuel was the self-belief that had been lacking earlier in the 1970s, when he was trying to train his unique vision into something suitable for the Beach Boys. He revealed that his goal was to produce 'a much bigger sound' than his group could ever achieve; he credited his influences as Beethoven, Wagner and Bach, besides, of course, his brother Brian. 'My album is more into poetry and music, listening to the sounds, the overall experience,' he added when it was finished, and that was not a description fitting any Beach Boys records from the second half of the 1970s.

It is ironic, or maybe just touching, that Brian and Dennis were reaching peak productivity at the same moment – and that their work was so starkly different from each other's. Dennis was completing *Pacific Ocean Blue* while Brian was recording *Adult/Child* in the same studio complex. 'Believe me, I've never felt so good about anything since the first Beach Boys single was recorded,' Dennis announced.

As the August 1977 release date for *Pacific Ocean Blue* grew closer, Dennis admitted to being 'scared. I really am. People say, "Don't worry, you're going to be a star". But that's not the point. I just want to do it well enough so I can do it again.' Artistically, there was no doubting what he had achieved: the sheer musicality and depth of his record was staggering. But it did not sound remotely like a Beach Boys album, nor was it overtly commercial, lacking the pop hooks and pristine vocalising associated with the mothership. Listening to *Pacific Ocean Blue* was like embarking on a relationship with Dennis Wilson: overwhelming, confusing, sometimes dark, often beautiful, an immersion of the senses and emotions.

By 1977, it was tough enough to sell Beach Boys albums, let alone a complex offering from the band's drummer. Initial reviews were often damning. One declared coldly that Dennis 'can't sing … can hardly keep on key', as if the critic had been expecting the Beach Boys of 1963. Even the positive responses viewed *Pacific Ocean Blue* as the beginning of a journey, not a destination. It soon became apparent that there was no danger of Dennis's record sales outstripping those of the group. 'I've been humbled,' he had to admit. 'You think you're a big shot in a big band and then you put out a solo record and expect everyone to play it right away.' There was no cult of *Pacific Ocean Blue* in 1977, no faction insisting that Dennis was the Beach Boys' secret genius: that would only happen decades after his death. Still, disappointed or not, Dennis was wise enough to understand the significance of what he had achieved: 'I used to be terrified the group would break up. Now it could break up and I wouldn't fall apart. Now I have my own career.' It was gratifying to hear his pride being admitted so openly. 'It's the first time in my life I've completed a significant project alone. Getting out there alone gives me a real sense of power and confidence.'

'Getting out there alone' involved more than recording. Dennis had booked a ten-city concert tour, set to open in New York during November 1977. Alongside him would be one active Beach Boy, his brother Carl, and one former member, Bruce Johnston – plus what Dennis described as 'a small orchestra'. Two days of rehearsals took place, as preparation for his first exposure, on the TV series *Don Kirshner's Rock Concert*. But that taping was cancelled at the last minute and, soon afterwards, the tour met the same fate – postponed initially until January, then taken off the agenda. There was talk that other Beach Boys – Mike Love was always in the frame on these occasions – had threatened that if he performed solo, then Dennis would be out of the band. That would have been hypocritical if it were true, because Mike had staged his own mini-tour in October with his band-in-progress, then still known as Making Waves. In any case, as Mike stated in his memoir about the supposed threat, 'that was not true. I was looking forward to writing more songs with Dennis for his solo efforts.'

As *Pacific Ocean Blue* was released, Dennis was indeed promising a second album within a matter of weeks. He certainly had the material, especially when he began to tackle a bunch of songs composed by one of his collaborators, Beach Boys keyboardist Carli Muñoz. (Like Jakobson, Muñoz baled out when Dennis lost control of his drug intake.) No record label in 1978 would have wanted a follow-up so soon, so Dennis kept recording through the first half of the year – until his sonic playground at Brother Studios had to be sold for financial reasons. Now he was forced to jockey for position at other commercial studios and pay professional rates for the kind of facilities he had effectively been enjoying for free. Already struggling through the circular disintegration of his marriage, and his increasing dependence on alcohol and narcotics, Dennis gave up hope of completing the second album, let alone the two further records he had been boasting about a few months earlier. Now, there was also less need for him to remain focused on music. Hedonism, and its attendant despair, could take control – and inevitably they did. The final outlet for his new music in his lifetime came when Carl and Bruce borrowed two of his songs, 'Love Surrounds Me' and 'Baby Blue', for the Beach Boys' *L.A. (Light Album).* They sounded magnificent, especially with Carl's vocal cameos. But it was a stunning sunset, not a fresh dawn.

At the time *Pacific Ocean Blue* was released, Dennis was still fantasising about a future in which he might compose a rock opera and open a recording complex in Hawaii named Bamboo. That moniker was passed on to his next album, and in turn to the bootlegs of semi-completed tracks that emerged after his death; years later, insiders asserted that the title should have been spelled *Bambu*. But despite the twenty-first-century unveiling of many unreleased songs, it isn't true that *Bambu* was ready for release back in 1978 – or, indeed, that Dennis had fixed upon a definite track listing. Like *SMiLE*, whatever *Bambu* might have been was open to speculation, then argument, and finally a lingering sense of loss that Dennis Wilson must have felt more keenly than any of us.

Christmas Comes This Time Each Year

The Beach Boys' strange seasonal gifts

The madcap pace of Beach Boys albums in the 1960s was not just a tribute to Brian Wilson's speed and proficiency in the recording studio. It was also a contractual obligation imposed by Capitol Records. They expected a teen sensation such as the Beach Boys to enjoy two or, at most, three years of slavish devotion from their fans, who would buy anything bearing their idols' name. After that, the group would either slide into commercial oblivion or, if they were smart, they would widen their appeal towards the adult easy listening market, hoping that at least some of their teenage fans would follow their stale new direction. In either case, a seasonal record of Christmas songs made financial sense. Teenagers would buy it out of loyalty and adults might discover a painless introduction to a harmony combo who could – who knew? – come to rival the Four Freshmen for longevity.

Capitol's avarice was a brutal weapon. During their early recording career, the Beach Boys were expected to deliver four long-playing albums per year. Even a composer/producer as prolific as Brian Wilson found that pace impossible to maintain, which is why 1964 saw them issuing a live record, followed closely by *The Beach Boys' Christmas Album*. Brian could have spent a couple of days creating *a capella* arrangements of Christmas carols – topped and tailed, perhaps, by the kind of singalong tunes that turned up on similar offerings by the likes of Frank Sinatra or Perry Como. Instead, he elected to fill one side of the album with original material and turn the other over to the man who had masterminded the Four Freshmen recordings. Dick Reynolds, Brian conceded, 'is practically a god to me', which is why he allowed the older man to handle the arrangements. The results were safe and square, but Brian relished the experience. His brother Dennis was also thrilled. 'Some of the things were really hard to do, but I felt like I'd just made a million dollars when I heard "Blue Christmas".'

Their 1964 fanbase were probably more impressed by the first side of the album, which kicked off with their quintessential Christmas single, 'Little Saint Nick' – a standard Brian Wilson car song, given a reindeer-and-sled twist, with sleigh bells to match. It has become as inescapable at Christmas time, in Britain at least, as those other Yuletide singles that refuse to die – by Wham!, Mariah Carey and the rest.

Markedly absent from the Christmas playlists that chime out from high-street stores is the Beach Boys' seasonal cash-in from 1974, 'Child of Winter (Christmas Song)'. If anyone had heard it at the time, they might have interpreted it as an artistic suicide note. It had been almost two years since the band's last new studio offering, the *Holland* album. 'Child of Winter' bore no relation to anything on that record – except, perhaps, Brian's 'Fairy Tale', though that sounded like a symphonic masterpiece by comparison with the Christmas single. The 'original' element of 'Child of Winter' comprised the simplest of two-chord patterns, repeated to the point of obsessive compulsion – in the same way that Brian was now turning up at friends' houses and treating them to marathon performances of two equally banal riffs that had lodged themselves in his imagination, 'Ding Dang' and 'Shortnin' Bread'.

The only variation was supplied when the song drifted into a revival of the vintage Gene Autry hit, 'Here Comes Santa Claus' (the composers of which were not credited on the Beach Boys' release). That sweet relief was all too brief as the deadening riff returned, Mike Love did his best to pretend he was still awake, and sundry Beach Boys repeated an almost clinically simplistic refrain. Towards the end, Brian reprised the squeaky, proto-Cartman voice he'd employed on the 'Fairy Tale' – but, by then, any sane listener would already have switched off their radio.

Not that this emergency tactic was much in demand at Christmas 1974. The Beach Boys ensured that the record wouldn't sell by holding back its release until 23 December. Nobody reviewed it, no station played it, nobody bought it – in fact, almost nobody knew it had been released.

Even that was a success in comparison to the next Christmas project. Not content with relocating the band (except for Carl and Dennis, who voted to remain on the West Coast) to the Maharishi's university in Iowa, Messrs Love, Jardine and Wilson (B.D.) decided it made sense to record two albums simultaneously in November 1977 – one of which, inevitably, was a seasonal record. Equally inevitably, it was taped too late for Christmas – although even more inevitably, that wasn't a problem this time, as Warner/Reprise vehemently refused to consider releasing it.

Most of *Merry Christmas from the Beach Boys* has since been smuggled onto compilation albums – enough to prove how disastrous a project this would have been. Two 'serious' songs were recorded: Brian's 'Winter Symphony', which was both elegant and intensely personal, and Dennis's 'Morning Christmas', perhaps the most funereal of the many achingly poignant ballads he cut in the late 1970s. The rest was a mixture of Christmas carols, performed with wives and children; leftovers from earlier sessions with no seasonal relevance, such as 'Seasons in the Sun' and 'Michael Row the Boat Ashore'; and rewritten Yule-themed versions of other unreleased songs. 'Loop de Loop' became 'Santa's Got an Airplane', 'Help is on the Way' mutated into 'Santa's on His Way', and Buddy Holly's 'Peggy Sue' somehow metamorphosed into 'Christmas Time is Here Again'. And what was that, propping up the track listing? Yes, the unfortunate 'Child of Winter'. No wonder Carl and Dennis stayed home.

Cousins, Friends and Brothers

The Beach Boys fall apart

While the Washington establishment was inaugurating a president, the 'best composer living in the world' (in his cousin's words) was taking the stage in the suburbs east of the city, at the Capital Centre in Largo, Maryland. Jimmy Carter's administration would end in humiliation four years later, but in January 1977, Brian Wilson and the Beach Boys could implode far more quickly than that.

Moments of chaos and tension littered the show in Largo. Dennis Wilson could carry off intoxication with ease, but throughout 1977, his younger brother Carl struggled to hide the same affliction. His usually flawless singing was slurred and incoherent, and his lead guitar so off key that Al Jardine winced and groaned as they set out to butcher 'Susie Cincinnati'. Through 'Surfer Girl', perpetually warring cousins Dennis and Mike Love glared at each other with ill-disguised contempt. Love messed with Jardine's microphone stand during 'Back Home', eventually planting it firmly on his bandmate's foot. Brian Wilson began the same song by shaking his microphone as if he was trying to kill it, then set off across centre-stage before the song had finished, throwing his bass guitar into Love's arms. His behaviour during the newly written 'Airplane' was even more bizarre, as he bellowed his vocal cameos like a lion announcing a kill. Wounded classics littered the stage; nothing escaped entirely unharmed.

Yet there would still have been so much to love if you'd been there, so much nostalgia compressed into the oldies, so much joy delivered almost by accident between the collisions and failures. Through it all, Mike Love maintained a showman's panache and ease, while Al Jardine delivered every vocal with perfect pitch and tone. The jazz master of the flute and saxophone, Charles Lloyd, conjured ecstasy out of the torn canvas of two of the band's most beautiful songs, 'Feel Flows' and 'All This is That'. And at the end, Dennis managed to forget his hatred for his cousin and blessed the crowd with the wrecked majesty of his solo rendition of 'You Are So Beautiful'.

The next day, with a new album set for release, Love set out on his six-month TM course, and the band ground to a halt. The plan was that they would return with a flamboyant run of stadium shows in Europe. But management chaos and Love's apparent unwillingness to return for rehearsals endangered the tour. And then, as Brian Wilson let slip to a reporter while his PR man panicked alongside him, 'tickets weren't selling' and all the concerts were cancelled. All, that is, except one. In one of the great Beach Boys acts of self-sabotage, the band still gathered in London to play at the CBS Records Convention in front of industry guests and friends – but none of their disappointed followers. 'Beach Boys Snub British Fans' was the verdict of a London newspaper.

For a band who hadn't seen each other for six months, the CBS show was surprisingly coherent. Brian had stopped wanting to savage his songs and was prepared to sing them; Carl was both sober and coherent, unlike the over-refreshed audience. OK, the harmonies were rough and, by the end, Mike had become so annoyed with Brian that he attempted to push his piano off stage. (The Beach Boys were playing 'Fun, Fun, Fun' at the time, appropriately enough.) But there was one breathtaking moment when four of the group, Brian and Carl, Al and Mike, gathered without instruments at the front of the stage and delivered an utterly flawless *a capella* version of 'Their Hearts Were Full of Spring', as if it was 1964 again and they couldn't help but ooze magic.

Then it was back to the US and two weeks of touring, which led them to New York's Central Park for a free afternoon concert. It was the usual affair – sloppy, chaotic when Carl's voice revealed that he was back under the influence – but still somehow joyful. The following morning, the group gathered at a Manhattan office for a traumatic business meeting. There was one item on the agenda. After months of managers arriving and leaving, should the band rehire the contender who had already caused Dennis and Carl most pain, and who was also their cousin: Steve Love?

Dennis returned to their hotel for an interview to promote his new solo album and announced that the evening concert on Rhode Island would probably be their last. By now, the band was so fractured that they travelled on two jets. One of them carried the clean-living contingent headed by Mike and Al; the other, the party animals, led by Dennis and Carl. Brian veered between one and the other, depending on who had made him the best offer. Sensing a juicy story, John Swenson of *Rolling Stone* magazine chose the more exuberant plane and was rewarded by Dennis and Carl at their most candid. It became apparent that at the morning meeting, Brian had voted sleepily with the Love/Jardine faction, and Steve Love was back at the helm. Carl and Dennis threatened to walk out; the others said that they had already chosen suitable replacements. Dennis told Swenson that he was about to witness the final concert. Carl admitted that he was 'incredibly sad. My heart is broken.'

Backstage at the venue, the two brothers tried to explain what had gone wrong to their mother Audree. As if they were still in grade school, she suggested they should try to mend the fences and stick the band back together. 'You have to communicate with the rest of the boys,' she told Dennis. He sighed and explained that he had tried. 'You were the last to know,' he told her. 'I wish you could somehow straighten it all out', she said quietly.

On stage, the Beach Boys were 'shaky', a reporter said, not least because Brian decided to walk off early in the set and not return until close to the encores. Nobody said a word about a crisis; the band soaked up the applause and headed back to Providence airport. In an attempt at healing, Dennis and his girlfriend joined the Steve Love faction on their plane, leaving Carl to sulk alone on the other jet. The entire band was scheduled to fly back to California via a connecting flight in Newark, but at the last moment Dennis and Karen Lamm announced they were going to stay in New York. Brian signalled that he liked that idea too. Perhaps they were terrified of what might happen to him if he was separated from them, perhaps they simply couldn't brook disobedience, but the Love/Jardine faction became incensed and commanded Brian to get on their plane. Dennis swore at Al Jardine, whose birthday it was, and Al told him that the band no longer needed him: 'We can make it without you.'

Dennis stomped off their plane and reported back to Carl, who was furious. Fired up by his brother's support, Dennis raced back towards the Love/Jardine plane. Meanwhile, John Swenson climbed into the limousine that Dennis had ordered for his ride into the city. The next minute, Dennis, Mike, Steve Love and the third brother, Stan, proceeded to scream at each other next to the limousine. Swenson got out to make sure he could hear it all: the threats, the insults aimed at Dennis, the Love brothers' repeated accusation that the drummer had been riding on the band's coattails for years.

Back at the *Rolling Stone* office, Swenson made calls to find out whether the Beach Boys had really called it quits. He located Dennis, who said that a critical meeting had been planned to decide the future – and Brian had chosen that moment to escape to Hawaii on vacation. The vote was split two-two and everything was left to cool down.

'Unfortunately, we happened to have an argument that was overheard by a guy from *Rolling Stone*,' Love commented after Swenson's account was published, 'and he made it into a *National Enquirer* article.' Love admitted that 'there are some very strong egos in the group', but insisted that 'the next couple of years will see a real blossoming of the Beach Boys as a group and as individuals'.

Days before the Rhode Island showdown, Dennis had told a reporter that if any of the three Wilson brothers left the Beach Boys, it would be the end of the group – that the departure of one would automatically trigger the departure of all three. Legally, he explained, all five members were required to sign off on a concert tour or an album: 'They can't do much without Carl and me.' But he was adamant that the band could only survive if the calibre of their own work improved. 'I think the Beach Boys haven't been making winner albums, and it hurts when you don't have a winner. I wasn't in total agreement with those albums [*15 Big Ones* and *Love You*]. They weren't as good as the guys can do. I told them, "Guys, maybe we should be taking more time with these records." They said, "Don't worry about it." We had some tense moments about that.'

Instead, Love and Jardine had relocated the band to the Maharishi's university in Iowa, where Dennis and Carl did not want to go. The result was almost certainly the worst (released) record of their career, the utterly banal *M.I.U. Album*. And the Beach Boys were also committed to a run of live shows either side of the first studio sessions, plus more performances in December. By common assent, these concerts were disasters. Dennis coped with the tension by drinking to excess and then drinking some more. In Johnson City, he began to insult the Southern audience, calling them 'slow' and 'dumb'. In Vancouver, he started ranting to the crowd about ice hockey and wouldn't shut up, so the band had to play over him. Brian would start to perform a song and then walk away from the microphone without warning, leaving Mike to cover for him. Band members would wander on and off the stage at the slightest provocation. Harmonies wavered on a scale between atrocious and non-existent. Audiences booed when the group attempted to play new songs. But at a hometown gig just after Christmas 1977, there was a family reunion of sorts, as all three Wilson brothers, their cousin Mike Love and his three sisters were all up on stage at the same time.

Through January and early February 1978, Dennis worked sporadically on a second solo record. Then the group prepared for a trip that would make their pre-Christmas tour seem like a vacation: almost a month in New Zealand and Australia. The Sex Pistols had just toured the US for the first time, their roadies wearing T-shirts that boasted 'This Sure Ain't the Beach Boys Tour'. But the Beach Boys were about to outstrip the Pistols when it came to excess.

All three Wilson brothers had reached crisis point at the same moment. Any lingering influence of Eugene Landy's therapy on Brian's psyche had vanished: the oldest brother clawed desperately at any stimulant or sedative that would stop him from hearing the destructive voices in his head. Dennis was a functioning alcoholic who couldn't draw the line between indulgence and oblivion. As he had already told a reporter the previous summer, 'I've been in moods where I'd do cocaine for a week, for the experience'. And those weeks now extended into months. And Carl, the peacemaker, the force of reason within the Beach Boys, the strict onstage taskmaster and perfectionist? He could no longer bear the tension of the band's internal dynamics, nor the physical pain inflicted by his chronic back complaint. He had confessed to taking cocaine: what he didn't tell the press was that, like his brothers, he was also falling prey to the seductive illusion of heroin.

The first drama on the tour came when Brian went down with a heavy cold and diagnosed himself as being unable to perform. Every night he would appear briefly on stage and then disappear without a word to the crowd or his colleagues. 'He doesn't hide his feelings,' Carl explained. 'He doesn't have the facility like other people of carrying on great and feeling dreadful inside. If he feels bad, everybody can tell.' And he always felt bad. He hated touring, he told a journalist, and wished he had been born with less talent, and less responsibility.

Carl's public version of the Beach Boys' current state verged on the idyllic. He admitted there were still arguments, 'but we don't want to hurt each other's feelings. There's more quality in our communication now, it's more complete.' Not as complete as the punch thrown at him by Rocky Pamplin, one of Brian's bodyguards, after the first Melbourne show, which knocked him out. Brian had scored some heroin – maybe from Dennis, with Carl's silent encouragement, maybe from an anonymous source – and drifted into unconsciousness, having to be revived with jets of cold water. Carl aimed a sarcastic comment at his minder. Exit the peacemaker.

The following night, Carl's black eye was heavily made up and his dosage of painkillers increased. Neither improved his performance. His voice was the central pivot of the group's harmonies, and that night in Melbourne, it was askew from the start. He swayed back and forth in front of his microphone, smiled and laughed at inappropriate moments, and lost the ability to tune his guitar. In an unlikely reversal of moral standards, Carl even swore loudly over the microphone and had to be reminded where he was by Dennis. Every song was a betrayal of the Beach Boys' legacy, despite all of Mike Love's showmanship and Al Jardine's professionalism. To his credit, Carl did attempt to sing: on 'God Only Knows', he concentrated so hard that he sounded like a choirboy sliding inexorably off a clifftop. By the time Love's voice vanished towards the end of the show, there was only one coherent performer on the stage, and Jardine's face betrayed the fact that he would rather be anywhere but there.

From there, the tour went downhill. The first show in Perth was the group's all-time nadir: they could cope with Brian's disappearing acts, and Dennis stumbling around the stage like a vaudeville drunk, but when Carl fell flat on his face while trying to sing 'Darlin'', and when he spent more time eyeing up the girls than playing guitar, the game was up. The following morning, he had to stage an apologetic press conference, taking full responsibility and blaming 'a Valium … and two Mai Tais'. He conceded that 'I was frightening the other members of the group', especially Brian, who had also been criticised in the local papers. 'I screwed everything up,' he insisted during the second show. 'It was my fault – and they got on Brian's case, and that wasn't even so.' They moved on to Sydney, where they performed during an apocalyptic downpour, and flew home via Hawaii, where a reviewer said that they 'sounded waterlogged – like hearing their records in warped condition'.

As Carl explained five years later, 'that was a very rough time for all of us. Relations were very strained and icy. Everyone was frightened and it came out as anger. Everything was falling apart in front of us. We got a chance to see if we really wanted to be a group or not. It became clear that we should put it back together.'

But, as Paul Simon could have told him, everything put together sooner or later falls apart …

Love, Love, Love

The other weird Beach Boys family

'There's a lot of estrangement in our family.'

In that single sentence, Stephen Love succeeded in summing up the sorry saga of the Beach Boys. Not to be outdone, his brother Stanley put it like this: 'Looking back on it, the Beach Boys, well, that was probably the worst thing that ever happened to us.'

Put even more simply, the Wilson clan did not own the monopoly in family conflict within the Beach Boys. There was only one Love in the band, but Mike and his two non-singing brothers succeeded in stirring up just as much controversy as Brian, Dennis, Carl and their father Murry. (By contrast, nobody seems to have had a word to say against the three Love sisters, all of whom appeared on Beach Boys records occasionally.)

For years, the Wilson and Love kids seemed to be repairing the rift between the elder generation, exemplified by the refusal of Murry Wilson to speak to his brother-in-law, Mike's father Milt, except at Christmas time. And although the Mike/Brian relationship was always going to be feisty, especially when artistry and money came into conflict, the wider Love family might have escaped the fallout without one strategic error: inviting Mike's younger brothers Stanley and Stephen to get involved with the Beach Boys.

Mike wasn't the only star in the Love family, as Stan Love staked out a successful career on the basketball court (as did his son Kevin from the next generation). He was a famously combative player, it seems, who carried much of that attitude with him beyond the sporting arena. He was also prodigiously tall, as his choice of sport suggested. Stephen Love wasn't afraid of physical activity either, displaying some talent for karate. But his area of expertise was business, which ensured that he would join the group's management in the 1970s after they parted company from Jack Rieley. It was Steve's proud boast that he was at the helm for the era of 'their greatest success' as a touring band around the time of the *Endless Summer* compilation. When Stan's basketball career slowed down, Steve offered him a crucial role in the group's organisation: helping to protect Brian Wilson from himself by keeping him from drugs and encouraging him to pursue physical fitness.

With Eugene Landy in the role of chief therapist, Stan joined the support crew tasked with ensuring that, as the publicity slogan put it, 'Brian's back'. 'Brian never wanted to be a star,' Stan confided in 1976 as the campaign began. 'He wanted to lay back and run things.' When Landy was fired for financial reasons (by Steve, according to Carl), Stan took over as Brian's minder-cum-controller. He complained that his cousin was still a teenager at heart: his task, Stan said, was to turn Brian into a man. There was also a monetary motive: 'Brian is like a musical oil well. We look after the oil well.'

Meanwhile, the rest of the oil industry was falling apart. Steve Love was fired by popular consent in 1977, only for Mike, Al and a mostly silent Brian to call him back – to the disgust of the other Wilson brothers. The group broke up over that quarrel, then gradually came together when both Steve and Stan were exiled from the group's inner circle. But Brian's condition deteriorated fast, and soon Stan was back in post as one of his support crew. He and fresh recruit Rocky Pamplin formed a hard-man partnership against anyone who threatened Brian's sobriety – including Dennis, whom they beat to a pulp in 1982. (An earlier fistfight, in 1977, saw the same Pamplin/Love combination intervening to stop Brian from punching Mike Love backstage. 'I was really hitting,' Brian confessed. 'Mike didn't hit me back. If he did, he would have knocked me unconscious.')

Meanwhile, a five-year land dispute had been bubbling beneath the surface – this time pitting Steve Love against his most famous brother. It concerned two acres of beachfront on the Hawaiian island of Kauai. Steve purchased the land, which was duly put in his name. He claimed he'd bought it for his own purposes; Mike insisted that Steve had been acting as a surrogate for him. Much embarrassing legal drama ensued, at the end of which Mike kept the property and Steve received his money back.

Steve's fortunes deteriorated when a second battle over land and its proceeds reached the courts. This time the property was in Santa Barbara County. In 1975, Steve (acting as the Beach Boys' business manager) formed a limited partnership to purchase the land. In 1980, after being fired by the band, he launched a lawsuit claiming breach of contract. At that point, the Beach Boys discovered that they no longer owned the Santa Barbara land: Steve had apparently sold it secretly and kept the proceeds for himself. Al Jardine claimed that Steve admitted, 'I was real bad. I took the money from the partnership and put it into real estate in Hawaii.' In 1988, Steve finally pleaded guilty to one charge of grand theft and was put on five years' probation. At this point, not surprisingly, Mike and Steve became permanently estranged.

This was not the end of the extended Love family saga. In 1990, Stan Love reappeared, staging a press conference to demand that Brian Wilson be removed from the care of Eugene Landy, whom he claimed was keeping Brian from the rest of his family. Instead, Stan wanted himself to be appointed as conservator/guardian. To Stan's amazement, Brian invaded the conference to announce that he was completely capable of making his own decisions: 'Stan's charges that I'm being controlled or taken advantage of are simply untrue'. Stan was 'visibly stunned' and told reporters: 'Brian Wilson has the look in his face like a prisoner of war coming back from Vietnam, or a hostage. He is totally controlled. He is a puppet right now. It's been that way for years.' Stan claimed to have tried to phone Brian more than a hundred times without being allowed to speak to his cousin once.

The following year, Steve and Stan admitted that they had been primary sources for Steven Gaines' highly controversial biography of the Beach Boys, *Heroes and Villains*. Meanwhile, the two brothers and their sisters spoke up to insist that Stan would be the best person to look after Brian. 'Fame is the worst thing that ever happened to us,' Stan said. 'A lot of us wish the Beach Boys had never happened.'

Time passed, disputes were settled, Eugene Landy was removed. Brian remarried and, in 2008, joined his contentious cousin Stan at courtside to watch young Kevin Love in a high school game. All was at peace, it seemed, although in his 2016 autobiography, Mike revealed that he and his brother Stephen were still estranged after the battles over land rights and money. And Stanley? Until his death in 2025, he remained in touch with brother Mike. But around 2021, Beach Boys fans on Reddit began to circulate what they claimed was a screenshot from Stan Love's Facebook feed, on which he allegedly wrote: 'I knew Dennis [Wilson] for 30 years … I have never met a bigger piece of shit drunken coke head. Wife beater. This guy was a real shit person. If you idolise this pos [piece of shit]. Your fucked also.' It proved that words of Love only go so far when you have to love the family you're with.

Who Wears Short Shorts?

Profile #8: Bruce Johnston

He never intended to be a Beach Boy. At the start, he was a stand-in, first for a night, then for a week. He was waiting for the message that it was time to go home, but until then, he kept turning up, and getting paid, and one day Brian Wilson invited him to join the group in the studio. For the rest of the 1960s, he drifted along on the fringes of the band: sometimes he'd skip sessions for a while and vacation in Europe. More recently, it's been suggested that other members of the Beach Boys spent much of the decade trying to send him into permanent exile. But he clung on until 1972, became a Grammy-award-winning songwriter, dropped by Beach Boys sessions and concerts from time to time, and was then invited to become a stand-in one more time, for one more tour. Instead, he upgraded that role to producer – and Bruce Johnston has been a Beach Boy ever since, racking up more active years with the group than anyone other than Mike Love.

He's an easy man to caricature: in fact, he does it himself. Bruce calls himself 'the all-round schlockmeister'. Publicist Derek Taylor dubbed him 'the Beach Boys' ambassador in tennis shoes'. For the past forty-five years, he's been up front, standing behind a skimpy keyboard wearing even skimpier shorts, his hands more often raised to lead the community clapping than ever touching the keys. Not that he is hiding any musical inadequacies: Bruce Johnston is the Beach Boy with the classical education, a master pianist and producer. His voice has less presence than those of his original bandmates, but it's always been infinitely flexible and he could hit higher notes than Brian without sounding remotely pained. For at least the last thirty-five years, he has been threatening to leave the Beach Boys and concentrate on composing songs. But then another tour rolls around and Bruce is back up there again, the band's in-house cheerleader, critic, peacemaker and all-around chilled guy. He still surfs, into his eighties. Maybe he was the perfect Beach Boy after all.

If Bruce sometimes presents himself as a man who can't believe he got so lucky, that's probably because it's true. He was born on 27 June 1942, to a single-mother college student in Illinois, under the name of Benjamin Baldwin. He was quickly adopted by a Los Angeles family with a business empire, who renamed him Bruce Arthur Johnston. Only after his adoptive parents died did he start to track down his blood relatives, discovering that he had three extra brothers and three new sisters.

Meanwhile, his new family had prospered to the point that his adoptive father became president of the Owl Rexall Drug Company. By 1967, it was being reported that Bruce was heir to 'two vast fortunes in medicine and canning', which is probably why he lacked the existential will to succeed of a Mike Love or Brian Wilson: it's hard to feel a sense of risk with an inheritance to rely on. For a man who's been known to carry himself like a well-mannered playboy, though, Bruce Johnston couldn't be accused of laziness, especially in the first two decades of his career.

He'd been tutored in piano at private school and Interlochen Arts Camp. He was supposed to graduate at UCLA, but slipped out of university after a few weeks to concentrate on something more pressing: rock 'n' roll. He fell into a small, rumbustious community of teenage musicians, any of whom might crop up in a variety of different guises and disguises. For a while, he was pianist in Kip Tyler and the Flips; he was almost a member of the Teddy Bears with Phil Spector, though he skipped the session for their first single to go on a date; he appeared behind stars such as Eddie Cochran and the Everly Brothers before his eighteenth birthday; and he helped his friend Sandy Nelson create one of the landmark instrumentals of the rock 'n' roll era, 'Teen Beat'.

'The first day I was in the business,' Bruce recalled, 'I did a demo with Sandy Nelson. This black guy who owned the label that Jesse Belvin was on, he asked us to come down to his office, and while we were there, someone came in and shot him. I was fourteen years old and I was witness to a murder!' The victim was John Dolphin, a noted impresario on the Hollywood R&B scene, who died on 1 February 1958 (when Bruce was fifteen years old). Press reports noted that three teenagers were in the office at the time: one of them was (supposedly) sixteen-year-old Bruce McCullough, who testified at the preliminary murder hearing. Was McCullough really Johnston, fearing for his safety and hiding behind a pseudonym?

This bizarre incident was not allowed to dampen the boy's enthusiasm. You could trace an accurate picture of the Los Angeles rock scene between 1958 and 1967 by deleting everything from history apart from the records Bruce Johnston played on. He wasn't a scene-maker like Kim Fowley, or an innovator like Phil Spector, or an intuitive composing genius like Brian Wilson, or even a star, really, prizing his anonymity even when he was a member of the Beach Boys. But he was there, riding every shift in pop scenery, shaping some of them, tailing along behind the rest, but always around, usually with a song up his sleeve to cash in on the latest pop novelty.

Before the Beach Boys, he was half of a writing/producing/performing team with Terry Melcher, another rock 'n' roller raised in privilege (his mother was, of course, Doris Day). They flooded the California record scene with singles in the early 1960s, cutting surf and hot rod and folk-rock and blue-eyed soul and anything else the market might require. Sometimes they were Bruce and Terry, which made sense; or else they were the Rip Chords (a real group, pushed aside to make way for their more talented producers); or the Hot Doggers, the Vettes, the Rogues or even Bob Sled & the Toboggans (for a surfing novelty retooled for the snow season). 'We were hired to be Columbia's rock 'n' roll department,' Bruce explained. Very little of this was remotely original, usually offering a pastiche of what the Beach Boys had done last month. But the experience required to be so versatile and so prolific was exactly what Brian Wilson needed in the studio, which was why he welcomed Johnston into the Beach Boys recording unit with such enthusiasm.

Bruce first met the Beach Boys at a Hawaii show in July 1963, after he'd bumped into Murry Wilson at the airport and squeezed a ticket out of him. That was a month after the release of *Surfers' Pajama Party*, a live album supposedly recorded at a UCLA fraternity house (elements of the record sounded suspiciously studio-based). Among its mix of frat-rock covers and instrumentals were an archetypal Johnston smoocher, 'Gee But I'm Lonesome', and one of the many variations of an authentically hard-rocking (for the early 1960s) dance novelty entitled 'Do the Surfer Stomp'. Issued a couple of weeks later was the Hot Doggers' LP *Surfin' USA*, with Bruce covering several Beach Boys hits; and within another month, there was yet another long-player, credited to Bruce alone. *Surfin' Round the World* extended the usual garage-rock sound to encompass some Latin rhythms, indications of the young man's broad musical tastes.

On all these records, Bruce did his best to masquerade as a fully-fledged pop star, a role he also relished in person. 'Having girls scream at you wasn't bad,' he explained half a lifetime later. 'I remember one girl who had me sign her arm after a show. So I signed my name and she said, "I'll never wash". About two weeks later, she came to another gig I was playing at and showed me that my name was still on her arm. I thought, "This isn't someone I'll be dating".'

As Bruce and Terry's studio expertise deepened, they were able to concoct such sophisticated fare as 'Carmen' from 1964, an astonishingly mature development of the Four Seasons sound. Later that year, they combined to transform Vegas entertainer Wayne Newton into a facsimile Beach Boy on the minor hit, 'Coming on Too Strong'. Any of these releases might have recommended Bruce to the group, but he could also boast a burgeoning friendship with Mike Love. When Glen Campbell opted out of touring as Brian Wilson's stand-in, Johnston was an obvious recruit. For him, the road began with a one-off April 1965 show in New Orleans, before he was dragooned full-time six weeks later. (Ironically, his first run of shows also featured Glen Campbell, but as a support act, not a surrogate Beach Boy.)

For his first Beach Boys show, Bruce was forced to don a pair of Al Jardine's spare trousers, which were four inches too short and three sizes too small. Personable, confident and reliably accurate as a singer, he eased himself effortlessly into the line-up. Within a year, he was single-handedly mounting a promotional mission for the *Pet Sounds* album in England and striking up a close relationship with key movers of the London scene, such as Keith Moon and Andrew Loog Oldham. 'He's very bouncy, effervescent,' Brian Wilson decided by 1966. 'Hams it up a lot. But he's very even-tempered, which is a good thing when you're recording.'

All outward appearances to the contrary, Bruce judged himself as being 'hard to get along with' in 1967, the first time that he seemed to be drifting away from the Beach Boys. As their publicist Derek Taylor noted, 'sometimes Bruce regrets the imprisonment of his individual spirit – the constriction of his desire to shine on his own'. Bruce himself highlighted social differences between him and the band: 'The others never telephone me. But then I suppose we have very little in common. They're all married and have their own circle of friends, and I have mine.' Mike Love aside, his closest relationship was also the least likely: privileged college kid and high school drop-out seemed unlikely to bond, but Bruce and Dennis discovered a mutual love for both surfing and fishing, and Bruce's affability ensured that their friendship remained solid. (So solid, in fact, that when Dennis briefly planned a solo tour in 1977, he invited Bruce to accompany him.)

In retrospect, it's apparent that Johnston was always planning for the moment when he was told it was time to leave. He set up independent production companies on both sides of the Atlantic and began to plot a relaunch of his solo career. He announced in early 1968 that he was working on an album that would include a cover of the Beatles' 'With a Little Help From My Friends', his rewritten version of the late 1950s hit 'Bluebirds Over the Mountain' (which subsequently emerged as a Beach

Boys single), and a remake of 'God Only Knows', slow and sultry with solo piano. Bruce was also able to sneak a guest vocal into the US chart when he joined other LA luminaries on Gary Usher's production epic *Present Tense*, issued under the name Sagittarius in 1967. He sang lead on 'My World Fell Down', which sounded like a condensed fantasy of how the *SMiLE* album might have ended up.

'I'd like to see us work for about five more years and then quit,' Bruce announced in 1971, by which point his trademark ballads had become a popular (if sometimes controversial) facet of Beach Boys albums. He planned to move to New Zealand, he said, to escape the California rat race, though he would establish a recording studio there and invite all his American friends down as his clients.

Instead, without any announcement, he glided out of the band as quietly as he had arrived, after an April 1972 show in Tampa. 'I fired Johnston,' claimed Jack Rieley, alleging that Bruce had 'stymied the group's creative consciousness'. (Rieley also made an outrageous accusation about his time managing the band: 'Bruce consistently displayed pure, shameless disdain for Brian Wilson, Carl Wilson and Dennis Wilson.' I don't believe that for a second, but of course I wasn't there ...)

A congenital peacemaker, Bruce Johnston usually credited his departure to his desire to work as a composer, though he also admitted that he spent his first year off the road in surfing and swimming. Carl, at least, took him at his word: 'We decided that since he always said that he wanted to compose more than anything, that he should really do what he wants to do. I find that the group is a little tighter for it, and that's not saying anything against Bruce at all.' Bruce admitted that 'I felt I wasn't being productive' and that as 'we all felt tense with each other, I'm surprised we didn't all quit'. Eventually, though, he let slip that he had found clear evidence of financial irregularities in the way that Rieley was handling the band. 'If that problem with the management hadn't happened, I probably would still be with them.'

Not that he was ever very distant. 'I've played a few Beach Boys concerts,' he confirmed in 1975. 'I have what I term my visitation rights.' He also sang on all but one of the Beach Boys' studio albums during his period of absence. More importantly, he offered band members the opportunities to work in fresh surroundings. By 1973, Bruce had formed another production partnership, Equinox Music, with Terry Melcher, assembling an amorphous collective of his peers, dubbed California Music, as the company's first signing. The group involved Bruce and Terry and any of their friends who were in the vicinity. Many of them also masqueraded as the Legendary Masked Surfers, under the loose leadership of Jan & Dean veteran Dean Torrence.

California Music was launched with a lazy, soft-rock revamp of 'Don't Worry Baby', which outraged Beach Boys purists but deserved a place on Top 40 radio. Aware that Brian Wilson was struggling creatively and personally, Bruce then gave him the chance to produce and/or perform any song he wanted under the California Music logo, without the pressure of representing the Beach Boys. 'We loaned him a production deal,' Bruce said. 'We gave him our advance – and he gave it to his wife! Unbelievable.' Brian could only muster a lumbering, awkward arrangement of 'Why Do Fools Fall in Love', which seemed like a parody or an insult – at least, until *15 Big Ones* a year later proved that this was simply his bizarre idea of how a commercial record should sound in the mid-1970s.

Bruce was more successful as an arranger, concocting Beach Boys-style banks of harmonies for the likes of Elton John ('Don't Let the Sun Go Down on Me', also employing Carl Wilson), Roger McGuinn ('Draggin'', with Bruce as a one-man Beach Boys) and Pink Floyd (vocal arranger on parts of *The Wall*). In 1974, when none of the Beach Boys appeared to be writing anything of consequence, Bruce composed by far the most successful song of his career. Widely believed to be a tribute to Brian Wilson, 'I Write the Songs' was actually Bruce Johnston thinking himself into the creative mindset of God – a stretch, even for a man who would end up producing the Beach Boys.

It was first recorded by his old friends, Captain & Tennille, as an album track – opening with a cascade of vocal harmonies that called out for the Beach Boys to take them over. Bruce then produced, arranged and sang (with Carl Wilson) on a rendition by David Cassidy, which was a hit in Britain but wasn't issued as a single in the States. Instead, that market was left open for Barry Manilow, who was reluctant to cut 'I Write the Songs' at first – after all, he hadn't actually written it – but was rewarded with a number one single. Bruce duly won the Song of the Year trophy at the 1977 Grammy Awards – the first of the Beach Boys to be recognised in that way. He has since claimed that he would never have composed 'I Write the Songs' if he had remained in the Beach Boys and that it might have killed the band's career if he had recorded it with them. All of this leaves an intriguing glimpse of an alternative 1970s, one in which that song takes the Beach Boys to number one, there is no need for the group to pretend that 'Brian's back' and Bruce Johnston becomes their mellifluous creative heart.

Instead, Bruce took advantage of his heightened commercial power to release what he described as his first solo album (though it was actually his third). Sadly, *Going Public* was a record for those who thought that the Beach Boys' version of 'Disney Girls' was too raucous. Dominated by an electric piano sound that dated almost immediately, it was so heavy in treacle that it was risky to dip so much as a toe into its mush, for fear of getting sucked into the sugary swamp. The record acted as a sampler of Bruce's sleepy balladeering and briefly nodded to the country market that – if he hadn't joined the Beach Boys – might have been his natural destiny. But there was one clear signal to the future: a penchant for MOR disco that produced a pleasant revival of the *Sunflower* tune, 'Deirdre', and a genuinely commercial dancefloor arrangement of the early '60s surf instrumental, 'Pipeline'. The latter was even a minor hit single.

Sadly missing from *Going Public* was a song that Bruce wrote but never officially released: an epic tribute to the Marx Brothers entitled 'Brand New Old Friends'. It fell into the hands of Curt Boettcher [aka Becher], Bruce's longtime friend and co-producer. Under the guise of California (a successor to the California Music brand), Curt crafted a sumptuous vocal arrangement that climaxed in a 90-second tag of sheer vocal joy. But the *Passionfruit* album for which it was intended was rejected, and the track only surfaced decades later as a lo-fi tape transfer.

Bruce Johnston never made false claims for *Going Public*: in fact, his publicity campaign involved dismissing the record as a trifle. 'This kind of album doesn't make it overnight,' he said with distressing accuracy. 'If anything happens with it at all, it will probably happen slowly. Who knows? The record company may even drop me.' More than a decade later, he admitted that he didn't like his own record. There was certainly no demand from Columbia for an immediate follow-up, while his separate production deal with RCA expired when the label complained that he hadn't brought them any hits. (His British and European success with David Cassidy clearly didn't count.)

Decisions about a solo career were shelved when the Beach Boys ran aground during the early sessions for a successor to the disastrous *M.I.U. Album*. 'Brian came up with the suggestion to have Bruce come down to Florida to help us with the vocals,' Mike Love explained – omitting the fact that Brian specifically wanted someone to cover the high parts he simply couldn't reach anymore. From there, it was an easy and, at the time, uncontroversial step for the band to invite Bruce to produce the project. As Mike admitted, 'he brought a certain outside objectivity and inside knowledge of how the group really works best'. But they weren't the only things Bruce brought down to Florida …

Murder on the Dancefloor

The Beach Boys at the discotheque

It began with Curt Boettcher. His 1960s credits included producing the debut album by the Association, collaborating with the likes of Gary Usher and Bruce Johnston on the inspired Sagittarius album, *Present Tense*, and channelling all his passion for soft-pop and vocal harmonies into a group called the Millennium.

A decade later, he was still working regularly with Johnston, having inherited Bruce's California Music project and streamlined its name to California (and his own to Becher). He was still obsessed with smooth, multi-tracked harmonies, but by 1977, his musical taste had switched to disco; it was he who encouraged Johnston to add dancefloor grooves to his solo album. Around the same time, Becher recorded a disco version of 'I Can Hear Music', based shamelessly on the Beach Boys' template.

Searching for a follow-up among the Beach Boys' catalogue, he hit upon the almost-forgotten 1967 album track, 'Here Comes the Night' (from *Wild Honey*). As he and Johnston began to map out a disco setting for the song, the Beach Boys came calling: they needed Bruce back, as a singer and a producer. Johnston agreed, bringing with him a rough mix of 'Here Comes the Night', as sung by Becher and his friends. Their vocals were either stripped out or mixed down to make room for the Beach Boys to add their own. 'I'm so proud of that track,' Johnston said more than twenty years later. 'There were no repeated loops and, of course, we had no sampler.' Disco was the strictest of masters. Every line had to be sung anew and aligned perfectly with the electronic dance beats.

'It was a chance to use that format to have a long cut on our album which enabled us to stretch out our vocals,' Johnston explained. Mike Love reinforced his view: 'The Beach Boys are known for their vocal prowess and Bruce thought to take that and apply it to disco would be pretty unique.' The group had already acknowledged the disco explosion in the lyrics to 'She's Got Rhythm', the eerie opening track to the *M.I.U. Album*. The scenario of that song involved Brian Wilson trying to pick up a stranger on the dancefloor and being rejected, in much the way that the album would be.

When 'Here Comes the Night' was released in a variety of mixes and formats in February 1979, the idea of pop or rock artists aiming straight at the dancefloor was anything but unique. The Bee Gees had pioneered the 'white disco' sound with 'Jive Talkin'' four years earlier, and since then artists as diverse as Abba, the Rolling Stones, Rod Stewart and Paul McCartney had been experimenting with its unwavering rhythmic pulse. In his 'Disco File' column in the industry magazine *Record World*, Brian Chin greeted the ten-minute-plus mix of the Beach Boys' song enthusiastically. 'The best moments happen when the group is just being itself,' he conceded, but 'instrumental passages carry very well with waves of strings and overwhelming thump, so what's to complain?'

Answers came from all directions, inside the group and out. By 1979, the backlash against disco control of the pop charts had spawned a reactionary, rowdy movement, which would culminate with the notorious 'Disco Demolition' riot at Chicago's Comiskey Park stadium in July. While disco stations put the Beach Boys' track into heavy rotation, old-school reviewers complained (to choose just one example): 'This is a terrible travesty of their music, commercial pandering of the vilest sort.'

That view was shared by at least some of the Beach Boys. Carl Wilson, who contributed an impeccably soulful lead vocal, said bravely that 'I like the idea of going out on uncharted water'. But within a couple of weeks, he was admitting that he was 'just kind of walked through' the session. His brothers missed it entirely. Brian spoke not a word, while Dennis savaged the single in the British press. 'You really want to know about the disco community?' he asked journalist Richard Williams. 'Well, the gay community has made a tremendous mistake. Just like Hitler used Wagner, it's unfair to take an art-form and use it.' He added: 'I'm not into disco … it reminds me of the "busy" signal on the telephone line.' Bruce Johnston replied: 'There are probably some things about disco that turn off the macho side of the listener. It's the whole gay thing that I'm not into, but I can understand it. Look how Macho City Dennis is.' And he claimed that Dennis 'came around' after he played the disco mix to his friends in Fleetwood Mac, who told him (quite rightly) that the vocals were amazing.

Yet more of the wider public shared Dennis Wilson's misgivings than Bruce Johnston's open-mindedness. The single made the Disco Top 30 and flirted with the upper half of the *Billboard* Hot 100 chart, but it represented no threat to Rod Stewart's 'Do Ya Think I'm Sexy' or the Bee Gees' 'Tragedy'. 'It's created controversy,' Mike Love said manfully, 'but I guess that's good. It means it isn't going unnoticed.' Just merely unsold.

The acid test came when the Beach Boys went out on the road in March 1979 to plug the single and prepare the world for their *L.A. (Light Album)*. Legend has it that, when the group debuted 'Here Comes the Night' at New York's Radio City Music Hall, they were booed off stage and the song immediately vanished from their live sets. But, as usual, the truth was more nuanced than that.

That show began with some ecstatically received oldies, none finer than Carl's soul-touching rendition of 'Caroline, No'. The audience relished these songs they knew, but were still prepared to shout out for such comparatively recherché album tracks as 'Disney Girls' and 'Surf's Up'. Instead, the electronic rhythm track from their disco single filled the hall, as Bruce Johnston announced 'This is our new record'. A sizeable number of young women squealed with anticipation.

The performance was not flawless: the sax player wandered way off key during his solo and some of the harmonies lacked the studio polish. But Carl's lead vocal was magnificent – drenched in soul, utterly committed to the moment. When it was over, the venue wasn't filled with boos, though the reception was noticeably less frenzied than for the 1960s classics that had preceded it. One or two male voices made themselves heard over the masses, calling out repeatedly 'You sold out' to the band and 'Don't buy it' to the audience. If it wasn't quite as dramatic a confrontation as Bob Dylan's 'Judas' moment from 1966, it did suggest that something was at stake and that some of the Beach Boys' fans felt as emasculated by the disco direction as Dennis Wilson had been. The track survived in the live set for several months, but nobody missed it when it was gone and the experiment was never repeated. 'Our fans hated it,' Bruce Johnston had to concede later that year. 'It was like having a very successful TV comedy show and then trying to do drama. It didn't work.' But as Bruce told me in 1990, 'it's a fabulous record', and I wouldn't disagree with him, then or now.

'We've always related to our songs being danceable,' Mike Love said as the furore died down. 'Disco just has a more prominent bass drum and more electronics. I wouldn't mind if we did a few more disco songs. But disco is just a rage; it'll die down by this fall … You'll still hear it as dance music for many more years. But it's not going to be as big an influence.' He was right, to a point: the disco movement epitomised by the Bee Gees and *Saturday Night Fever* was already on the verge of collapse. But that more prominent bass drum? Those electronics? The passion for dance music? They never disappeared. Luckily for the Beach Boys, neither did nostalgia.

Brand New Old Friends

Bruce Johnston reshapes the Beach Boys

Being a Beach Boy in 1978 was anything but fun fun fun. The group had survived their airport break-up the previous year and somehow crawled to the end of their Australian tour without any of the Wilson brothers overdosing on heroin, becoming terminally pickled in booze or conjuring up other ways of summoning the grim reaper.

By this point, Brian Wilson's very existence was a cry for help. Some segment of the group's management reckoned it was a bright idea to put him up for interview on an evening TV magazine show named *PM*. His segment, taped at an Oakland show in late May, was titled, with brutal honesty, 'The Tension Behind the Music'. He was grossly fat, grotesquely greasy, ill-at-ease, but still somehow desperate to please, despite coughing up his lungs between almost every sentence (a bout of laryngitis, apparently, though it seemed to last all year).

He was asked about his role as a shaper of modern music. Brian winced apologetically and said, 'I'm not really a shaper of modern music at all'. He sounded resigned, he sounded desperate. The interviewer tried an equally inappropriate tack: did he think he was a genius? Brian had no illusions left, no defences, just the truth. 'That doesn't describe me, I don't think. I never thought of myself as a genius.' Then he almost chuckled to himself, the way a man might do when he knows the horizon is disappearing. 'They say write about the things you do,' he explained, 'but the things I do, it doesn't seem that I would want to write about them.' He smiled with barren amusement, stretched beyond the borders of his endurance. How much more honest could he be?

Within a matter of weeks, while the Beach Boys caravan continued to trek its remorseless way across North America, Brian escaped, or disappeared. It seems to have been a journey with no destination: who knows if he ever imagined coming home again. Travelling without possessions, he caught a bus down to Mexico, then rode another bus back across the border to San Diego. Several days later, a man in severely dishevelled state, virtually comatose, barely able to identify himself, was found slumped on a park bench in the city's Balboa Park. Somebody recognised that he was Brian Wilson and contacted the Beach Boys' management. Brian was immediately taken to Alvarado Hospital, where he was treated for alcohol poisoning among other ills. Then he was driven back to Los Angeles and straight into a series of recording sessions with the other Beach Boys.

Over the next few weeks, the entire Beach Boys universe was reorganised. Jerry Schilling, fresh from several traumatic years with Elvis Presley's management team, was invited to guide the Beach Boys' affairs. Somehow, he succeeded in meeting the approval of the entire band, a feat that no one else had achieved for years. He conferred with Marilyn Wilson, who agreed that rather than attempting to function as a Beach Boy, Brian urgently needed to be placed under full-time psychiatric care. This time, he was hospitalised for several months. No sooner had he been admitted than Marilyn, driven beyond the point of despair, filed for divorce. This seems to have triggered Carl and Dennis's wives to make the same move, although both those relationships were patched up and staggered on for another year or so.

Schilling was convinced that the music the Beach Boys had been recording in recent months did not equate to an album worthy of the name. To prove the point, he asked the band to assemble a reel of their best material and then arranged a playback for the president of Columbia Records, the irrepressibly foul-mouthed Walter Yetnikoff. Yetnikoff listened silently to the music, which ranged from Dennis Wilson ballads to a pointless Brian Wilson revival of 'Calendar Girl', and delivered the legendary verdict: 'Gentlemen, I think I've been fucked.'

To his credit, Yetnikoff didn't attempt to have the Beach Boys' contract annulled. Nor did he panic when he realised (as he must have done) that Brian was in no shape to oversee any kind of album. He recognised the good sense in inviting Bruce Johnston to return, not just to handle Brian's high harmonies but also as producer. Left in place, though, was the contractual clause that insisted a certain percentage of the music on each new Beach Boys album must be written by Brian. (Brian is said to have cried when he realised the implications of the deal.)

With Brian absent, Bruce tried to discover exactly what he had to work with. Every member of the band was sitting on songs, but they didn't necessarily tell Bruce about them. He had to delve into the tape archives to discover what had been logged recently, a task he shared with the band's former manager, Jim Guercio. During this process, Bruce was also reminded how much vintage material remained unreleased. He ran a few tapes for Guercio to hear, only for Jim to declare that the band's first album for Columbia should be filled with out-takes from *SMiLE*. Bruce wasn't enamoured with that suggestion, but he did toy with retrieving 'Can't Wait Too Long' (aka 'Been Way Too Long') from the reject pile – or maybe re-recording it, adding a shimmer of disco, making it contemporary?

In the event, neither of these bizarre ideas made the grade. Dennis celebrated Bruce's return by going into rehab and then immediately resuming his hedonistic drug and alcohol regime. He did agree, however, to hand over tracks he'd almost completed for his second solo album. Meanwhile, Bruce had identified Dennis's delivery of a new Carl song, 'Angel Come Home', as a potential hit single. He also suggested that the band might delve cautiously into the disco market, as it was so hot …

The controversy over 'Here Comes the Night' aside, Johnston succeeded in creating something that would not have been conceivable if Brian Wilson was in the room: a genuinely democratic Beach Boys album. To that extent, it was the follow-up to *Holland*, although it lacked that record's progressive rock edge. The currency of the collection that Carl insisted for spiritual reasons on calling *L.A. (Light Album)* was adult contemporary – alias hip easy listening. Apart from one of Brian's endless incarnations of 'Shortnin' Bread', it shared none of the juvenile worldview of recent Beach Boys output: there were no schoolgirls in the lyrics or kookiness in the arrangements. Carl and Dennis returned as active contributors for the first time since *Holland*, Carl offering two highly mellow but otherwise luscious ballads, Dennis his by now customary romantic intensity. Mike Love was represented by the sickly but heartfelt 'Sumahama', inspired by a new (and soon superseded) fiancée. Al Jardine's love song to his wife, 'Lady Lynda', also seemed to doom the couple's union, but it did provide the band with their first new British hit since 'Cottonfields' in 1970.

And Brian? That would have been the question on Yetnikoff's lips. This is where subterfuge took over. The album began with a slight but at least comparatively recent (1974) Wilson composition entitled 'Good Timin'' and ended with the infernal 'Shortnin' Bread'. Otherwise, his only appearance in the writing credits was on 'Here Comes the Night'. By unbalancing the album with the full-length disco mix of that tune, Johnston ensured that Brian's name was on about half the record's running time – even if his musical contributions were effectively zero. As Bruce admitted, 'Brian's key involvement was getting me'.

This time, there were no Wilson brothers confessing disgust or even mild misgivings as the album was released. Dennis and Carl were represented in authentic contemporary form and there was no pandering to the belief that the Beach Boys mustn't sing anything but summer and surfing songs.

Any feeling on behalf of Jardine and Love that the album didn't reflect their version of the Beach Boys was probably appeased with the creation of an old-school soundtrack song: 'It's a Beautiful Day' from the tiresome movie satire, *Americathon*. The record might have sold if the film had been a hit; after all, Love's side project, Celebration, had recently delivered a Beach Boys soundalike, 'Almost Summer', which reached the US Top 30. Perhaps Mike was feeling sidelined by both

Bruce's return and the renaissance of the younger Wilson brothers as writer/producers. During the period when Johnston was at work, Love not only completed a second Celebration album, but also two full-length solo sets, *First Love* and *Country Love* (neither of which has ever been released, aside from Mike's tribute to his cousin, 'Brian's Back').

Bruce Johnston was adamant that 'I'm sure that I won't rejoin the band' after completing the *Light Album*. Later, he revealed that he had quit as producer several times during the sessions but was begged back every time. 'I think this is a really good album,' Bruce declared. 'But I think I can do even better on the next one. I want to deliver the Beach Boys equivalent of [Fleetwood Mac's] *Rumours* for the next one, and I think I can.' And maybe he could have done, except for one fatal flaw: he was dealing with the Beach Boys.

Looking Back With Love

Mike Love's best ideas

While the other Beach Boys were squabbling over exactly who and what the Beach Boys were supposed to be at the end of the 1970s (and beyond), Mike Love kept his eye on the prize. He never forgot that the Beach Boys was, more than anything else, a brand – and that brands were a sure-fire way of making money.

August 1979: Love says the Beach Boys will soon be making a movie: *California Beach Party*. 'We all have acting roles, but the real star will be the beach. During the filming, we will throw a giant, free, Woodstock-style concert on a West Coast beach. On the bill with us will be half a dozen big names, and we expect half a million people to turn up.' And there is a plotline, of sorts: 'It's loosely the story of four girls who come from different corners of the US and who meet up in California. And all the action takes place against a backdrop of Beach Boys music.' There will be more beautiful girls in this movie than any film ever made, he promises. Also on the horizon: *Sumahama*, a film based on Mike's latest romance with a young Korean woman. Within a year, the couple have separated.

September 1980: *California Beach Party* is back. 'My idea is to come up with a film that's in the spirit of the Hope and Crosby *Road* films,'

Mike explains, 'combining the good times, the laughs, the scenery and great music.'

May 1981: *California Beach Party* is now set to be the biggest concert of all time, with an estimated audience of one million people this July. Then the group will launch a Broadway show – the Beach Boys equivalent to the highly successful jukebox musical, *Beatlemania* – but with the group themselves providing the music, not actors. Needless to say, none of this happens.

July 1981: *Looking Back with Love* is not just Mike's new solo album, but also 'something I envision as a whole retrospective of the '60s, with an audio-visual presentation of personalities and news events of the decade, projected onto a screen, while my band performs the songs of the era.' Nope, didn't happen. Meanwhile, the *California Beach Party* lives on: 'I'd like to get the Blues Brothers to be our road managers for a day, things like that to make it more fun.'

July 1982: The manufacturers of the soft drink Sunkist have been using 'Good Vibrations' for years in their TV ads. Now it's the turn of 'Wouldn't It Be Nice', rewritten for a Tropicana Chugger ad. Mike doesn't take any of this too seriously: 'The guy from Sunkist asked me, "Mike, do you ever drink Sunkist?" I said, "Well, let me put it to you this way. If my car broke down in the Gobi Desert and I had some Sunkist with me, I'd first drain my radiator and drink the fluid before I'd touch a Sunkist."'

May 1984: Mike wants the Beach Boys to record a twenty-fifth anniversary album featuring twenty-five tracks with twenty-five different guests. 'We'd like the Four Seasons, Barbra Streisand, Kenny Rogers, Neil Diamond, B.B. King, people like that. Imagine the Jacksons and the Beach Boys doing "Good Vibrations" … with the proceeds going to something that benefits the environment. Or humanity. Or both.'

July 1985: Mike has had a vision of raising $4 million via five free concerts – with funds from donations and concessions going towards feeding starving people around the world and helping to restore the Statue of Liberty. He forms the Love Foundation to make it happen.

Ultimately only two concerts take place, and although together they attract 1.5 million people, the Foundation's expenses were so high, and the charitable donations at the shows so paltry, that everyone ended up out of pocket. Promised guest stars such as James Brown and Eric Clapton fail to show up, and a third show, in Dallas, has to be cancelled when it becomes apparent that nobody has told the rest of the Beach Boys about it. More proof of the organisation's attention to detail: a giant banner across the stage at the Washington DC show, which reads: 'American Airlines – Sea to Shinning [sic] Sea'. At the same time, Mike has filed for personal bankruptcy.

September 1987: Chevrolet announces that it is sponsoring the Chevrolet Heartbeat of America Beach Boys Tour, a venture so successful that it is extended into 1988. 'The Beach Boys will help Chevrolet continue to reach a young audience,' the company claims. Mike says: 'I loved the Chevrolet commercial because we got Corvettes.'

June 1988: Mike tantalises fans with what turns out to be one of rock's great lost projects: 'We're thinking of a children's Smurf album where we'd do songs like "Smurfing USA" and "Smurfer Girl".'

October 1988: Coming next year, according to Love: concerts in Moscow's Gorky Park and China's Forbidden City. But both ideas are forbidden. The changing political situation in the Soviet bloc also forces the cancellation of a proposed collaboration in 1990 with the Leningrad Philharmonic Orchestra.

October 1988: Mike launches a genuinely charitable enterprise for Project Teach, which is designed to encourage minority students to join the teaching profession. The Beach Boys play benefit concerts for the cause over the next few years. 'I want to capitalise on the momentum of "Kokomo", in terms of philanthropy and leadership,' he says, 'which is the highest and best use of your celebrity.' Before a Santa Barbara benefit in 1990, he explains: 'The people in the front line of the war against ignorance are teachers, so the whole teaching infrastructure needs to be encouraged, uplifted, bolstered and reinforced.' But at the show, the Beach Boys are accompanied on stage by cheerleaders. 'The older the group gets, the slower we are at catching them,' Mike tells the audience.

June 1989: The Beach Boys combine with Sheraton Hotels for a Get Around America Summer Value promotion. The company explains: 'The Beach Boys work perfectly for us – they're extremely popular with couples and families, our prime prospects.' Hotels will broadcast Beach Boys songs in their lobbies and elevators, and feature Beach Boys-themed menus and cocktail bars.

January 1992: Mike talks about persuading Bart Simpson – yes, *that* Bart Simpson – to duet with him on the next Beach Boys album. He's chosen the perfect song: 'Summer of Love'. 'Bart talks about how he's out in California,' Mike promises. 'He hears reports that they've got a lot of year-round water sports. [He starts singing] "I'm gonna check myself into one of those fine resorts and if they don't like how I'm dressed, they can eat my shorts". I don't know if it will be a big hit record, but it will be a big novelty record.' Sadly, Bart turned the offer down.

August 1993: Love helps to promote *Camp California*, an animation project designed to boost children's awareness of environmental issues. 'The whole concept of *Camp California* is timeless,' he says, 'just like Beach Boys songs.' The actors who voice the characters on screen also provide vocals for an album, *Camp California: Where the Music Never Ends*, which features covers of surfing hits by the Beach Boys and others. 'It's all about positive fun and all-American, clean-cut kinds of themes,' Mike promises.

September 1993: The Beach Boys' latest sponsorship deal is with the manufacturers of Tone soap, the Dial Corporation. In return, the group makes appearances at participating supermarkets, attends special backstage parties for the sponsors and even invites Tone retailers on stage to sing 'Barbara Ann'. Dial intend to repeat the idea next year with another of their businesses, Premier Cruise Lines.

August 1996: Mike announces plans for a franchised string of venues called Club Kokomo. 'It'll be like House of Blues,' he explains, 'but more upscale and with better food … a *Cheers* at the beach kind of place.' Initial plans are for the Love-themed clubs to open in around twenty-five venues. A year later, that has been honed down to two ventures in Hawaii, where the renamed Mike Love's Club Kokomo will soon appear in Honolulu and Lahaina. The chief executive officer of the scheme says the menu will be 'California meets Caribbean on the way to Hawaii'. And there is also talk of another Club Kokomo in Orange, California, where there will be a resident Kokomo Club House Band. Members will include Mike Love, Bruce Johnston, Dean Torrence of Jan & Dean and occasional Beach Boys drummer (and actor) John Stamos. But don't hurry to book: Club Kokomo isn't there. Other abandoned Club Kokomo ideas include becoming an ISP provider and selling branded clothing and eyewear.

July 2024: The Club Kokomo brand is alive and well as a line of spirits, offering rums and pre-mixed rum cocktails. Love originates the idea in 2022 when he's enjoying a mojito with his wife and thinks: 'Kokomojito! Why not?' And a new money-making scheme is born.

End of the Show

The decline of Dennis Wilson

By summer 1979, nobody could pretend that Dennis Wilson was a functioning member of the Beach Boys. On that spring's *L.A. (Light Album)*, he contributed songs in the spirit of his mighty solo record from 1977. But that was his last shot. Divorced from Karen Lamm for the second time, he took up with Christine McVie of Fleetwood Mac. Their relationship was romantic – Dennis was prone to extravagant gestures of love, like filling her garden with roses, though he left her to pay the bill. On another occasion, he arranged for a symphony orchestra and grand piano to gather beneath the bedroom window of her Beverly Hills home, ready for him to sing 'You Are So Beautiful' – and then he got drunk, ended up in the pool and the performance never happened. His constant binges on alcohol and cocaine outstripped the endurance of even a hardened road warrior like McVie, and despite promises of engagement, marriage and joint recording projects, their union was doomed. Any songs they wrote together remain locked in McVie's archive.

There was no longer any pivot in Dennis's life. Excess seeped into everything and the Beach Boys usually bore the brunt. At a Tennessee show in April 1979, Dennis passed out in the touring bus and never made it to the stage. On the occasions that he did show, he would crash away at the drums like Animal from *The Muppets*, setting tempos that were frenzied, erratic or both. His cousin Mike Love deplored his reckless behaviour on stage, like his penchant for threatening to expose himself in front of audiences. During a week-long arena run in Los Angeles that June, Wilson and Love stumbled into a fistfight in full view of the crowd. For almost the next year, Dennis was secretly exiled from the touring band, having to beg special permission for his occasional cameos in public.

Even out of the limelight, he could not avoid trouble. While on a California fishing trip in August 1979, he was arrested for public drunkenness and disturbing the peace by a lake near the remote community of Lone Pine. Several weeks later, Scott Mathews from the new wave band the Dūrocs was recruited to replace him, perhaps on a permanent basis. 'Dreams do come true,' Mathews said as he took part in a session at Al Jardine's ranch in Big Sur. Wilson and McVie countered by promising to appear as a duo at a televised benefit concert for victims of famine in Cambodia – but didn't show up.

Dennis's absence from Beach Boys concerts was also noted by fans. The group made excuses over the microphone: the drummer had missed the plane, or overslept, had suffered an obscure injury, or was at home battling the flu. Meanwhile, Dennis and Christine were being featured in the celebrity magazines, kissing passionately at airports or, in March 1980, staging a public engagement ceremony at a Hawaii restaurant. The next day, the Beach Boys were visible on prime-time TV with a documentary about their latest projects, over-optimistically entitled *Going Platinum*. Dennis was neither visible nor even mentioned as a member of the band.

Quizzed about his brother's whereabouts, Carl claimed that Dennis was still attending tour rehearsals (he wasn't) and was going to rehab (he wasn't, or at least not yet). 'Dennis has some behaviour stuff to work through,' he said euphemistically. 'He's kind of re-evaluating his life right now.' When the band flew to Britain in June 1980, Dennis accompanied them, and for the first and last time, the six primary Beach Boys shared a London stage. They also headlined an outdoor festival at Knebworth, where Dennis drove the group ferociously through a succession of hit singles. Even this triumphant show was chaotic, however. For the ballad

'Surfer Girl', he took his place centre-stage at a vocal microphone, crooning croakily while making doe-eyes at his cousin and *bête noire,* Mike Love. Irritated by this overtly sarcastic behaviour, Love managed to unplug Wilson's mic mid-song. Dennis laughed it off, but had to restrain the normally peaceable Carl, who lunged angrily at Mike as the song ended.

The drummer's unpredictable conduct was signalled to a national audience when the group made the mistake of heralding their twentieth anniversary year with a live interview on ABC's *Good Morning, America.* The satellite-linked conversation was marred by a faulty connection, but that did not explain why the segment began with Dennis bent almost double on the sofa, apparently unable to sit up straight. Soon afterwards, he slumped back in his seat, although he did manage to force his body towards a microphone long enough to ensure the nation that 'we love one another'. The Beach Boys' new manager, Jerry Schilling, was left to insist how professional the group were, while the man next to him slid into semi-consciousness. In the *Palm Beach Post*, a reader asked the paper's showbiz columnist what had been wrong with Dennis. 'The general consensus,' came the reply, 'was Dennis Wilson had a few too many Quaaludes prior to interview time.' With Brian staring at the camera like a cornered animal, and Mike Love barely able to speak with frustration and rage, it was an ill-omened launch to what was supposed to be a year of celebration. Shortly afterwards, Carl left the group for a year, complaining that 'the Beach Boys are basically unmanageable'.

And so 1981 continued to prove. In Hartford, Dennis devoted himself to throwing water at the band's roadies, rather than playing drums. At the Greek Theatre in Los Angeles, he was (as a reviewer complained) 'ill-behaved and offensive', to the point that Love launched himself at him backstage and another fistfight ensued. After that, he was more often absent than not, leaving his colleagues to raid the medical dictionary again as they reached for excuses.

Meanwhile, Brian was also slipping into incoherence as he gorged himself on whatever stimulants or sedatives he could find to protect himself from the real world. Mike's brother, Stanley, and another member of the band's milieu, Rushton 'Rocky' Pamplin, discovered once too often that it was Dennis who was supplying Brian with cocaine, heroin and other narcotics. The Beach Boys prided themselves on being family, but sometimes their family dynamics started out toxic and soured quickly into pure vitriol.

According to Dennis, Love and Pamplin broke down the door to his Venice Beach home and 'pursued me through three rooms of my house, breaking windows and damaging furniture'. One of his assailants held him down, Wilson continued, while the other beat him until he lost consciousness. When he came round, he was struck in the face with a telephone and passed out again. As a result, he was living in 'constant fear of further attack' and worried that his intruders might impose similar punishment beatings upon other members of the Beach Boys. Stanley Love, however, simply described that he had been forced to act to protect Brian from his brother, who was regularly buying him cocaine. (Hence the title of *The Cocaine Tapes* given to the pair's chaotic bootleg recordings from this period.) The violent dispute, he added, had been 'a personal family matter and was not done to harass Dennis Wilson in any manner whatsoever'. Dennis disagreed: he argued that the assault was provoked by the fact that the Beach Boys had filed a lawsuit against Stanley Love over financial matters. Judge Jacqueline L. Weiss, presumably hoping that she would never have to meet any of these people again, imposed a mutual restraining order, preventing the parties involved from creeping closer than 100 yards to each other's homes.

Mike Love was not alone among the Beach Boys in believing that his drummer cousin was now an active menace to the group's career. 'Dennis is currently drunk,' he told the *Daily Oklahoman* in June 1982. 'He's battling alcoholism. I don't know if he'll make it or not.' He sounded callous, but was presumably just resigned. As ever, Carl tried to strike a more positive note. 'Dennis has been going through some behaviour stuff,' he explained a month later, just as he had in 1980. 'He just needs to get himself straightened out a little bit.' Occasionally, Dennis was able to control himself sufficiently to attend a run of shows, still thrilling elements of the Beach Boys' audience by dragging himself to the microphone during the encore and growling 'You Are So Beautiful' as if he was sending out a personal message to every woman in the house.

By 1983, press attention was focused on the dissolute appearance and shambolic performances of Brian, at least until Eugene Landy reappeared in his life. But nobody who met Dennis that year could ignore that his once stunningly attractive face had become bloated, his eyes puffy and vacant, his legs barely able to function as he swigged constantly from bottles of orange juice that were 80 per cent cheap vodka, his voice so ravaged that it could hardly be described as singing. In a desperate attempt at repair, doctors submitted him to a series of throat operations and procedures that year, but his self-abusive lifestyle undercut anything that medical science could achieve. Aware that he was suffocating himself in alcohol, Dennis agreed to try his hand at rehab, but lacked the will-power to persevere. 'He has been working real hard at it,' Carl insisted in August. 'He'll fall off the wagon and then get back on and be really OK. Right now, he looks great.' Photographs and his rare public appearances suggested otherwise. One of the band's limo drivers recalled a July show where 'Wilson crapped his pants while he was on stage … He walked around the hotel with a beer in each hand … and didn't eat. He was a total problem. He was always the last one out of the hotel.'

On 26 September 1983, Dennis showed up for a gig at the LA County Fair in Pomona, though he didn't really attempt to sing and there were two drummers on stage besides him, so his contribution was symbolic rather than musical. He stumbled back to the same venue the next night, apparently laying waste to everything around him, and was restrained from mounting the stage. His life as a Beach Boy was over. Now only the inevitable remained.

Keep the Summer Alive

The end of the original Beach Boys

Even by the dysfunctional standards of the Beach Boys, the early months of 1979 were strange. Brian was in a mental hospital; Dennis was about to be exiled for a year; Bruce wanted to go disco; and the world's most unstable band had just issued an album of (disco aside) mellow, soporific, adult easy listening.

Even when Brian rejoined the outside world, he was hardly a functioning adult. He hired a full-time carer, Carolyn Williams, who soon insinuated her way deeper into his life. (Her reward was to be arrested at an airport in 1982 while carrying supplies of cocaine for her 'boyfriend'.) Although Bruce Johnston had planned to return to his swimming pool after completing the *Light Album*, there was nobody available to take over his role. 'Brian has handed me the baton for the time being,' Bruce said euphemistically. 'I think that what I will do will probably make him want to come back into it. If I'm successful, I will make myself obsolete.' He never left the band again.

But what constituted success for the Beach Boys in 1979? And whose version of the band would take priority? If he'd been remotely sober, this is the moment when Dennis could have seized creative control of the band, supported by Carl. But his decade-long outpouring of tortured ballads had run dry. There was no appetite for another disco experiment, either. Mike Love recognised that this was his opportunity. He informed Brian that the pair of them, and brother Carl, were going to take a trip to Hawaii so they could write the next album. 'I said, "Write songs? Ugh",' Brian recalled. 'But we went, Michael and Carl and myself, and it really worked.'

At this point, Mike's priority was the *California Beach Party* project, which might be a movie or a tour or simply an album, but would definitely require old-style Beach Boys songs. Like *15 Big Ones*, it was briefly envisaged as a double-album: half cover versions from the '50s and early '60s (Brian's appetite in that direction was undimmed) and half fresh material. The Beach Party never took place, although Mike propelled the band in that direction for the remainder of its life. But songs did emerge, all vaguely familiar without quite alarming the copyright lawyers. Two of the new Wilson/Love songs showed real potential: 'Some of Your Love' and the fabulous 'Goin' On'. The latter was the last great Wilson/Love composition – a confection of marvellous hooks and shifts and tags, crowned with a cathartic sax solo by Phil Spector's vintage sideman, Steve Douglas.

If ever an album appeared to have been titled by Mike Love, it was *Keepin' the Summer Alive*. But it was actually the invention of Carl Wilson and former Bachman–Turner Overdrive frontman Randy Bachman, who also contributed a country lope called 'Livin' with a Heartache'. (This was a record full of dropped 'g's.) 'I was surprised they chose it for the album,' Carl reflected of the latter song. He was equally baffled by the inclusion of 'When Girls Get Together', a leftover from the *Sunflower* album ('I guess Bruce just liked that song'), not to mention Johnston's own 'Endless Harmony', a tribute to the group that had originally been written as 'Ten Years of Harmony' back in 1972. 'I felt kind of funny singing our part,' Carl said, 'because we have never had the idea of singing about us.' Little did he know that Mike Love would obsessively pursue exactly that tactic for the next four decades.

The concept, such as it was, of *Keepin' the Summer Alive* was illustrated by a painting of the band performing inside a sealed bubble situated in a polar landscape. The only spectators? Two polar bears, one penguin (poles apart, of course). As one reviewer said, 'it figures that no one else is around. Who else would want to listen?' He concluded that the album was 'the final insult. Give up. The Beach Boys are over the hill.' Another critic interpreted 'Endless Harmony' as 'a suicide note. It will be the last song on the last Beach Boys album.' And perhaps it should have been.

Keepin' the Summer Alive appeared in March 1980, alongside the 'Goin' On' single. Both climbed just far enough into the US Top 100 charts to prove that they had flopped. Brian Wilson emerged from hospital in time to join the promotional tour. In Portland, a reviewer noticed that he 'seemed genuinely frightened by his audience. It was as if he believed that, by the time the song ended, the crowd was going to rush up on stage and consume him, totally.' Before one show, Johnston and Al Jardine gave a lecture for kids about the evils of smoking. Then Brian took to the stage and puffed his way through a pack of twenty. At least he was there: once again, the group had to channel their imaginations into dreaming up excuses for Dennis's absence. (To be fair, he hadn't appeared on the album, either.)

'Brian shouldn't be regarded as a freak show,' Bruce pleaded that summer. But Wilson didn't make it easy. Backstage in Dayton, a reporter told Brian earnestly that *Pet Sounds* had changed his life. Brian glared back at him and demanded: 'You don't have any speed, do you?' By now, Mike Love had given up on making excuses for his cousin: 'Permanent schizophrenia is not something you can just get over,' he told a London reporter starkly.

For their first full European tour in almost a decade, Dennis was admitted back into the ranks – but only because concert promoters demanded it. English critics were as cruel as their reputation suggested: some of the band, declared the *Observer*, 'are so gross and podgy these days that they'd sink any surfboard they boarded'. At Wembley Arena in June, I had my sole opportunity to witness all six of the 'classic' Beach Boys together – well, briefly, as Dennis and Brian kept leaving the stage. Dennis would at least wait until the end of a song; Brian looked confused, bored and distressed, and would then walk in front of his bandmates while they were just starting to sing. The setlist was full of 1960s hits and there was no hint of the early 1970s sound I loved so much. But it was still an event, and the Beach Boys could not help but reach a certain level of competence. At their outdoor festival at Knebworth a couple of weeks later, they managed even better than that. Nobody knew it, but it was the end of an era: the last gasp of the original Beach Boys.

Things disintegrated quickly after that. Back in the States, Carl couldn't face another year of non-creativity with the group, so he cut a solo album. He summed up his frustration with the travelling circus succinctly: 'All you really have to do is show up and the audience takes care of the rest. Your singing can be way off, and they'll fill in the harmony by themselves.' He was determined not to offer a pastiche of the Beach Boys on his own record. He collaborated with Myrna Smith, the girlfriend of his manager Jerry Schilling. She did her inexperienced best to reflect Carl's worldview in the lyrics she penned for his melodies. The *Carl Wilson* album was beautifully sung, of course, but its mix of soulful rockers and gentle ballads was rarely more than pleasant listening. The exception was 'Heaven', a classic slow song that would earn its place in the Beach Boys' setlist.

To mark the spring 1981 release of his album, Carl took a sabbatical from the Beach Boys. If he'd turned it into a PR event, he might have won some much-needed publicity. As it was, *Carl Wilson* didn't sell and he struggled to half-fill the small clubs in which he performed. By the time he was ready to explain himself in public, it was too late. But his statement that July summed up the situation perfectly. 'I do not plan on touring with them until they decide 1981 means as much to them as 1961. I'm putting my energies into something positive for me. I feel the Beach Boys aren't at peak energy now.'

Before Carl could consider returning to the group, there were 'three issues I had raised [that] remained unchanged. First, I wanted the Beach Boys to make a new rock 'n' roll record of new songs, rather than just relying on the hits of the past. Second, I wanted the guys to rehearse thoroughly before a tour because there's hardly been a full Beach Boys rehearsal in more than a year. Third, I didn't want a major thrust of Beach Boys touring to be multi-night engagements in Tahoe and Las Vegas and places like that.' It was a damning indictment of the group's collective complacency.

Not that Carl was entirely blameless. He had repeatedly reinforced the message that Mike Love had propagated the previous year, that 'Brian is writing as creatively right now as he has in the last ten years'. Carl claimed that his brother 'had just finished a demo of a song that sounds a lot like "Good Vibrations"'; it remains unidentified. It was true that Brian did prepare a stunning demo of a new composition in early 1981: 'Stevie', a love song for Stevie Nicks, which had all the vibrancy of his best work from 1965. But the song was also deeply disturbing. 'It's OK, come inside my mind,' Brian sang. 'You might be surprised by what you find.' It was not exactly an enticing prospect. He was probably fortunate to escape without a restraining order.

As the Beach Boys set out on a summer tour without Carl, Brian voiced his doubts that his youngest brother would ever return to the band. 'I don't trust him,' he said. Neither was he impressed by Carl's album: 'I didn't like that too much. I liked Dennis's album, though.' (Nearly forty years later, he would claim on camera that he had never heard Dennis's record.)

Mike Love remained typically optimistic (or deluded). 'The Beach Boys are on the verge of a new plateau of awareness and creativity,' he claimed. 'There is health and harmony within the group.' But it was not apparent in their music. Brian was now being asked to take up the slack left by Carl's desertion and he was not always up to the task. In Indianapolis, for example, he performed 'Don't Worry Baby' and, a reviewer noted sadly, 'destroyed it'. In Los Angeles, a sudden noise from an amplifier made Brian flee the stage in panic just as he began to sing 'God Only Knows'. Al Jardine scampered behind him, trying to cut him off, while a startled Bruce Johnston was left to rescue the song.

The group's fragile status was revealed to a national audience on 5 July 1981, when a show alongside the *Queen Mary* at Long Beach was broadcast live on TV. The group had just stepped off a plane from

Washington DC and they seemed dazed. 'It made me feel real bad to see the guys,' Carl lamented. Mike looked permanently anxious, Dennis played drums as if he was demolishing furniture and Brian occasionally delivered a near-perfect vocal but stared ahead blankly as if he'd been heavily sedated. Only Al Jardine appeared both competent and confident. The star vocal performance of the night came from Bobby Figueroa, the band's second drummer, who rose elegantly to the task of delivering 'Sail on Sailor'. It was the only occasion on which the Beach Boys came close to Carl's wish that they should 'return and expand on the sound we were doing in the early '70s'.

Nothing in the Beach Boys' world made much sense anymore. Out of nowhere, the group achieved two Top 20 hit singles – the first time they'd managed that since 1967 – without raising a finger. The first was a 'Beach Boys Medley' that sounded as if it had been assembled by a small child with a roll of sticky tape. Certainly, Carl complained that 'the edits are real tacky'. The rest of the group mimed to its incoherence on *American Bandstand*, with Brian laughing out loud at the stupidity of it all and Dennis hanging his head as if desperate not to be recognised. Then Al Jardine's revival of the Del-Vikings' 1950s doo-wop hit, 'Come Go with Me' (first issued on the *M.I.U. Album*), was plucked from a compilation and also charted. As gracefully as possible, Al tried to point out that he'd wanted to release it as a single back in 1978 but had been overruled.

These successes convinced the group that oldies were the way to go. In late 1981, a Mike Love solo album finally reached the shops. *Looking Back with Love* was professional, perhaps too keen to sound modern, with its Fairlights and syn-drums, but competent enough. It was also stuffed with covers, none of which matched the originals. The one genuinely impressive song on the album, 'Paradise Found', was ignored by everyone in the world. Carl named his second album, *Youngblood*, after a 1950s R&B hit by the Coasters. He also revived John Fogerty's 'Rockin' All Over the World'. The record was tougher, tighter and more commercial (in theory) than its predecessor, but it only sold to Beach Boys diehards. Mike Love travelled to England to remake hits from the early 1960s with Adrian Baker, a harmony freak slipped into the touring group to provide the vocal accuracy that the original members could no longer achieve. (Their relationship culminated in one of the most unnecessary records in pop history, Mike's 1983 revival of 'Jingle Bell Rock'.) Mike and Dean Torrence also created a compilation of 'new' (in other words, revived) material entitled *Rock 'n' roll City* – issued only on cassette by a chain of hi-fi stores. It included that modern rarity, a competent new Beach Boys recording – a cover, of course, as Al Jardine sang the Mamas and the Papas' 'California Dreamin''. Certain that this was the group's optimum direction of travel, Jardine added Del Shannon's 'Runaway' to their live setlists and announced that it would be the group's next single. (It was never released.)

In 1982, these embarrassing nods to the past were the Beach Boys' only sign of life. Carl returned to the group, hypnotising himself into believing that the ethos had changed; it hadn't. Dennis appeared only sporadically and tended to cause chaos when he did. Brian's health and wellbeing deteriorated to the point that he was in danger of dying from either obesity or drug addiction; it was just a question of which got him first. 'I wrote a song called "Brian's Back",' Mike Love lamented, 'but it's not the truth. Mentally, sometimes he's here and sometimes he's not. Physically, he's not there at all.' Not that Mike was immune from criticism this year. In one memorable review, the *Hartford Courant* joked that he 'seems to have undergone a bizarre operation in which all of his sinuses were replaced by kazoos. He soon will be able to sing entirely through his nose.'

This was the Beach Boys in 1982: sick, discouraged, self-deluding, desperate, increasingly unable to convince even the most party-crazed audiences that they were a functioning band. Two of the original members seemed to be flirting with death every day. But only one of them could be saved.

Farewell My Friend

The fall of Dennis Wilson

'I'll never make the headlines or the evening news,' Dennis Wilson sang on his *Pacific Ocean Blue* album, but he was wrong.

'He was hooked on alcohol,' Mike Love recalled. 'It ruled his life. It ruled it in the morning, when he got up, until the evening, when he passed out. Sometimes he didn't make it to the evening. It was a tragedy, but he was hooked, just like an addict hooked on anything. We tried to get him to seek help, but he would only do it his way. Which was: he was a rebel.' And how did that manifest itself? Love said that Dennis would 'get drunk, then try to sober up for shows. It got to be a real drag. The tragedy is that he didn't live life to the fullest.'

Bruce Johnston agreed: 'He was in a lane faster than the fast lane. The way he lived, if you could average it out in years, Dennis was probably 150 years old. He was paying the bill. He was one of the most handsome men I have ever known. He had love affairs with some of the most gorgeous women. He had it all. He could have been a movie star. He could do anything he wanted. But sometimes people don't feel worthy.'

'Dennis had been talking about not reaching his next birthday,' added his friend Gary Cook, who claimed to have been working with the drummer on a biography. 'He had talked about suicide.' Beach Boys manager Jerry Schilling denied that he had heard Dennis sounding that desperate but admitted that 'he entered rehab programs two or three times in the last three months, but he never completed them'.

Locked out of his Venice Beach home in the final weeks of 1983, distanced from his teenage wife Shawn and their toddler son Gage, banned from attending Beach Boys shows, broke, sick and aimless, Dennis wandered from bar to bar through Marina Del Rey, the harbour inlet behind the beach. Most days he would end up at Nick's Liquor Store, hanging out with the locals, many of whom no longer recognised him as a celebrity. He would cadge drinks from strangers and friends, crash on the boats moored in the slips, or maybe charm a young woman to take him home for a few nights, until he became too smashed or rowdy to endure. Shawn and Gage were a couple of miles away at a cheap Santa Monica hotel. He called on them on his birthday, 4 December, drunk as ever. 'I asked him what he wanted,' Shawn recalled. 'He said, "I want to stop hurting myself".'

Almost three weeks later, on 23 December, he took a decisive step towards that goal. Dr Joe Takamine worked at the rehab clinic for drug and alcohol abuse at St John's Hospital in Santa Monica. 'I talked with his agent for months about getting him onto a program,' the doctor said. 'Finally, Dennis started talking seriously about it and he was admitted. I laid it out. I said, "You're thirty-nine, you better pull your act together." He said, "I know, I want to go on the program."' He admitted having been drinking and taking cocaine, and he was placed on a detox regimen. But on Christmas Day, he was visited by friends who told him that Shawn and Gage were being thrown out of their hotel for being unable to pay the bill. Dennis immediately announced that he was going to rescue them. 'He became quite agitated, quite anxious,' Takamine recalled, 'although he was sedated and the nurses tried to talk him out of it. We thought he'd come back. He'd done this before.'

Dennis tracked down his wife and son at her mother's home, but was refused permission to stay there. Instead, he wandered back towards the beach, winding up at the Santa Monica Bay Inn. There he lumbered his way into a fight with a male friend of Shawn's who was many years younger and in far better physical shape. A friend pulled him out of the melee, although not before Dennis had been badly beaten. While he mumbled drunken, dazed threats of reprisals, the friend phoned St John's and begged that Dennis should be readmitted. The duty doctor refused, apparently telling Wilson's friend: 'He's just too much trouble.' Wilson was taken back to Marina Del Rey, where a hospital salved his wounds, and he was held for the night. In the morning, he was back on the street, managing to track down a friend and part-time lover, Colleen McGovern.

On 27 December, Dennis phoned his friend Bill Oster, whose yacht the *Emerald* was moored at the marina alongside the berth once occupied by Wilson's own sailboat, the *Harmony*. Oster and his girlfriend Brenda Clugston welcomed him and Colleen aboard, and Dennis relished their hospitality (and the vodka that was his constant companion) to the point that he passed out. His friends took this as their cue to sleep, but Dennis was soon awake and restless. He spent the night calling acquaintances and family from a payphone, desperate for anything to occupy his disturbed mind.

In the morning, his friends hid the remaining vodka, but Wilson's appetite gave him the tracking skills of a bloodhound. The four of them rowed out into the harbour for a while, exploring all the different slips and basins, before returning to the *Emerald* for lunch. Dennis picked fitfully at his turkey sandwich and kept swigging his vodka. Then, visibly unsteady, he wandered along the jetty to see another boat-dweller, Nicky Morris. Almost twenty years older than Wilson, she admitted that 'he was kind of a weirdo, but you couldn't help liking the guy'. He told her he was going to dive down and look for items he'd thrown overboard from the *Harmony* a few months earlier. Like the crew of the *Emerald*, she warned him the water was too cold, but he waved their objections away.

Dennis threw himself into the murky water again and again, congratulating himself on the fact that he found a photo frame in which he'd once kept a picture of his previous wife, Karen. Then, to his friends' relief, he climbed back onto the *Emerald* and applied himself once more to the bottle of vodka. It was nearing sunset, but he threw off his shirt and, wearing only his cut-off shorts, plunged beneath the water. Oster watched anxiously, saw Dennis come close enough to the surface to wave his hand, and then vanish. 'He was having fun,' Oster recalled. 'I thought he was clowning and he would come up. [But] after several minutes, I still didn't see him – he just never came up.' He and the two women called his name, searched desperately around the basin in case he was hiding behind another craft and then waved down a passing Harbour Patrol boat.

Officers were unable to see through the dark mass of the water, so they dived twelve feet to the bottom and began to feel with their hands along the harbour bed until they located a body, lying on its back. They pulled it to the surface and, at 5.45pm on 28 December 1983, Dennis Carl Wilson was pronounced dead, some eighty minutes after he had disappeared. His body was zipped into a bag and pushed away on a gurney; that was the image repeated on the TV newsflash. His face was bruised and slightly cut (presumably from the earlier fistfight, though it was also possible that, in the murkiness of the sea, he had collided with the bottom of the *Emerald*'s rowboat), but there was no sign of foul play. 'Underwater pressure causes nitrogen to be absorbed into the blood, which results in euphoria,' concluded the celebrity coroner Thomas Noguchi. 'Wilson went down only twelve feet, but unfortunately there was another biological factor in his system encouraging euphoria: alcohol. Therefore, he stayed down much longer than he would have if he had been sober.'

The news reached the Beach Boys' management and spread among his family and bandmates. Carl had invited Dennis to stay with him and their mother over Christmas, but Dennis had promised to arrive for New Year instead. 'My mother was with us at my home in the [Colorado] mountains when it happened,' Carl recalled. 'I had to be the one to tell her and it wasn't easy.' Jerry Schilling phoned Brian, who was with some of Eugene Landy's minders. 'I felt real strange,' Brian said afterwards. 'It's a weird feeling when you hear about a death in the family, a weird trip. It's not something you can really talk about or describe. I got tears after a half-hour. Then I saw it on the news and thought, "Oh God, there he is, lying there, dead." I was blown out by the whole idea that he drowned, although I just let it lay. I didn't think too much about it.'

'He took it quite well,' Carl felt. 'He did great.'

Bruce Johnston's sadness was overwhelmed by frustration, even anger. 'I sat up all night in my chair next to my piano, swearing at him for being so dumb. What he did was so typical of him – the risks, the fast lane. You don't go swimming in 58-degree water without a wetsuit. You don't go diving in a marina, looking for junk you threw off your old boat years before. He was very, very stupid to do that. If he were here, he'd agree.' But Johnston was quick to insist that 'he had the biggest heart. If you met Dennis, you'd really like him. If he had a million dollars in his hotel room, and you needed it, he's the kind of guy – I swear to God – that he'd just give it to you. He'd figure, "I can make more". And he could.'

Mike Love's reaction to his cousin's death mingled psychology and spirituality. 'He defied the laws of nature and of man. You can get away with breaking man-made laws, but nature is unforgiving. I think that put him on the path to his so-called accidental drowning. I don't think it was an accident at all. I think he was very unhappy.' But he stated his belief that, freed from the limitations and frailties of his body and psyche, Dennis would finally be at peace. 'I feel the presence of his soul or spirit much stronger. After a few hours, alcohol leaves the body. I'm sure if you're disincarnate, it gives you time to think, without the inhibiting values of drugs and alcohol and stuff.'

There was an immediate and official statement on behalf of the Beach Boys as an entity, delivered by publicist Sandy Friedman: 'We are saddened by the sudden death of Dennis Wilson. He was one of the most sensitive and gifted musicians in pop music. Dennis was our brother and our friend. We love him and we will miss him.' Almost two weeks later, the surviving Beach Boys staged a press conference, where Carl explained that 'we are not disbanding' because that was not what Dennis would have wanted, but, as Al Jardine added, 'we are waiting for our hearts to mend'. 'Emotionally we wanted to wait a little before we sang "Fun, Fun, Fun" again,' Mike Love declared. (Their pause lasted another five weeks, until they fulfilled a week-long engagement at a Lake Tahoe casino hotel. 'We all thought that Dennis would have wanted it that way,' Jardine said.)

As he had when his father died, Brian felt unable to attend the funeral service on New Year's Eve, though he did take part in a private service at the chapel. Dennis's teenage widow, Shawn, insisted that he had wanted to be laid to rest in the ocean, though it took a personal intervention from President Reagan for that to be allowed. Fitting though it might have seemed for Dennis's body to be consumed by the ocean he loved so much, Brian was appalled by the decision. 'I thought that took on a very scary effect,' he said. 'Burying out at sea just didn't seem like the proper way to bury someone. I went through a lot of changes there.' Not that he was prepared to wallow in grief. 'For me, the mourning is over,' he announced at the group's press conference. He was planning to channel his sorrow into a song: 'I could write a song for Dennis right here. I could go to a piano and take ten minutes to get it off my chest.' But no tribute song ever emerged. Instead, the Beach Boys dedicated something in their live show to their lost drummer – usually Carl's affecting ballad, 'Heaven'.

'At least his essence is locked up in the music,' Bruce Johnston felt. 'There were 50,000 people at our show in San Diego, and two of Dennis's sons, Mike and Carl, were there. They saw what their dad had created.' But there was also a barely expressed (though Mike Love came closest) sense of relief that an unpredictable force of nature had been removed from the band's working environment. 'It was a stress on the whole group,' Mike said of Dennis's behaviour in recent years, adding that they had told him to 'take some time off and get yourself together. But he never did.' The hurricane had passed, although the Beach Boys were still quite capable of concocting crises without Dennis Wilson. His talent, however – no matter how poorly he had served it in the final five years of his life – could never be replaced. Neither could his spirit, that relentless fire that lit up the stage when he was there. 'I miss that strong beat,' Al Jardine admitted. 'But we'll get by. We always seem to.'

Sweet Insanity

Brian Wilson and Eugene Landy, part 2

Everybody wanted to save Brian Wilson from himself. But what were they saving him for? For Carl Wilson, his brother's life transcended his music. 'I really don't care if he writes another note of music, unless it nurtures him. He's been through so much pain. I just want him to get well.' For the Beach Boys as a collective entity, Brian represented security and commercial viability. And for Eugene Landy, reinstalled as Brian's saviour in 1983? He could see a payout that would accumulate like a snowball rolling down a Himalayan peak.

Just as he had in 1976, Landy insisted that his client should be exposed to the outside world as soon as his recovery began to pay dividends. It was part therapy for Brian, part advertisement for Landy's magical powers. Faced by reporters in 1983 and 1984, Brian mostly voiced the platitudes he'd just been taught, although his insecurities were impossible to ignore. The reporter Jonathan Taylor met Brian in late 1983 and was shocked to encounter a man with 'shaking hands, scared eyes and often disjointed conversation … all but incapable of completing a full thought'. In front of Taylor, Brian told his mentor disconsolately: 'I think ultimately I'm just a sound. I don't know if I'm a human being.' In another interview, he looked stricken at the suggestion that one day Landy might not be there. 'I'd be scared out of my mind. I wouldn't want to walk out my front door.' The self-reliance that Landy saw as Brian's goal was far from reality.

The therapy-cum-comeback involved returning to the stage with the Beach Boys, where he behaved like someone who had never learned how to act in front of the public. He was able to unveil some new material, although it was so simplistic that it was as if he had been locked in a room for a year with only an album of 1950s R&B ballads for nourishment. The most affecting song was 'It's Just a Matter of Time', which ended with an anguished confessional yell: 'I've been to hell / It's been hell for me'. (Those lines were omitted when he recorded the song with the Beach Boys.)

What nobody realised until they read the small print on the 1985 album *The Beach Boys* was that Brian now had a permanent co-writer: Eugene Landy. The therapist was initially taking 25 per cent of Brian's writing royalties off the top, whether he was involved in the process of creation or not, and then an additional half of the rest if his name appeared on the song. By 1985, Brian's lawyer was able to negotiate down that 25 per cent premium, but Landy now insisted that he should be credited for everything Brian wrote – even though, as the lawyer grumbled, 'I haven't ever seen [Landy] write a song'.

Brian's grasp on reality was as tenuous as his hold on his earnings. Al Jardine was disturbed by a conversation he caught behind the scenes: 'Just before we went on stage the other night, I heard Brian turn to Carl. He said, "There's one brother left". Carl turned to Brian and said, "No, Brian, there's two".' But at the same time that he could erase himself from the scenery, he was also capable of making wild pronouncements about his plans and possibilities. When *The Beach Boys* appeared in June 1985, Brian proclaimed his intention to release a solo album before Christmas. 'I want to shave my beard soon, practise hard and get back into action with people like David Bowie and Cyndi Lauper,' he declared.

To achieve anything coherent, anything worthy of his name and legacy, Brian needed a collaborator who didn't see him as both a psychiatric client and a cash-cow. His fan and friend David Leaf, author of a controversial 1978 biography that staked Brian's claim to be the persecuted heart and soul of the Beach Boys, negotiated with Brian's early 1960s collaborator, Gary Usher. The writing team that had spawned 'Lonely Sea', 'In My Room' and 'We'll Run Away' was reunited for a turbulent ten-month partnership. (Stephen J McParland's book *The Wilson Project*, based on detailed input from Usher, chronicled the turmoil in excruciating detail.) As with so many periods of Brian's post-*SMiLE* life, historians have tended to interpret this era as a golden age of creativity, which was blocked, subverted and finally capsized by Dr Landy. Musical evidence, in the form of leaked demos and half-completed songs, doesn't suggest that Brian was in any shape to write classic songs. But Usher's reminiscences of sessions that were constantly interrupted or cancelled by Landy are harrowing, as are his memories of brief encounters with the Beach Boys during the same period.

Few outside the Landy camp have ever doubted Usher's motives. He was, at the very least, clear-eyed about the challenge he faced. When Brian first played him some songs in progress, Gary realised: 'It was obvious that Brian was out of tune with what was happening in the record market.' The pair would work on a collaboration one day, plan to resume the following morning, only for Brian to show up with a completely different, Landy-selected song in mind, and the almost robotic statement: 'This is what we're doing'. One or more of Landy's assistants, usually Kevin Leslie, would attend every session, while Landy would demand to be updated about progress at regular intervals. If any song ever neared completion, Landy would stake his claim to writing and production credits. Usher was left to fight his corner without Brian's support or financial aid.

One significant event occurred during the *Project* sessions. In August 1986, Wilson and Usher double-dated at a Moody Blues concert. Brian's partner that evening was a car saleswoman named Melinda Ledbetter. 'She and Brian had as much in common as apples and bananas,' a confused Usher recalled. So did Usher and Landy. Under the circumstances, it is remarkable that any recordings were finished, let alone Brian's first solo single for more than twenty years: 'Let's Go to Heaven in My Car'. Clumsy and gauche, it was still an entertaining trifle, wildly out of place on the soundtrack of the film comedy *Police Academy 4*. Wilson, Landy and Usher shared the writing credits and were all listed as producers of various kinds. (Amidst the constant historical revisionism that surrounds this period, Usher lost his tag as 'co-producer' after his death.)

If that single was charming, albeit uncommercial, the other Wilson/ Usher creation to reach the public in 1987 was simply banal. 'The Spirit of Rock & Roll', so Brian imagined, 'sounds like a Top 10 record. I can't see it not being Top 20.' We'll never know, as the Beach Boys' recording (with no Carl or Al) was restricted to the closing sequence of the band's misbegotten twenty-fifth anniversary TV special. Still, to his amazement, Usher's name did surface as co-producer when the final credits unfurled.

By then, Brian had been signed to Sire Records (part of the Warners group) by president Seymour Stein: a two-album deal overseen by Warners veteran Lenny Waronker, who had championed Van Dyke Parks' work for two decades. Wilson did not exactly bless the deal with optimism, admitting that 'I've exhausted my creative abilities ... I rely on my past achievements so much. Otherwise, I'd be too scared to write. I wouldn't think it will be good enough.' Immediately there was a flurry of claims and counterclaims about who exactly would be steering Brian's solo debut home. Usher was soon exiled and left to nurture his disillusionment until his tragically early death in 1990. Songwriter and musician Andy Paley emerged as Brian's closest surrogate and aide. Stein and Waronker each submitted their own fantasies about how Brian should sound. And through it all, Eugene Landy (and his girlfriend/ co-writer, Alexandra Morgan) jousted with all the creatives to retain control and the financial rewards.

As the sessions continued, Landy was suddenly forced to defend himself on an entirely new plane. On 17 February 1988, he was served with notice of a legal action: a complaint that he had broken multiple rules governing the psychology profession. The charges were brought by one Thomas O'Connor, who was (pause for breath) the executive officer of the Psychology Examining Committee of the Division of Allied Health Professions of the Board of Medical Quality Assurance of the State of California. At issue was Landy's conduct with two of his clients: a woman named RG and a male musician called BW. At stake was the official licence allowing him to practise legally in California. Until the matter was decided, Landy's licence was suspended, meaning that he was no longer able to treat Brian Wilson. Did that stop him? Does that question need to be answered?

The details of the way Landy handled RG were appalling. It was alleged that the doctor had given his client cocaine and amyl nitrate on many occasions, drugs he had shared with her. He also began a sexual relationship with her, raped her, attended orgies with her and forced her to give him blow-jobs on demand, even when he was driving.

There were no sexual charges against Landy in the case of BW. Instead, Landy had exhibited 'Gross Negligence by being in a dual, triple or even quadruple relation with BW while remaining his therapist: business manager, business adviser, executive producer, co-songwriter.' The accusation spelled out this unethical involvement in great detail, noting Landy's claim to have co-written more than a dozen songs with Brian. It was said that, since January 1987, Landy had been representing Brian on the Beach Boys' Management Advisory Committee, for which he was also being paid. Almost as an aside, the complaint also noted that Landy was illegally prescribing Brian drugs and exerting an immoral degree of control over his client's everyday activities. It concluded by asserting that Brian had suffered 'severe emotional damage, psychological dependency and financial exploitation'.

This legal action must have registered on the horizon of the Sire/Warners executives who were liaising daily with Dr Landy. But there was too much money invested in Brian's solo album for such trivialities to endanger potential profit. Everyone concerned with the record pretended that nothing had changed – even when Brian was sent out on a lengthy series of media encounters that exposed both his recovery and his continued instability. Although every interview saw Brian paying exuberant tribute to his therapist and collaborator, he could not help himself from sending up distress flares. It was soon apparent that Landy's regime prohibited Brian from contacting his mother Audree, his daughters Carnie and Wendy, or his brother Carl. 'Dr Landy doesn't like me to be in touch with my family,' Brian explained confusedly. 'He thinks it's unhealthy.' Landy immediately denied saying any such thing. Asked why he and Carl apparently weren't speaking to each other, Brian said that he didn't know.

Michael Goldberg met Wilson and Landy for *Rolling Stone* magazine as the *Brian Wilson* album was released. He also spoke to another of Brian's therapists, the psychiatrist Dr Solon Samuels, who described Landy as 'emotionally explosive' and exhibiting 'a personality problem'. As if to prove the point, Landy told Goldberg that he was now Eugene Wilson Landy; Brian had become Brian Landy Wilson. 'We've exchanged names,' Landy explained. 'We've kind of merged. I've taken from him and he's taken from me.' Half of that last sentence is true. The pair formed a production company named Brains (for Brian) and Genius (Gene). Brains gave way to Genius on all occasions: Brian called his therapist 'scary', 'my boss', 'frightening' and admitted that he had 'total superiority over me'. He sounded proud to be in that position of subjection to a greater force. Genius also claimed writing credits for half the album and executive producer rights over the entire package. (A Stalinist rewriting of history ensured that Landy's name was omitted entirely from the package when the album was reissued in 2000.)

Various inquisitors picked up on the distance between Brian and his daughters. 'I don't want to get involved with them right now,' Brian said, claiming that he would resume contact with them in two years. 'I don't think they understand very well.' Three years passed and there was no reconciliation. By 1991, Carnie Wilson could hold back her anger no longer. 'I think that Dr Landy has really taken advantage. That will end soon. Because karma is the most powerful thing on earth, and the rat is going to get it. He is going to get it real good.' Another year on, her sister Wendy struck a sadder tone. 'He never calls us. We don't have a relationship with him. He withdrew from Day One. He was never a father figure. He didn't know how to be.' The two young women had now become stars, as two-thirds of the vocal trio Wilson Phillips. Eventually, Brian was persuaded to attend one of their shows: 'My mom saw him crying hysterically at the soundboard,' Wendy said, 'his face in his hands.' But he was still unable to connect with them as people.

The *Brian Wilson* album was supposed to redeem all of his failings as a parent and a human being. Critical opinion leaned towards ecstasy, with only occasional detractors. Diehard fans relished the record's melodic verve, its subtle throwbacks to vintage Wilson motifs, most especially the conceptual suite, 'Rio Grande', assembled at the request of Lenny Waronker to revive memories of *SMiLE*. It was an unusual record all round, dogged by tinkling computer noises and slightly too obvious recreations of the Phil Spector sound, with massed Wilson vocal harmonies that were both stirring and somehow artificial. With the passing decades, the album's flaws have become more apparent, its hybrid of *Pet Sounds* and *Love You* more contrived. But there were still moments of magic to be found, from the heart-tearing poignancy of 'Melt Away' to the pop perfection of 'Baby Let Your Hair Grow Long'. The opening cut, 'Love and Mercy', would become Brian's anthem, his gentle pathos capturing the tender, wounded soul beneath the tabloid exposes.

Somehow, none of this translated into popular appeal beyond those already primed for satisfaction. The other Beach Boys were not included in that number. Mike Love expressed his disappointment and belief that the album would have been improved if Brian had collaborated with him, not Landy. Bruce Johnston was even more critical. 'It was a tremendous disappointment to me,' he said. 'We got this meandering, strange album where he multi-tracked his voice and he sang in these funny arrangements. It sounded like he had creative cholesterol. It sounded so out of touch with what was going on in the world.' The album reinforced Bruce's slightly jaundiced view of the Beach Boys' maestro. As he told me in 1990, 'we've been talking about Brian for twenty years. It's like he had this five-year career and we've been talking about it ever since.' Bruce also admitted that he used Brian as a warning to his young sons – to stay away from narcotics.

It was unfortunate for Brian, to say the least, that the lukewarm commercial reception of his album coincided with one of the Beach

Boys' triumphs: a number one single with 'Kokomo'. In interviews, Brian complained that he had not even been told about the recording session – or, alternatively, that he was told so late that it would have been impossible for him to attend. The group countered that Landy would never put through their calls or pass on messages. As Bruce put it succinctly, 'when you can't get through to someone on the phone, their conclusion is that they're not invited'. More damaging for Brian was that 'Kokomo' convinced the group that they could succeed without him. Why would they go through the misery of trying to record with Brian, when that entailed dealing with his psychiatrist Siamese twin?

Landy had not abandoned hope of being the creative partner of one of the world's biggest stars. He was also inviting backers to bid for the rights to a stage musical based on the story of his epic journey with Brian. Until that happened (which it never did), he exerted even more control over the making of what was intended to be the second album in Brian's deal. In a moment of either extreme stupidity or rampant honesty, Landy insisted that the record should be titled *Sweet Insanity*. Maybe the adjective should have been 'Strange', as this was an album swamped in weirdness – and the most aggressive form of late 1980s percussion sounds, exploding apparently at random across every song. Anyone who thought that Brian had reached a peak of eccentricity in the late 1970s clearly hadn't heard his rap tune, 'Smart Girls', which he delivered without any sense of rhythm – or any sense, for that matter. Worse still, the track was intercut with endless clips from Beach Boys records, which sabotaged the beat. Other songs borrowed so heavily from the past that they were weighed down by familiarity: 'Water Builds Up' used the same melody as 'Let's Go to Heaven in My Car', while 'Someone to Love' seemed to have been constructed around brother Dennis's 'San Miguel'. 'The Spirit of Rock and Roll' featured a bizarre cameo from Bob Dylan, like a handful of gravel in a treacle tart. Most egregious of all was 'Brian', in which the lyrics (probably not written by Brian) attacked Audree and Carl Wilson, and claimed: 'They're not happy, cos I'm different, more creative, independent'. But only if Landy said so, of course.

Brian and Landy submitted the album to Warners and Sire in every expectation that the executives would be thrilled. Both sides of the corporate partnership turned it down. Howie Klein of Sire summed up their reaction. 'It was pathetic. Eugene Landy's lyrics were full of psychological mumbo-jumbo. When Brian brought the tapes in, I thought it was a joke, but it wasn't. It was awful.' 'We went with our hopes up,' Brian recalled, 'so we were disappointed they didn't like it.'

The demise of *Sweet Insanity* seemed to herald the downfall of Landy's reign, even if the edifice took another eighteen months to crumble. In legal terms, the foundations were demolished as early as March 1989, when the professional standards committee barred Landy from practising psychology in California for two years. The doctor's sins were, they declared, 'heinous'. For a sober, academic body, the verdict could hardly have been more damning.

Through 1990 and 1991, Brian held fast to Landy's shirttails. As the doctor had told him, the Beach Boys were the evil empire across the bay. 'They probably want control of me,' Brian said of his foes (band and family) in 1991, 'but they will not get it. I say let sleeping dogs lie.' Then, bizarrely, he repeated the line that had so often been credited to Mike Love: 'If the formula works, don't goof with it. That's been one of my major philosophies in life. It's been working.' Mike must have choked on his macrobiotic breakfast when he read that one.

And talking of reading ... The moment when Dr Landy overplayed his hand and destroyed the increasingly fragile Brian Wilson industry was the publication of a book that purported to be Brian's autobiography. *Wouldn't It Be Nice* was 'co-written' by celebrity journalist Todd Gold and its lengthy, often harrowing text delineated, in appalling detail, the many sins and injuries visited upon its narrator by his family and musical colleagues. Everything was someone else's fault, with particular emphasis on Murry Wilson and the individual members of the Beach Boys. Not a single word of the book read as if it had been spoken by Brian Wilson. It was full of factual inconsistencies and errors, and it had all too obviously been drawn from other writers' accounts of their meetings with Brian and the other band members. Anecdotes were extended and exaggerated; accidents were described as deliberate acts; Brian's failings as the inevitable consequence of his ill-treatment. Both Carl and their mother Audree launched libel suits against Brian, his ghost-writer and the publisher. TV journalist Diane Sawyer devoted a lengthy segment of *Primetime Live* to an expose of the book's many flaws. Meanwhile Brian's family, led by Stan Love, intervened legally to demand that he be released from Landy's control. It was revealed that Brian had been persuaded to rewrite his will, awarding most of his estate and publishing rights to Landy and his girlfriend.

Brian was sent out on a book tour to defend and promote the book. It was a disaster. During a conversation with Karen Heller of the *Philadelphia Inquirer*, he fell asleep six times, was unable to say how old he was and spoke in a voice that was 'slurred, his lips somewhat frozen, as if he's recovering from a stroke'. He explained that he thought Eugene Landy might be God and said that his therapist could 'control just about everybody else, but not the Beach Boys'. Why didn't he contact his daughters? Because, Brian said, they 'give me bad memories … I can't see them, it's just I pulled the curtain on them'. Heller concluded a disturbing encounter by listing the prescription drugs that Brian was being given by Landy: 'Xanax is an anti-anxiety and anti-depression medication. Eskalith is used to control manic depression. Navane and Serentil are given to curb anti-psychotic behaviour. And Cogentin is used to control the side effects of anti-psychotic drugs. Used together, they could cause small seizures and muscle spasms.'

Other interviews were equally traumatic, as Brian compulsively downed multiple bottles of mineral water, failed to respond to questions or asked for them to be repeated several times, and kept trying to get away from the minders who stalked his every move. Sometimes his eyes would roll back in his head so that only the whites would show. If he disliked the tone of the interviewer's voice, he would simply get up and walk away. He talked about being threatened physically by Mike Love; being reluctant to talk to Carnie and Wendy because they didn't like him; admitted to being 'addicted' to Dr Landy; claimed to be afraid of the Devil, although the Devil was also afraid of him. In a rare moment of freedom from Landy's aides, he confessed: 'I'm lost, I'm lonely – and I don't know where I'm headed. A lot of people haven't been real good to me. I'll probably come out of this OK – but I don't know.' It was not a good advertisement for nine years of Eugene Landy's therapy and medication.

What few of the interviewers were told was that Brian and Dr Landy had already parted company, by court order, although Landy was not (yet) prohibited from keeping tabs on his client and partner via a collection of minders. Then, in early December 1991, the separation became permanent: therapist and client were legally bound to keep their distance from each other and all their financial ties were cut. In Landy's place, a conservator was installed to mind his affairs and keep watch over his safety. Otherwise, Brian was free to live his life as he chose – the most terrifying prospect of all.

It was a complete break from Landy, but the past kept reverberating and throwing Brian off his axis. There were court cases about writing credits and royalties, and alleged defamatory comments in his 'autobiography': different suits in different jurisdictions, all of them sapping his income and unsettling his psyche. But Brian was being supported through the first half of the 1990s by three key figures: Don Was, who was making a documentary film and album entitled *I Just Wasn't Made for These Times*; Andy Paley, now able to resume the writing partnership he had tentatively begun with Brian in the previous decade; and, most significantly for Brian, Melinda Ledbetter. In 1995, they were married and began to adopt a series of small children, five in all. The Don Was project enabled Brian to reconnect with his elder daughters. He was also seen singing with his mother and brother at the family piano, just as he had as a child. Did these reunions signal a happy ending? Of course not. By 1998, Carnie Wilson was openly referring to her stepmother as 'Melandy'. Was Brian being saved or controlled? The debate began again.

Rock and Roll to the Rescue

The Beach Boys face a future they don't understand

Only weeks after the death of Dennis Wilson, their promoter/adviser Tom Hulett trumpeted his belief that 'we've become America's Band. After all, what could be more wholesome than the Beach Boys?' This was clearly a concentrated effort to distance the group from the tragedy. The music of the Beach Boys, claimed Bruce Johnston, was 'about being healthy, being young, being about as radical as *Animal House* was and as innocent as *Sesame Street* is.' He added: 'I always described us to the guys as the missing ride from Disneyland. And that missing ride is out on the road.' Carl Wilson winced as if he was in the dentist's chair every time Bruce hit that nerve. Cousin Mike chimed in: 'We've got the artistic side covered with Brian being our musical genius, and yet we symbolise a lot of positive fun things – the manifestation of the California myth.'

It was time to take stock. At the start of 1984, Brian Wilson was in recovery, although Eugene Landy was beginning to convince him that he no longer needed the Beach Boys. Carl Wilson had abandoned his dreams of solo glory – in fact, almost any dreams at all. Al Jardine was keeping his head down and looking for more oldies to remake in his own image. Mike Love was upbeat, optimistic, in control. And Bruce

Johnston's role as the band's in-house critic widened to the point where he became the jester who could speak truth to the kings: the one man who kept insisting that the Beach Boys were only worth preserving if they created new music. Mike could always float a fantasy or two about the future, but it was Bruce who made it happen. This time, he wasn't going to be the producer. That uncomfortable role was awarded to one of the hottest names on the pop scene: Bruce's friend Steve Levine, fresh from overseeing a series of global hits by Boy George and Culture Club.

Placed inside a recording studio, the Beach Boys could still sing. A handful of recent recordings emerged in 1984 to prove the point. Four years earlier, Frankie Valli of the Four Seasons complained that he had never met the Beach Boys. He suggested that the two groups should tour together: 'Call it *East Meets West.* What an important part of rock 'n' roll history that would be. We could film it. You could do a double-album that would sell 10, 12, 15 million copies. It's a once-in-a-lifetime concept.' Not even once, as it turned out: the tour that Valli hoped might 'do grosses beyond anything that's ever been seen' never took place. But the two groups did make a single together, which was indeed called 'East Meets West'. Bruce Johnston hated it, he told me: 'Oh God. I don't know why we ever did that. Those guys never understood harmony. It was like World Cup beer-drinking harmony compared to ours.' To an uninformed outsider, though, it sounded corny, a little crass, but genuinely thrilling – the way a Seasons/Boys all-star match-up should have been.

The single made zero commercial impact, just like the soundtrack album from the merely passable comedy film *Up the Creek*. That included one of Carl's most impassioned lead vocals, on a generic piece of modern rock entitled 'Chasin' the Sky'. The fact that he was being forced to record just a few days after his brother's death probably explained the emotional intensity of his performance. By contrast, the group showed up at a Julio Iglesias session the following month and seemed utterly anonymous as they crooned 'The Air That I Breathe' with the Spanish heartthrob.

Their persistent touring aside, the Beach Boys' chief focus was their album project with Steve Levine. 'We're all writing songs,' Bruce Johnston explained in May 1984, 'but I'm sure Brian will sort through it [all], laugh at it, get us all embarrassed and then we'll sing all the parts.' Sessions began a few weeks later at Red Bus Studios near London's Regents Park. How many Beach Boys turned up? Just one. Eugene Landy was insisting that he should be the album's executive producer, even if he didn't contribute anything, and that he and Brian Wilson would only attend the initial sessions if no other Beach Boys were there. ('We were totally separated from Brian at that point,' Carl revealed later.) Levine had no choice but to agree. The recording process would begin with individual members of the band presenting their songs. Carl arrived first, in June 1984; Brian (and Landy, of course) in July; Al Jardine in September. Then the location switched to California, where the band cut their vocals.

The album was awarded the definitive title of *The Beach Boys*. It coincided with a retrospective documentary film, *An American Band*. ('I didn't think that was very good at all,' Johnston admitted later.) First, there was a single, the deliberately nostalgic 'Getcha Back', concocted by Mike Love and their old friend Terry Melcher. The vocal blend was unmistakeable and the product effervescent, and the single reached the US Top 30. Sadly, the album was less successful, at least commercially, though Levine ensured that the record gleamed with so-called Adult Contemporary perfection. If there were weak points, they were the songs contributed by Boy George and Stevie Wonder, and the new material from Brian Wilson and his co-writers, Eugene Landy and his girlfriend. 'Brian's writing songs,' Bruce conceded after the album had been released, 'but that doesn't mean they're good.' In an interview with *Modern Recording* as the album was released, Bruce went further. 'I'm not very happy with this album,' he admitted. 'I think we've let everybody down. We really don't deserve to have a hit album with this album.' Ultimately, *The Beach Boys* was proficient and acceptable, though it didn't revitalise their recording career or alter their trajectory.

Only afterwards was it apparent how fraught the creative process had been. Brian's verdict begged questions: 'We got along good. We spoke to each other. We were peaceful. We didn't fight. We didn't have arguments. Nobody got hit. Nobody got hurt.' (What had he been expecting?) Carl talked airily about the 'obstacles' that the group had been forced to overcome, one of which was undoubtedly the barrier that Landy placed between Brian and his comrades. Much later, members of the group confessed that their collective behaviour had sometimes driven Levine to tears. The producer was obviously scarred by the experience. 'It was an absolute nightmare from start to finish. And if I'd known it was going to take as long as it did, I wouldn't have done it, because I was driven mad by them.' One problem, it seemed, was the quality of their vocals. Brian was outraged when Levine informed him that he needed to take singing lessons. 'The legend is that they're the best singers in the world,' the producer said, 'but actually they're among the worst, with the exception of Bruce Johnston and Carl Wilson.'

The Beach Boys' triumphant performance at Live Aid, just as their album was released, did little to suggest that there was anything wrong. But it was rooted in the past – they, of all people, were not going to make the mistake of exposing that audience to unfamiliar material. This was the decade of MTV, when all veteran acts faced the challenge of whether to ignore the dominant pop medium of the age, the video, or confront the modern generation at their own game. The Beach Boys, consciously or otherwise, repositioned themselves as a band for whom nothing mattered but hit singles, and they no longer mattered that much.

Not that the trickle of new music entirely ran dry. In 1986, the Love/Melcher team concocted the chaotic but undeniably amusing 'Rock 'n' Roll to the Rescue', featuring a surprisingly energised Brian. Their 1980s revival of 'California Dreamin'' was souped up with the addition of Byrds founder Roger McGuinn. 'It wasn't as big as I thought it would be,' Al Jardine admitted. Bruce Johnston described their 1987 collaboration with the Fat Boys on the (suitably enough) fatuous 'Wipe Out' as 'really stupid' – and he was being kind. But it was a worldwide hit. Bruce then stripped out parts of his song 'Brand New Old Friends' to make 'Happy Endings', a disastrous collaboration with one of the founders of rock 'n' roll. Little Richard over-emoted like a soap star while syn-drums clattered around him and, far in the distance, the Beach Boys tried to make themselves heard.

Even fans were struggling to maintain focus on the group's recordings, which were irrelevant and easily ignored. But some gestures were so large that they couldn't be missed, no matter how hard one tried. The Beach Boys ended 1986 by taping a twenty-fifth anniversary TV concert so crass that it was almost an act of auto-destruction. It was set in Hawaii, in an imaginary world where the aging group were irresistible to bikini-clad models and movie stars. The group mimed their entire set, although some of the lead vocals were live. Only two men emerged with any credit: Carl Wilson, who delivered 'Heaven' as if it meant something, and Ray Charles, whose 'Sail on Sailor' transcended the tackiness of the setting because he was a great singer.

Mike Love had struck up a close friendship with a young soap star named John Stamos, who was both an amateur musician and a Beach Boys fanatic. The group made cameo appearances on his shows and he reciprocated, occasionally taking over the drum stool for an encore. In February 1987, Mike staged a press conference to announce that Stamos was now officially the replacement for Dennis Wilson. This was news to the rest of the Beach Boys. Carl described the event as 'curious' and mustered a courageously polite response: 'He's a nice young man, but he's not a member of the band.'

Mike Love was only getting warmed up. On 20 January 1988, the Beach Boys were inducted into the Rock & Roll Hall of Fame. 'We failed to musically exploit the experience,' Al Jardine complained afterwards. 'First, we played "Barbara Ann", a stupid two-minute cover of the Regents' song. We should have played "Good Vibrations", something that symbolises us. Then, because one of my partners rambled on and on, all I got to say was "Thank you". I would like to have that evening back again.'

'Rambled' was a most delicate description of Love's speech that evening. Maybe someone had stood on his big toe backstage or compared his voice to a kazoo; maybe he had been fasting too long, like he did back in 1970. Whatever the cause, he chose this moment to launch into a diatribe against some of the most famous musicians in the world – the Beatles and the Supremes, because key members had failed to show up for the ceremony, and the Rolling Stones because, in his overexcited imagination, Mick Jagger was 'chickenshit' scared to get up on stage against him and the Beach Boys. Bob Dylan was inducted afterwards and pointedly thanked Mike for not having mentioned him. The fracas went round the world, consolidating Love's reputation among his detractors as one of the most obnoxious men in rock 'n' roll. The critic Dave Marsh said that Mike's remarks 'were said with the venom of spiritual fascism'. Nobody said a word in his defence.

Nobody, that is, except Mike Love. The problem, he explained, was that although he had taken up almost all the Beach Boys' allotted time, he hadn't been given long enough. 'What I was trying to say,' he explained, 'was that there's too many groups hiding behind their images and management. The music business has become too regimented, too dependent on celebrity, status and image, and that's not what rock and roll should be.' After this, nobody was much clearer. Love's grudge against Mick Jagger continued, though. By 1990, he was gratuitously attacking him during Beach Boys concerts as 'the skinny guy with the big lips who runs around trying to be black'. He also rekindled an age-old rumour about Jagger's relationship with another English superstar: 'He never gave me no satisfaction,' Love sneered, 'but I heard he gave some to David Bowie.' Every time he sniped at the Stones' frontman, Carl Wilson seethed, apparently powerless to shut his cousin down.

In the wake of the Hall of Fame disaster, the last thing anyone expected was that the Beach Boys would release one of the biggest (US) hits of their career. Maybe there was no such thing as bad publicity – or maybe 'Kokomo' was just a very commercial record. 'We wanted to do something that was meaningful and purposeful to the times,' Love claimed, but the joy of 'Kokomo' was that it had no significance whatsoever. It took four men to write: John Phillips of the Mamas and the

Papas to coin the original idea, Scott McKenzie to flesh it out, then the Love/Melcher team to transform it into a song. It is still fashionable for Beach Boys fanatics to hate 'Kokomo', but that is as pointless as hating Christmas. It might not be to everyone's taste, but lots of people loved it, which is why it became their first chart-topper since 'Good Vibrations'. It was just unfortunate – rather than a cunning Mike Love plot – that its movie-based release (on the soundtrack of *Cocktail*) coincided with the appearance of Brian Wilson's first solo album. Critics voted for Brian; the public loved the Beach Boys.

The single's success sparked renewed interest in a Beach Boys album from Capitol Records. The concept of *Still Cruisin'*, issued a full year after the hit, was that it would assemble all their movie contributions. There were enough of them, stretching back to 'The Monkey's Uncle' in 1964. But the project was diverted when Wilson and Landy demanded that one of their songs be included, and the album wound up as an unholy mix of over-familiar 1960s oldies (was there anyone in the world who didn't already own 'California Girls'?) and random modern tracks. Of those, the only significant offering was 'Somewhere Near Japan', penned by the team behind 'Kokomo'. Supposedly it was dedicated to John Phillips' disturbed actor daughter, Mackenzie, who would later pen a memoir claiming that she had been abused by her father since she was a teenager. Capitol said that the album's success was 'pivotal' to the group and demanded that it should produce three hit singles – which proved to be three more than it could muster.

Nobody was likely to buy the group's appalling 1990 single, 'Problem Child', either. It's a toss-up whether that was more embarrassing than their solitary 1991 release, a cacophonous assault on 'Crocodile Rock' for an Elton John tribute project. But one man at least was keeping his eye on the prize, or at least the fantasy that one day there might be a prize. Bruce Johnston had a vision: 'to somehow throw everybody into the room and come up with a California version of [Paul Simon's] *Graceland*, something with a lot of thought and intelligence and interesting sounds, maybe with some environmental point of view to it.' This was not quite how things turned out.

The good news was there was a Beach Boys album in 1992, one that was superbly packaged, with a pronounced environmental theme. Just as Bruce Johnston had wanted, *Summer in Paradise* was the product of a single vision carrying everything before it. But perhaps Bruce hadn't banked on the vision being entirely provided by Mike Love. Perhaps too there was no alternative. Bruce was always talking about recording another solo album, but there was scant evidence that he had the songs. Al had become locked into a mode where he tinkered with the same handful of tunes for decades at a time, Brian was lost in Landy-land and Carl Wilson had elected to divert all his creative urges into a tentative collaboration with two friends, Gerry Buckley from America and Robert Lamm from Chicago. None of them thought they would make a hit record, but they shared mutual respect, something that had been missing within the Beach Boys for way too long.

So that only left Mike Love, and his modern-day running mate, Terry Melcher. In the absence of any competition, they took full creative responsibility for *Summer in Paradise* and they have to be held responsible for its disastrous commercial performance. So negative was the response to the initial American release that the album was overdubbed and heavily remixed for Britain and Europe. But the album still only sold in Australia and Germany, and, even in those territories, it could not have been classified as anything as vulgar as a hit. Love set the tone when he considered saddling the record with that Bart Simpson cameo. As if that wasn't enough, he decided to update the first Beach Boys single, 'Surfin''. 'We'll be recording that with a more modern, more of a hip-hop or house music kind of beat, and rock 'n' roll guitar. The teenage kids of today will relate to it because the beat is going to be contemporary.'

Sure enough, the first sound on the record was the metallic clank of a syn-drum. The entire production was like a duet between synthesised percussion and Beach Boys samples. Strip away the instantly dated soundscape and even Mike Love's rap, 'Summer of Love', would not be too offensive. (It's certainly classier than his cousin's 'Smart Girls'.) In a different context, the title track and 'Strange Things Happen' might have ranked among the more impressive songs from the band's post-Dennis era. The vocals were superb throughout, but they were doomed by the quintessentially 'modern' sound effects. The record was also weighed down with unnecessary covers: classic hits by Sly & the Family Stone, the Drifters and the Shangri-La's (full marks for musical taste, if not the arrangements), and a totally redundant revival of Dennis's 'Forever', sung by the actor who Mike wanted as his replacement, John Stamos. Displaying considerable grace, Carl said only that 'I prefer to go for the originals' – new material in other words – 'but the other guys are not encumbered by that attitude'. (Neither Carl nor Al contributed songs to the album, incidentally.) As ever, Carl searched desperately for some good tidings: 'I think we at least brought a newness, a new energy.' This was the most positive thing anyone ever said about the last proper Beach Boys studio record for twenty years.

After that, almost everything was a revival. Brian was effectively estranged from the group for most of the 1990s, but he did invite Carl to join him on a cover of 'Proud Mary' – which was never completed. The year 1993 was dominated by a superb retrospective box set, *Good Vibrations*, after which – to everyone's amazement – the touring group dared to acknowledge that their catalogue extended beyond their hit singles. The Beach Boys ended the year with a short tour that included an 'unplugged' segment, in which they tackled choice 'deep' cuts from the past with acoustic guitars and superb harmonies. Among their choices were 'All This is That', 'Vegetables' and 'Add Some Music to Your Day'. It was a fanatic's fantasy and it dissolved just as quickly as a dream.

By now, the Beach Boys had abandoned the tactic of throwing random singles against a wall and expecting them to do anything but drop to the ground. Their film soundtrack opportunities seemed to have dried up, although some of the group did jump at the chance for a cameo appearance in an episode of *Baywatch* in 1995. Carl and Brian opted out of that one, while David Marks appeared on TV as a Beach Boy for the first time since 1963 – although, as they were miming, it was irrelevant who was in front of the cameras.

The holy grail, it seemed, was an album with Brian. Bruce Johnston continued to talk up the possibilities of something with 'a cutting edge. You have to stay current.' Mike Love considered yet another Beach Boys Christmas album, but was fortunately restrained from seeing it through. More encouraging was a brief Wilson/Love reunion in 1995, where they were joined by Carl as they worked through Brian's latest songs. Mike and Brian were filmed together by *Entertainment Tonight*, singing 'Do It Again' at the piano, while Brian enthused about cutting a new tune called 'Dancin' the Night Away'. Mike got excited too, calling the song 'a cross between "Do It Again" and "Surfin' USA".' But the reunion fell flat. A few months later, Mike conceded that one of Brian's songs, 'Soul Searching', was 'great' but that the rest were 'really inane'.

That didn't prevent the entire group gathering with Brian and producer Don Was in late 1995. 'They were just thrilled,' Was said after he was sent by Brian to request their presence in the studio. They started to work on a handful of tunes, 'Soul Searching' among them. 'We have so much momentum, professionally and personally,' Brian declared when the reunion was first mooted. But then Carl supposedly stepped away from the sessions, ostensibly because he thought the material was sub-par. There was also tension caused by the competing creative agendas of Don Was and Andy Paley, Brian's chief collaborator during the post-Landy fall-out. A year later, Bruce Johnston was still promising the project would happen, but he admitted that 'we can't sign the deal because Brian has to make his [second] solo album. It would be more beneficial to him to do a Beach Boys album first. But the people that surround Brian, telling him how great he is, think otherwise.' Not for the last time, one of his former colleagues was questioning the influence of Brian's new wife, Melinda Ledbetter. (As one of Brian's musical helpers told me around that time, 'you have to be suspicious about anyone who would choose to be with Brian, but she really does seem to have his best interests at heart'.)

There was one more Beach Boys album with both Brian and Carl on board: an utterly pointless collaboration with contemporary country music stars, who each tackled the lead on a Beach Boys hit from the 1960s. Only one song betrayed any magic and it was the first to be recorded: a beautiful reading by Willie Nelson of 'The Warmth of the Sun'. The rest was bland, lukewarm, professional, redundant – and released as *Stars and Stripes Vol. 1*. If it had sold (which it didn't), there would have been a second collection of country duets – or, as Mike suggested a few months later, a similar set of liaisons with contemporary pop stars or soul singers. All of them would be a distraction from the Beach Boys' utter lack of progress. None of these dead-end projects ever happened. And fate was about to throw a curveball that brought the entire future of the band into question.

Like a Brother

The loss of Carl Wilson

He had looked unwell for a while, his speaking voice a little gruffer, his face slightly bloated. Like his father and both his brothers, he had suffered from back pain for years, exacerbated by the solid-bodied electric guitars that weighed him down at every live performance. More recently, he had also been diagnosed with gout. Carl Wilson was approaching his fiftieth birthday in 1996, but he held and moved himself like an elderly man.

During the winter of his landmark birthday, which was celebrated on 21 December, he and his family took a long vacation at their holiday home in Hawaii. Carl was the most private of men, carrying burdens quietly rather than sharing his problems with the world. But it is believed that (at the least) he suffered from dizzy spells and crippling headaches on that trip, accompanied by increasingly severe neck pain. The doctor on duty at the local hospital diagnosed a trapped nerve.

Unconvinced by this verdict, he checked into the Cedars-Sinai Medical Center when he was back in Los Angeles. After a series of tests with progressively more ominous outcomes, he was told that there were malignant tumours in his brain and his lungs. He was given radiotherapy and put onto a routine of monthly chemotherapy – a regime that debilitated him and caused him the loss of his hair. 'Apparently they caught it early,' his publicist Alyson Dutch announced at the start of April. 'His spirits are really great and that's nice.'

It was easy for outsiders to locate a primary cause for Carl's cancer, as he had been smoking heavily since his early teens. But anyone who believed that psychological strain could exacerbate physical illness could point to the pressure he had endured for as long as he had been addicted to nicotine. Carl had always been the family peacemaker, a role that was carried forward into the Beach Boys. He was the still, quiet core of the band when all hell might be raging around him. And even when he was being treated for cancer in the spring of 1997, tremors from the past continued to unsettle his life – not least his ongoing court battle with his often-estranged brother Brian, over what had been written in the latter's book.

That May, there was a legal dispute over a taped interview Carl had given in 1978, in which he apparently admitted buying heroin during the group's infamous Australian tour. Brian's lawyers accused Carl of a 'cynical misuse' of the court process; Carl's representatives insisted that 'he was portrayed wrongly in his brother's book as an alcohol and drug abuser who didn't care about his brother'. None of this was designed to aid his recovery, or his relationship with Brian.

Late May was also when the Beach Boys were able to resume touring after a pause to allow for Carl's intensive early treatment. They set out on a month-long trip with their old buddies in the band Chicago. Their keyboardist and vocalist, Robert Lamm, was particularly close to Carl. Together with America vocalist Gerry Beckley, the pair had formed an occasional recording trio named, factually enough, Beckley-Lamm-Wilson. They had first combined to cut a song for a Nilsson tribute album, after which they scheduled recording sessions when the three men's touring schedules allowed. 'It was kind of a tag team thing,' Lamm explained. 'There was never a sense of urgency. It was just something we were doing for fun, for our own satisfaction.'

By Lamm's account, satisfaction (or the lack of it) had long been an issue for Carl within the Beach Boys. He felt 'constrained and limited' by his position in the group, Lamm believed. Carl's last real creative input to a Beach Boys album had come in 1985, since when he had loyally shouldered his duty as bandleader on stage, providing the same vocal parts that had been his since the 1960s. Not long before he was taken ill, Beckley-Lamm-Wilson completed the material for an album and now they were waiting for him to get well so they could pitch the record to interested parties. None of Carl's contributions to the record were composed or sung with the awareness that he was seriously ill. But, as Lamm believed, 'the subconscious and the spiritual world is a crazy thing. I think there was a sense in Carl of longing, of wanting to impart his feelings and love for his family – his siblings, offspring and his wife Gina. The title song, "Like a Brother", was a homage to Brian.'

When the album was eventually released, in the summer of 2000, it sounded exactly the way that a Beckley-Lamm-Wilson collaboration always would do: smooth, adult contemporary rock with impeccable harmonies and radio-friendly power ballads. While the song for Brian was disappointingly bland, there was one authentic Carl Wilson gem: 'I Wish for You', a song in the tradition of Bob Dylan's 'Forever Young', offered from father to sons. Intriguingly, Carl's publishing company at the time of his death was named Murry Gage Music, in tribute to his own tortured father.

None of those Beckley-Lamm-Wilson songs made it into the Beach Boys' 1997 setlists; in fact, it was a marvel that Carl was there himself. For most of the summer shows, he would start out sitting down, before dragging himself to his feet for his showcase performances: 'God Only Knows', 'I Can Hear Music', 'Sail on Sailor' and 'Good Vibrations'. Night after night, Mike Love would introduce 'God Only Knows' with a variation on the same speech: that Carl had been battling cancer, that his doctors were saying he was doing well. 'I don't know whether he's courageous or he's crazy,' Mike would say, 'but he's here tonight.' As if he was being powered by the love he felt from the band's audiences, Carl's 1997 performances were as magnificent as any he had delivered in his prime. Lung cancer did not seem to have robbed him of his vocal power or any of his range. And, night after night, Carl would thank the crowds for their support and tell them: 'Your prayers have been answered.'

He was still preaching the same message in late August, telling a Syracuse audience, for example, 'I'm winning this thing'. Hearing him sing, it was impossible not to believe him. But on 29 August 1997, Carl performed a show in Atlantic City, which he knew would be his last for a while because he had to fly home for more chemo. Before he left the group's hotel, Al Jardine taped Carl's final recorded vocal on a song entitled 'Waves of Love'. Only now did his voice betray a hint of frailty.

It soon became apparent that, despite all the positivity and love, Carl's health was failing. Family believed that he was somehow keeping himself alive so that his eighty-year-old mother, whose own health was declining fast, would not have to endure the heartache of losing a second son. Audree Wilson passed away on 1 December, and, little more than two months later, on 6 February 1998, Carl Wilson also died, surrounded by his close family.

For anyone who regarded Carl as the heart of the Beach Boys, the band's finest and most soulful voice, a songwriter who had all too seldom expressed his creativity within the context of the Beach Boys, the initial obituaries were gallingly vague. His death lacked the shock or scandal associated with brother Dennis's final days, although those who had not kept pace with Carl's health issues were appalled that he could have died at the ridiculously early age of fifty-one. Slowly, his friends and associates came forward to state his case, as if his musical legacy didn't already speak loudly enough. Brian's relationship with his kid brother had been difficult for a decade, but nonetheless he announced that 'I'm dedicating my future music' to Carl. 'The world has lost a beautiful voice and one of the most spiritual people I've ever known,' Brian said. It was some kind of comfort to him that he had been with Carl just a few days before his death, a bond repaired and renewed at the last.

Of those who didn't know Carl personally, perhaps the most touching tribute came from Don McLeese of the *Austin American-Statesman*. 'Carl was plainly the soul of the Beach Boys,' he wrote, 'the choirboy vocalist who deserved to be remembered with the best singers of the rock era … The part of the Beach Boys that Carl represented – the Beach Boys of "God Only Knows" and "Good Vibrations" – was the best part … The timeless, transcendent quality of the Beach Boys' music was shaped by Brian's vision, but it was sung in Carl's voice.'

Like a Brother

Art isn't supposed to be a competitive sport, but I struggle to imagine hearing a more beautiful sound in my life than Carl Wilson singing. His tone was raw with emotion but also tightly controlled: the perfect synthesis of technique and soul, refined talent and heart. The phrase has become a marketing man's cliché, but on Carl's gravestone in Westwood Memorial Park, Los Angeles, it says 'The Heart and Voice of an Angel'. Everyone who was touched by the man or his music will recognise the truth in that. The second half of the inscription is equally apposite: 'The World is a Far Lesser Place Without You'. So, sadly, were the Beach Boys, who could keep Carl's spirit alive, but never come close to replacing his presence or his sound.

Sea of Lawsuits

Brian Wilson and Mike Love go to war

Lawyers love disputes over the writing credits for hit songs, because right and wrong are so difficult to prove and the suits drag on for a long time. In the case of any band, there are usually at least three people involved in composing a hit: the person whose name appears on the record; the bandmate who thinks they should have been credited as well; and the total outsider who comes out of nowhere and claims that they wrote the song first. Plus at least two dozen lawyers, obviously.

'Fun, Fun, Fun' was one of the least contentious credits in the Beach Boys' catalogue. Mike Love and Brian Wilson agreed they'd written it together, and both men's names were listed on the original single. But, twenty-seven years later, enter Bill Gray. He had been a barber in Hollywood at the time the Beach Boys were starting out, and he remembered Brian and his dad coming into his shop one day for haircuts. He claimed they got talking about songs and Gray sang them one of his. Soon afterwards, he turned on his radio and there it was – his song, twisted around a little bit, and retitled 'Fun, Fun, Fun'. The reporter from the *North Country Times* who unearthed Bill in 1990 stood all the lawyers down: 'Gray says he doesn't feel like the Beach Boys stole the song from him. He's still a little disappointed he never got credit or royalties from it, but on the other hand, he doesn't take credit for any of the songs he writes.' No, as far as Bill Gray was concerned, the real composer was God and he has always been famously easy-going about copyrights.

Sea of Lawsuits

One of the things that Murry Wilson did to protect the Beach Boys' interests back in 1962 was to form the Sea of Tunes Music Company. This handled most of the early songs written by the group, with especial emphasis on his composer son, Brian. The first Beach Boys record to bear the 'Sea of Tunes' credit was '409', the flipside of their debut single for Capitol, 'Surfin' Safari'. And the last? The songs written by Brian Wilson for the 1969 album, *20/20.* A few months later, Murry sold the company to Irving Music – and Brian's signature appeared on the sale documents.

From that decision arose a lifetime's resentment, and two major lawsuits more than twenty years later. According to Brian's first and more spurious autobiography, he discovered about the sale in November 1969 (three months after it had been announced in *Billboard* magazine). The book includes a dramatic account of what supposedly happened next: a confrontation between father and son, broken crockery, shattered glassware and a final act of paternal cruelty that left Brian sobbing on the floor. 'I pounded my fists on the ground and kicked, screamed and cried like a child.'

We can crawl forward twenty years, arriving in November 1989 when Brian rather belatedly filed a suit against Irving Music and its parent company, A&M. His lawyers demanded $100m for the alleged underpayment of his royalties since 1969. His affidavit made other very serious claims: his signature on the 1969 agreement was a forgery; and in any case, he had been suffering with mental illness at the time and was legally incapable of making business decisions. To make sure the blame was placed elsewhere, he said that his disturbance had been caused by being given LSD by an employee of the William Morris Agency.

Behind the lawsuit was the silent figure of Eugene Landy, who stood ready to claim his managerial percentage of any damages Brian received. Soon the case was widened, as Wilson filed suit against the law firm who had handled his interests in the sale that he claimed not to know had been happening. It took Mike Love's 2016 memoir to explain the full background to the case. It transpired that a lawyer acting on behalf of the Beach Boys at the time of the 1969 sale was also representing

Irving/A&M, which sounded like a flagrant breach of practice. The Wilson v. Irving case was settled out of court in 1992, with Brian receiving damages that were quoted as being at least $10m.

Just another case of success breeding corporate greed, you might think. But the Sea of Tunes was about to become much more disturbed. In August 1992, Mike Love also filed suit – not against Irving Music, but against his cousin, Brian Wilson. As one can of worms was removed, another popped open and multiple lawyers gathered to chase them (and the consequent fees) around.

Before the lawsuits, Mike Love's official position on the relative creativity of Brian and the rest of the Beach Boys was neatly expressed in this 1981 quote: 'We're just a bunch of middle-class kids who wrote a bunch of songs. I happen to have a cousin who's a genius.' When it came to his own writing, he had this to say in 1974: 'I write music now and I never did that before. I always felt kind of shy about it because Brian was such a total, screaming, musical genius. So I wrote the words and was confident about that.' Sure enough, his name appeared alongside Brian's on many of the Beach Boys' best-known songs, Mike taking a smaller cut of the royalties than Brian to reflect that genius/average guy divide.

But there were other songs, right back to the beginning of the group, on which Brian's name appeared alone. In 1984, Mike tentatively began to address the issue of sole authorship: '[Brian] never did any song completely by himself. He would create melodies, and the rest of us would help on lyrics, arrangements, whatever.' Arrangements don't result in writing credits and royalties, except in the case of songs classed as 'traditional'. But lyrics certainly do. Having touched this nerve, he slowly began to assert some moral rights to songs that bore Brian's name alone – elements of 'Be True to Your School', for example, in a 1987 interview; the lyrics of 'California Girls' and the chorus of 'I Get Around' the following year.

But it was only in 1991 that he made public a grudge that he claimed (in his memoir) to have been raising in private for decades. 'My uncle [Murry] was doing the publishing and logging the songwriting,' he said, 'and he was pretty mad at me because Brian and I had fired him as our manager in the early days. So, to get even with me, he cheated me out of recognition.' He added that Brian 'is definitely a musical genius but he didn't have the concept and the lyrical abilities to carry off No. 1 hits by himself'. This story didn't entirely ring true, if only because some of the songs that he claimed credit for had predated Murry's sacking, so the 'pretty mad' motive didn't make sense. But it was apparently common knowledge among the Beach Boys that Mike felt aggrieved at having his name omitted or overlooked on songs he had co-written. He claimed that he consistently raised the issue with Brian, who either promised that it would be sorted out, or blamed his father and said the legalities were beyond his control.

When Mike saw Brian being awarded multiple millions in back-payments for songs that he felt he'd also helped to write – well, he saw red and then saw dollar signs. Now he too was demanding the missing royalties, the reinstatement of his name on the offending songs and punitive damages as recompense for his years of frustration. A few weeks later, he added another layer of accusations: defamation suits against Brian, his co-author and the publisher of his first autobiography. (The book included a section in which 'Brian' spelled out in detail how upset Mike had supposedly been when he had been frozen out of the writing process for the songs in question. It was almost as if the Wilson camp had smelled a lawsuit coming.) Even given the bizarre family dynamics of the Beach Boys, this was a novelty: cousin was about to take on cousin in court.

Soon, everyone in the vicinity was chiming in. Bruce Johnston claimed that it was all just business, not personal, and that the disputes would not harm the Brian/Mike relationship. His explanation of Love's late decision to sue was that 'Mike was a young lead singer chasing after girls when all this was happening, and he really didn't think about it'. The author Timothy White recalled Dennis Wilson telling him many years earlier about Mike's anger at being excluded from the credits. Al Jardine didn't take sides as such, but he did note that 'Brian's very easily led. He'll believe anything anybody tells him. He's one of the most gullible people I've ever known.'

All the time, Love ramped up the rhetoric. His uncle Murry was 'a very devious person and Brian went along with it. I never considered that my uncle and my cousin would cheat me the way they did. It's a sick situation.' And again: 'The history of this band is like the history of Russia. It's been written under a regime that distorts the past. I have lived with the inaccuracies and the lies, but when I read [Brian's] book, I decided it was time to act. What's funny is that when it came to the court deposition, Brian was forced to admit he'd made it all up.' The Wilson camp put up one of Brian's current creative partners, Andy Paley: 'The Love lawsuit has totally freaked Brian out. He really wants him off his back. It's not Brian's fault that Murry stole the publishing' – at which point Brian's case was effectively lost.

The great rapprochement came in stages. First there was a legal settlement, again out of court, over the allegations in Brian's book. Mike was said to be 'very satisfied' with the result. Meanwhile, the dispute over Love's missing credits and royalties trundled on. In October 1994, jury selection was undertaken and testimony began to be heard. It was long, slow and painful, but the crux of the dispute came down to this: Mike Love's signature was on a sale document from 1969 in which he testified legally that the existing writing credits were accurate. Mike explained that he had been told that his name could only be added to the other songs he'd co-written if he signed that agreement first – but then nothing was done. 'I signed it under duress,' he insisted.

At issue in the case were more than seventy songs. Ultimately, far too late to avoid enormous legal bills, another settlement was reached, after the initial jury ruled in Mike Love's favour. His name would be added to the credits of thirty-five of the contentious songs, among them such hits as 'Be True to Your School', 'I Get Around', 'Little Saint Nick', 'Help Me, Rhonda', 'Dance, Dance, Dance' and 'California Girls'. He was also awarded joint lyrical copyright for the *Pet Sounds* song 'Wouldn't It Be Nice' – which came as a shock to Tony Asher, who thought he had written most of that lyric. Mike could have been awarded the punitive damages he'd originally sought, but instead he agreed to settle for a $5m pay-off based on the $10m Brian had won from Irving. The big loser was Brian, who could have settled the case with much lower legal costs if he had agreed to give Mike the $3m he was originally demanding. 'The lawsuit ripped my heart right out,' Brian said afterwards. 'But it turns out that the trial was actually a godsend, because it totally put us together'.

That's right – Brian and Mike were writing together again. 'It's a miracle,' Brian conceded. 'Michael has always been one of my idols.' But, soon enough, the Wilson/Love reunion fell apart and Brian ended up remembering the lawsuits like this: '[Mike] tried to annihilate me and put me in the poor house. He's cost me a great deal of time and money and dragged my dignity through the mud.' Mike, meanwhile, took advantage of his victory and began to march slowly into Brian's territory, claiming full authorship of 'Surfin'' from 1961 and three-quarters of the credit for 'Surfin' Safari'. The lawyers briefly got excited again, but fortunately the two kissin' cousins managed to stay out of court this time, and the Beach Boys' proud history of Endless Harmony resumed.

Love and Mercy

Brian Wilson wakes up

For ten years, Brian Wilson's every move had been answerable to Eugene Landy or his assistants. Then Landy and the minders were withdrawn. To the person who has been under constant surveillance, nothing is more desirable than freedom – or more terrifying.

It was naïve to assume that liberation from a controlling therapist would unleash a torrent of creativity. Brian's natural state had become stasis, verging on depression. His relationship with Melinda Ledbetter provided physical and basic psychological stability: a safe haven for a tortured soul. But it did not offer him a purpose. That stimulation had to come from elsewhere – from Don Was while he was making his documentary about Brian, *I Just Wasn't Made for These Times*, and from Andy Paley, with whom Brian was occasionally writing songs.

Another old friend was alarmed by what he saw when he came to call. 'Brian was doing nothing,' Van Dyke Parks said. 'I saw him lying face up in a bed during the day with the surf behind him, and I thought there was something terrifically wrong with this picture.' Parks was never short of requests for collaborations or guest appearances, but it had been several years since his last major album or soundtrack assignment. He sifted through his accumulation of songs to select those that might benefit from Brian's voice and invited him to a recording session. 'I felt that our friendship had suffered too long from a failed attempt to work together,' Parks reflected, inevitably harking back to *SMiLE*.

Wilson was apparently puzzled when he realised that his old friend was not asking him to write or produce, but merely to provide vocals. Over the period of more than a year, he multi-tracked harmony parts on more than a dozen songs – a tortuous process for both men, as it turned out. The result was *Orange Crate Art*, that beautiful but not immediately commercial project, which delighted those who relished Parks as a composer, but did little to extend the range of that cult following. 'It's a great album,' Brian conceded, 'but I don't like my voice on it. I'd never play it, because I don't think I sound good.'

The Wilson/Paley partnership was beginning to assemble sufficient new material for an album, but Brian's experience of working with Chicago producer Joe Thomas on the Beach Boys' *Stars and Stripes* project persuaded Melinda – now Brian's second wife – to suggest that he would be a more beneficial partner. Meanwhile, Bruce Johnston was trying to persuade Brian that he, and the Beach Boys, should work with the Irish writer/producer Sean O'Hagan – whose band, the High Llamas, had recently released two albums, *Gideon Gaye* and *Hawaii*, consciously built upon the foundations of the Beach Boys' *SMiLE* era.

O'Hagan stepped into these troubled waters aware that it would be almost impossible for an outsider to satisfy all the Beach Boys' competing desires and ideas. Invited to meet Brian, he discovered that Joe Thomas was also at the meeting. 'The whole thing was absurd,' O'Hagan recalled. 'As far as I can see, Joe Thomas hasn't got a clue about Brian Wilson and his legacy. He wanted Brian to make a big '80s ballad record, all cavernous snares. He kept referring to Brian's potential as an Adult Contemporary crossover artist. I said, "Don't you realise that Brian Wilson is essentially a twentieth-century avant-garde pop genius?" And he went, "Avant-garde? Not the Brian Wilson I know."' O'Hagan's conclusion was that Thomas had been chosen because he was 'a father figure' to Brian, who made him feel 'safe and comfortable'. It was also difficult not to conclude that Melinda Wilson was more interested in her husband appealing to modern radio tastes than in maintaining the Brian Wilson music tradition that ran back to the 1960s. Another MW – Murry Wilson – might have approved.

The Wilson/Thomas team warmed up by working on a couple of tracks for *The Wilsons*, the first duo album by Brian's daughters, Carnie and Wendy. Their personal relationship with their father was still difficult, but they were able to connect at the microphone. Brian and Tony Asher wrote 'Everything I Need', a perfect vehicle for their reunion. The vocals were touching, but Joe Thomas sugar-coated the results to the point of anonymity.

The ties between the Wilson and Thomas families became so close that they bought houses next to each other in the Chicago suburbs. (Brian wasn't totally enamoured of his new location: 'I don't like the snow – it reminds me of something I don't want to think about'.) Sessions running from late 1996 through to 1998 produced *Imagination*. Brian was initially entranced by the album: 'It was the most unbelievable record I've ever made in my life. It might not be my best record, but it's the most interesting.' But little more than a year later, he reconsidered, calling it 'a flat album. I don't think it had the energy it should have had. I don't think it was up to par. I can do better.'

As the official follow-up to the *Brian Wilson* album a decade earlier, *Imagination* was hotly anticipated. Its songs had been dragooned from a variety of sources: two remakes of Beach Boys classics, one collaboration with Andy Paley, and a sneak preview of the four-man writing team who would concoct the Beach Boys' reunion single in 2012. There were guest appearances from unexpected artists, including Jimmy Buffett and J.D. Souther. Fans with long memories were drawn to Brian's reimaginings of two unissued Beach Boys songs: 'My Solution', which mutated into 'Happy Days' (Brian called the chords of the original tune 'terrible'), and 'Sherry She Needs Me'. This mid-'60s collaboration with Russ Titelman had already been revived unsuccessfully in the '70s. Now it was altered again, emerging as the smooth but still effortlessly tuneful 'She Says That She Needs Me'.

The back stories were milked for publicity purposes: how Brian wrote 'Cry' after a row with Melinda sparked him into demanding a divorce; how 'South American' had been contrived to impress the Beach Boys, presumably because it sounded a little like 'Kokomo'; and, most poignantly, how he wrote the elegant ballad 'Lay Down Burden', of which Brian said coldly: 'After Carl died, the song was about him. Before he died, it was just about me.' The album kicked off with 'Your Imagination', as if 'Love and Mercy' had been fed through a twenty-first-century AI program. Critics leaped onto the emotional impact of Brian singing 'I miss the way I used to call the shots around here', but Brian cut them down. 'I did not write that line. Joe did.' In any case, the 'shots' weren't that effective: the song showed up on US Adult Contemporary radio stations, but the album climbed no higher than number eighty-eight in the *Billboard* charts. Sales weren't improved much by an *Imagination* promo show, at which his old colleague Bruce Johnston appeared. Most of its music was overdubbed after the event to cover obvious flaws, as were all of Brian's close-up shots, to hide his permanent expression of fear on stage.

Within less than a year, however, Brian was embarking on an American tour. In late 1994, he had attended a tribute concert in California at which the experimental pop band the Wondermints were performing. That initial connection was favourable and, four years later, he was persuaded to join the band on stage at an album launch. Their multi-instrumental capabilities and obvious vocal prowess – not to mention their absolute respect for his work – convinced him that they would be able to represent his music in concert better than anyone had done before. Not that he was going to cast off all his safety nets: the presence of Joe Thomas was required before Brian would allow the tour to go ahead, with Thomas bringing several extra musicians along for the ride. There was a week of shows in March, several more in June, followed by a brief trip to Japan – for which Joe Thomas was absent – and then a longer run in the autumn. Some nights Brian seemed disengaged or otherwise out of sorts; on others, he was visibly caught up in the music and the astonishingly rich arrangements overseen by the Wondermints' keyboardist, Darian Sahanaja. Their repertoire lent heavily on Brian's past, but this was no Mike Love-style hits show. Once the band had proved their credentials, they were allowed to suggest material as unexpected as 'This Whole World' and the instrumentals from the *Pet Sounds* album. Anything related to *SMiLE* was strictly off limits.

As befits every step of this California saga, progress was inevitably sabotaged from within. The web of legal complications enveloping Brian was made more claustrophobic when Melinda (acting as her husband's personal manager) and Thomas launched lawsuits at each other. She accused him of using Brian 'to further his own interests and/or raise his profile in the entertainment industry … and reap profits not commensurate with [his] contributions'. He responded that she was the one manipulating Brian and alleged that she had robbed him of some of his rightful songwriting credits. (Does this scenario sound strangely familiar?) Thomas continued to accompany Brian on tour through 1999.

Ever the master publicist, Brian once again complained to the press that his artistic inspiration was running low. 'I can't understand why I can't write melodies anymore,' he claimed, adding: 'I think my life was a waste.' With new material at a premium and Thomas isolated from Brian in 2000, the only possible road forward was a concert album. *Live at the Roxy* was taped that April, showcasing two mediocre but unheard songs which (upon closer observation) proved to have been written in 1995 and 1983. Also added to the palette was a brief extract from Barenaked Ladies' ironic tribute 'Brian Wilson'. (Years later, Brian claimed never to have heard of the song.)

Any creative inertia on Brian's part was cunningly disguised by the decision that he and his superb band should perform the entire *Pet Sounds* album, in sequence, with orchestral accompaniment. Shows were played across the US in 2000. The following year, Brian toured the nation again as support act to Paul Simon, but in 2002, the *Pet Sounds* revival show was transported to Britain (where a live record was taped during the first of two visits that year), Europe, Japan and Australasia. Brian's interviews continued to entertain. Asked whether he had felt like a visionary when he cut *Pet Sounds* back in 1966, he took the question entirely at face value: 'Right, exactly. A Christ figure type of thing. When we did *Pet Sounds*, I said, "Hey! This is Jesus Christ stuff."'

Even a visionary would have struggled to predict his next move. When Brian attended London's Ivor Novello Awards in May 2003, he shocked an industry crowd by announcing that he would be returning to Britain the following year: to perform *SMiLE*. Such grandiose statements had been made before, but gradually it became clear that he really did intend to complete, and perform, the most legendary lost album in rock history.

As a subsequent documentary film illustrated, the journey from concept to the stage of the Royal Festival Hall in London was predictably turbulent. Darian Sahanaja was left to provide the creative impetus, once it became apparent that Brian was unable to explain how he had originally intended to finish and sequence *SMiLE* back in 1967. Though he had always abhorred the idea of revisiting the project that had pained him so much, Van Dyke Parks was persuaded to lend his expertise, reminding Brian of lyrics that had been written but not recorded, and supplying fresh words when requested. Sahanaja coaxed Brian through the agonising process of giving *SMiLE* form: the pair concocted a three-suite framework that led the listener from the opening glory of 'Our Prayer' to a finale of 'Good Vibrations'.

As the world premiere in London grew closer, Brian's nerves frayed and broke. One day, he walked out of the rehearsals and took up residence for the day in the A&E department of a nearby hospital, though he was never admitted. His anxiety was exposed in the documentary and not entirely assuaged by the triumphant response to the first show. (The *LA Times* described the complete *SMiLE* as 'a glorious piece of music whose grand ambition is outstripped only by its inherent beauty and cumulative power'.) I saw the second night's performance and was blown away by the dexterity of the new arrangements, and the remarkable skill with which they were delivered. It was a phenomenal, deeply emotional show to witness, but Brian still occupied the stage like a man expecting to be arrested for crimes against artistic integrity. Only after the London run was he prepared to accept *SMiLE* as 'the most important piece of music that I ever composed'.

The initial year of *SMiLE* performances around the world was probably the pinnacle of Brian's career as a live performer. The new studio recording of the concert suite, *Brian Wilson Presents SMiLE*, was also ecstatically received. Bizarrely, it won Wilson his first Grammy Award, with 'Mrs O'Leary's Cow' (alias the infamous 'fire' section of the 'Elements' suite) acclaimed as the year's best instrumental piece. Without this revival, it is highly unlikely that the 2011 Beach Boys box set of *The Smile Sessions* would ever have been brought to fruition. Brian gave his official support to that project, before promoting it by saying: 'I prefer the one I did with my band. They're better musicians' – better than the Beach Boys and the cream of the mid-1960s Los Angeles session community.

It was either unfortunate or deliberate that between the first *SMiLE* shows and the *Presents SMiLE* album, another Brian Wilson record was quietly slipped onto the market. *Gettin' in Over My Head* existed only to prove that he hadn't been joking when he claimed a year or two before that he had lost his creative spark. It was filled with songs first attempted during his 1980s/1990s collaborations with Andy Paley and even Eugene Landy (though the therapist was obviously not mentioned in the credits). A full decade after the song was written, Brian finally released 'Soul Searchin'', complete with a lead vocal from his late brother Carl. The only other highlight on a glossy but mediocre collection was 'City Blues' – not because of Brian, whose efforts were painful, but because guest guitarist Eric Clapton played lengthy solos as if it was 1966 again. Other celebrity cameos, by Elton John and Paul McCartney, were less rewarding.

Subsequent Brian Wilson releases were mostly makeweights: a Christmas album in 2005; an album of Gershwin songs in 2010, including two tracks on which Brian added a minimal something to unfinished tunes by the master; and then a less ambitious collection of Disney tunes, weighted towards the modern (Randy Newman and Elton John/Tim Rice) rather than the classic. Like so many of Brian's solo offerings, they were filled with gratuitous attempts to remind listeners of the golden days of the Beach Boys. The only gold among this dross was provided by an album suite entitled *That Lucky Old Sun*. It was built around the late 1940s song that had become a jazz/pop standard and incorporated recitations penned for Brian by Van Dyke Parks, as well as briefly reviving the post-*SMiLE*-era Beach Boys outtake 'Can't Wait Too Long'. The remainder was composed by Brian with his band member Scott Bennett (later imprisoned for raping a woman after a Wilson band show in Tulsa). Only those two men know exactly what their individual contributions amounted to, but they did succeed in creating arguably the most enjoyable 'new' solo album in Brian's catalogue. One would certainly like to believe that the heartbreaking melodic shifts and cathartic release of 'Midnight's Another Day' came from Brian's imagination: they deserved to.

That Lucky Old Sun seemed as if it might be a final display of the 'classic' Brian Wilson sound. But by the time the Disney album was released, in October 2011, it was becoming clear that completing *SMiLE* wasn't destined to be his only twenty-first-century miracle. He had decided to outdo it by rejoining the Beach Boys for a world tour and a studio album that he alone would produce.

Getcha Back

The fight for a Beach Boys reunion

Who were the Beach Boys if there were no Wilson brothers – two dead, one permanently absent? The answer, it seemed, was simple. There was now only one essential Beach Boy (according to David Marks): the irrepressible frontman, the alpha male, the oldest of the pack, Mike Love. 'The audience don't know our names anyway,' Mike said modestly, but Marks insisted that Mike was the one with the 'distinctive voice'.

Yes, David Marks: last seen as an active Beach Boy in 1963, he had been recruited in 1997 to fill the guitar gap while Carl Wilson was undergoing chemotherapy. 'I knew Carl couldn't play all those dates,' Mike explained, 'but he tried his best to hang in there. David came in and started playing those guitar leads just like the originals and just like the old days. In fact, Carl said there's nobody who knows those leads better than David.' Marks had endured his own problems with drugs and alcohol in the intervening decades. He admitted that 'the Beach Boys have helped sustain me through my life as far as royalties, and I feel like maybe this is my chance to give something back'.

Mike had the power to rehire Marks, but Bruce Johnston's effort to recruit former Chicago vocalist Peter Cetera to replace Carl's vocal presence came to nothing. Instead, Mike engineered a situation whereby another veteran member could be jettisoned. He had already refashioned his occasional solo vehicle, the Endless Summer Beach Band, into a new format: the California Beach Band (which tied in with that movie project he'd been trying to spark into life since the early 1980s, *California Beach Party*). It soon became apparent that the new Love band (CBB for short) was an exact replica of the current, Carl-less Beach Boys, with one exception: there was no place for Al Jardine.

Matters came to a head twelve days before Carl's death, when it was confidently asserted in the press that the Beach Boys would be performing at a Super Bowl pre-game show in San Diego. Al Jardine, the papers explained, had 'decided to pass on today's performance' – which was news to him, as he hadn't been invited. Instead, none other than the substitute Beach Boy from 1964–65, Glen Campbell, performed as a special guest. (Insofar as anyone performed, in fact, as the musical portion of the show was pre-recorded in a studio.) Jardine watched the show at home, as did Brian and Carl, together for the final time.

Then Carl died and, as Mike Love explained on behalf of the band, 'we did take a deep breath'. Although not that deep a breath, it transpired, as the California Beach Band were back on stage within a week. (When Dennis died, there had been a pause of no less than seven weeks.) 'I don't think there was any serious thought about calling it quits,' Mike added. But he did concede that he had given due consideration to a total rebrand of the group, from the Beach Boys to 'Mike Love, with America's Band'. 'The promoters didn't seem to like the idea,' he said. 'I guess they want to keep it all in historical perspective.'

Carl's death exposed a fissure that had been widening for the previous couple of years – between Love and Jardine. 'Michael and I had been touring for a while together,' Al explained, 'and it just didn't seem to be fulfilling, so we had a creative parting of the ways. We were like a travelling jukebox, and then we added cheerleaders to the jukebox, and it started to look like an overly decorated Christmas tree. It just got to be too much of a circus and I wanted to put the music back in the show.' Love replied that Jardine had been unenthusiastic and on occasions positively obstructive during recent years – no loss, in other words. And Brian, quizzed about the prospects of a reunion, declared: 'I would if Mike Love wouldn't be so egotistical. And same with Al Jardine. Very egotistical. Grumpy.' Pushed on the subject, Brian claimed that 'I haven't talked to Mike since Carl died' and that when it came to continuing without Carl, 'I don't agree with Mike. I don't think he should do that. But if he wants to, he can.' Mike was asked if it was possible to have a Beach Boys with nobody called Wilson in the band. 'There's a significant amount of demand for the Beach Boys,' he said curtly. But, of course, 'there's plenty of goodwill'.

Questions about the direction, operation, ownership and future of the Beach Boys could be delayed no longer. The original members had long since handed over management of their affairs, and their name, to a corporate board who controlled Brother Records Inc on behalf of the musicians. Those executives opted to award a touring licence for using the Beach Boys' name to Love, the band's irrepressible frontman. But Jardine also won the right to exploit the group's title and legacy – or so he thought. (Likewise, Brian Wilson, though he did not attempt to tour under the Beach Boys name.) Brother Records disagreed over the terms, and objected to Jardine's insistence that he would proceed with his plans regardless of what they decided. And so legal warfare began.

In effect, the CBB had now become the BBs, so the California Beach Band name disappeared (although Mike still smuggled an occasional Endless Summer Beach Band show into the schedule, to keep everyone confused). Al defiantly stood alongside Mike at a Beach Boys cancer benefit in May 1998, after which the new era began. Al wouldn't work professionally as a Beach Boy for another thirteen years, while Mike, Bruce Johnston and David Marks launched their officially licensed line-up at the altogether appropriate venue of the Trump Marina Casino in Atlantic City on 4 July.

Plans were everywhere. Mike wanted to cut an orchestral album of Beach Boys songs, with Brian producing (Bruce had already produced a symphonic tribute to the group with the Royal Philharmonic Orchestra). Al was working on a family project with his two sons, while Bruce was preparing the solo record he'd been promising for more than a decade. Mike and British singer Adrian Baker taped new versions of many Beach Boys classics and threatened a set of original songs. And

Brian toured to promote his *Imagination* album, while complaining: 'They don't call me. Bruce called me on my birthday, but Mike never calls me.'

By the end of 1998, Jardine was ready to launch his rival concern: Alan Jardine's Beach Boys Family and Friends. He could only boast one actual Beach Boy, whereas the official line-up had three, of various vintages. But his support crew was impressive and could claim strong bloodlines back to the original group. 'I hired back all the best players I could find,' Al explained. 'I had the back-up band the Beach Boys had in the '60s and '70s.' His musical director was Daryl Dragon, not just one-half of Captain & Tennille but also a Dennis Wilson co-writer and frequent Beach Boys auxiliary member.

The emotional pull came from the 'Family' element of the ensemble. Brian's two daughters, Wendy and Carnie, were there, likewise some of the children of both Carl and Dennis. Also on stage was Owen Elliot, the daughter of Mama Cass Elliot, which gave the group the freedom to perform their only non-Beach Boys number: 'Monday Monday'. They debuted at a benefit for a Los Angeles spiritual foundation just before Christmas and, in the final days of 1998, they were performing in Las Vegas – which was also, strangely enough, where Mike Love's Beach Boys were winding up their year.

There were changes in Jardine's line-up: Daryl Dragon soon quit, pleading the time-honoured 'creative differences', the Wilson boys dropped by only occasionally and Owen Elliot went on maternity leave. But Al remained buoyant. 'We have this wonderful pool of talent – I call it the gene pool – and we all have something to harness, all this energy. It's like the early days of the Beach Boys with all these creative people. These are not all the original harmonies. These girls, Wendy and Carnie, give it some depth. Female singers can give it a whole different perspective on the harmonies.'

Jardine also staked his claim to the Beach Boys' artistic spirit. 'Carl and I were the music police. When Carl left, it left me standing somewhat alone in that great field of music. You could basically say [Mike and I] split along creative lines, and business differences caused the split.'

Love, he maintained, only wanted 'a clone band'. Jardine respected the music.

Sadly, that was not the verdict of many people who attended the first Family and Friends show of 1999, at the annual Strawberry Festival in Plant City, Florida. The first problem was that tickets for the shows listed the artists performing as the Beach Boys. The second was that the ensemble took a while to settle into their repertoire, although the spirit was there – and so was Brian's ex-wife Marilyn, who stepped out for the encore. But Al made the mistake of describing the first concert of the day as 'a paid rehearsal', which only exacerbated the disappointment of those who thought they had paid to see the entire Beach Boys band. The *Tampa Tribune* laid it on thick: 'What these relatives and near-relatives did to a few of the loopy, surfside lullabies may not have been villainous, but it sure wasn't victorious either. It seemed to boil down to this. An apparent lack of rehearsal. An unfocused eye to detail. A very real sluggishness. And a fundamental fear of the classics.'

Jardine struggled on, with a shift of ethos. Now the rationale of his group was to explore the Beach Boys' deeper catalogue of songs, the material that fans and critics loved but which the Mike Love hit machine would never dare to sample. Bruce Johnston, maintaining open communication with everyone in the Beach Boys' world, admitted that 'Al is doing something I wouldn't have the courage to do … They are all tremendously talented, so it sounds great.' But the reality was that anyone attending a Jardine show and expecting an array of so-called 'deep cuts' was going to be disappointed. Like the official band, Family and Friends concentrated almost exclusively on material from 1962–1966, and the rarities were album tracks and B-sides from the same era. Meanwhile Mike Love's band was extending its repertoire by taking in oldies from other performers, such as Gene Chandler's 'Duke of Earl' and the Four Seasons' 'Sherry'. Meanwhile, the real collector's gems were coming from Brian Wilson, whose rejuvenated shows offered such off-the-wall numbers as Harry Nilsson and Phil Spector's 'This Could Be the Night' and the two instrumentals from the *Pet Sounds* album.

In his role of in-house critic/philosopher, Bruce Johnston offered an intelligent and emotional view of where the Beach Boys stood at the end of the century: 'I miss Carl. I miss Al. I miss Dennis. I miss their voices. But the ironic part of all this is that I've discovered that even without them, the star of the Beach Boys is the music. The music is so good that it can't not be good.'

With one exception, it seemed. In late November 1999, while the Family and Friends were staging a lengthy run at the MGM Grand Hotel in Las Vegas, Brother Records Inc filed a suit against Al Jardine in the Los Angeles branch of the U.S. District Court. This followed an earlier suit in which Brother accused Jardine of infringing its trademark in the Beach Boys. The new legal papers noted that, by utilising female vocalists, Family and Friends were also breaking away from the classic Beach Boys sound, one which revolved around certain themes: 'i.e. cars, surf, girls and fun'. (This definition effectively erased everything the group had achieved between 1966 and 1973 and chained them to their early 1960s catalogue.)

'I don't see why I should relinquish my interest in the Beach Boys name,' Jardine replied. 'I've earned it. I'm the victim of a typical corporate takeover.' He added: 'I think Mike has become all the things that he is telling people Brian has become. He's paranoid and he's scared to death we're going to succeed.' There was a retort from Love's attorney: 'Jardine is destroying the trademark. It's deception in the marketplace.'

The District Court issued a preliminary injunction in March 2000, which prohibited Al Jardine from using the name 'Beach Boys' anywhere in his promotions, except when referring to his personal history 'in a descriptive fashion'. Johnston was quizzed about the decision and insisted that he and Love had not been involved in the lawsuit in any way: it was merely a corporate concern, he said. By then, however, a second ex-Beach Boy was shifting sides. David Marks had now left Love and Johnston's touring band. He conceded that 'I like Mike as a person', but concluded that 'he's a little underhanded ... Mike just aced Al out so he could control all the money, basically.' But then Marks recommended fans should ignore both the Love and Jardine bands and watch Brian perform instead.

Meanwhile, the lawyers got rich. Jardine appealed the 2000 decision against him and lost. He had already launched a rival suit, claiming that by not inviting him to take part in recent Beach Boys concerts, Mike Love, Brian Wilson (who was not touring with the band), the Carl Wilson Estate and Brother Records were freezing him out of the group, of which he was an original member. This unlikely-sounding case crawled along for more than a year, before Jardine lost – only to appeal, be countersued, be refused the opportunity to be heard before the US Supreme Court and then, in October 2003, end up before the California Court of Appeal. There, to many observers' surprise, it was determined that the other parties had acted unlawfully in excluding Jardine (a signatory to a prior partnership agreement of 1993) from claiming a share of proceeds from Beach Boys concerts, just as Brian was able to do. Jardine was jubilant and claimed that he must be owed tens of millions of dollars in damages. But, he added, 'it's about much more than money. I want to be able to tour again, and to be able to identify myself as a Beach Boy again.'

Everybody now seemed to have sued everybody else, and everybody seemed to have both won and lost, even those (like Brian) who had not taken an active role in the Californian legal saga. Love's meditative skills had already come in useful: 'I would suggest he read some Buddhist literature,' he said of Jardine. 'He's been pretty contentious.' Johnston noted that lawsuits were 'not what music is all about'. And we were only in 2003. Submissions and writs and appeals and further dockets of documents moved sluggishly around the legal world for another four years or more. Eventually, in March 2008, the representatives of Mike, Al, Brian and Carl's estate reached the compromise that should surely have been possible a decade earlier – and settled all their litigation. One of the lawyers involved commented: 'Mr Love and Mr Jardine are looking forward to bringing more great Beach Boys music to the United States and around the world, particularly as they approach their fiftieth anniversary.'

The statement cut to the point: after almost a lifeline of disputes and onstage bickering and brotherhood and harmony and discord, was it really possible for all the surviving Beach Boys to forget the past and combine their talents one more time? It was the question that each member had found inescapable since Carl's death.

'Carl died, and that was the end of the group for me,' said Brian in 2001, and he rarely steered away from that opinion over the next decade. 'I don't care what they do,' he added. 'I'm not going to work with them.' Even when his guard was lowered, and (as in December 2002) he was prepared to admit that a reunion was not only inevitable but desirable, he found it impossible to imagine how their collective relationship might be repaired. 'I don't even like them,' he said of Love and Jardine in 2004. Not that Bruce Johnston was neglected: he was 'out of my life', Brian declared.

After which, a little thawing was detectable in the wall of ice. Brian acknowledged late that year that he had just spoken to Al Jardine 'for the first time in eight years. I told him I'd see him some time.' A few months later, Brother Records business forced Mike and Brian into the same lawyer's office and, to Love's amazement, Brian 'gave me a shoulder rub'. 'We had a great talk,' Brian conceded. But any cousinly love was soon dissolved when Mike launched another lawsuit against Wilson, this time for promoting his *SMiLE* album in a way that 'shamelessly misappropriated Mike Love's songs, likeness and the Beach Boys' trademark'. Mike defended himself: 'I'm known as the bad one in this band, but it's not true. I'm just different from the Wilsons.'

In 2006, the fortieth anniversary of the release of *Pet Sounds* provided a rare occasion on which corporate aims outranked personal squabbles. Five of the seven surviving Beach Boys – Brian, Mike, Al, Bruce and David, but not Blondie or Ricky – gathered on the Capitol Records rooftop in Los Angeles to receive the latest gold discs earned by the label's ceaseless programme of repackages. 'It's always good to do this while we're living,' Al agreed. Mike was asked if all the hatchets had been buried. He pointed to his back and said, 'They're right here'. But at least nobody fell out while the cameras were rolling.

A year later, and another celebration, this time sparked by a Beach Boys exhibit at the Rock & Roll Hall of Fame Museum in Cleveland. Mike played nice – 'There is a relationship there. It transcends just about anything. Given the opportunity to get together again, good stuff could come out of it' – to which Brian responded: 'People want to see the Beach Boys get back together, but I don't think it's going to happen. I really don't. I don't like Mike. And he doesn't like me!' Ever the peacemaker, Bruce Johnston opined that a new Beach Boys album wouldn't make sense, in any case, because Carl and Dennis weren't there.

In 2008, Mike and Al were discussing the prospect of working together. The following year, Mike and Brian went out for dinner with their wives. But Brian's disapproval remained adamant: 'We thought about it, we talked about it, we hashed it over, but then we decided not to do it. There's no way I could ever work with the Beach Boys again. No way.' Come 2010, and Al was saying that everyone had agreed to perform one reunion show; Brian denied it. 'Let the past go already,' he commented. 'I'll never do that.' But in 2011, one major fault line was repaired when the Beach Boys were asked to perform at a concert to mark what would have been President Ronald Reagan's 100th birthday. To his obvious delight, Al took the stage alongside Mike and Bruce to perform six of the band's biggest hits, his performance demonstrating how much his vocal presence had been missed.

By then, a full reunion of the five participants in the Capitol rooftop ceremony had been agreed. *Billboard* magazine broke the news that summer: there would be a new album from the band in 2012. Not that Brian seemed to remember making the decision – 'I don't know anything about that', he said helpfully. Did he want to take part? 'Not particularly.' But his co-writer/producer Joe Thomas was already three months into the process of assembling the songs that the band might perform. In December 2011, when not just the record but a fifty-date world tour were confirmed, Brian's publicity machine made the appropriate noises on his behalf. But how did he really feel? His wife Melinda let slip that her husband's opinions were mercurial. 'You know Brian. From day to day, it changes. From hour to hour, it changes. What do I think he really wants to do? I don't know. I haven't asked him today.' Meanwhile, his old writing partner Van Dyke Parks declared that the planned reunion was 'a transparent worship of the God of Mammon' and (in case that was too subtle) 'beyond mawkishly mercenary'. In 2012, did the Beach Boys mean anything more than money?

Do it Again

The Beach Boys are back ...

If a satirist was going to imagine a Beach Boys reunion, they would probably envisage the survivors of the group deciding to stride boldly into the future by stepping immediately back into the past. And what song could be more symbolic of this strange project than 'Do It Again'? Back in 1968, it was a self-conscious throwback to the good old days of just five years earlier. In 2011, it had a much wider meaning.

First, it entailed recording 'Do It Again' – again. This was the try-out, its familiarity designed to show whether the original Beach Boys could still sound like themselves. 'I felt the love from the guys, that's all I can tell you' was Brian's impeccable PR response the following year. Besides a professional rendering of their 1968 hit, the group (augmented by long-time 'anonymous' Beach Boy, and touring friend of Brian, Jeff Foskett) tackled the *a capella* piece that Wilson had written with none other than Joe Thomas, 'Think About the Days'. As Thomas, eventually credited as the album's 'recorder' rather than producer, explained, 'that was the moment we all went, "Wow, these guys can still sing".' It was true that some Auto-Tune might need to be applied to these elderly men's rough edges, but the blend had survived – and, with it, Brian Wilson's instinctive ability to place their voices into their optimum harmonic blend.

Even after these initial sessions, Brian continued to deny all knowledge of the reunion and exuded anything but enthusiasm. It was only when an official announcement came in December 2011 that his PR executive firmly took control. Now, someone by the name of Brian Wilson was apparently saying, 'this anniversary is special to me because I miss the boys, and it will be a thrill for me to make a new record and be on stage with them again'. Like everything Brian said and did in modern times, though, his declaration begged questions. Some of the early sessions for the album seem to have taken place while both the Beach Boys and Brian were on tour. Who was in charge of the reunion? And who was setting the agenda?

Mike Love had long been the group's official spokesman, augmented by Bruce Johnston, and he was adamant that the way to reform the Beach Boys was to reunite the Wilson/Love writing partnership. Strangely, Brian never quite seemed to be available for that kind of collaboration around the piano, the way they used to work. Then Mike discovered that, as far as his cousin was concerned, the songs for the new record had already been written – around 1997/98. And although Brian had a co-writer, it wasn't Mike Love, but Joe Thomas.

'Brian was very specific,' Thomas explained. 'He had two or three songs that he did not want to do solo. He wanted to do them with the Beach Boys. One of them was "That's Why God Made the Radio".' That song was composed when Wilson, Thomas, studio engineer Larry Millas and Jim Peterik (guitarist with the arena rock band, Survivor) got together one night after a Chicago White Sox baseball game. Brian was given the credit for coining the title at a café or a bar. It was enough to carry all four men to Peterik's home studio, where they quickly concocted a rough demo.

The tale of a song or two sidelined for the boys gradually expanded, until Thomas was claiming that Brian had set aside somewhere between ten and fifteen hours of song ideas – no words, but occasionally an idea for a title or even a chorus hook. It was Thomas's task to sieve through them and present the most coherent ideas to Brian. Thomas added some lyrics and Jeff Foskett was recruited from Brian's live band to sing simple piano demos of half a dozen songs. It was these recordings that enticed the Beach Boys' old label, Capitol Records, to offer them a twenty-first-century deal. The next stage was to enlist Mike Love's support. Brian invited his vegetarian cousin to join him at a steakhouse ('Brian didn't quite get the memo on that,' Thomas said wryly), where an agreement was made that Mike would be able to compose lyrics for some of the new material. Mike was still imagining that poignant piano moment, but instead was sent almost complete songs and asked to add or tweak a line or two. In the immediate aftermath of the reunion, Mike politely expressed his disappointment; but as time passed, he became more explosively vocal on the subject: 'It was kind of fraudulent. I did end up writing a couple of lines for a song here and there, but it wasn't like the old days.'

To maintain the pretence of democracy, albeit under autocratic rule, the non-Wilson Beach Boys were invited to submit material for consideration. At this stage, there was solid talk of representing the lost members, Carl and Dennis, via unreleased tracks. Towards that end, Al Jardine offered 'Waves of Love', on which he had captured Carl's last vocal performance. He was still pushing that song forward without success when the tour began several months later. Strangely, Love and Johnston went even further back into the past. Bruce's offer was that the group should remake 'She Believes in Love Again', a song he performed on the 1985 album, *The Beach Boys*. Mike exhumed 'Daybreak Over the Ocean', which he had originally recorded for his unissued solo record, *First Love*, back in 1979. Bruce's song was rejected, but Mike's thirty-year-old tune did make the final cut.

'It was like putting a puzzle back together,' Bruce Johnston said of the process of translating Brian's vintage fragments into coherent songs. The small print in the CD booklet revealed the piecemeal approach, hinting that several of the basic tracks were carried forward intact from previous projects. Only two of the Beach Boys played on the album: David Marks, who was a non-singing guitarist on most tracks, and Jeff Foskett, also on guitar, but as vital to the harmonic blend as he was on stage with both the group and Brian's solo band. The album couldn't have been made without him, although he didn't feature in the photos or publicity material.

Joe Thomas revealed that Brian's working title for the album was taken from the final track, 'Summer's Gone'. It had been written, Joe explained, 'as the last Beach Boys song ever'. He added: 'Everybody was getting along so well and the creativeness started flowing again, [so] he shelved the idea of this being the last song on the last Beach Boys record. He was having too good of a time.' Brian claimed that they had prepared basic tracks, at least, of something like twenty-seven songs for the album. But evidently only twelve were completed. The last four represented a large segment of what Wilson and Thomas had intended as a suite – something that Brian was apparently always about to complete in subsequent years.

In the final week of April 2012, the title track, 'That's Why God Made the Radio', was released for airplay. 'It sounds like 1965 again,' Mike crowed. 'It's very déjà vu. We sound like we sound.' He wasn't lying. Maybe the lyrics were outdated in the era of internet radio, but the vocals were scintillating, and the melody flowed, and the arrangement ebbed and grew, as if they'd been in the middle of creating *The Beach Boys Today!* or *Summer Days*. If there was a flaw, it was that the vocal blend was so tight, and so processed, that it was difficult to single out individual voices. Elsewhere on the album, the distinctive sounds of Wilson, Love, Jardine and Johnston could be heard in isolation, delivering the personal connection between artists and fans that the latter were so desperate to find.

Nowhere was that emotional link so touching as during that final quartet of Wilson/Thomas songs. If you ignored the writing credit, and the doubts it conjured up, the music sounded 'authentically' Brian Wilson, from the same personal strand that began with *Pet Sounds* and carried forward to 'Midnight's Another Day'. (Just don't ask who wrote those lyrics, either.) 'Pacific Coast Highway', brief and elegiac, seemed to bid the world farewell, while 'Summer's Gone' maintained the mood, albeit signalling sufficient optimism to hint that the narrator would not be alone at the setting of the final day.

Of the intervening material, 'Isn't It Time' was the keeper and could have slotted easily into the sequence for *15 Big Ones* (and improved it).

'Spring Vacation' and 'Beaches in Mind' were textbook Love-era Beach Boys: summer fun, to the last. Only one song made Brian and his band sound out of time: 'The Private Life of Bill and Sue', which was both banal and tiresome. The rest of the album was never less than enjoyable, and often genuinely thrilling – a landmark that nobody ever expected to find.

When it was released during the reunion tour and raced to number three in the US charts, all the Beach Boys hymned the joys of *That's Why God Made the Radio*. It was only later, when the mood had soured, that Mike Love's dissenting voice made itself heard. It was he who exposed the emptiness of the songwriting 'reunion', before letting slip exactly how distant he and the other non-Wilson band members had remained from the finished product: 'They put the album out without me getting a chance to listen to it, which is pretty insulting.' That's also more or less how Bruce Johnston felt when Joe Thomas put together a double live album from the reunion tour and slathered the group in Auto-Tune so blatant that it made them sound like robots. Once again, he hadn't been consulted. There was, it seemed, still one word that would always attach itself to the Beach Boys: dysfunction.

Summer's Gone

The Beach Boys lose their way home – again

Of course, the Beach Boys' reunion ended in disarray. How could it have been any other way?

'Nobody was enemies,' Bruce Johnston believed as the 2012 tour began to gather steam. 'Everyone's had fake judo fights over the years, but there's a lot of padding, so no one got hurt. The part that you think would be difficult, to turn the friendship light back on and then get back into the music, that was pretty easy.' Joe Thomas, the reunion facilitator, agreed. 'The band loves each other. It really is a tight-knit family group. Right now, everything is really wonderful.'

On the same day that the participants hymned the joy of revisiting the past, Mike was sent an urgent email by Brian's wife, Melinda, which spelled out her response to the demand from promoters that the tour schedule should be extended. 'No more shows for Wilson,' she insisted. As Love revealed later, 'very early on, Brian was just going to join the tour for a few dates in big cities. We finally settled on fifty dates in fifty major markets' – after which a further twenty-five were added. The representatives of Love and Johnston, the previous touring Beach Boys, began to schedule dates for a resumption of normal business: autumn and winter shows in the kinds of clubs and casinos that were way too small for the reunion package.

Three weeks later, Love reported, Melinda sent him another email, going back on the previous decision. But, by then, contracts and guarantees had been exchanged. The reunion tour could not be extended without financial loss and damage to the pre-existing Beach Boys brand promoted by Love and Johnston. Melinda Wilson's first email prompted both men to confirm the limited duration of the reunion, via interviews carried out in the first week of June. 'I think this is a special, one-time-only thing,' Love said, to which Bruce Johnston added: 'Brian's not going to be a touring guy. He would never tour as much as we do. He would hate it.' At that point the position was clear: 'one special tour', in Johnston's phrase, followed by the original status quo. There was no argument, no controversy: just one reunion to be savoured for its unlikely and inarguable pleasures.

On the opening night, in Tucson, Arizona on 24 April 2012, any misgivings about the value of a fiftieth anniversary celebration were quickly dispelled. Reviewers were dazed by the perfection of the group's harmonies, aided in large part by the accomplishments of the touring band. This was almost entirely made up of the multi-talented crew who regularly accompanied Brian on the road. Having handled the complexities of the entire *Pet Sounds* and *SMiLE* projects earlier in the decade, a joyous parade of the Beach Boys' hits presented few challenges.

'The unsung workhorse of this show,' according to the *Los Angeles Times*, was Jeff Foskett. For nearly thirty years, he had provided vocal support for the Beach Boys and then Brian's solo shows. As Al Jardine explained, 'Jeffrey is invaluable to keeping the continuity between the various component parts. He has Brian's confidence and basically makes it possible to have Brian Wilson on the road with us.' The full extent of that 'confidence' emerged with time: Foskett was rooming with Brian, ensuring he rose and ate on schedule, providing psychological consolation if his mentor's morale began to droop. Not that his importance was entirely appreciated by the rest of the group, who also expected Jeff to monitor and collect their stage laundry for each show. On stage, his role was to duplicate the swooping, soaring falsetto that would once have been Brian's forte, while being prepared to intervene if the veteran stumbled or preferred not to attempt a tricky vocal line.

Brian's performance was the acknowledged weakness of that first show. The *LA Times* reckoned he 'didn't seem to be having much fun … There's a reason why he stopped touring with the Beach Boys. He obviously doesn't like it.' Another reviewer noted that 'several times he lost his place and came in too early or too late', while looking 'horribly frustrated'. But so rich were the arrangements that only keen students of the show were aware that anything was wrong. Asked afterwards how he felt the tour would go, Brian concentrated on the fans: 'They sense that we love each other and that we really want to share that love with them.' Included in that love, by band and audience alike, were the two missing Wilson brothers, both of whom were present on a big screen to provide vintage lead vocals on showcase tunes ('God Only Knows' for Carl; 'Forever' for Dennis). The family vibe was extended in southern California, where there were cameo appearances by California Saga – an eight-piece vocal group made up of Wilson, Love and Jardine children.

Audiences were almost universally delighted by what they heard in a setlist that ranged wide and, at times, deep. Songs ranged from the sublime ('This Whole World', 'All This is That', 'I Just Wasn't Made for These Times') to the nostalgic delights of such period classics as 'Shut Down', 'Wendy' and 'Kiss Me, Baby'. Selections were pulled from almost every album in the Beach Boys catalogue to build a programme as diverse as could be imagined within the arena-show format. 'When we step onstage and hear that first beat of the drum of "Do It Again",' Al said, 'it's a clarion call, and everything else just goes away. You're totally energised.'

Collective zeal for the music dragged the group across North America for three months, then around Europe and on to the Far East and Australia. The final leg comprised a short burst of shows in England, designed as a celebration in front of the band's most loyal audience. Instead, the build-up to the farewell shows at the Royal Albert Hall and Wembley Arena was overshadowed by the internal warfare that was apparently inevitable whenever more than two Beach Boys were gathered in one place.

The shocking news that fizzed around the world in a digital second was that Brian Wilson had been fired from the band by Mike Love. Beneath the headlines was something slightly more nuanced: the Beach Boys would be continuing their tour without Wilson, Al Jardine or David Marks. As the spokesperson for Love's touring band explained, 'the 50th Reunion Tour was designed to be a set tour with a beginning and an end to mark a special fifty-year milestone for the band.'

Of course, that was exactly what had been decided and (quietly) announced almost four months earlier. Nobody should have been surprised, least of all any members of the Beach Boys. But the 'firings' presented an ideal opportunity for the media, and two of the apparently spurned Beach Boys, to revive all the accusations they had been aiming at Mike Love since 1997. Al supported a Facebook petition designed to change Love's mind, while Brian told CNN: 'I'm disappointed and can't understand why [Mike] doesn't want to tour with Al, David and me. We are out here having so much fun. After all, we are the real Beach Boys.'

What Wilson and Jardine failed to address, or had maybe even chosen to forget, was that the tour was never meant to extend beyond September. Moreover, it had been Brian's wife who had insisted that her husband would not be touring beyond that point. Unwilling to inflame the situation before the last shows, Love merely replied that it made commercial sense for another reunion tour to wait a year or two for fresh momentum and demand to build. But he maintained that he was perfectly ready to start work on a second reunion album.

At the Royal Albert Hall, Brian offered his most eloquent comment on the dispute when he walked out for the encore before his bandmates and launched into what was apparently an unscheduled rendition of his poignant ballad, 'Summer's Gone'. He didn't need to say any more, as outrage spread around the globe. Once more, Mike Love was the Beach Boys' villain and Brian Wilson the creative genius who was being victimised by his jealous and selfish cousin.

Mike had already withstood decades of blame and contempt from fans who believed that Brian could do no wrong. Now seventy-one years old, he was no longer prepared to let the world dump its prejudices on his shoulders. His riposte was an op-ed in the *Los Angeles Times*, published in early October. He recounted how he had boarded the plane home from England, 'buzzing with excitement, and I start reading a lot of nasty gossip and I'm heartbroken. I didn't want the divisive and ugly rumours of the last week to tarnish the experience of fans and the high note we ended the tour on.'

His explanation was curt and direct: 'I did not fire Brian Wilson from the Beach Boys. I cannot fire Brian Wilson from the Beach Boys. I am not his employer. I do not have such authority. And even if I did, I would never fire Brian Wilson from the Beach Boys. [Well, except in 1982, of course.] I love Brian Wilson. We are partners. He's my cousin by birth and my brother in music.' Then he spelled out the details that all his bandmates understood, adding with pointed restraint: 'I was surprised that Brian and Al said they were surprised by this announcement.'

He ended with possibly the most emotional statement of his entire life about what the reunion tour had meant to him. 'The great thing about getting older is that you get a chance to tell the people in your life who matter what they mean to you. Throughout the course of the tour, Brian said some really kind things to me about how my early songs gave him the freedom to go deeper musically. His words meant so much to me and I returned the praise every chance I could.' Then he picked up on the message of 'Summer's Gone' and offered its mirrored reflection: 'The Beach Boys are bigger than those who created it. When all of us remaining founders have turned to dust, the band will live on in the hearts of those who relish the sounds of summer. You see, summer's never really gone. And neither are the Beach Boys.'

Four days later, the same newspaper hosted a response from Brian. He reiterated his shock, disgust and disappointment, claimed to have known nothing about the finite nature of the tour, and wondered why the rest of the band hadn't been included in Mike's decision-making. 'I welcome Mike to call me,' he insisted, making the point that he and Al Jardine 'would like to be included in the continuous promotion' of the reunion album. He ended with a rather hypocritical plea for discussions to be carried out in private rather than via the press – but who was it who had made the original 'fired' story public?

The result of this open conflict was that any form of reunion, on record or stage, was swept off the table. For the next few years, Wilson and Jardine continued to bitch about Love's selfishness, while Love offered increasingly barbed hints about the power behind the Wilson throne who was using her influence to make sure that the two camps remained separated.

Here was Al the following summer, after being told that Mike still wanted to work with him and Brian [sarcasm alert]: 'Well, what a wonderful thought. I'd like to work with Mahatma Gandhi, too. I'd like to work with George Gershwin. Those are the things we wish for, but wishing is one thing and actually doing it is another. So, if you really mean it, you come out and work for it.'

And here was Mike Love in 2014, asked if he had spoken to his cousin since the reunion tour. 'No, Brian is controlled and still medicated. It used to be the indiscriminate use of street drugs, but now it's prescribed drugs. He speaks very highly of me and I have no issues. If just he and I could speak alone, it would be great, but Brian is controlled. Some of those around him think that to build Brian up, you must put everyone else down involved with him.'

As each year passed, the divide grew. Both sides were convinced they were right – and careful selection of the evidence proved that they were. The Beach Boys kept touring, preserving the image of Mike Love's choice: the ultimate summer party band. Brian Wilson's band offered another vision: the Beach Boys as art project. Al Jardine was torn between the two, but felt more loyalty towards Brian than Mike. And Brian? He kept saying that he wanted to rock – you know, rock and roll, rock real hard. It was his last remaining ambition and nobody wanted to accept it was the only dream left in his head.

The Last Song

The legacy and loss of Brian Wilson

Dennis Wilson's death was sudden and inevitable. His brother Carl's was shocking and inescapable. But Brian Wilson's decline – physical, mental, emotional, artistic – stretched back over many agonising decades.

Reading his future into the Beach Boys' earliest television appearances, one can recognise hints of his frailty and vulnerability even in his youthful prime. If anyone glanced at their television screen in 1964 and thought, even for a second, *That young man seems uncomfortable*, there would have been a dozen explanations at hand. He was inherently shy; nervous of the cameras; self-conscious about his appearance; wary of his sudden lurch into the snake-pit of fame. Early biographical knowledge would have filled in some gaps: his deafness in one ear, the weight of his multi-faceted creative role and the oppressive presence of his bullying father. But from the vantage point of six decades' hindsight, knowing what we could never have known then (even he was unaware of it), it's clear that Brian's awkwardness and discomfort was rooted in a profound, corrosive, suffocating, almost cancerous form of psychological illness. He spent the rest of his life outrunning it, battling it, treating it, surrendering to it, endlessly suffering from it, until his body could no longer sustain the burden. What courage to have survived so long and endured so much; what unimaginable agony to function as any form of public artist when he was being undermined both by scrutiny and extreme self-doubt, not on a single occasion but on every conscious day of his life. And no wonder that, for years, he chose to escape consciousness via any route he could find, no matter how ruinous they might prove to his excruciatingly prolonged existence.

If any man deserved a gentle immersion beneath what Bob Dylan once called 'the waters of oblivion', it was Brian Douglas Wilson. But the same fate that chained his almost surreal talent to a wounded psyche made sure that he was being tortured all the way down. Decades after his survival first seemed unlikely, he lived long enough to witness the deaths of his parents and his two younger brothers, most of his closest friends and collaborators (although none of the other Beach Boys) and, finally, the year before his own demise, his second wife. Melinda, whether you read her role in the saga as saviour or villain, had been his psychological crutch, defender and helpmate for the best part of four decades. So, of course she had to die, suddenly, just when Brian's years of mental disturbance were finally coalescing into a diagnosis of dementia (or a close cousin of the same).

Melinda passed away on 30 January 2024, a year that also brought Brian the loss of two of his closest solo collaborators: Joe Thomas and Andy Paley. One can only hope that he was gradually shedding his awareness of exactly how much he had lost. The death of Melinda removed not only his partner, but also his legal guardian and protector. Within three weeks, his management team had filed official papers requesting that they should be appointed as his conservators, with the approval of his children and (apparently) Brian himself. He was enabled to remain in his home, under the loving daily supervision of Gloria Ramos, who had been his housekeeper since the dawn of his second relationship with Dr Landy. There, his children assure us, he was free to exist (at last) beyond the pressure of his fame and his genius, watching basketball games, tinkering at the piano and enjoying his favourite restaurants. His kids would drop in and out, hoping that he would remember them, and occasionally one of the other Beach Boys would stop by. Mike Love remembered a final meeting less than a month before Brian's death, at which his cousin insisted that the two old men should sing some of the band's landmark hits one last time.

A similar episode in nostalgia was carried out in September 2023, when the five surviving members of the 1960s Beach Boys – Wilson, Love, Jardine, Johnston and Marks – attempted to recreate their harmonic blend before a film crew. A little of the footage (but none of the soundtrack) was slipped into *The Beach Boys*, a Disney+ film documentary that retold the sanitised version of the group's story: all surf, sun and summer fun, with little room for chaos, trauma or other adult complexities. Brian's only public appearance after Melinda's death came on 22 May 2024, when he was wheeled into a Los Angeles theatre for the movie premiere. The audience stood and roared; Wilson appeared not to notice, or indeed to greet the other Beach Boys with anything more than vague recognition. He was now unable to stagger more than a few steps without physical support, the victim (so his daughter Wendy explained) of two 'really shitty' back surgeries. That particular family weakness, shared with his father and both brothers, accompanied him to the end.

After that, there was a year of silence, broken only by the news that Al Jardine was going to take over the Brian Wilson touring band in the summer of 2025. Meanwhile, Mike Love and Bruce Johnston continued to represent the Beach Boys around the world. Mike was at last revealing inevitable signs of age upon his vocal range and strength (Jardine remains the almost supernatural exception to that rule of nature). But so well-trained was the Love/Johnston vehicle that it was easy to imagine a time, a year or two hence, when the last remaining veterans might slip quietly out of the touring line-up, while the Beach Boys juggernaut motored into eternity, as irrepressible as the subjects of all those vintage car songs. One day, all the original Beach Boys will be gone, but long live the Beach Boys, and the particularities of history be damned.

Yet one real Beach Boy, at least, will still qualify for the history books. There was no element of surprise when the death of Brian Douglas Wilson was announced by his family on 11 June 2025. His end had come at home a little after 6 a.m., attributed by doctors to an ugly cocktail of frailties, among them respiratory arrest (or lung failure), sepsis and cystitis. His body had effectively gone into shutdown, its vitality sapped by multiple chronic conditions exacerbated by his dementia-like curse.

Those closest to him were heartbroken, especially his children. Mike Love had posted an incredibly touching message online after Melinda's death, promising Brian that 'we are family and I will always be there for you … we are here to support you in any way you need'. Because so many people prefer to find evil in everything Mike does, there was predictable 'outrage' that he continued to perform with the Beach Boys a couple of days after Brian's own death and that he didn't treat the crowd to a tearful obituary tribute. The reason was obvious: this loss was too profound to be expressed in simple words, beyond those attributed to Mike online: 'I'll miss you forever, my beloved cousin.' Al's grief was not haunted by the same ambiguities and guilt that Mike must have felt, and his tribute was more measured, though still sincere: 'I'll always feel blessed that you were in our lives for as long as you were … You were a humble giant who always made me laugh.'

Brian's community – his family, friends and collaborators – had long been prepared for this day. But the world at large, those who had not tracked the inexorable decline in his health across a decade or more, reacted to his demise with genuine shock and grief. It was as if it took Brian's departure to remind people how much his music had mattered in their lives. Removed from the turmoil of his private affairs, his achievements (particularly in the 1960s) stood loud and proud. At last, it seemed as if all the qualifications that had coloured critical opinion were stripped away and only the staggering beauty of his music remained. It was irrelevant now to complain, as some people always had, that his songs and productions were too lush, too soft, too juvenile, too commercial, too far removed from the radical rhetoric of the rock revolution. All that mattered was that Brian Wilson assembled chords, melodies and harmonic layers with an intuitive genius and finesse beyond the grasp of any of his peers. That talent had inspired the ageless hits with which Mike Love and Bruce Johnston continued to tour the world, but also the richer, more sophisticated fare that was brought to life via the masterful contributions of his touring band.

It was in concert, after all, that the full scope of his achievements was finally exposed. His records with the Beach Boys (and sometimes beyond) were often ecstatic and brilliant, but they were almost too complex and miraculous for an ordinary mind to process. The great achievements of the live band assembled by Darian Sahanaja were reproducing those arrangements in public, without sacrificing any of their intricacies, while analysing them, if you like, exposing their constituent parts. The results were breathtaking to hear, of course, but also confirmed the dazzling, daredevil scale of the imagination that first conjured them into life.

Brian Wilson invented and imagined that music. And, as behind-the-scenes rehearsal footage confirmed, he remained absolutely certain about how he wanted it to be performed. Yet one of the saddest elements of his story is that he was unable to take so little apparent pleasure when it was being enacted around him. I began this book by remembering that London performance in 2006, when Brian was suddenly confronted by the hidden meaning of one of his most famous compositions. What I didn't mention earlier was my profound sense of unease when the concert ended. As ever, Brian greeted the audience adulation as an assault rather than a blessing and fled into the sanctuary of his family's embrace as soon as he could escape the public gaze. I felt guilty at having taken part in a ceremony that clearly cost Brian so much psychological anguish.

But the touring continued, for another sixteen years, and so did the increasingly arduous process of forcing Brian Wilson to play the puppet role of the star. His promotional interviews, always awkward, became monosyllabic and then wordless. His final albums, culminating in a characterless set of piano instrumentals, sounded anonymous and forced. On stage, his participation level decreased. For years, his piano had been nothing more than a prop. But in his final years on the road, it was also a barrier to prevent the fans from seeing how little Brian was capable of offering to the music. There were good tours and bad, and a false reprieve in 2021 when he briefly appeared to be engaged in and connected with the music again. But the final shows, in the summer of 2022, were like the modern equivalent of a visit to a Victorian asylum. Brian sat motionless and silent amidst his magnificent musicians, his presence at the heart of the stage like a gaping sinkhole which the other performers pretended not to see. For perhaps a couple of songs a night, he would emerge from his semi-conscious state to deliver a few lines of lyrics, but meanwhile life outside went on all around him. There were years when it was impossible not to wonder whether Brian was a willing or knowing participant in what was happening. In 2022, the question didn't even need to be asked. It was a sweet relief when he was allowed to slide into an unacknowledged retirement.

Just as it did in his final concerts, Brian Wilson's music continues without him. The Beach Boys, whoever they will be in years to come, will carry one image of his genius around the world: complex emotions compressed into a cavalcade of two-minute pop gems. For the rest, a little excavation may be required and future scholars will no doubt be exploring the surreal landscape of his creations for decades and maybe centuries ahead. Until then, the music survives best in the hearts and souls of everyone who has been touched by it, enriched by it, opened themselves to all its emotional ambiguities and riches. Nobody else made music like Brian Wilson; nobody ever could.

Notes

INTRODUCTION

xiv: 'We're pretty low on money': *Disc & Music Echo*, 31 May 1969

xiv: 'A lot of the guys': ibid

xv: 'We are not bankrupt': *Des Moines Tribune*, 9 July 1969

WE'RE TOGETHER AGAIN

4: 'I couldn't believe it': *Beach Boys Stomp*, December 1988

5: 'Every day I go through': *Bay Area Music*, 12 August 1988

THE BOYS ON THE BEACH

8: 'A lot are pseudo gigolos': *New York Daily News*, 22 November 1964

9: 'Being a beach boy': ibid

RIDE THE WILD SURF

10: 'the kookiest, wildest': *Billboard*, 29 June 1963

10: 'It's a fad that belongs': ibid

13: 'It's dangerous': *Daily Telegraph*, 2 September 1995

13: 'Dennis tried to get me': *Victoria Times Colonist*, 31 July 1993

13: 'knew how to ride a wave': Love, *Good Vibrations*, p. 35

14: 'I don't like it': *NME*, 7 September 1968

14: 'really resented us': *North County Times*, 25 January 1998

15: 'Surfing is out now': *Daily Mirror*, 3 November 1964

15: 'probably be a tag': *Wilmington Morning News*, 21 April 1965

15: 'Surf City has gone punk': Associated Press, 4 September 1981

CALIFORNIA CALLING

16: *Life* magazine quotes: 22 October 1945 and 9 October 1962

17: 'Our songs tell stories': *Los Angeles Times*, 28 June 1965

17: 'Brian created': *Musician*, October 1983

17: 'I've always had the feeling': *Detroit Free Press*, 28 May 1982

18: 'Myths the size of California': *LA Weekly*, 5 November 1990

18: 'Tell everybody to think': *The Tennessean*, 6 April 1969

18: 'the worst weather': *Life*, 9 October 1962

18: 'there is smog on the basin': *Los Angeles Free Press*, 13 September 1968

18: 'Everyone feels the alienation': *Los Angeles Times*, 10 December 1967

19: 'It was totally into': *Daily Utah Chronicle*, 25 February 1975

19: 'bringing a new optimism': the *Observer*, 20 June 1993

19: 'The Los Angeles': the *Independent*, 17 March 1990

20: 'Now you get murdered': the *Independent*, 25 February, 1996

HOME ALONE IN HAWTHORNE

22: 'It gelled so quickly': *Modesto Bee*, 3 October 2014

22: 'Listening to a group': *NME*, 29 April 1966

22: 'The five of us': ibid

23: 'It was my guitar': *Musician*, October 1983

24: 'Dennis was thrilled': ibid

24: 'I threw it all away': *Modesto Bee*, 3 October 2014

25: 'Our street was the border': *The Columbian*, 12 November 1980

25: 'I'd been practising': ibid

25: 'Brian was the lone guy': ibid

26: 'The beach scene': *Billboard*, 9 June 1962

26: 'The hardest part': *Fort Worth Star-Telegram*, 12 March 1987

WE GOT LOVE

31: 'We fight, we really do': *Newcastle Evening Chronicle*, 7 November 1964

31: 'Dennis fucked my first wife': Muñoz, *A Fool's Journey*, p. 114

31: Barry Robinson quotes: *Asbury Park Evening Press*, 12 July 1965

32: 'the most serious-minded': *Wilmington Morning News*, 21 April 1965

32: 'the old man': *Los Angeles Times*, 20 March 1966

32: 'worldly, sarcastic': ibid

32: 'shrewd with money': *Melody Maker*, 6 May 1967

32: 'I was a sheet metal': Associated Press, 30 June 1975

I JUST WASN'T MADE FOR THESE TIMES

34: 'dropped me in my infancy': Wilson, *Wouldn't It Be Nice*, p. 20

34: 'local kid called Seymour': Wilson, *I Am Brian Wilson*, p. 138

34: 'it's a damaged ninth nerve': *Rolling Stone*, 4 November 1976

34: 'I've always been afraid': *Record Mail*, November 1964

36: Rich Sloan & Fred Morgan quotes: *Daily Breeze*, 4 January 1981

36: 'bent me out of shape': *San Francisco Examiner*, c.23 July 1998

36: 'My whole life was given over': ibid

38: 'I think that record production': *KRLA Beat*, 30 April 1966

38: 'the most creative person': *Anaheim Bulletin*, 26 November 1966

38: 'I got bored with it': *Vancouver Sun*, 27 August 2005

SURF CITY, DRAG CITY

40: 'A new album': *Daily Northwestern*, 1 November 1962

40: 'one of the worst albums': *Indianapolis Star*, 11 November 1962

41: 'there are plenty of musicologists': Wilson, *Wouldn't It Be Nice*, p. 71

41: 'It was the first record': *Memphis Press-Scimitar*, 19 December 1980

41: 'It was the first time': *Musician*, October 1983

43: 'Promoters created': *Fort Lauderdale News*, 28 March 1975

43: 'has a real spiritual': *Musician*, October 1983

44: 'There's something about that song': *San Luis Obispo Tribune*, 24 June 1987

44: 'The lyrics change': *Los Angeles Evening Citizen News*, 23 November 1963

THE WANDERER

46: 'Dennis is crazy': *Disc & Music Echo*, 28 May 1966

47: 'I don't understand it': *Honolulu Star-Advertiser*, 5 August 1965

48: 'a complete outgoing': quoted *Los Angeles Times*, 20 March 1966

48: 'I like showing them': *Harvard Crimson*, 30 November 1965

48: 'I'm really a sick guy': ibid

48: 'nature boy': *KRLA News*, 14 January 1967

48: 'the most messed-up person': *NME*, 26 August 1966

48: 'It's like everyone else': ibid

BABY LET YOUR HAIR GROW LONG

50: 'hair bleached blond': *Billboard*, 29 June 1963

50: 'We weren't very creative': *Los Angeles Times*, 12 May 2000

50: 'Everyone was bleaching': *Musician*, October 1983

50: 'We just picked up': *Los Angeles Times*, 12 May 2000

51: 'The scene was fantastic': *Los Angeles Times*, 30 June 1996

51: 'long-maned': *Kansas City Star*, 2 June 1963

51: 'unkempt': *Indianapolis Star*, 11 November 1962

52: 'shaggy-haired': *Fresno Beat*, 4 August 1964

52: 'beatnik': *Oakland Tribune*, 28 July 1966

52: 'a normal haircut': *Wilmington Morning News*, 21 April 1965

52: 'He appears to wonder': *Los Angeles Times*, 20 March 1966

52: 'I hate to shave': *Memphis Commercial Appeal*, 17 April 1966

53: Anne Nightingale quote: *Disc & Music Echo*, 12 November 1966

53: 'white, pubescent': *Los Angeles Times*, 1 October 1968

53: 'Wait a second': *Ithaca Journal*, 25 November 1972

53: 'the huge bearded figure': *Everett Daily Herald*, 21 December 1976

53: 'a mirrored Arabian vest': *Contra Costa Times*, 17 December 1976

54: 'Never has a rock group': *Honolulu Star-Advertiser*, 21 March 1978

54: 'Brian Wilson looked more': *Daily Utah Chronicle*, 23 July 1981

54: 'backsliding, getting fatter': *Daily Oklahoman*, 13 June 1982

54: 'Hawaiian shirts': *Winston-Salem Journal*, 22 May 1987

BUGGED AT MY OLD MAN

55: 'Murry Wilson was a hard': quoted in *Rolling Stone*, 4 November 1976

56: 'Brian and Michael': ibid

56: 'When they are travelling': *Melbourne Age*, 20 January 1964

56: 'The basis of surfing': *Billboard*, 29 June 1963

57: 'He would take his belt': *Melbourne Age*, 8 December 1996

58: 'We changed from our father': *NME*, 30 October 1964

58: 'destroyed him': *Rolling Stone*, 4 November 1976

59: 'He says he is deaf': *Nottingham Evening Post*, 28 August 1964

59: 'I've always written tunes': *Record Mirror*, 1 December 1967

60: 'I am now a millionaire': *Daily Express*, 30 November 1967

61: 'You know, there's a streak': *Washington Post*, c.8 May 1979

61: 'Our father beat the shit': *Rolling Stone*, 4 November 1976

62: 'He was always telling me': *Detroit Free Press*, 2 November 1991

YOU'RE WELCOME

63: 'vanguard of wholesome living': *Tacoma News Tribune*, 13 September 1985

64: 'My mother bought me': *Billings Gazette*, 6 October 2006

65: 'it turned into surf music': *Washington Post*, 3 October 2013

65: 'He saved me': *The Plain Dealer*, 2 August 1985

65: 'While the other Beach Boys': *Los Angeles Times*, 20 March 1966

65: 'a sort of father image': *Syracuse Post Standard*, 30 July 1966

65: 'the most sincere smile': *NME*, 26 August 1966

65: 'He keeps his opinions': ibid

66: 'He is our anchor': *Melody Maker*, 6 May 1967

SPECTRE OF THE STUDIO

68: 'bringing in drums and saxes': *Music Business*, 15 August 1964

68: 'where you hear something': *KRLA Beat*, 30 April 1966

68: 'Brian just adored Phil': *Musician*, October 1983

69: 'Every day, every morning': *Daily Telegraph*, 2 September 1995

70: 'He was very egotistical': *Daily Telegraph*, 5 January 2002

70: 'What if it's real?': *Cheetah*, October 1967

71: 'Brian was (apparently) oblivious': *Gadfly*, June 1998

71: 'We relied on Spector': *New York Daily News*, 5 February 1987

71: 'I looked to Spector': *New York Daily News*, 22 October 1991

71: 'I was paralysed with fear': the *Observer*, 6 January 2002

72: 'Yeah, sometimes I think': *Los Angeles Times*, c.21 November 1999

72: 'I don't know if it's possible': *Daily Telegraph*, 5 January 2002

72: 'So we went over to his mansion': the *Guardian*, 23 December 1988

72: 'Phil's voice is scary': Wilson, *I Am Brian Wilson*, p. 2

LET'S GO TRIPPIN'

73: 'only for those who have purchased': *Los Angeles Evening Citizen News*, 24 October 1962

73: 'They played on a very': *Fort Worth Star-Telegram*, 12 March 1987

YOU NEED A MESS OF HELP

78: 'I was run down mentally': *Tiger Beat*, April 1967

78: 'Brian was suffering': *Melody Maker*, 18 November 1967

79: 'He's very shy': ibid

LET HIM RUN WILD

80: 'We had no idea': Blaine/Goggin: *Hal Blaine & the Wrecking Crew*, p. 77

80: 'Murry Wilson was often': op cit p. 78

83: 'We're just gonna stay': *Record Mirror*, 7 November 1964

83: 'I have lately become very aware': *NME*, 5 August 1966

84: 'I just kind of floated': *Morristown Daily Record*, 30 June 2002

84: 'has something of a new sound': *Charlotte Observer*, 15 July 1965

85: 'was getting into a very expansive': *Musician*, October 1983

85: 'my concept of what most people': *Melody Maker*, 3 December 1966

85: 'will probably be our most': the *Observer*, 6 September 1998

85: 'When I die': ibid

85: 'I would have made the rhythm': *Rapid City Journal*, 8 October 2004

86: 'Capitol said they wanted': *Record Mirror*, 28 May 1966

87: 'It wasn't even a produced record': *Melody Maker*, 19 March 1966

87: 'I was explicitly warned': *Fort Worth Star-Telegram*, 24 April 1982

WHY DO FOOLS FALL IN LOVE?

88: 'That way I could make sure': Wilson, *I Am Brian Wilson*, p. 117

88: 'Women come after': *Philadelphia Inquirer*, 23 October 1991

88: 'I'm singing – and this may surprise': *Billboard*, 3 April 2015

89: 'Can you imagine what': *San Francisco Examiner*, 8 January 1984

89: 'I was a skinny little guy': *San Luis Obispo Tribune*, 24 June 1987

89: 'I was definitely no Don Juan': ibid

90: 'the bikinied schtick': *Hartford Courant*, 29 June 1992

90: 'I'll be standing there': *San Luis Obispo Tribune*, 24 June 1987

90: 'sex orgies': *Louisville Courier-Journal*, 14 February 1965

90: 'Dennis sat at the end': *Daily Hampshire Gazette*, 3 January 1984

92: 'his dick was too small': Jack Rieley post on *Pet Sounds* online message board, 2 November 1996

93: 'It's a cute song': *Greenville News*, 1 May 1977

94: 'Empty beer bottles': *Arizona Daily Star*, 25 May 1978

94: 'We have to keep our mouths shut': *New York Daily News*, 25 June 1978

HOLD ON DEAR BROTHER

96: 'I've always been the one': *Musician*, October 1983

97: 'Even when he was a senior': *NME*, 29 April 1966

97: 'A friend of my parents': ibid

98: 'I can hardly express': *NME*, 26 August 1966

I KNOW THERE'S AN ANSWER

100: 'Brian Wilson's evolutionary': *Rolling Stone*, 22 June 1972

101: 'He was really the first': *Musician*, October 1983

101: 'They gave it a real lukewarm': ibid

102: 'a new plateau for us': *Corpus Christi Times*, 18 March 1966

102: 'Personally, I think the group': *Melody Maker*, 19 March 1966

103: 'It's like I'm right in the golden era': ibid

104: 'I paid attention': Valerie Simadas blog on Wordpress, 2023

104: 'prayed every night': *Montreal Gazette*, 5 July 2016

104: 'The band didn't like it': *Arizona Republic*, 26 June 2016

104: 'It was quite a big deal': ibid

104: 'Carl and Al were yelling': *Daily Telegraph*, 2 September 1995

104: 'Michael hated *Pet Sounds*': *The Item* [Lynn, MA], 9 November 2006

105: 'Brian's "ego" music': Gaines, *Heroes and Villains*, p. 146

105: 'Who's gonna hear this?': ibid

105: 'Who's gonna hear this shit?': *Dallas Morning News*, c.25 July 2000

105: 'Some of what Brian did': *New York Daily News*, 17 July 1997

105: 'I worked very hard': *Arizona Republic*, 26 June 2016

105: 'a real dictator': *Vancouver Sun*, 28 November 1997

105: '*Pet Sounds* is the most creative': ibid

106: 'I'm trying to be as harmonic': *KRLA Beat*, 30 April 1966

106: 'a collection of art pieces': *Melody Maker*, 7 May 1966

106: 'the finest piece of art': ibid

107: 'That's a strange cut': *The Rocket*, 6 October 1999

107: 'the best song we ever recorded': *Modesto Bee*, 18 June 1999

107: 'faintly comic': *Evening Standard*, 16 July 1966

107: 'a load of old junk': *Bristol Evening Post*, 23 July 1966
107: 'We should have put': *The Item*, 9 November 2006
108: 'The biggest mistake': ibid
108: 'First off, one of them': *San Diego Union*, 13 May 1966
108: 'the goats were terrible': *Record Mirror*, 28 May 1966
108: 'They wanted *Shut Down Volume Six*': *Daily Utah Chronicle*, 25 February 1975
108: 'they said it wasn't commercial': *Fort Worth Star-Telegram*, 7 October 1979
108: 'the first "I guess your career's over"': *Dayton Daily News*, 1 February 1991
109: 'I think it killed': *Arizona Republic*, 2 May 1985
109: 'Brian just lost faith': *Vancouver Sun*, 28 November 1997
109: 'too artistic for comfort': Associated Press, 16 April 1976
109: 'I was smoking marijuana': *Detroit Free Press*, 2 November 1991
110: 'In Brian's heart': *Chicago Tribune*, 6 September 1996

GETTIN' IN OVER MY HEAD
113: 'feels are brief': *Melody Maker*, 7 May 1966
114: 'tried to make a pocket symphony': ibid
114: 'This took ninety hours': *Sunday Mirror*, 6 November 1966
114: 'When I heard Good Vibrations': *Toronto Star*, 19 August 1983
114: 'Michael didn't write': *Musician*, October 1983
114: 'We'd double or triple': ibid
114: 'I don't call it complicated': *NME*, 18 November 1966
115: 'the needles in the control panel': *Lincolnshire News*, 10 December 1974
115: 'I was so excited': *Sunday Mirror*, 6 November 1966
115: 'everyone blew their minds': *Detroit Free Press*, 10 February 1967
115: 'Tempo varies between': *NME*, 28 October 1966
115: 'not so much a record': *Liverpool Echo*, 22 October 1966
116: 'a scary record': the *Observer*, 6 January 2002
116: 'It's too weird for me': the *Observer*, 6 September 1998
116: 'will contain lots of humour': *NME*, 18 November 1966
117: 'there are about six different': *NME*, 8 July 1967
117: 'At any time, Wilson': *Disc & Music Echo*, 25 March 1967

118: 'I arrived and no one': *Los Angeles Times News Service*, 15 July 1967

118: 'the announcer said': *Honolulu Advertiser*, 25 February 1983

118: 'it should have been a hit': ibid

118: 'I am left with the impression': *Liverpool Post*, 5 August 1967

119: 'Brian blurted it out': Jack Rieley post on *Pet Sounds* online message board, 18 October 1996

WORDS WE BOTH COULD SAY

120: 'kids in the States': *Suffolk Free Press*, 30 July 1964

120: 'The lyrics are about': *Louisville Courier-Journal*, 14 February 1965

121: 'it's all soft': quoted in *Santa Barbara News-Press*, 16 July 1966

123: 'You must remember': *Calgary Herald*, 9 October 2004

123: 'writes vague, alliterative': *Daily Utah Chronicle*, 25 February 1975

123: 'The lyrics didn't make sense': *Tyler Morning Telegraph*, 16 June 2000

124: 'sometimes people get too far out': *Daily Utah Chronicle*, 25 February 1975

THE SMILE YOU SEND OUT...

127: 'In my opinion, it makes': *NME*, 11 November 1966

128: 'God is love': ibid

129: 'children's songs': *Detroit Free Press*, 28 October 1966

129: 'little musicals': ibid

129: 'I think that buying': *KRLA Beat*, 11 June 1966

130: 'when he gets home': *Los Angeles Times*, 27 November 1966

131: 'a perfectionist thing': *Detroit Free Press*, 10 February 1967

131: 'a bunt instead of a grand slam': *Billboard*, 24 July 1976

131: 'We had to sit back': *Hamilton Spectator*, 17 July 1971

132: 'hardly a track isn't marred': *Evening Standard*, 21 October 1967

132: 'the most beautiful rock': *Cheetah*, November 1967

132: 'Brian Wilson got bored': *Los Angeles Times*, 18 February 1968

132: 'We decided not to have': *Indianapolis Star*, 25 September 1967

132: 'We didn't scrap': *Los Angeles Times*, 8 October 1967

132: 'We got very paranoid': *Record Mirror*, 21 December 1968

133: 'Carl and I got': Jack Rieley post on *Pet Sounds* online message board, 15 October 1996

133: 'What happened is that Brian': *Daily Utah Chronicle*, 25 February 1975

133: 'a rather painful experience': *Fort Lauderdale News*, 28 March 1975

133: 'curled up': *Rolling Stone* syndication, 17 February 1978

133: 'Brian just couldn't thread': *Musician*, October 1983

134: 'We're going to fix up *SMiLE*': *Bay Area Music*, 12 August 1988

134: 'only a couple of cuts': ibid

134: 'SMiLE doesn't strike me': *Boston Globe*, 27 August 1988

134: 'only greed or vanity': *St. Louis Post-Dispatch*, 17 November 1995

134: 'I hate that fucking album': *Kansas City Star*, 28 October 1999

LET IT BE?

135: 'The mystique of the English': *Melody Maker*, 3 December 1966

135: 'anybody singing today': *NME*, 4 August 1964

135: 'the Beatles sensation': *Los Angeles Times*, c.29 August 1985

136: 'the Beatles showed our band': *Detroit Free Press*, 11 February 1984

136: 'Moans of disappointment': *Wilmington Morning News*, 16 March 1964

136: 'a clean-cut, virile': *Charlotte Observer*, 15 March 1964

136: 'I had this mop': *Fresno Bee*, 4 August 1964

137: 'something like a dozen pigs': *Oakland Tribune*, 15 March 1964

137: 'Compared to the Beach Boys': *Fresno Bee*, 4 August 1964

137: 'they like surfing': *Philadelphia Daily News*, 13 February 1965

137: 'The Beatles are getting old': ibid

137: 'I think the Beatles' influence': *KRLA Beat*, 6 November 1965

137: 'great harmonic ability': *Chicago Tribune*, 22 July 1966

138: 'They're trying to put everybody on': *Omaha World-Herald*, 12 August 1966

138: 'frightful in its pseudo-sanctity': *San Francisco Examiner*, 29 December 1966

138: Reviewer in Omaha: *Omaha World-Herald*, 26 August 1966

138: 'Show business will vibrate': *NME*, 3 December 1966

139: 'were tremendously concerned': *Newsday*, 6 April 1984

139: 'When I heard Joe Cocker': *NME*, 30 November 1968

139: 'The result may be': *Thanet Times*, 2 April 1968

140: 'The Beatles were focused': Jack Rieley post on *Pet Sounds* online message board, 19 October 1996

141: 'I've been crazy': *North County Magazine*, 1 December 1983

141: 'I used to rely': *Sunday Oregonian*, 5 September 2010

141: 'He's the guy who wrote': *Atlanta Journal-Constitution*, 1 August 2011

141: 'fools. They went from': *Newsday*, 6 April 1984

THE WALRUS WAS BRIAN

143: Fred LaBour story: *Michigan Daily*, 14 October 1969

HANG ON TO YOUR EGO

144: 'I think there will be more': *Disc & Music Echo*, 3 September 1966

144: 'I have lately become very aware': *NME*, 5 August 1966

144: 'We believe in God': *NME*, 11 November 1966

144: 'is the deepest expression': *Stoke-on-Trent Evening Sentinel*, 19 November 1966

144: 'a 23-year-old cherub': *Los Angeles Times*, 27 November 1966

145: 'I could kill the guy': *Rolling Stone*, 4 November 1976

145: 'Brian's trip happened': ibid

145: 'it blew his mind': *Daily Utah Chronicle*, 25 February 1975

146: 'was just the wrong person': *Hartford Courant*, 19 July 1981

146: 'and it almost destroyed him': *New York Daily News*, 27 March 1983

146: 'all these pressures': *Musician*, October 1983

146: 'had some very bad experiences': *Vancouver Sun*, 28 November 1997

146: 1989 affidavit: from court papers filed 18/9/89, Wilson v. Irving Music et al.

146: 'Brian and LSD': https://collapseboard.com/odd-comment-left-on-brian-wilson-blog-entry/

148: 'feels a strangely paternal': *Melody Maker*, 6 May 1967

148: 'I started to feel really conscious': interview with Jamake Highwater, 11 January 1968

WHEN I GROW UP

150: Bruce feigning femininity: Valerie Simadis blog on Wordpress, 2023

150: Dennis and arthritis: *Harvard Crimson*, 30 November 1965

150: 'I'd clear all American soldiers': ibid

150: 'I would not be drafted': *Fort Worth Star-Telegram*, 19 May 1967

151: 'I spent a day in jail': *Indianapolis Star*, 25 September 1967

151: 'My duty to God': *Los Angeles Free Press*, 9–15 June 1967

151: 'They seemed at a complete loss': *NME*, 6 May 1967

152: 'I want to do something good': *KRLA Beat*, 29 July 1967

152: 'I am not going to find a man': ibid

152: 'an institutional worker': Associated Press, 1 August 1967

153: 'I feel this is an opportunity': Associated Press, 15 September 1971

TIME TO GET ALONE

154: 'I think, basically': *Honolulu Advertiser*, 25 August 1967

155: 'will probably have to do': *Honolulu Advertiser*, 27 August 1967

156: 'Brian asked me to get more involved': *Billboard*, 24 July 1976

156: 'I understand. The Beach Boys were gods': *McAllen Monitor*, 15 October 2004

158: 'We'd like to pull out': interview with Jamake Highwater, 11 January 1968

JAI GURU DEV

160: 'I was really freaked out': *Cheetah*, October 1967

160: 'a way to educate man': *Los Angeles Times*, 11 October 1966

161: Mike Love on meeting the Maharishi: syndicated article published [in different versions] in *Hartford Courant*, 27 April 1968, and *Baltimore Sun*, 2 May 1968

161: 'the purest, most honest': *NME*, 3 December 1967

162: 'They inspire the young': *Chicago Daily News Service*, 20 January 1968

163: 'it would be a festival': Reuters, 25 May 1968

163: 'It is the idea': *Liverpool Daily Post*, 27 March 1968

163: 'The Maharishi got our vibrations': *Memphis Commercial Appeal*, 2 May 1968

163: 'downing a noonday Bloody Mary': ibid

164: 'tranquil music': *Philadelphia Inquirer*, 12 April 1968

165: 'The music, the air-conditioning': *Philadelphia Inquirer*, 7 May 1968

165: 'to meditate with moviemakers': *Berkshire Eagle*, 6 May 1968

165: Maharishi in Israel: *Honolulu Star-Bulletin*, 11 May 1968

165: 'a mild case of pneumonia': *Los Angeles Times*, 9 May 1968

165: 'resting in Santa Barbara': *Los Angeles Times*, 10 May 1968

165: 'are rapidly sinking': *Ottawa Journal*, 10 May 1968

165: 'He expected it': *Record Searchlight*, 29 July 1968

165: 'I don't think we should have got involved': *Melody Maker*, 7 September 1968

166: 'are a bit like circus dogs': *Chicago Tribune*, 7 July 1968

166: 'has trouble getting out of his house': *NME*, 7 September 1968

SEVENTEEN GIRLS FOR EVERY BOY

168: 'I'm a drop-out': *Record Searchlight*, 29 July 1968

169: 'Dennis went through a lot': *Boston Globe*, c.1 January 1984

170: 'a big nothing': *Record Searchlight*, 29 July 1968

170: 'We did a garbage run': Associated Press, 6 February 1971

170: 'told them he was a songwriter': *Bridgeport Telegram*, 4 December 1969

171: 'me and Charlie': *San Francisco Examiner*, 8 January 1984

171: 'heavy taxes and expenses': UPI news agency, 15 May 1969

171: 'I look at it as my mind': *Rave*, September 1969

171: Dennis Wilson interviews on Manson: *Record Mirror*, 21 December 1968 and 5 July 1969

174: 'I could pass a car wreck': *Hamilton Spectator*, 22 July 1969

174: 'Fear is nothing but awareness': *Rave*, September 1969

174: 'he and I worked': quoted in *Edmonton News*, 8 February 1987

175: Mike Love on Manson: Love, *Good Vibrations*, p. 209

176: Steve Desper on Charles Manson: Manson/Dennis Story thread at smileysmile.net forum

176: 'thought [Dennis] was nuts': O'Neill, *Chaos*, p. 114

176: 'it would be big news': op. cit. p. 110

177: 'Dennis Willson': https://www.mansonblog.com/2022/10/william-ray-cole-and-dennis-willson.html

177: 'he was pulled from the vehicle': *The Desert Sun*, 13 February 1980

177: 'the drummer of the Beach Boys': quoted in Marynick, *Charles Manson Now*, unpaginated

177: 'Do you remember how Dennis': ibid

WHICH SIDE ARE YOU ON?

179: 'stay in school': *Lincoln News Messenger*, 31 October 1963

180: 'to show that not all': *Tulsa World*, 14 April 1969

180: 'We plan to visit Moscow': *Daily Oklahoman*, 2 May 1969

181: 'They just whistled': *Montreal Gazette*, 23 June 1978

182: 'had Carl and I blushing': Jack Rieley post on *Pet Sounds* online message board, 9 October 1996

182: 'a singing group popular': UPI news agency, 2 May 1971

182: 'nonwhites': Associated Press, 29 February 1972

182: 'we're the only rock group left': *Montreal Gazette*, 11 September 1971

183: 'Beach Boys to Desegregate': *Charlotte News*, 2 March 1972

183: 'Beach Boys Break Color Barrier': *The Province*, 1 March 1972

183: 'It took us a while': *Washington Daily News*, 29 March 1972

183: 'Most of these guys here': ibid

183: 'When it comes to the point': *Ithaca Journal*, 25 November 1972

184: 'We are so mid-stream': Associated Press, 30 June 1975

185: 'He seemed to us': *Fort Lauderdale News*, 27 February 1980

185: 'shared the same concerns': *Miami Herald*, 7 March 1980

186: 'teenyboppers': *Baltimore Sun*, 18 May 1980

186: 'you can't really judge': *Detroit Free Press*, 28 May 1982

186: 'When I caught the headline': *Sacremento Bee*, 14 October 1983

187: 'Now they are OK': *Los Angeles Times*, 10 May 1983

187: 'The whole thing has stimulated me': ibid

187: 'the Beach Boys have never': *Kansas City Star*, 4 June 1984

187: 'needs an image in the world': *Scranton Times-Tribune*, 3 July 1985

188: 'I hate to say I disagree': *Boston Globe*, 19 January 1989

188: 'such a cool': *Kansas City Star*, 20 June 1989

189: 'a renewed commitment': *North Jersey Herald and News*, 21 August 1992

189: 'were just so insulting': *Los Angeles Times*, 12 September 1992

189: 'That whole mess of everybody': *Kamloops This Week*, 24 March 2006

189: 'Kennedy was elected': ibid

189: 'liberal' as an all-purpose insult: *Tucson Citizen*, 3 October 1996

190: 'a poolside pre-show': *Palm Beach Post*, 6 March 1997

ADD SOME MUSIC?

192: 'one of our really good records': *Musician*, October 1983

192: 'at the very height of his creativity': ibid

193: Mo Ostin statement: *Record World*, 7 February 1970

195: 'It wasn't really fashionable': *Lexington Herald-Leader*, 17 August 1986

196: 'I gave him 50 per cent': author interview

SUPERMAN COMES TO THE SUPERMARKET

197: 'produced a number of Prince albums': *Boston Globe*, 1 April 2001

198: 'Colonnaded Ruins Domino': *Brattleboro Reformer*, 4 October 2001

200: 'I look at us as a whole new group': *Los Angeles Times*, 31 October 1970

200: 'he got into a horrible fight': *Record World*, 28 July 1973

201: 'was a divide-and-conquer': author interview

202: 'Brian Wilson, Dennis Wilson': Jack Rieley post on *Pet Sounds* online message board, 7 October 1996

202: 'encouraged the Wilsons': ibid

202: 'follow my car': Jack Rieley post on *Pet Sounds* online message board, 2 November 1996

202: 'under seriously powdered conditions': op. cit., 14 October 1996

203: 'I AM the Beach Boys': op. cit. 13 October 1996

203: 'Upon my departure': op. cit. 7 October 1996

MAKE IT GOOD

205: 'resting but still very uncomfortable': *Los Angeles Times*, 7 November 1970

205: 'We actually recorded that album': author interview

205: 'We're trying to rub some': *Evening Standard*, 21 November 1970

206: 'recently people have rediscovered us': *Hamilton Spectator*, 17 July 1971

207: 'the most important piece of music': *Indianapolis News*, 2 October 1971

207: 'Carl is the heavy on this album': *Montreal Gazette*, 11 September 1971

208: 'It is Reprise–Brother': ad in *Los Angeles Times*, 12 September 1971

208: 'We were joining a band': author interview

209: 'It was the first occasion': author interview

209: 'a large, classical work': Radio Veronica interview aired 15 July 1972

210: 'felt different every time': Muñoz, *A Fool's Journey*, p. 116

211: *Montreal Star* review: 17 February 1973

211: 'proves conclusively': *Los Angeles Free Press*, 2–12 February 1973

211: 'I heard it': *Record World*, 28 July 1973

211: 'we do concept albums now': *Baltimore Evening Sun*, 10 September 1973

211: 'somehow he ended up': author interview

Notes

LET US GO ON THIS WAY

213: 'When I first heard that Capitol': *Arizona Republic*, 30 December 1974

214: 'The surfing sound': *Regina Leader-Post*, 22 August 1968

214: 'We are a bit fed up': *Disc & Music Echo*, 14 December 1969

214: 'If people in the audience': Lisa Robinson syndication, 13 March 1971

214: 'We do the old stuff': *Newsday*, 20 May 1971

214: 'If we played just our old hits': *Press & Sun-Bulletin*, 15 March 1972

214: 'I enjoy doing the old ones': *Baltimore Evening Sun*, 10 September 1973

214: 'You want us to progress': quoted in *Ottawa Citizen*, 16 September 1976

214: 'Our only problem': *Green Bay Press-Gazette*, 29 December 1974

214: 'We're nostalgia now': *Fort Lauderdale News*, 28 March 1975

215: 'We could easily have wound up': *Miami News*, 28 March 1975

215: 'When you think of the Beach Boys': *Los Angeles Times*, 27 June 1976

215: 'We've stopped resisting our past': *Indianapolis News*, 8 January 1977

215: 'What worried us the most': UPI news agency, 2 January 1981

215: 'It ends up being a show': *Baltimore Sun*, 17 July 1981

215: 'I disagree with what Carl says': *Miami News*, 4 September 1981

215: 'The audiences have locked us': *South Bend Tribune*, 4 October 1981

215: 'We have to keep playing': *Santa Cruz Sentinel*, 4 December 1981

215: 'It gets wearisome sometimes': *The Californian*, 3 May 1984

215: 'In order to have old music': *Kennebec Journal*, 30 May 1984

216: 'I guess we feel semi-boxed in': *Boston Globe*, 19 January 1989

216: 'I don't want the Beach Boys': *Los Angeles Times*, 26 May 1989

216: 'We can be a life raft': ibid

216: 'We try to do all our Top 10 hits': *Bangor Daily News*, 19 July 1989

216: 'I take the money': the *Observer*, 20 June 1993

216: 'I would like to do': *Charlotte Observer*, 16 November 1993

THEY SAY BRIAN IS BACK

218: 'That's Brian': *Montreal Gazette*, 11 September 1971

218: 'He's a very spacy person': *Montreal Star*, 14 January 1977

219: Grave story: Jack Rieley post on *Pet Sounds* online message board, 26 October 1996

219: 'the Howard Hughes of music': *San Bernadino County Sun*, 15 March 1973

219: 'he figured': *Los Angeles Times*, 17 June 1973

219: 'He won't let me': *Record World*, 28 July 1973

219: 'only wants to be left alone': *Boston Globe*, 10 December 1972

220: 'It was more therapeutic': Blaine/Goggin, *Hal Blaine and the Wrecking Crew*, p. 82

220: 'He's brilliant when he wants to be': *Daily Utah Chronicle*, 25 February 1975

221: 'Everything he did was funny': *Rolling Stone*, 4 November 1976

222: 'in a funky sort of bag': *Cincinnati Post*, 22 November 1975

222: 'People will say the group': Associated Press, 16 April 1976

223: 'our music will sound like': ibid

223: 'whether he admits it or not': *Rolling Stone* syndication, 16 May 1976

223: 'I know it's weird': *Modern Recording*, June–July 1976

223: 'the most fully realized': *San Francisco Examiner*, 27 June 1976

223: 'I was unhappy with the oldies': *Crawdaddy*, September 1976

224: 'Well, I've recorded enough': ibid

224: 'decided to make the record': *Oui*, December 1976

224: 'Each song is different': *Philadelphia Inquirer*, 8 August 1976

TOO MUCH SUGAR

227: 'porky': *Harvard Crimson*, 30 November 1965

227: 'balloon': *Los Angeles Times*, 20 March 1966

227: 'the biggest appetite': *Reading Evening Post*, 12 November 1966

227: 'He goes into phases': *Anaheim Bulletin*, 26 November 1966

227: 'vegetables are the best thing': ibid

227: Brian Wilson story: 'Vibrations – Brian Wilson Style', *KRLA Beat*, 17/ December 1966

228: 'honey, milk and bran': *Ottawa Citizen*, 3 August 1968

228: 'twelve different kinds': *Salt Lake City Sun-Chronicle*, 3 July 1969

229: 'a big pain': *Chicago Tribune*, 5 June 1977

229: 'I wanted to purge': Love, *Good Vibrations*, p. 228

229: 'I bit Stephen': op. cit. p. 229

229: Love's absence 'conspicuous': *Everett Daily Herald*, 3 March 1970

230: 'subsisting on candy': *Los Angeles Times*, c.26 August 1985

230: 'I got scared': *New York Times*, 26 June 1988

230: 'His diet is all messed up': *Fort Worth Star Telegram*, 22 November 1982

230: 'the Brian Wilson Diet': *San Francisco Examiner*, 11 July 1988

230: 'He couldn't see his feet': ibid

231: 'He's taught me things': *Rolling Stone*, 4 November 1976

231: 'Stop eating red meat': *Daily Oklahoman*, 28 August 1988

231: 'All he wanted to do': *Daily Telegraph*, 16 May 1998

231: 'My favourite thing': *Daily Telegraph* 5 January 2002

FORGET HIM, HE'S CRAZY

232: George Benson memories: https://amhistory.si.edu/jazz/Benson-George/Benson_George_Transcript.pdf

233: 'I first smoked grass': *Honolulu Star-Advertiser*, 7 September 1972

233: 'This is a lost generation': ibid

233: 'Steiger couldn't even': *Honolulu Star-Bulletin*, 12 May 1980

233: 'What I saw was a man': *Los Angeles Times*, 26 June 1983

234: 'I was hiding in my bedroom': *Los Angeles Times*, 27 June 1976

234: 'We teach people': *Honolulu Star-Bulletin*, 12 May 1980

235: 'I'd have been a goner': *Rolling Stone*, 4 November 1976

235: 'Is marijuana a drug?': *Washington Post* syndication, 7 September 1976

235: 'Do you have any uppers?': *Oui*, December 1976

236: 'I would give up my total career': quoted in *Los Angeles Free Press*, 7–13 January 1977

236: 'Brian was just getting back': *Musician*, October 1983

236: 'he was fascinated': *New York Daily News*, 25 June 1978

237: 'I started taking drugs again': *Los Angeles Times,* 26 June 1983

237: 'he was too self-destructive': *Fort Lauderdale News*, 20 March 1983

237: 'I told the other guys': *Los Angeles Times*, 26 June 1983

237: 'His lung capacity': ibid

237: 'leaving town on a retreat': Associated Press, 23 February 1983

237: 'I will be back as soon': ibid

ADULT CHILD

239: 'He's got some heavy songs': *Passaic Herald-News*, 13 August 1976

241: 'just sitting down at the piano': *Atlanta Constitution*, 8 January 1977

241: Pat Collins story: syndicated radio interview with Dave Herman, 1977

241: 'I would love to do a crooner album': ibid

241: 'I've been experimenting': *Memphis Commercial Appeal*, 24 April 1977

242: 'there was a problem with Mike': *Bay Area Music*, 12 August 1988

242: 'the best album since *Pet Sounds*': *Los Angeles Free Press*, 15–21 February 1977

242: 'a lyrical disaster': *Miami Herald*, 14 April 1977

242: 'abysmal songs': *Montreal Star*, 16 April 1977

243: 'one of the more woeful': *Philadelphia Inquirer*, 17 April 1977

243: 'the weakest album': *Wichita Falls Times Record News*, 30 April 1977

243: 'a piece of trash': *Edmonton Journal*, 23 April 1977

243: 'probably the worst album': ibid

243: 'Like some of the best': *Ottawa Citizen*, 5 May 1977

TM IN THE A.M.

244: 'I wrote the song for the Maharishi': *Billboard*, 24 July 1976

245: 'corny': *Rolling Stone* syndication, 16 May 1976

246: 'a University of California': UPI news agency, 5 September 1974

246: 'We've found it to be really helpful': *Indianapolis News*, 7 June 1972

246: 'One night I walked into a dressing room': *Ottawa Journal*, 23 June 1978

248: 'maximise energy and creativity': *Albuquerque Tribune*, 13 May 1978

248: 'is said to have succeeded': *Sydney Morning Herald*, 11 March 1978

248: Love's foam rubber: *Waterloo Courier*, 10 February 1978

249: Love dematerialising: *Daily Record*, 21 September 1979

249: 'the people who complained': *Flint Journal*, 2 January 1977

249: 'I spend an hour praying': *Rapid City Journal*, 23 August 1981

249: 'easily intimidated': *Albuquerque Journal*, 19 June 1995

249: 'It's like surrendering yourself': *Charlotte News*, 28 July 1978

249: 'field of energy': *Newsday*, 6 May 1984

250: 'I tell people I may be forty-six': *Indianapolis News*, 30 December 1987

250: 'Rather than just accepting': *Philadelphia Daily News*, 16 September 1993

HOLY MAN

251: 'He was so totally un-self-conscious': https://www.youtube.com/watch?v=swro47PQvxE

255: Dennis/Karen fight: *Bryan College Station Eagle*, 29 January 1976, and *Indiana Gazette*, 31 January 1976

255: 17-year-old: UPI news agency, 6 October 1976

255: 'just another Beach Boys album': *Ithaca Journal*, 24 May 1977

256: 'Dennis comes into the studio': *Rock Magazine*, May 1977

256: 'self-indulgence': *Ithaca Journal*, 24 May 1977

256: 'a much bigger sound': *Detroit Free Press*, 28 August 1977

256: 'My album is more into poetry': ibid

256: 'Believe me, I've never felt': *Toronto Star*, 30 August 1977

256: 'scared. I really am': *Rock Magazine*, May 1977

257: 'can't sing': *Richmond Independent*, 19 August 1977

257: 'I've been humbled': *Los Angeles Times*, 16 October 1977

257: 'I used to be terrified': ibid

257: 'a small orchestra': ibid

257: 'that was not true': Love, *Good Vibrations*, p. 273

CHRISTMAS COMES THIS TIME EACH YEAR

260: 'is practically a god to me': *Music Business*, 15 August 1964

260: 'Some of the things were really hard': Associated Press, 26 November 1964

COUSINS, FRIENDS AND BROTHERS

263: 'tickets weren't selling': the *Guardian*, 29 July 1977

263: 'Beach Boys Snub British Fans': *Evening Standard*, 28 July 1977

264: John Swenson story: *Rolling Stone*, 20 October 1977

265: 'Unfortunately, we happened': *Santa Rosa Press Democrat*, 18 November 1977

266: 'They can't do much': *Los Angeles Times*, 16 October 1977

266: 'I think the Beach Boys haven't': ibid

267: 'I've been in moods': *Detroit Free Press*, 28 August 1977

267: 'He doesn't hide his feelings': *Sydney Morning Herald*, 11 March 1978

267: 'but we don't want to hurt': ibid

268: 'a Valium … and two Mai Tais': recording of Perth press conference, 15 March 1978

268: 'sounded waterlogged': *Honolulu Star-Advertiser*, 21 March 1978

269: 'that was a very rough time': *Musician,* October 1983

LOVE, LOVE, LOVE

270: 'There's a lot of estrangement': *Sunday Oregonian*, 21 July 1991

270: 'Looking back on it': ibid

271: 'Brian never wanted to be a star': *Oakland Tribune*, 13 June 1976

271: 'Brian is like a musical oil well': *Sydney Morning Herald*, 11 March 1978

271: 'I was really hitting': Wilson, *I Am Brian Wilson*, p. 199

272: 'I was real bad': UPI news agency, 17 December 1985

272: 'Stan's charges': *San Pedro News-Pilot*, 8 May 1990

272: 'Brian Wilson has the look in his face': ibid

273: 'Fame is the worst thing': *Sunday Oregonian*, 21 July 1991

273: 'I knew Dennis': https://www.reddit.com/r/thebeachboys/comments/r4hi1u/stan_love_going_off_in_a_dennis_wilson_group_on/

WHO WEARS SHORT SHORTS?

274: 'all-round schlockmeister': author interview

274: 'the Beach Boys' ambassador': *NME*, 20 May 1966

275: 'two vast fortunes': ibid

276: 'The first day I was in the business': author interview

276: Reports of shooting: *California Eagle*, 27 February 1958

276: 'We were hired to be': author interview

277: 'Having girls scream at you': *Ventura County Star*, 2 August 2007

278: 'He's very bouncy': *NME*, 26 August 1966

278: 'hard to get along with': *Nottingham Evening Post & News*, 5 September 1967

278: 'sometimes Bruce regrets': *Melody Maker*, 6 May 1967

278: 'The others never telephone me': *NME*, 20 June 1967

279: 'I'd like to see us work': *Hamilton Spectator*, 17 July 1971

279: New Zealand plans: ibid

279: 'I fired Johnston': Jack Rieley post on *Pet Sounds* online message board, 7 October 1996

279: 'Bruce consistently displayed': Jack Rieley post on *Pet Sounds* online message board, 8 October 1996

279: 'We decided that since': *Asbury Park Press*, 22 June 1973

279: 'I felt I wasn't being productive': *Lincolnshire News*, 10 December 1974
279: 'we all felt tense': *Old Grey Whistle Test* TV show, 24 January 1975
279: 'If that problem': *Los Angeles Times*, 19 June 1977
279: 'I've played a few Beach Boys concerts': *Old Grey Whistle Test* TV show, 24 January 1975
280: 'We loaned him a production deal': author interview
282: 'This kind of album': *Los Angeles Times* 19 June 1977
282: 'Brian came up with the suggestion': *Rochester Democrat & Chronicle*, 13 May 1979
282: 'he brought a certain outside': ibid

MURDER ON THE DANCEFLOOR
283: 'I'm so proud of that track': *Florida Today*, 11 December 2000
284: 'It was a chance to use': Associated Press, 30 March 1979
284: 'The Beach Boys are known': *New York Daily News*, 28 February 1979
284: 'The best moments happen': *Record World*, 24 February 1979
284: 'This is a terrible travesty': *New York Daily News*, 5 March 1979
284: 'I like the idea of going out': *Newark Star-Ledger*, 15 March 1979
285: 'You really want to know': *Melody Maker*, 24 March 1979
285: 'There are probably some things': *Austin American-Statesman*, 21 May 1979
285: 'It's created controversy': *New York Daily News*, 28 February 1979
286: 'Our fans hated it': *Wichita Eagle*, 28 September 1979
286: 'it's a fabulous record': author interview
286: 'We've always related': *Lexington Herald-Leader*, 26 April 1979

BRAND NEW OLD FRIENDS
287: Brian Wilson on *PM*: https://www.youtube.com/watch?v=yV1X4i_jF04
290: 'Brian's key involvement': *Asbury Park Press*, 20 May 1979
291: 'I'm sure that I won't rejoin': *Wichita Beacon*, 15 June 1979
291: 'I think this is a really good album': *Asbury Park Press*, 20 May 1979

LOOKING BACK WITH LOVE
292: 'We all have acting roles': *Daily Mirror*, 20 August 1979
292: 'My idea is to come up': *Philadelphia Daily News*, 1 May 1981

293: 'something I envision': *Oakland Tribune*, 2 July 1981

293: 'The guy from Sunkist': *Philadelphia Daily News*, 16 September 1993

293: 'We'd like the Four Seasons': *New York Daily News*, 6 May 1984

294: 'The Beach Boys will help Chevrolet': press release, 17 September 1987

294: 'I loved the Chevrolet commercial': *Philadelphia Daily News*, 16 September 1993

294: 'We're thinking of a children's': *Boston Globe*, 16 June 1988

294: 'I want to capitalise': *Arizona Daily Star*, 14 October 1988

294: 'The people in the front line': *Modesto Bee*, 14 October 1990

295: 'The Beach Boys work perfectly': *New York Daily News*, 25 June 1989

295: 'Bart talks about': *Reno Gazette-Journal*, 30 January 1992

295: 'The whole concept': *Detroit Free Press*, 30 August 1993

295: 'It'll be like House of Blues': *Myrtle Beach Sun News*, 12 July 1996

296: 'California meets Caribbean': *Honolulu Star-Bulletin*, 14 March 1997

296: Kokomojito launch: forbes.com, 10 July 2024

END OF THE SHOW

298: 'Dreams do come true': *San Francisco Examiner*, 18 November 1979

298: Cambodia benefit: *Fresno Bee*, 3 February 1980

298: 'Dennis has some behaviour stuff': *Dayton Journal Herald*, 17 April 1980

299: *Good Morning, America*: https://www.youtube.com/watch?v=d9ghYXXXx1I

299: 'The general consensus': *Palm Beach Post*, 17 January 1981

299: 'the Beach Boys are basically unmanageable': *Rolling Stone*, 14 May 1981

299: 'ill-behaved and offensive': *San Pedro News Pilot*, 21 July 1981

300: 'pursued me through three rooms': *Los Angeles Times*, 20 March 1982

300: 'a personal family matter': ibid

300: 'Dennis is currently drunk': *Daily Oklahoman*, 13 June 1982

300: 'Dennis has been going through': *Chicago Tribune*, 13 July 1982

301: 'He has been working real hard': *Indianapolis News*, 18 August 1983

301: 'Wilson crapped his pants': *Vancouver Sun*, 26 May 1984

KEEP THE SUMMER ALIVE

302: 'Brian has handed me the baton': *Austin American-Statesman*, 21 May 1979

303: 'I said, "Write songs? Ugh"': *Philadelphia Inquirer*, 18 April 1980
303: 'I was surprised they chose it': *Indianapolis News*, 19 April 1980
303: 'I guess Bruce just liked that song': *NME*, 19 April 1980
303: 'I felt kind of funny': *Indianapolis News*, 19 April 1980
304: 'it figures that no one else is around': *Bloomsburg Morning Press*, 29 March 1980
304: 'a suicide note': *Fond Du Lac Reporter*, 15 June 1980
304: 'seemed genuinely frightened': *Biddeford Journal Tribune*, 28 March 1980
304: 'Brian shouldn't be regarded': *Evening Standard*, 6 June 1980
304: 'Permanent schizophrenia': ibid
304: 'are so gross and podgy': the *Observer*, 29 June 1980
305: 'All you really have to do': *Austin American-Statesman*, 11 March 1981
305: 'I do not plan on touring': *Rochester Democrat & Chronicle*, 14 July 1981
305: 'three issues I had raised': ibid
306: 'Brian is writing as creatively': *Spokane Spokesman-Review*, 12 December 1980
306: 'had just finished a demo': *Kansas City Star*, 16 February 1981
306: 'I don't trust him': *Fort Lauderdale News*, 15 May 1981
306: 'The Beach Boys are on the verge': *El Paso Herald Post*, 3 July 1981
306: 'destroyed it': *Indianapolis Times*, 26 June 1981
307: 'It made me feel real bad': *Baltimore Sun*, 17 July 1981
307: 'the edits are real tacky': *Morristown Daily Record*, 11 September 1981
308: 'I wrote a song called "Brian's Back"': *Tampa Bay Times*, 24 March 1982
308: 'seems to have undergone': *Hartford Courant*, 24 November 1982

FAREWELL MY FRIEND

309: 'He was hooked on alcohol': *Newsday*, 6 May 1984
309: 'get drunk, then try': *New York Daily News*, 6 May 1984
309: 'He was in a lane': *Buffalo News*, 14 May 1984
309: 'Dennis had been talking': *The Californian*, 30 December 1983
309: 'he entered rehab programs': UPI news agency, 31 December 1983
310: 'I asked him what he wanted': *The Californian*, 30 December 1983
310: 'I talked with his agent': *San Pedro News Pilot*, 31 December 1983
311: 'He's just too much trouble': *Rolling Stone* syndication, 27 May 1984

311: 'he was kind of a weirdo': *Los Angeles Times*, 29 December 1983
312: 'He was having fun': *San Pedro News Pilot*, 29 December 1983
312: 'Underwater pressure': *Fort Worth Star-Telegram*, 27 March 1986
312: 'My mother was with us': *Indianapolis News*, 14 April 1984
312: 'I felt real strange': *Los Angeles Times*, c.27 August 1985
312: 'He took it quite well': *Indianapolis News*, 14 April 1984
313: 'I sat up all night': ibid
313: 'he had the biggest heart': *Buffalo News*, 14 May 1984
313: 'He defied the laws of nature': *Newsday*, 6 May 1984
313: 'I feel the presence of his soul': ibid
313: 'We are saddened': UPI news agency, 29 December 1983
313: 'We all thought that Dennis': Knight News Wire, 19 February 1984
314: 'I thought that took on': UPI news agency, 10 January 1984
314: 'At least his essence': *The Morning Call*, 25 May 1984
314: 'It was a stress on the whole group': *Newsday*, 6 May 1984
314: 'I miss that strong beat': Knight News Wire, 19 February 1984

SWEET INSANITY

315: 'I really don't care': *New York Daily News*, 27 March 1983
315: 'shaking hands, scared eyes': *North County Magazine*, 1 December 1983
316: 'Just before we went on stage': *Calgary Herald*, 27 January 1985
316: 'I want to shave my beard': *Los Angeles Times*, c.29 August 1985
317: 'It was obvious that Brian': McParland, *The Wilson Project*, p. 4
317: 'She and Brian had as much': op. cit. p. 30
318: 'sounds like a Top 10 record': Associated Press, 4 February 1987
318: 'I've exhausted my creative abilities': ibid
318: Court papers: McParland, *The Wilson Project*, pp. 119–134
319: 'Dr Landy doesn't like me': *New York Times*, 26 June 1988
320: 'emotionally explosive': *Sacramento Bee*, 27 July 1988
320: 'total superiority': *Bay Area Music*, 12 July 1988
320: 'I don't want to get involved': *Daily Oklahoman*, 28 August 1988
320: 'I think that Dr Landy': *Rolling Stone*, 2 May 1991
320: 'He never calls us': *The Tennessean*, 31 May 1992
320: 'My mom saw him': ibid

321: 'It was a tremendous disappointment': *Melbourne Age*, 20 November 1992

321: 'we've been talking about Brian': author interview

322: 'when you can't get through': *Melbourne Age*, 20 November 1992

323: 'It was pathetic': *Evening Standard*, 17 June 1993

323: 'They probably want control of me': *Washington Post*, 1 December 1991

324: 'slurred, his lips': *Philadelphia Inquirer*, 23 October 1991

325: 'I'm lost, I'm lonely': *Detroit Free Press*, 2 November 1991

325: 'Melandy': *Uncut*, June 1998

ROCK AND ROLL TO THE RESCUE

326: 'we've become America's band': *White Plains Reporter Dispatch*, 20 January 1984

326: 'about being healthy': *Indianapolis News*, 13 April 1984

326: 'We've got the artistic side': ibid

327: 'Call it *East Meets West*': *Mamaroneck Times*, 20 July 1980

327: 'Oh God. I don't know why': author interview

328: 'We're all writing songs': *Atlanta Constitution*, 2 June 1984

328: 'We were totally separated': *Detroit Free Press*, 19 June 1987

328: 'I didn't think that was very good': author interview

328: 'Brian's writing songs': *The Tennessean*, 6 October 1985

328: 'I'm not very happy with this album': *Modern Recording*, October 1985

329: 'We got along good': *Bay Area Music*, 12 August 1988

329: 'obstacles': *Moline Dispatch*, 12 July 1985

329: 'It was an absolute nightmare': *Fort Worth Star Telegram*, 2 November 1986

329: 'The legend is that': ibid

329: 'It wasn't as big': *Tallahassee Democrat*, 10 April 1987

329: 'really stupid': *Boston Globe*, 19 January 1989

330: Carl on John Stamos: *San Francisco Examiner*, 8 February 1987

330: 'We failed to musically exploit': *Raleigh News & Observer*, 17 June 1992

331: 'were said with the venom': *Independence Examiner*, 22 January 1988

331: 'What I was trying to say': *Memphis Commercial Appeal*, 24 August 1990

331: 'the skinny guy': *Asbury Park Press*, 6 August 1990

331: 'He never gave me no satisfaction': recording of 3 September 1990 show

331: 'We wanted to do something': *Palm Beach Daily News*, 6 October 1988

332: 'to somehow throw everybody': *Detroit Free Press*, 8 February 1991

333: 'We'll be recording that': *Reno Gazette-Journal*, 30 January 1992

334: 'I prefer to go for the originals': *Detroit Free Press*, 4 September 1992

335: 'a cutting edge': *Indiana Gazette*, 25 March 1993

335: 'a cross between': *Billboard*, 18 March 1995

335: Mike on Brian's songs: *Quad City Times*, 27 August 1995

335: 'They were just thrilled': *Orange County Register*, 1 October 1995

335: 'We have so much momentum': *Billboard*, 18 March 1995

335: 'we can't sign the deal': *Winston-Salem Journal*, 11 October 1996

LIKE A BROTHER

337: 'Apparently they caught it early': Associated Press, 3 April 1997

338: 'cynical misuse': *Albuquerque Journal*, 20 May 1997

338: 'he was portrayed wrongly': ibid

338: 'It was kind of a tag team thing': *Philadelphia Daily News*, 20 July 2000

340: 'I'm dedicating my future music': *Endless Summer Quarterly*, March 1998

340: 'Carl was plainly the soul': *Austin American-Statesman*, 11 February 1998

SEA OF LAWSUITS

342: 'Gray says he doesn't feel': *North County Times*, 12 November 1990

343: 'I pounded my fists': Wilson/Gold, *Wouldn't It Be Nice*, p. 188

344: 'We're just a bunch': *Allentown Morning Call*, 24 July 1981

344: 'I write music now': *Daily Utah Chronicle*, 25 February 1975

344: '[Brian] never did any song': *New York Daily News*, 6 May 1984

344: 'My uncle': *Ottawa Citizen*, 20 August 1991

345: Not writing with Mike: *Wouldn't It Be Nice*, p. 90

345: 'Mike was a young lead singer': *McAllen Monitor*, 27 September 1992

345: 'Brian's very easily led': *Victoria Times Colonist*, 31 July 1993

346: 'a very devious person': *Tulsa World*, 11 April 1993

346: 'The history of this band': the *Observer*, 20 June 1993

346: 'The Love lawsuit': *Evening Standard*, 17 June 1993

346: 'I signed it under duress': *Los Angeles Times*, 29 October 1994
347: 'The lawsuit ripped my heart': *Los Angeles Times*, 17 January 1995
347: 'It's a miracle': ibid
347: 'tried to annihilate me': *The Item* [Lynn, MA], 9 November 2006

LOVE AND MERCY

348: 'Brian was doing nothing': *Calgary Herald*, 9 October 2004
348: 'I felt that our friendship': *St. Louis Post-Dispatch*, 17 November 1995
349: 'It's a great album': *Los Angeles Daily News*, 26 August 1995
349: 'The whole thing was absurd': *Daily Telegraph*, 16 August 1998
350: 'I don't like the snow': *Chicago Tribune*, 31 May 1998
350: 'It was the most unbelievable': *Daily Breeze*, 19 June 1998
350: 'a flat album': *Kansas City Star*, 28 October 1999
351: 'After Carl died': *Daily Breeze*, 19 June 1998
351: 'I did not write that line': ibid
352: 'to further his own interests': *Birmingham Evening Mail*, 27 August 1999
352: 'I can't understand': *Los Angeles Times*, c.21 November 1999
352: 'Right, exactly': the *Guardian*, 1 June 2002
353: 'a glorious piece of music': *Los Angeles Times*, 23 February 2004
353: 'the most important piece': Associated Press, 20 August 2004
354: 'I prefer the one I did': *Boston Globe*, 30 October 2011

GETCHA BACK

356: 'The audience don't know': *Melbourne Age*, 8 December 1998
356: 'distinctive voice': ibid
356: 'I knew Carl couldn't play': *Asbury Park Press*, 28 June 1998
356: 'the Beach Boys have helped': *Los Angeles Times*, 11 October 1997
357: 'decided to pass': *North County Times*, 25 January 1998
357: 'we did take a deep breath': *Philadelphia Inquirer*, 3 July 1998
357: 'I don't think there was any serious thought': ibid
357: 'The promoters didn't seem': ibid
357: 'Michael and I had been touring': *Tampa Bay Times*, 26 February 1999
357: 'I would if Mike Love': *Chicago Tribune*, 31 May 1998

358: 'I haven't talked to Mike': *Daily Breeze*, 19 June 1998
358: 'I don't agree with Mike': ibid
358: 'There's a significant amount': *Santa Maria Times*, 23 June 1998
359: 'They don't call me': the *Observer*, 6 September 1998
359: 'I hired back all the best players': *Flint Times*, 11 June 1999
359: 'We have this wonderful pool': ibid
359: 'Carl and I were': ibid
360: 'a paid rehearsal': *Tampa Tribune*, 1 March 1999
360: 'What these relatives': ibid
360: 'Al is doing something': *Modesto Bee*, 18 June 1999
361: 'I miss Carl': *Lexington Herald-Leader*, 10 October 1999
361: 'i.e. cars, surf, girls and fun': *Los Angeles Times*, 28 November 1999
361: 'I don't see why I should': *Sunday Telegraph*, 5 December 1999
361: 'Jardine is destroying': *Newsday*, 30 December 1999
361: 'I like Mike as a person': *Des Moines Register*, 2 September 2000
362: 'it's about much more than money': *Victorville Daily Press*, 14 November 2003
362: 'I would suggest he read': *Appleton Post-Crescent*, 1 May 2003
362: 'not what music is all about': *Daily Item* [Lynn, MA], 31 July 2003
362: 'Mr Love and Mr Jardine': *The Province*, 21 March 2008
363: 'Carl died, and that was the end': *Minneapolis Star Tribune*, 24 June 2001
363: 'I don't even like them': *Tampa Tribune*, 15 October 2004
363: 'out of my life': *Rapid City Journal*, 8 October 2004
363: 'for the first time in eight years': *Palm Beach Post*, 17 October 2004
363: 'gave me a shoulder rub': *Cedar Rapids Gazette*, 23 June 2005
363: 'We had a great talk': *Victoria Times Colonist*, 16 August 2005
363: 'shamelessly misappropriated': Associated Press, 5 November 2005
363: 'I'm known as the bad one': *Asbury Park Press*, 2 December 2005
364: 'There is a relationship there': *The Plain Dealer*, 17 June 2007
364: 'People want to see the Beach Boys': ibid
364: 'We thought about it': *Hackensack Record*, 5 November 2009
364: 'Let the past go already': *Sunday Oregonian*, 5 September 2010
364: 'I don't know anything about that': *Billboard* syndication, 1 August 2011
364: 'You know Brian': *Boston Globe*, 30 October 2011

DO IT AGAIN

366: 'I felt the love from the guys': *Orange County Register*, 1 April 2012

366: 'that was the moment': *Ventura County Star*, 25 May 2012

367: 'this anniversary is special to me': Reuters, 17 December 2011

367: 'Brian was very specific': *Ventura County Star*, 25 May 2012

368: 'Brian didn't quite get the memo': ibid

368: 'It was kind of fraudulent': *Reno Gazette-Journal*, 26 May 2015

368: 'It was like putting a puzzle': *Philadelphia Inquirer*, 20 May 2012

369: 'as the last Beach Boys song ever': *Ventura County Star*, 25 May 2012

369: 'It sounds like 1965 again': *USA Today*, 28 April 2012

370: 'They put the album out': *Reno Gazette-Journal*, 26 March 2015

SUMMER'S GONE

371: 'Nobody was enemies': *Billboard*, 2 June 2012

371: 'The band loves each other': ibid

371: 'No more shows for Wilson': Love, *Good Vibrations*, p. 403

371: 'very early on, Brian': *Los Angeles Times*, 6 October 2012

372: 'I think this is a special': quoted *Akron Beacon Journal*, 7 June 2012

372: 'Brian's not going to be a touring guy': ibid

372: 'The unsung workhorse': *Los Angeles Times*, 26 April 2012

372: 'Jeffrey is invaluable': *Los Angeles Times*, 2 June 2012

373: 'didn't seem to be having': *Los Angeles Times*, 26 April 2012

373: 'several times he lost': *Arizona Daily Star*, 25 April 2012

373: 'They sense that we love': Associated Press, 29 April 2012

373: 'When we step onstage': *Toronto Star*, 17 June 2012

374: 'the 50th Reunion Tour': quoted *Independent*, 26 September 2012

374: 'I'm disappointed and can't understand': ibid

375: Mike Love op-ed: *Los Angeles Times*, 6 October 2012

375: Brian Wilson op-ed: *Los Angeles Times*, 10 October 2012

376: 'Well, what a wonderful thought': *Pittsburgh Post-Gazette*, 18 July 2013

376: 'No, Brian is controlled': *Springfield Republican*, 10 August 2014

Bibliography

Abbott, Kingsley (ed.): *Back to the Beach: A Brïan Wilson and the Beach Boys Reader* (London: Helter Skelter, 1997)

Abbott, Kingsley: *The Beach Boys' Pet Sounds: The Greatest Album of the Twentieth Century* (London: Helter Skelter, 2001)

Badman, Keith: *The Beach Boys: The Definitive Diary of America's Greatest Band on Stage and in the Studio* (San Francisco: Backbeat Books, 2004)

The Beach Boys: *The Beach Boys by the Beach Boys* (Guildford: Genesis Publications, 2023)

Blaine, Hal & David Goggin: *Hal Blaine and the Wrecking Crew* (Emeryville, CA: Mix Books, 1990)

Carlin, Peter Ames: *Catch a Wave: The Rise, Fall & Redemption of the Beach Boys' Brian Wilson* (London: Rodale International, 2006)

Cavanagh, Dwight: *The Smile File* (North Strathfield NSW: PTB Productions, 1994)

Chidester, Brian & Domenic Priore: *Pop Surf Culture: Music, Design, Film, and Fashion from the Bohemian Surf Boom* (Santa Monica: Santa Monica Press, 2008)

Davis, Mike: *City of Quartz: Excavating the Future in Los Angeles* (London: Verso, 2006)

Dillon, Mark: *Fifty Sides of the Beach Boys: The Songs That Tell Their Story* (Toronto: ECW Press, 2012)

Doggett, Peter: *There's a Riot Going On: Revolutionaries, Rock Stars and the Rise and Fall of '60s Counter-Culture* (Edinburgh: Canongate, 2007)

Doggett, Peter: *Electric Shock: From the Gramophone to the iPhone – 125 Years of Pop Music* (London: The Bodley Head, 2015)

Elliott, Brad: *Surf's Up: The Beach Boys on Record, 1961–1981* (Ann Arbor, MI: Pierian Press, 1982)

Fusilli, Jim: *Pet Sounds* (New York: Continuum Books, 2005)

Gaines, Steven: *Heroes & Villains: The True Story of the Beach Boys* (New York: New American Library, 1986)

Golden, Bruce: *The Beach Boys: Southern California Pastoral* (Van Nuys, CA: Newcastle/Borgo Press, 1976)

Granat May, Kirse: *Golden State, Golden Youth: The California Image in Popular Culture, 1955–1966* (Chapel Hill NC: University of North Carolina Press, 2002)

Henderson, Richard: *Song Cycle* (New York: Continuum Books, 2010)

Leaf, David: *The Beach Boys and the California Myth* (New York: Grosset & Dunlap, 1978)

Leaf, David: *The Beach Boys* (Philadelphia: Courage Books, 1985; extended edition of above volume)

Love, Mike (with James S. Hirsch): *Good Vibrations: My Life as a Beach Boy* (London: Faber & Faber, 2016)

McParland, Stephen J.: *The Wilson Project* (North Strathfield, New South Wales: PTB Productions, 1992)

McParland, Stephen J.: *Our Favourite Recording Sessions: In the Studio with Brian Wilson and the Beach Boys* (North Strathfield, New South Wales: California Music, 2000)

McParland, Stephen J.: *The California Sound: An Insider's Story: The Musical Biography of Gary Lee Usher* Vols. 1–5 (North Strathfield, New South Wales: California Music, 2000–2001)

McParland, Stephen J.: *Bull Sessions with the Big Daddy* (North Strathfield, New South Wales: California Music, 2001)

Milward, John: *The Beach Boys Silver Anniversary* (New York: Dolphin Books, 1985)

Muñoz, Carli: *A Fool's Journey: To the Beach Boys & Beyond* (Northampton, MA: Interlink Books, 2023)

Murphy, James B.: *Becoming the Beach Boys, 1961–1963* (Jefferson, NC: McFarland & Co., 2015)

O'Neill, Tom (with Dan Piepenbring): *Chaos: The Truth Behind the Manson Murders* (London: Windmill, 2020)

Preiss, Byron: *The Beach Boys* (New York: Ballantine Books, 1979)

Priore, Domenic: *Smile: The Story of Brian Wilson's Lost Masterpiece* (London: Sanctuary Publishing, 2005)

Searles, Malcolm C.: *The Beach Boys: Back Through the Opera Glass: The Stories Behind the Album Covers Parts 1–3* (online: dojotonepublications.com, 2017–2022)

Starr, Kevin: *California: A History* (New York: Modern Library, 2005)

Stebbins, Jon: *Dennis Wilson: The Real Beach Boy* (Toronto: ECW Press, 1999)

Tobler, John: *The Beach Boys* (London: Phoebus, 1977)

Webb, Adam: *Dumb Angel: The Life and Music of Dennis Wilson* (London: Creation Books, 2001)

White, Timothy: *The Nearest Faraway Place: Brian Wilson, the Beach Boys and the Southern California Experience* (New York: Henry Holt, 1995)

Williams, Paul: *Outlaw Blues: A Book of Rock Music* (New York: E.P. Dutton & Co., 1969)

Williams, Paul (ed.): *The Crawdaddy! Book: Writings (and Images) from the Magazine of Rock* (Milwaukee: Hal Leonard Corporation, 2002)

Wilson, Brian (with Todd Gold): *Wouldn't It Be Nice: My Own Story* (New York: HarperCollins, 1991)

Wilson, Brian (with Ben Greenman): *I Am Brian Wilson: The Genius Behind the Beach Boys* (London: Coronet, 2016)

Wise, Nick: *The Beach Boys in Their Own Words* (London: Omnibus Press, 1994)

[illegible]

[illegible]

[illegible]

[illegible]

[illegible]

[illegible]

[illegible]

[illegible]

[illegible]

[illegible]

[illegible]

[illegible]

[illegible]

[illegible]

[illegible]

[illegible]

[illegible]

Acknowledgements

The music of the Beach Boys has been a constant emotional and physical presence in my life for more than half a century, and this book can never repay all the joy their work has given me. In my professional life, I have been lucky enough to spend time with three of the group – Brian Wilson, Bruce Johnston and Ricky Fataar – and also with many of their collaborators, some more crucial and positive influences than others. They have included Van Dyke Parks, Tony Asher, Don Was, Derek Taylor, Leon Russell, Roger McGuinn, David Crosby, John Phillips, Jimmy Webb, Al Kooper, Andrew Loog Oldham – and, yes, even Eugene Landy.

Down the years, I have discussed the Beach Boys and their music with many people, all of whom contributed in various ways either to this book or to my appreciation of their work. Thanks therefore to Kingsley Abbott, Keith Altham, Stuart Batsford, Sean Body, Debbie Cassell, Clinton Heylin, Brian Hogg, Andy Miller, Johnny Rogan, Andrew Sclanders, John Tobler, Kieron Tyler and Paul Williams. Special thanks to Mike Grant, former editor of *Beach Boys Stomp* magazine, for his generosity over many years. And I also need to thank Cindy Lee Berryhill, composer of the classic Brian Wilson tribute, 'Song for Brian', on her 1994 album *Garage Orchestra*.

Pete Selby's enthusiasm for this project at New Modern made the book happen; my agent Matthew Hamilton made the connection and the deal. Many thanks to them both – and also to James Lilford and Dusty Miller PR.

Acknowledgements

This book was written during a sometimes thrilling, sometimes tumultuous period of our family life. Thanks to all relatives and friends for their support, especially the Doggetts in Coventry and the Gawleys in Hampshire. Much, much love to Becca, Max and the amazing Phoebe; and to Catrin, James and the equally amazing Cora, born on the day that the final proofs of this book were completed. These are the most exciting times of our lives, thanks to all of you.

Gilbert and George provide non-stop four-pawed entertainment as they defend their territory against invaders, feline, imaginary or otherwise. But, as ever, the biggest thanks and deepest love must go to Rachel Baylis, whose irrepressible creative spirit and energy have survived recent illness fully intact, and whose presence in my life continues to seem both entirely natural and miraculous. As the song says, God only knows what I'd be without you.

The team at New Modern would like to thank the following individuals:

Nige Tassell for copy-editing
Sophie Lazar for proofreading
Marie Doherty for typesetting
Paul Palmer-Edwards for cover design
Amanda Russell for image research
Dusty Miller for publicity
Marie Lecouturier, Charlotte Rose, Andreina Brezzo and the team at Simon & Schuster UK for sales and distribution